Christianity and the Leaders of Modern Science

Karl Alois Kneller S.J.

REGIS
UNIVERSITY
Learners Becoming Leaders

CHRISTIANITY

AND THE

LEADERS OF MODERN SCIENCE

A CONTRIBUTION TO THE HISTORY
OF CULTURE IN THE NINETEENTH CENTURY

BY

KARL ALOIS KNELLER, S. J.

TRANSLATED FROM THE SECOND GERMAN EDITION BY

T. M. KETTLE, B. L., M. P.

WITH AN INTRODUCTION BY REV. T. A. FINLAY, S. J., M. A.

WITH THE APPROBATION OF THE MOST REV. ARCHBISHOP OF FREIBURG.

B. HERDER
PUBLISHER TO THE HOLY APOSTOLIC SEE
LONDON, W. C. 1911 ST. LOUIS, MO.
FREIBURG IM BREISGAU.

INTRODUCTION.

A few days ago the newspapers announced that Mr. Edison had declared himself a materialist. He had satisfied himself that the physico-chemical forces at work in the brain, with the resultant electrical effects, were sufficient to account for all the phenomena of conscious life in man. This was the first public intimation that the distinguished inventor had turned philosopher. He had previously been known as an ingenious contriver of useful mechanisms. He had invented the phonograph, megaphone, kinetoscope, and had introduced many important improvements in telegraphy. His success in bending the forces of Nature to his will had won him a deserved celebrity; he was recognised as an adept in the application of science to practical ends, if not in science itself. Such fame notwithstanding, his profession of materialism left the world wholly unperturbed. No believer saw in it a new menace to his faith; no unbeliever found in it a new justification of his unbelief. The incident passed with a tribute of comment from the press scantier than would be accorded to a horse race or a prize fight.

This attitude of the public mind seems to indicate a healthy spread of sober thought, a growing capacity to appreciate at their true value the pronouncements of "science" on the supreme problems of life.

The study of the inorganic and organic worlds leads men irresistibly to speculate on the ultimate causes of the phenomena they investigate. The necessity is imposed by an inherent tendency of thought. With every fresh advance this constraining impulse becomes more imperative. But progress along the lines of empirical research brings with it no new light on the issues of deepest import to man. The discoveries of chemistry have enabled us to substitute molecules, atoms, electrons for the elemental earth, air, fire, and water of the Greeks; but the problem of the constitution of matter has become only more perplexing for the change. In biology we have got down to the cell as the basal element in living structures; but vital activity in the cell is as mysterious and inexplicable as in the most complicated organisms; the cerebral movements which accompany the functions of mind have been, in some measure, determined; but this gives no new help towards an explanation of consciousness; in this respect the most accomplished physiologist has no more effective data at command than the man who knows only that we see by means of eyes and hear by means of ears. The question whether the universe is ordered on a preconceived plan is not brought nearer a solution by discoveries which merely multiply for us the elements constituting it; the question whether there is an immaterial soul in man is not elucidated by an increased knowledge of the complexities of structure and movement in the organism within which the phenomena of sensation and thought manifest themselves. In face of these problems the man of science and the man of normal human experience stand upon the same plane. In both the answer will be given by that spontaneous process of inference which decides, for learned and unlearned alike, the urgent issues of life, and which is so largely influenced by the perfections or the defects of individual character. We may attempt a logical analysis of the process, endeavour to follow step by step the path which the mind has traversed with lightning speed. But whatever the result of this attempt, be it satisfactory or otherwise, the assent to the conclusion is not thereby affected. Doubt as to the correctness of an analysis of our own act of reasoning is one thing; doubt as to the validity of the inference itself is quite another.

It stands to the credit of the founders of modern science — the master minds of the 17th and 18th Centuries — that they had a salutary sense of the limitations of empirical methods. Their discoveries, which opened the way to all subsequent progress, did not interfere with their faith in God, or their belief in the spirituality and immortality of the human soul. If anything, their reverence for the Mind that reveals Itself in Nature grew more profound as their knowledge of natural phenomena became deeper. The more enlightened of their successors in the 19th Century have upheld their conception of Nature's God, and of man's place in Nature. This it is the purpose of Father Kneller's book to demonstrate. The thoroughness with which he has executed his task is obvious on every page; he has rendered a conspicuous service to Christianity and to Science.

Dublin, October 1910.

T. A. Finlay.

CONTENTS.

INTRODUCTION.

"Many excellent people", said the distinguished physicist Lord Rayleigh[1] on one occasion in a public speech, "are afraid of science as tending towards materialism. That such apprehension should exist is not surprising, for unfortunately there are writers, speaking in the name of science, who have set themselves to foster it. It is true that amongst scientific men, as in other classes, crude views are to be met with as to the deeper things of nature; but that the lifelong beliefs of Newton, of Faraday, and of Maxwell, are inconsistent with the scientific habit of mind, is surely a proposition which I need not pause to refute." We might have adopted these words of the eminent scientist[2] as the motto of our work, for they give a clear statement of the fundamental idea which we seek to develop here. In Germany also we have a great many writers, who, announcing themselves as champions of

[1] Report of the 54th Meeting of the British Association for the Advancement of Science, held at Montreal in August and September 1884. Presidential Address 22. London 1885.

[2] John William Strutt, since 1873 Lord Rayleigh, born in 1842, was Maxwell's successor as Professor of Experimental Physics at Cambridge. He is one of the greatest recent authorities on Natural Philosophy in England. He attained a world-wide reputation when in 1894 he discovered a hitherto unknown constituent of the atmosphere, namely argon.

science, proclaim in its name and on its authority the irreparable defeat of religion and Christianity. Scientific discoveries, we are assured, have undermined the very foundations of religion — belief in the existence of God, and in the presence of a spiritual soul in man — and in short we must either renounce religion altogether or cast about for a new form of it, more in harmony with the results of the modern interpretation of nature. Assertions of this kind are to be met with everywhere. Newspapers and brochures are full of them; popular works on science treat them as self-evident, and seize every opportunity of insinuating that no one of any scientific standing any longer troubles about religion. Nor does it need any deep knowledge of human nature to understand how greatly representations of this kind contribute to the spread of Materialism. It is not only in matters of dress and outer things that fashion rules, and that society takes its tone from certain 'circles'. Those who by wealth, nobility of birth, or erudition stand out from the common mass, exercise, by word and example, the most far-reaching influence in graver questions also, questions in which least of all their influence ought to be felt. How then could the average man fail to be startled when, following an exposition of the brilliant discoveries of modern research, he is assured, or at least given to understand, that every eminent mind that has contributed to such marvels has rejected Christianity and welcomed in Materialism and Atheism the light and the salvation of the future?

The essential value of such an argument is indeed very slight. Even if it were true that modern scientists as one man stood out against Christ and the Church, this would offer no disproof of Christianity. In earlier days, at all events, Natural Science took up no such position, and the fact that a certain opinion is for a period generally accepted cannot be held to guarantee its truth.

The leaders of Physics, Chemistry, Geology speak with authority as regards the actual facts and empirical laws of their own special provinces. But Materialism, Atheism, Positivism are not observed facts, but systems of philosophy, inferences from facts, and inferences which fall, properly speaking, within the province not of Science but of Metaphysics. And as regards conclusions of this order, the scientist is not, as such, the authoritative judge. Other people have quite as good, and indeed better claims to be heard. "I do not think", says Lord Rayleigh elsewhere, "that he has a claim superior to that of other educated men, to assume the attitude of a prophet. In his heart he knows that underneath the theories that he constructs there lie contradictions he cannot reconcile. The higher mysteries of being, if penetrable at all by human intellect, require other weapons than those of calculation and experiment." Further it is a fact of history that many an opinion which represented itself as the only truly scientific opinion, has none the less fallen in course of time into contempt; and that very often the higher synthesis by no means confirms the brilliant pretensions of 'culture'. Our Lord Jesus Christ had ranked against him, solidly and with a complete self-consciousness, the Science of the Jews. But, in spite of this, the wisdom of the scribes and their Talmudic erudition is to-day utterly disregarded; Christ was right, the Science of His day was wrong. In a later century Neo-Platonism spoke of Christianity, although borrowing largely from it, as the product of a barbarian brain[1]; the Gnostic and the Manichean thought themselves exalted far above the orthodox theology when, instead of the teaching of Christ, they proclaimed as the Higher Wisdom a medley of Greek and Oriental speculations, glossed over with Christian ideas. To-day we repeat of those discoveries the contemptuous words of St. Jerome touching the Greek philosophers of his time: "At most a few old bookworms, who would otherwise be unoccupied, still concern themselves about it in the seclusion of their libraries. But with our rustic and uncultured fishermen the whole world resounds."[2] As far as material culture goes, the Arabs of the early Middle Ages could boast themselves superior to the Christian nations, as later the Anabaptists and the Mormons surpassed the rest of Christianity in industrial pursuits. The comparison becomes still clearer, if we look back to the remotest ages. In the Old Testament as often as Israel came in contact with the dazzling culture of Egypt, Assyria or Greece, multitudes of the chosen people yielded, as if bewitched, to the intoxicating appeal to the senses. They felt in comparison with it rude and primitive, grew ashamed of the religion of their fathers, flung themselves into the arms of attractive idolatries, and laboured as in the time of the Maccabbees to obliterate the last trace of adherence to the old faith. But who to-day doubts that the many, who so acted, bartered their treasure and their heritage for mere tinsel, in a blindness all but inconceivable, and that as a world-philosophy the religious system of

---

[1] Ἀ βάρβαρον τόλμημα. Porphyrius in Euseb., H. E. 6, 19.

[2] Vix in angulo otioso eos senes recolunt. Rusticanos vero et piscatores nostros totus orbis loquitur, universus mundus sonat (S. Hieron., In Gal. l. 3 init.).

Israel was far loftier than the nature-worship of Greece and the Orient?

A thousand times in the course of history material culture has advanced the claim to formulate also the general philosophy of life. But on every occasion this claim has been withstood by countless believers, and for the most part in the process of history its pretences have been punished. Humanity has continued to seek the sources of the higher life less in the palaces than in the catacombs of Rome, less in the philosophical schools of Athens and Alexandria than in the solitudes of the Thebaid.

If then there is in fact hostility between Christianity and the Science of to-day, that is to say, Natural Science, why must it be assumed that the truth lies on the side of Science? It is idle to say that things do not stand as in previous conflicts of this kind, that in former times what passed for the criticism of Christianity was mere metaphysical speculation, soon dissipated, but that the Science of to-day relies on facts which can certainly never be refuted. It is not the facts that are hostile to Christianity, but the philosophy which it is sought to ground on them; and this is as unstable a structure as any philosophy of the past.

But we must not delay here over any further consideration of these points. As against the apostles of Materialism, mentioned above, we desire to develop the thought suggested by Lord Rayleigh in his reference to Newton, Faraday, and Maxwell. We call in question not the inference from the alleged enmity between science and religion, but the fact of this enmity itself. From the writers who represent themselves as the champions of science we wish to turn to those who are recognized as such in the largest sense of the word, those to whom the advance of science is due, the veritable pioneers. These, before all, we desire to question concerning this conflict between scientific research and religious belief. If it exists, it will naturally be found most patent to minds of the first order. And if on the other hand we find among the great investigators, the very pioneers of science, many firm and fervent believers, and many others who admit the fundamental truths on which Christianity is founded, we shall not set a very high value on this pretended antagonism between knowledge and belief.

Our standpoint has, we hope, been now made clear. Our object is not to set forth an argument for Christianity, but to point out the emptiness of a familiar objection urged against it. We seek, not to collect the testimony given in favour of Christian belief by great scientists, but to repel the hostile inference drawn from the alleged unanimity of Science in its disfavour. Nor do we aim at exhibiting the question in every light, but only in one, limiting ourselves, namely to the contention that such unanimous opposition simply does not exist.

We confine our survey to the savants of the 19th Century. For nobody thinks of calling in question the Christian faith of the earlier scientists, of Copernicus, Galileo, Kepler, Newton, Leibniz, Euler, Boyle, Mariotte, Haller and Linnaeus. Living contemporaries ought not, perhaps, to be dealt with in this connection, but we satisfy our scruples by referring only to discourses pronounced publicly by them in the ear of the whole world.

I. A FUNDAMENTAL LAW: THE CONSERVATION OF ENERGY.

The greatest conquest of the 19th Century in Physics, its richest gain on the theoretical side, is beyond question the mechanical theory of heat, and what is intimately bound up with this theory, the Law of the Conservation of Energy. The formulation of this theory was not only a great advance in our knowledge of a single natural force, but a light on the constitution of matter in general, full of significance for every branch of exact science.

It had long been known that beneath the changes, incessant and manifold of the material world, organic as well as inorganic, beneath the perpetual formations and disintegrations, the underlying matter merely moves hither and thither and never diminishes or increases in the minutest degree. It was now proved that a similar law holds good of the force operative in matter. The kindling of a fire produces heat and light. But that which issues in the form of light and heat from the burning material was already present in it, as the energy of the discharged arrow was present in the bent bow. If we burn coal to set a steam-engine in motion, we may say similarly that we produce motion. But this production is not a creation out of nothing, but a transformation. As much mechanical work can be done as there is power to do work in the burning material, and no more. This law applies to all changes, physical or chemical. If the work of the steam-engine be translated into electricity, this again into light or heat, and the light or heat into any form of "Motive-power" or "Energy", all these are simply transformations; an increase or diminution of the existent sum of energy is as impossible as an increase or diminution of the originally created sum of matter.

Haeckel[1] combines the two laws, the Conservation of Matter and the Conservation of Energy, under the single "Law of Substance", and not only calls this "the supreme and basal law of the Cosmos" in which are synthesized "all the most important results" and intellectual conquests of modern science, but sets it down further as "Paragraph I of the Monist Religion of the future". He expresses himself full of contempt that the great physicist Von Helmholtz was buried at Berlin "amidst the tolling of church-bells" and in the presence of the highest people of the land. "Did none of these 'first people in the land', then, suspect that these honours were being heaped on a 'Freethinker', who to their eyes must appear as an iconoclast, an obstinate 'heretic' of the first order? Did none of them know that Helmholtz's greatest achievement, the Law of Substance, is Paragraph I of the Monist Religion?"

Now we are very far indeed from taking such rhetoric seriously. For what does Haeckel really mean to say? Does he assert that the Law of the Conservation of Energy is in contradiction with some Christian dogma? This would be a completely unintelligible assertion, for

---

[1] Die Zukunft III, Berlin 1895, 199.

what doctrine of Christianity could forbid my acceptance of the 'Law of Substance' if the evidence in its favour seemed to me conclusive? Or does he mean to make it a reproach against Christianity that it has not taught the Law of Substance? That would be even more unintelligible, for the Christian Revelation has not been given to impart truths of the natural order; these are to be acquired by human reason. What does Haeckel mean?

But we are straying a little from our subject. Our aim with regard to this pretended incompatibility of science and religious faith is not to discuss the question directly, but rather to ascertain what was thought by the leaders of science themselves of the supposed anti-Christian character of their discoveries. Let us turn first of all to the brilliant scientists to whom we owe the Mechanical Theory of Heat, and the Law of the Conservation of Energy, and ascertain whether they gave the same account of the significance of their discoveries as is given by Haeckel.

The first inquirer who was led by his researches to suggest that heat is a form of matter, and so to prepare the ground for the later view that it is a form of motion, was Count Von Rumford. His discovery was confirmed by Davy. The more modern determination of the relation between heat and mechanical work, and the first general statement of the Law of the Conservation of Energy we owe to the German scientist Robert Mayer. Independently of Mayer, perhaps, Helmholtz also enunciated the Law; and original statements of the relation between heat and mechanical work were also made in France by Hirn, and in England by Joule. The consequences of the Law of the Conservation of Energy for the whole Cosmos were expounded by Clausius and William Thomson (Lord Kelvin).

Whatever is to be said of the American Benjamin Thompson, Count Von Rumford († 1814), who pursued his epoch-making researches in Munich, he certainly was no precursor of Haeckel. "Whatever were the feelings of Rumford towards men", writes G. Cuvier of him, "they did not diminish his respect for the Deity. In his writings he neglects no opportunity of expressing his pious admiration for Providence, and of proposing to the admiration of others the innumerable variety of safeguards which it has adopted for the conservation of its creatures." [1]

Of Sir Humphry Davy († 1829) precisely the same can be said. His opposition to Materialism, and his conviction of the immortality of the soul and the existence of God find, more than once, clear and unambiguous expression. Thus in his "Last Days of a Philosopher" [2], a volume in dialogue form, written in

---

[1] Quels que fussent au reste les sentiments de M. de Rumford pour les hommes (he had rather pessimistic and misanthropical views on this subject), ils ne diminuaient en rien son respect pour la Divinité. Il n'a négligé dans ses ouvrages aucune occasion d'exprimer sa religieuse admiration pour la Providence, et d'y offrir à l'admiration des autres les précautions innombrables et variées par lesquelles elle a pourvu à la conservation de ses créatures (Cuvier, Recueil des éloges historiques lus dans les séances publiques de l'Institut Royal de France II, Strasbourg-Paris 1819, 230). Cf. J. B. Dumas, Discours II 253; Allg. deutsche Biographie XX 655. For a general view of Rumford cf. Bence Jones, The Royal Institution: its Founders and its First Professors, London 1871, 1—113.

[2] Consolation in travel or the Last Days of a Philosopher, in The Collected Works of Sir Humphry Davy, edited by his brother John Davy, IX, London 1840, 213.

his leisure hours towards the end of his life, Philalethes, who, in these conversations — as in another connection "the Unknown" — represents Davy's own views, says in the Fourth Dialogue, "Proteus or Immortality"[1]:

"The doctrine of the materialists was always even in my youth, a cold, heavy, dull and insupportable doctrine to me, and necessarily tending to atheism. When I had heard with disgust in the dissecting rooms, the plan of the physiologist, of the gradual accretion of matter and its becoming endowed with irritability, ripening into sensibility and acquiring such organs as were necessary, by its own inherent forces, and at last rising into intellectual existence, a walk into the green fields or woods by the banks of rivers brought back my feelings from nature to God; I saw in all the powers of matter the instruments of the Deity. . . . Then my own mind I felt connected with new sensations and indefinite hopes, a thirst of immortality. These feelings, though generally considered as poetical, yet, I think offer a sound philosophical argument in favour of the immortality of the soul."[2]

Of religion "the Unknown" says in the same Dialogue:

"Its influence outlives all earthly enjoyments, and becomes stronger as the organs decay and the frame dissolves; it appears as that evening star of light in the horizon of life, which, we are sure, is to become in another season a morning star, and it throws its radiance through the gloom and shadow of death."[3]

In the next Dialogue, Davy defends the Science of Chemistry, and attempts to paint an ideal picture of the investigator in this field:

"It is surely", said the Unknown, "a pure delight . . . to produce as it were a microcosm in the laboratory of art,

---

[1] Concerning the identity of Philalethes and the "Unknown", cf. ib. I, London 1839, 433—438.

[2] Ib. IX 345. [3] Ib. IX 347.

and to measure and weigh those invisible atoms, which, by their motions and changes according to laws impressed upon them by the Divine Intelligence, constitute the universe of things. The true chemical philosopher sees good in all the diversified forms of the external world. Whilst he investigates the operations of infinite power, guided by infinite wisdom, all low prejudices, all mean superstitions disappear from his mind."[1] "I do not mean that he should affix written prayers and inscriptions or recommendations of his processes to Providence, as was the custom of Peter Wolfe, who was alive in my early days; but his mind should always be awake to devotional feelings, and in contemplating the variety and the beauty of the external world, and developing its scientific wonders he will always refer to that infinite wonder, through whose beneficence he is permitted to enjoy knowledge; and, in becoming wiser, he will become better; he will rise at once in the scale of intellectual and moral existence, his increased sagacity will be subservient to a more exalted faith, and in proportion as the veil becomes thinner, through which he sees the causes of things, he will admire more the brightness of the divine lights, by which they are rendered visible."[2]

These passages were written by Davy for publication. But in his diaries and letters we find the same ideas. We cite a few examples:

"April 6. 1827. Did not shoot, but returned thanks to the Great Cause of all being for all His mercies to me, an undeserving and often ungrateful creature, but now most grateful. May I become better and more grateful and more humble-minded every day.

September 2. I took my exercise well with less fatigue, and certainly feel better. Offered up my thanksgiving to the O. O. O.[3] with tears of gratitude and feelings of intense adoration.

---

[1] Collected Works LX 361. [2] Ib. IX 367.

[3] Instead of the name of God, Davy writes, here as elsewhere, O. O. O., instead of "Thanks be to God", he writes frequently only G. O. O. O., i. e. gratias Omnipotenti or Omniscienti.

September 27. St. Goar. . . . As I have so often alluded to the possibility of my dying suddenly, I think it right to mention that I am too intense a believer in the Supreme Intelligence, and have too strong a faith in the optimism of the system of the universe, ever to accelerate my dissolution. The laurel-water, laudanum, and opium that are in my dressing-case are medicines. I have been and am taking a care of my health which I fear it is not worth, but which, hoping it may please Providence to preserve me for wise purposes, I think my duty G. O. O. O.[1]

June 3. 1828. Aussee in Steiermark. I indulge in the idea that you are well and happy and enjoying a life which I can say I only support supposing that it please Omniscience to preserve me for some ends which I cannot understand, but which I trust belong to the great plan of goodness and mercy belonging to the Divine mind."[2]

For the Protestant religious ethos Davy showed little liking, at least in the latter part of his life. But it is worthy of note that he regarded the Catholic Church and the Catholic spirit with the greatest friendliness. The influence of the Catholic religion on the mass of the people, the hearty festive joy of their Sunday in contrast to the Puritanical restraint of the English Sabbath impressed him vividly. In this connection his brother writes[3]:

"The obedience which the Church requires, the submission of reason, the unlimited faith, he considered favourable to religious feeling, and the securest harbour for the unfortunate and afflicted, the strongest hold against popular schism, scepticism, and fanaticism; and in accordance with the faculties and wants of the human mind, especially as regarding its affections. On the latter point he expresses him-

---

[1] Memoirs of the Life of Sir Humphry Davy, by his brother John Davy, in Collected Works I 345 376 381.

[2] Letter to his brother John, ib. I 388.

[3] Collected Works I 431.

self strongly in his diary on the 14th of June, 1827, at Aussee, on occasion of that beautiful ceremony, the Fête-Dieu. His words are: 'Struck with the affecting nature and superiority of the Catholic religion, which gives joy and comfort to the human heart, by making a festivity and not a hard duty of worship, — it is the Fête-Dieu.' His views of the weakness and fallacy of reason on the subject of religion might have promoted a bias in his mind in favour of this church; and having travelled much in Roman Catholic countries, and witnessed the powerful influence which religion there has over the people, as regards habits of life and daily feelings, the bias might have been confirmed from seeing the positive civil and social advantages which it gives in comparison with the Protestant; its levelling, unaristocratic nature; its being no distinguisher of persons, its bringing all classes of people together, without distinction, in mixed worship, under the same roof, its throwing open the most splendid churches to the populace and allowing them to be made an asylum to the pauper."

The discovery of Davy and Rumford did not take its place among the accepted truths of science until about the middle of the 19th Century, when the genius of Julius Robert Mayer pressed it conclusively to the front. With him, therefore, we must occupy ourselves more closely [1].

Born at Heilbronn on November 25th 1814, the son of an apothecary, Robert devoted himself to the study

---

[1] Die Mechanik der Wärme Gesammelte Schriften von Robert Mayer. Dritte, ergänzte und mit historisch-literarischen Mitteilungen versehene Auflage, herausgeg. von Dr. Jakob J. Weyrauch, Stuttgart 1893. Kleinere Schriften und Briefe von Robert Mayer. Nebst Mitteilungen aus seinem Leben. Herausgeg. von Dr. Jakob J. Weyrauch, Stuttgart 1893. Rumelin, Erinnerungen an R. Mayer, in Allgemeine Zeitung, Stuttgart u. Augsburg 1878, Beil. Nr. 120—122, p. 1761 1778 1795. Also printed in "Leopoldina" XV, Halle 1879, 34 50. Cf. ib. XIV, Halle 1878, 82.

of medicine, and on the completion of his course in 1840 made a voyage as ship's doctor to Batavia. While engaged bleeding the seamen, he found that the blood in the veins of the arms was not, as in our latitudes, dark, but, on the contrary, rather bright. The attempt to explain this simple fact gave Mayer the first impulse to his discovery. The blood changes colour according as it combines in the lungs with the oxygen of the atmosphere, and this combination is a kind of combustion, which has for outcome the natural warmth of the body. Thus by the consequent thinking-out of his observation, Mayer was led on to the question of the origin of bodily heat and of heat in general. What is meant, he asked himself, by saying that heat arises? Is this origination a starting out of nothing, is the cessation of heat a veritable annihilation, or are both merely a transformation of a something already in existence? These questions troubled him incessantly.

"I threw myself", he writes, "so eagerly into the investigation, that I (and many a one will laugh at me for it) busied very little to collect information about the remote region in which I was, but preferred to stay on board, where I could pursue my work without interruption. Often I felt as it were inspired: such a feeling as I do not remember to have ever experienced before or after. Certain ideas which flashed into my mind in the roadstead of Surabaja were followed up and led to further questions. Those days are gone: but the systematic establishment of what then suggested itself to me, taught me that truth is that which is not only subjectively felt but can also be objectively demonstrated. . . . The time will certainly come when these truths will belong to the common stock of science, but who will establish them, or when, who can say?"[1]

---

[1] Weyrauch, Kleinere Schriften 212—213.

The day of recognition came at last, but not till after a long and weary struggle. No review would accept his first essay, a fact for which Mayer's style was to blame, for although his scheme of thought was clear and sequent enough he omits, in reducing it to writing, so many connecting links as to produce the impression of incoherence. His early essays on the Theory of Heat attracted hardly any notice. This and his cruel treatment at the hands of the reviewers threw him into a sort of nervous tumult so violent that he had at times to be confined in a lunatic asylum. But his ideas gradually made their way.

"No greater genius", declared Tyndall in 1891, "than Robert Mayer has appeared in our century. Some men who now overshadow him will undoubtedly be placed beneath him in the future history of science."

And to the discoverer himself he writes in 1866: "I am a plain blunt man who speaks his mind, and therefore you must accept my words without a trace of flattery, when I say that I never turn to your scientific writings without wonder. That you, in a small provincial town, and occupied with the duties of your profession, should have shot so far in advance of all other men, is to me astonishing. I know no similar case in the history of science." [1]

Clausius expressed himself in similar terms. As soon as his attention had been drawn to Mayer's writings he corroborated Tyndall's opinion of them. He was "amazed at the multitude of just and beautiful ideas contained in them" [2].

---

[1] Weyrauch, Kleinere Schriften 212—213.

[2] Clausius, Die mechanische Wärmetheorie I[3], Braunschweig 1887, 396; II[2], ib. 1879, 326.

What Robert Mayer thought of Materialism and Christianity, we shall learn from himself. "The anti-materialistic standpoint which I have assumed, and which I will never renounce (Mt. x. 32)[1], is naturally maintained here also", he writes on June 15th 1871, in forwarding to a friend his "Discourses on Natural Science". Nor did Mayer keep his Christianity locked up in his heart. At the Scientific Conference held at Innsbruck in 1869 he was invited to pronounce a discourse, and he spoke of the conclusions which could be deduced from his theory in the various departments of knowledge[2]. He claimed that the new conception of the Conservation of Energy necessarily implied the existence of a spiritual soul in man.

"The French physicist Adolphe Hirn, who like Joule, Holtzmann and Helmholtz discovered independently the mechanical equivalent of heat, classifies all existences, in my opinion, justly and beautifully, under the three categories: 1. Matter, 2. Force, and 3. the Soul or spiritual principle. When once we have come to understand that there exist not only material bodies but also forces, forces in the stricter sense known to modern science, just as indestructible as the elements of the chemist, there needs but one more logical step to the recognition and acceptance of spiritual realities. In the non-living world we speak of atoms, in the living world of individuals. But the living body is made up, as we now know, not solely of material particles but

[1] "Everyone, therefore, that shall confess Me before men, I will also confess him before My Father Who is in heaven. But he that shall deny Me before men, I will also deny him before My Father Who is in heaven."

[2] Copy of a discourse in the Journal of 43rd Assembly of German Naturalists and Doctors in Innsbruck from 18th to the 24th Sept. 1869, Innsbruck 1869, 40—44. Also printed in "Ausland" 1869, 1061 to 1065.

also, in its essence, of forces. Now neither matter nor force is capable of thought, feeling, or volition. But Man thinks."

He maintains "that in the living brain, physical changes designated by the name of molecular activity are continually taking place, and that the spiritual functions of the individual are connected in the most intimate manner with these cerebral processes. But it is a gross blunder to identify these concurrent activities. An example will demonstrate this unequivocally. Telegraphic communication cannot, as every one knows, be established without a simultaneous chemical process. But the message delivered by the wire, the contents of the telegram, can by no means be regarded as a function of this electro-chemical process. This holds with still greater force of the relation of thought to the brain. The brain is not the soul, but only the instrument of the soul. And the soul, not coming within the reach of sense-perception, is not an object of investigation for Physics or Anatomy. Thought subjectively accurate is also objectively true. Were it not for this inalterable harmony, pre-established by God, between subject and object, all our thinking would necessarily be without fruit. Logic is the Statics, Grammar the Mechanics, and Language the Dynamics of thought".

"Let me here conclude. With heartfelt conviction I say it: A sound philosophy must and can be nothing else than a propaedeutic to Christianity."

The conviction expressed in these words was with Mayer a life-long one, and we find it also proclaimed during his East Indian voyage, when the germinal idea of his theory first flashed into his mind.

He writes to his parents on Feb. 25th 1840 shortly before the sailing of his ship: "I will send up under all skies incessant prayers to the Almighty that He may keep my beloved parents safe and well."[1] And two days later: "Now for a time good-bye, my dearest father and mother; my childlike gratitude for your unwearied kindness to me, my most

[1] Weyrauch, Kleinere Schriften 85.

earnest appeal for forgiveness for my many faults and failings, my most ardent prayers for your constant welfare. Weeping I cast myself on your breasts." [1]

How he occupied himself during the voyage appears from certain entries. "On the ninth (of March) I succeeded in extricating my box of books from between-decks. . . . Triumphantly I waved on high my Bible and my hymn book, for which before all others I had longed, and which every day procure for me some blessed hours. The heart withdrawn from the tumult of the world, is drawn to meditation, and, living before the glorious face of nature, there is nothing more beautiful than to elevate one's thoughts to the Creator." [2]

"Thanks to the All-Good", he writes home on June 8th 1840 on reaching the Straits of Sunda, "Who has vouchsafed me these little trials without which life cannot go on, and has granted me also the grace never to grow weary of praising his wisdom." [3] And on July 25th: "To the All-Wise Providence of God, so evident in the ordering of my life, I confidently commit the future also; if He grants me only one prayer I will cheerfully let all else pass by me: but in this regard alone I cannot yet sincerely pray: Thy Will be done. I speak of the hope of once again clasping my dear ones to my breast." [4]

Nor did his years of trial alter in any way this attitude of mind:

"My early feeling", he writes on Dec. 31st 1851, "that scientific truths are to the Christian religion much what brooks and rivers are to the ocean, has become my most vital conviction. Tempted as I was to drift with the tempest of passion, I had made shipwreck in these latter years, had not in my heaviest hours the Mercy of God, through your instrumentality, kept me always on the right path. How indifferent to me are many things which had else been so important!" [5]

---

[1] Ib. 88. [2] Ib. 92. [3] Ib. 95.
[4] Ib. 97. [5] Ib. 339—340.

Mayer, nevertheless, experienced at times certain of those confusions which are as it were the patrimony of Protestantism. He says incidentally, that "in the supernatural sphere" he "never succeeded in coming to perfect agreement with himself"[1]. The passage occurs in a letter of thanks to Moleschott, and must have in some degree tempered the hostility of the latter towards the known religious opinions of Mayer. On another occasion he has words of recognition for a brochure of D. F. Strauss[2], apparently the latter's "Two Essays in Conciliation: 'Perishable and Permanent Elements in Christianity'; 'On Justinus Kerner'". On the death of his mother he writes to a friend[3]:

"The firm conviction which I have — based on scientific facts and without any reference to Revelation — of personal immortality, and of a higher direction of human life, was my greatest consolation when I clasped the cold hand of my dying mother."

But our object here is not to criticise Mayer's religious belief, but merely to show that he always upheld firmly those truths which form the basis of Christianity. To this end a passage such as that last cited is almost more valuable than the pious utterances to be found in his letters to his parents, or the fact that on his death-bed he comforted himself with the frequent repetition of that verse of the Bible: "Blessed are the dead who die in the Lord."[4]

In his scientific correspondence we find also incidental recognitions of personal immortality, or such expres-

---

[1] Weyrauch, Kleinere Schriften 362

[2] Ib. 92, Letter of March 1840.

[3] Ib. 20. [4] Ib. 485.

sions as: "The planetary system, the whole stellar system in general, are ordinances of Divine wisdom."[1]

Towards the Catholic Church, Mayer was very amicably disposed: "The idea of authority", says his friend Rümelin[2], "was so dominant with him, that for a time he dreamed of a fusion of Catholic discipline with Protestant dogma. . . . At this time (the time of his convalescence), he also took great pleasure in the company of Catholic priests." When Professor Huefner paid him a visit at the beginning of his seventieth year, Mayer's nephew begged him not to talk to his uncle about Darwin or politics. "Darwin's theory he cannot endure, and in politics he is a vigorous Ultramontane."[3] In a conversation on politics with Ringseis in 1869 he declared: "Nobody but the Pope can help us." For a time he had thoughts of becoming a Catholic, but contented himself with the reflection that internal communion was enough[4].

Very different was his estimate of modern German philosophy. "He had", writes Rümelin[5], "till 1841, never read a volume of philosophy, nor, so far as I know, did he ever read one after that year. When I brought him Hegel's Logic and the volume of the Encyclopaedia which contains the Philosophy of Nature, he returned both in a few days saying that he had not

---

[1] Weyrauch ante 423, Letter of 3. Aug. 1869. Ib. 139, Letter dated 17. July 1842.

[2] Allgemeine Zeitung 1878, Beilage Nr. 122, p. 1795; "Leopoldina" XV (1879) 54

[3] Hovestadt in "Natur und Offenbarung" XL (1894) 15.

[4] Erinnerungen des Dr. Joh. Nep. v. Ringseis, herausgeg. von Em. Ringseis IV, Regensburg 1891, 139.

[5] Obituary Notice: Allgemeine Zeitung 1878, Beilage Nr. 121, p. 1778.

understood a single syllable, and would not, even if he were to keep on reading them for a hundred years." Many another, indeed, has had a similar experience, but it is a token of Mayer's sincerity that he was not ashamed to admit it with the greatest frankness.

His criticism of Darwin may also find a place here:

"What from my standpoint I have to urge against Darwin's Theory is above all this: We see with our own eyes innumerable new individuals coming continually into existence in the vegetable and animal worlds by propagation and fertilisation. But how this comes about is for Physiology a completely insoluble riddle, a secret beyond our discovery. It is a case in which the well-known couplet of Haller finds the fullest application:

'Ins Inn're der Natur dringt kein erschaffner Geist;
Zu glucklich, wem sie noch die äuss're Schale weist.' [1]

"But although in these matters which lie so immediately beside us we are compelled to confess complete ignorance, the good Darwin, like another Lord God, offers us a complete explanation of a far more fundamental problem, the most fundamental of all, namely, the origin of organic life on our planet! This to my mind goes so ludicrously beyond the limits of human capacity, that I think of certain words of St. Paul. Beyond doubt the Darwinians are good propagandists, and the theory has won so many adherents in Germany on this sole account, that capital could be made out of it for Materialism." [2]

In England not Mayer but Joule († 1889) is regarded as having established the modern Theory of Heat[3]. James

---

1 "No created mind can penetrate the secrets of nature;
Too happy is it if it can know the outer shell."

2 Weyrauch, Kleinere Schriften 460, Mayer to Schmid, 22. Dec. 1874.

3 Osborne Reynolds, Memoir of James Prescott Joule: Memoirs and Proceedings of the Manchester Literary and Philosophical

Prescott Joule was born on Dec. 24th 1818, at Salford, near Manchester. His father was a wealthy brewer, and Joule was never under the necessity of earning his bread, nor did he interest himself at any period of his life in the business of the brewery. After preparatory studies with a private tutor he attended lectures in Chemistry given by Dalton, and then devoted himself to experiment and research. The most noteworthy fruits of his great patience and perseverance are sufficiently well-known, namely, the formulation of the mechanical equivalent of heat and the important law, known as Joule's Law.

The first preliminary account of his experiments on the Theory of Heat was submitted by Joule to the Meeting of the British Association held at Cork on July 23th 1843. In an addendum to this paper dated August 1843 we read:

"I shall lose no time in repeating and extending these experiments, being satisfied that the grand agents of nature are, by the Creator's Fiat, indestructible, and that whatever mechanical force is expended, an exact equivalent of heat is always obtained."[1]

On other occasions also Joule gladly invokes the name of the Creator, whether to base on His Will the indestructibility of Energy or to exalt the Divine Omnipotence and Wisdom manifested in the constitution of

---

Society. Vol. VI. Fourth Series. Manchester 1892. Cf. Scientific papers of J. P. Joule, 2 vols, London 1884 1887 (vol. I contains Joule's treatises, vol. II his correspondence on scientific matters). Das mechanische Wärme-Äquivalent. Gesammelte Abhandlungen von J. P. Joule. Ins Deutsche ubersetzt von J. W. Spengel. Braunschweig 1872. Nature XXVI (26. Oct. 1882), Nr. 678.

[1] Reynolds, Memoirs VI 71.

the world. Thus we find at the end of his essay "On the Alteration of Temperature consequent on the Rarefaction or Condensation of the Atmosphere", read before the Royal Scientific Society on June 20th 1844:

"Believing that the power of destroying things belongs to the Creator alone, I entirely co-incide with Roget and Faraday in the opinion that any theory which, when carried out, demands the annihilation of force, is necessarily erroneous."[1]

In a lecture on "Matter, Vital Force, and Heat", delivered in 1857, Joule states that he regards the argument against the destructibility of matter drawn from the fact that matter is the outcome of creation as of itself all but conclusive:

"We might reason a priori, that such absolute destruction of living force cannot possibly take place, because it is manifestly absurd to suppose that the powers with which God has endowed matter, can be destroyed any more than that they can be created by man's agency; but we are not left with this argument alone, decisive as it must be to every unprejudiced mind."[2]

A whole sub-division of the discourses in question is devoted to an exposition of the "wonderful arrangements of creation" which depend on the interchange of vital force and heat.

"He turns first to stellar space ... (phenomena) which speak in language which cannot be misunderstood of the wisdom and beneficence of the Great Architect of Nature."

"Thus it is that order is maintained in the universe — nothing is deranged, nothing ever lost, but the entire machinery,

---

[1] Reynolds, Memoirs VI 88.

[2] On Matter, Vital Force and Heat. By J. P. Joule. A Lecture at St. Ann's Church Reading Room 1847. Reynolds ante VI 2.

complicated as it is, works smoothly and harmoniously. And though, as in the awful vision of Ezekiel, wheel may be in the middle of wheel, and everything may appear complicated and involved in the apparent confusion and intricacy of an almost endless variety of causes, effects, conversions, and arrangements, yet is the most perfect regularity preserved — the whole being governed by the sovereign will of God." [1]

Joule employed his theory of the transformation of heat into work to explain the ignition of meteorites on their entry into our atmosphere. The friction of these bodies, travelling with the velocity of a planet, is so great as to kindle them to a glow. The intensity of the heat at last bursts them asunder, and so renders them powerless to injure the earth. The consideration of these facts leads Joule on to say:

"I cannot but be filled with admiration and gratitude for the wonderful provision thus made by the Author of Nature for the protection of His creatures. Were it not for the atmosphere which covers us with a shield, impenetrable in proportion to the violence which it is called upon to resist, we should be continually exposed to a bombardment of the most fatal and irresistible character. To say nothing of the larger stones, no ordinary buildings could afford shelter from very small particles striking at the velocity of eighteen miles per second. Even dust flying at such a velocity would kill any animal exposed to it." [2]

Another investigator who must be named in connection with the Mechanical Theory of Heat is the Alsatian engineer G. A. Hirn († 1890)[3]. Among his

---

[1] Reynolds ante VI 12—13.

[2] On Shooting Stars: Philosophical Magazine 1848. Reynolds, Memoirs VI 112.

[3] Gustave-Adolphe Hirn 1815—1890. Notice biographique avec documents divers concernant la vie, la famille et les travaux de

numerous essays on physical and mechanical subjects, the most interesting, next to the work on the Theory of Heat, is that in which he discusses the conditions of equilibrium of the Ring of Saturn, and proves, by mathematical considerations, that it need not necessarily be a connected whole but may be merely an aggregate of many smaller independent bodies. Hirn shows himself in these works a physicist of the first order, and his estimate of the philosophical implications of the discoveries made by modern science is for that reason highly valuable. In this connection he stands among the great figures of modern research. As his philosophic mind loves to pierce down to the basal principles of modern Physics, of force, of ether, of the kinetic theory of gas, so he occupies himself also with the relations of Physics on the one hand to philosophy and on the other to religion [1]. His last work published posthumously bears the title "Modern Science and the Question of a Future Life". In all his writings Hirn is a resolute opponent of Materialism.

M. Hirn, par M. le Docteur Faudel et M. Emile Schwoerer, ingénieur: Mitteilungen der naturhistor. Gesellschaft in Colmar, N. F. I, Jahre 1889—1890, Colmar 1891, 181—235.

[1] La notion de la Force dans la Science Moderne: Revue Scientifique XXXVI, Paris 1885, 129—141; XXXVII, 1886, 252—253; Recherches expérimentales sur la relation qui existe entre la résistance de l'air et sa température. Conséquences physiques et philosophiques qui découlent de ses expériences: Mémoires de l'Académie des Sciences de Belgique XLIII, Bruxelles 1882; Réflexions critiques sur la théorie cinétique de l'Univers — Réfutation scientifique de la doctrine matérialiste, ib.; etc. — His most important work on the subject: Constitution de l'espace céleste, Bruxelles 1889, contains a cutting criticism of the assumption of a material ether, which fills all space.

In the work in which he recounts his researches into the nature of heat [1] he treats also of the consequences which result from the new discoveries for the whole modern conception of the world; this latter question is developed later in a separate book [2]. And what are these consequences? According to Hirn all the attempts to explain reality are reducible to three systems: Materialism, for which there exists but matter; Pantheism, for which all things are God; Spiritualism whose characteristic is "that it admits a multiplicity of substances, ranging from matter to pure spirit, and, above all, maintains the immutability and individuality of these substances" [3].

The outcome of Hirn's investigation is to dismiss both Pantheism and Materialism, and, after his fashion, to establish Spiritualism. The earlier of the works named concludes with the statement:

"Spiritualism drawn down by reason from the cloudy regions whither it had soared only too often on the fatal wings of mysticism: Spiritualism fashioned to the requirements of the data furnished by empirical science, is, as things stand, the only one of our three systems at once acceptable to the reason and imposed on us by the facts, and is alone to be called rational." [4]

---

[1] Recherches sur l'équivalent mécanique de la chaleur, présentées à la société de physique de Berlin, par G. A. Hirn, ingénieur civil, Colmar 1858.

[2] Théorie mécanique de la chaleur. Conséquences philosophiques et métaphysiques de la thermodynamique, par G. A. Hirn. Analyse élémentaire de l'univers. Paris 1868.

[3] Ib. 3—4.

[4] Le spiritualisme arraché par la raison des régions nuageuses où il n'est allé que trop souvent se perdre sur les ailes du mysticisme; le spiritualisme, plié aux exigences des faits fournis par les sciences

This citation would be enough for our purpose, but we add another:

"The most trivial phenomenon of the inanimate world implies the presence of two distinct elements, the material element and the dynamic element: the most trivial being of the animate world implies the presence of a third element, in this case individualised in unities specifically different, the animic element. . . ."

"Either the universe as we know it to-day is in its present condition for the first time, or it has passed through such conditions an indefinite number of times. If the elements of the universe exist from all eternity, then from all eternity they have obeyed the laws of their constitution and their qualities. Now however long we suppose the period necessary to allow them to group themselves into the worlds which exist to-day, though we heap aeon on aeon, this period remains none the less finite; we are therefore forced to admit that the elements themselves remained inactive during an indefinite period, and did not begin to enter into relations until a given moment. The other horn of the dilemma, the idea of a closed circle of recurrent phenomena, does not indeed imply an absurdity; it is possible to say that the worlds which people space, and which have been formed by the condensation of the nebulae or cosmic substance will one day be destroyed and dispersed in space so as to reconstitute similar cosmic nebulae, and that the same series of phenomena will be repeated *ad infinitum.* But let it be clearly understood that this second clause of the dilemma is founded on no fact, on no analogy, however remote, derived from known facts: it would constitute in the physical sphere an article of faith, with which reason has no more to do than with any other article of faith." [1]

---

d'observation, est donc pour le moment la seule de nos trois doctrines qui à la fois soit acceptée et imposée, et qui puisse recevoir le nom rationnelle (Hirn, Recherches sur l'équivalent 337).

[1] Hirn, Théorie 165.

The necessary inference from this is evident; matter came into existence at a definite point of time and through an act of creation.

Later in the work Hirn casts about to find an argument for the immortality of the soul[1]: creatures are to him realised thoughts of the Creator[2], and he always by preference designates God "the Creator"[3].

It is obvious that this whole line of thought is derived from Christianity, and if logically pursued leads to Christianity, although Hirn himself in regard to Christianity was full of prejudices and misconceptions. This however does not affect our argument: it is enough that a Physicist, completely master of his special department and constantly occupied with the metaphysical interpretation of physical discoveries, finds it in no wise necessary to attach himself to Pantheism and Materialism, but on the contrary declares both these systems irreconcilable with the facts. "With his dying hand", wrote A. Slaby[4] (Berlin) in an obituary notice of Hirn, "he wrote on his last work as a Confession of Faith the lines:

---

[1] Ib. 167. [2] Pensées réalisées du Créateur (Hirn, Théorie 517).

[3] Ib. 475 507 511 etc.

[4] Mitteilungen der naturhistor. Gesellschaft in Colmar, N. F. I 335. Cf. p. 212. C'est contre ce matérialisme, renouvelé avec peu de modifications de celui d'Épicure, de Lucrèce, que Hirn n'a cessé de lutter de toutes ses forces dès l'origine de ses travaux, mais avec des armes de plus en plus puissantes, toutes tirées de faits aujourd'hui connus appliqués à l'aide d'une méthode neuve aussi. La Force, ou pour nous exprimer plus exactement, ce qui dans l'Univers établit les relations d'attraction, de répulsion, de lumière, de chaleur, d'électricité . . . entre les corps, est un Élément spécifiquement distinct de la Matière, une réalité objective, et non plus une sorte d'entité métaphysique ou un simple mouvement de la Matière.

'Hoch über der Zeit und dem Raume webt
Lebendig der höchste Gedanke,
Und ob alles in ewigem Wechsel kreist,
Es beharret im Wechsel ein ruhiger Geist.'"

Far from unimportant was the contribution to the Theory of Heat of the English engineer W. J. Macquorn Rankine († 1872). P. G. Tait writes of him in the biography prefixed to his edition of Rankine's writings: "He was profoundly attached to his parents; and one of the most touching notes in his journal is the brief record of his lasting obligations to them for early instruction in the fundamental principles of the Christian Religion and the character of its Founder." [1]

Perhaps the greatest of recent Physicists is Sir William Thomson (Lord Kelvin), born in 1824 in Belfast. As early as 1846, at the age of twenty-two, he was appointed Professor of Natural Science in the University of Glasgow; and in 1855 he was, in the words of Von Helmholtz, "one of the first Mathematical Physicists in Europe". He is the author of more than three hundred important works.

Concerning Lord Kelvin's position among scientists, the Berlin Academy of Science expressed itself as follows n an "Address to Lord Kelvin on his Golden Jubilee, July 15th 1896".

"Rich indeed are the acquisitions made by Physics in the last fifty years: but foremost among these great conquests are the establishment and development of the Mechanical Theory of Heat, and the vast extension of the Theory of

---

[1] Miscellaneous Scientific Papers. By W. J. Macquorn Rankine. With a Memoir of the author by P. G. Tait, edited by W. J. Millar, London 1881, xx. — Abbé Moigno says: Rankine was one of the busiest letter writers in the world (Les Mondes XXX, Paris 1873, 2).

Electricity with its various applications. To all these victories you have in a supreme degree contributed. . . ."

"We marvel at the boldness and accuracy with which in your works you reach your conclusions, whether you are engaged in synthesizing experiments of the laboratory, or in deducing the density of ether from the energy of radiation: in concluding from the times of the tides to the stability of the globe, or in employing the laws of the conduction of heat to unveil the remote past of our planet. . . ."

"In a supreme measure you have become a teacher of our generation, and among living Physicists there must be few indeed who have not sat at your feet and who do not with heartfelt gratitude acclaim you as their Master."

Not an unimportant proof of the far-reaching and comprehensive penetration which is here praised in Lord Kelvin is the fact that he recognised from the purely scientific point of view the necessity for the existence of a Creator. He does this in the paper in which, beginning with the everyday phenomena of motion, heat, and light, he tries to arrive at their ultimate mechanical antecedents [1].

If motion, heat, and light, are according, to modern theories of Physics, only different forms, in which the supply of "living force" or "energy" existing in Nature, manifests itself, if any one of these forms of energy can pass into another, the question naturally arises: Which form of energy is at the beginning of the series, and is to be regarded as the source of the others? Sir W. Thomson gives as first consequence the following opinion, which forms the subject-

---

[1] Sitzungsberichte 1896, 729. The renowned German Physicist, H. v. Helmholtz, wrote in 1855 concerning W. Thomson, whom he had visited in Kreuznach as follows: "Er ubertrifft ubrigens alle wissenschaftlichen Grössen, welche ich persönlich kennen gelernt habe, an Scharfsinn, Klarheit und Beweglichkeit des Geistes, so dass ich selbst mir neben ihm etwas stumpfsinnig erscheine" (L. Königsberger, Hermann v. Helmholtz I, Braunschweig 1902, 255).

matter for further discussion: "We must regard the sun as the source from which the mechanical energy of all the motions and heat of living creatures, and of the motions, heat and light derived from fires and artificial flames is supplied." [1]

Those who have never reflected on the matter, may indeed be astonished when they are told that the sun gives the soldier strength to march, and the blacksmith power to deal mighty blows on his anvil. But Lord Kelvin proceeds to explain his views. All modes of life derive their bodily heat and energy from chemical changes which are due to the food which they have taken. The food of man and of animals comes ultimately from the vegetable kingdom, that of the herbivorous creatures directly, and that of the carnivorous indirectly. But how do plants grow and build up their organisms? Except the fungus, they draw in the greater part of their substance from the air and the soil by the decomposition of carbonic acid and water. This decomposition can however only go on under the influence of light. Thus the plant is directly the child of the sun, as is the plant-eating animal. Furthermore from the sun is derived every species of artificial light and heat. "Coal composed as it is of the relics of ancient vegetation, derived its potential energy from the light of distant ages. Wood fires give us heat and light which has been got from the sun a few years ago. Our coalfires and gas lamps bring us for our present comfort heat and light of a primeval sun which have lain dormant as potential energy beneath seas and mountains for countless ages." [2]

Is the sun then to be regarded as the sole source of life on earth? No. For the natural movements of earth and water, we must admit, besides the effect of the sun, a second cause, namely the motion of the earth, the respective movements and mutual attractions of the earth, sun, and moon.

---

[1] On Mechanical Antecedents of Motion, Heat, and Light. Mathematical and Physical Papers by Sir W Thomson II, Cambridge 1884, 34—41.

[2] Ib. II 35

Thus we seem to have arrived at a twofold source of all power and energy. Might not both be traced back to one common source? Sir W. Thomson tries to prove that this is really the case. He attributes the motion of the planets as well as the heat of the sun to gravity, a view which, with one important correction by Von Helmholtz, concerning the source of the sun's heat, is to-day the one most generally received. To develop his suggestion, Thomson had to go back to the first stage of the planetary system; he shows at the outset that we have a right to speak of an evolution of the planetary system, and to follow this development back wards and forwards from its present condition. We meet however with one obstacle, when we review the different steps of the planetary system and seek to deduce one from the other.

"All such conclusions are subject to limitations, as we do not know at what moment a creation of matter or energy may have given a beginning beyond which mechanical speculations cannot lead us. If in purely mechanical science we are ever liable to forget this limitation, we ought to be reminded of it by considering that purely mechanical reasoning shows a time when the earth must have been tenantless; and teaches us that our own bodies, as well as all living plants and animals and all fossil organic remains, are organised forms of matter to which science can point no antecedent except the Will of a Creator, a truth amply confirmed by the evidence of geological history." [1]

In these words it is laid down as self-evident, that matter and energy can only come into existence by being created, and that without God the origin of life is inexplicable. We find the same thought expressed by Lord Kelvin in other passages, for example:

---

[1] Ib. 37—38.

"It is impossible", he says, "to understand either the beginning or the continuance of life, without an overruling creative power; and therefore, no conclusions of dynamical science regarding the future condition of the earth can be held to give dispiriting views as to the destiny of the race of intelligent beings by which it is at present inhabited." [1]

In the same paper he says that living beings could not have come into existence spontaneously from inorganic matter.

"I need scarcely say", he writes, "that the beginning and maintenance of life on the earth is absolutely and infinitely beyond the range of all sound speculation in dynamical science. The only contribution of dynamics to theoretical biology is absolute negation of automatic commencement or automatic maintenance of life." [2]

In the year 1871 when Darwinism still occupied the fore-ground in scientific discussions, and the question of the origin of life held the minds of all in suspense Lord Kelvin had occasion to express his opinions on this subject before a meeting of the British Association in Edinburgh. Of evolution within the world of organisms, he knows nothing at first hand, but that system of evolution which takes its name from Darwin, he declares to be unsatisfactory.

"Darwin", he says, "concludes his great work on the Origin of Species with the following words: 'It is interesting to contemplate an entangled bank clothed with many plants of many kinds, with birds singing on the bushes, with various insects flitting about, and with worms crawling

[1] On the Age of the Sun's Heat. Popular Lectures and Discourses I. 198.

[2] Ib. 314.

through the damp earth, and to reflect that these elaborately constructed forms, so different from each other, and depending on each other in so complex a manner, have all been produced by laws acting around us.'

There is grandeur in this view of life with its several powers having been originally breathed by the Creator into a few forms or into one; and that, whilst this planet has gone cycling on according to the fixed law of gravity, from so simple a beginning endless forms most beautiful and most wonderful have been and are being evolved. With the feeling expressed in these two sentences I most cordially sympathise. I have omitted two sentences which come between them, describing briefly the hypothesis of 'the Origin of Species by Natural Selection', because I have always felt that this hypothesis does not contain the true theory of evolution, if evolution there has been, in biology. Sir John Herschel . . . objected to the doctrine of natural selection that it was too like the Laputan method of making books, and that it did not sufficiently take into account a continually guiding and controlling intelligence. This seems to me a most valuable and instructive criticism. I feel profoundly convinced that the argument of design has been greatly too much lost sight of in recent zoological speculations. Reactions against the frivolities of teleology, such as are to be found not rarely in the notes of the learned commentators on Paley's Natural Theology, have, I believe, a temporary effect in turning attention from the solid and irrefragable argument so well put forward in that excellent old book. But overpoweringly strong proofs of intelligent and benevolent design lie all round us; and if ever perplexities, whether metaphysical or scientific, turn us away from them for a time, they come back upon us with irresistible force, showing to us through Nature the influence of a free will, and teaching us that living beings depend on one ever-acting Creator and Ruler." [1]

[1] Report of the Forty-First Meeting of the British Association for the Advancement of Science held at Edinburgh in August 1871: Address by the President Sir William Thomson, London 1872, cv.

One must refer to Jonathan Swift's Gulliver's Travels to find out how books are made in Laputa. The trend of "that excellent old book" Paley's Natural Theology can however be gathered from its second and more detailed title, Evidences of the Existence and Attributes of the Deity [1].

More recently, in the beginning of May 1903, Lord Kelvin emphatically voiced his opinions on the theme "Science and Religion".

"The Times" contain the following report of his speech [2]:

"In connection with University College Christian Association the first of a course of lectures on 'Christian Apologetics' was delivered last Friday, in the botanical theatre at University College. Lord Reay, President of University College, occupied the Chair, and the large theatre was filled to over-flowing, many visitors being unable to find seats.

The Rev. Professor G. Henslow, who was the lecturer, spoke on the subject of 'Present-day Rationalism, an Examination of Darwinism."

Lord Kelvin in moving a vote of thanks to the lecturer, said he wished to make a personal explanation. He had recently had occasion to make use of the expressions ether, atoms, electricity, and had been horrified to read in the press that he had spoken of ether-atoms. Ether was absolutely non-atomic; it was absolutely structureless and homogeneous. He was in thorough sympathy with Professor Henslow in the fundamentals of his lecture, but he

---

[1] Natural Theology, or Evidences of the Existence and Attributes of the Deity, London 1802 and subsequent editions. Between 1836 and 1839, Lord Brougham and Sir Charles Bell were occupied in publishing an annotated edition.

[2] The Times. Weekly edition. Vol XXVII, Nr. 1375, London, May 8th 1903, Supplement III.

could not say that with regard to the origin of life science neither affirmed nor denied creative power. Science positively affirmed creative power. Science made everyone feel a miracle in himself. It was not in dead matter that they lived and moved and had their being, but in the creating and directive power which science compelled them to accept as an article of belief. They could not escape from that when they studied the physics and dynamics of living and dead matter all around. Modern biologists were coming once more to a firm acceptance of something, and that was a vital principle. They had an unknown object put before them in science. In thinking of that subject they were all agnostics. They only knew God in His works, but they were absolutely forced by science to admit and to believe with absolute confidence in a directive power — in an influence other than physical, dynamical, electrical forces. Cicero had denied that they could have come into existence by a fortuitous concourse of atoms. There was nothing between absolute scientific belief in creative power, and the acceptance of the theory of a fortuitous concourse of atoms. Was there, he asked, anything so absurd as to believe that a number of atoms by falling together of their own accord could make a crystal, a sprig of moss, a microbe, a living animal? People thought that given millions of years, these might come to pass, but they could not think that a million of millions of millions of years could give them unaided a beautiful world like ours. They had a spiritual influence, and in science a knowledge that there was that influence, in the world around them. He admired the healthy, breezy atmosphere of free thought in Professor Henslow's Lecture. Let no one, he urged, be afraid of true freedom. They could be free in their thought, in their criticisms, and with freedom of thought they were bound to come to the conclusion that science was not antagonistic to religion, but a help for religion."

In a letter to the "Times" two days later Lord Kelvin made certain corrections touching upon the differences between the possible origin of crystals and that of living organisms.

"I desired to point out that while 'fortuitous concourse of atoms' is not an inappropriate description of the formation of a crystal, it is utterly absurd in respect to the coming into existence, or the growth, or the continuation of the molecular combinations presented in the bodies of living things. Here scientific thought is compelled to accept the idea of creative power. Forty years ago I asked Liebig, walking somewhere in the country, if he believed that the grass and flowers which we saw around us grew by mere chemical forces. He answered, 'No, no more than I believe that a book of botany describing them could grow by mere chemical forces'. Every action of human free will is a miracle to physical and chemical and mathematical science."

In printing, in the "Nineteenth Century" for June 1903, his own version of his speech, Lord Kelvin concludes with the exhortation:

"Do not be afraid of being free-thinkers! If you think strongly enough, you will be forced by science to the belief in God, which is the foundation of all religion. You will find science not antagonistic but helpful to religion." [1]

Lord Kelvin's utterances brought down on him a crowd of objections; most of them however were composed in the heat of anger and are beside the point in question [2].

As Haeckel appeals to Helmholtz († 1894), a passage from a letter of the latter may fitly be quoted.

"We Mathematical Scientists", writes Helmholtz to his father, "are disciplined to the most anxious precision in the

---

[1] Reprinted from the Nineteenth Century in The American Catholic Quarterly Review XXVIII, Philadelphia 1903, 603. Cf. Stimmen aus Maria-Laach LXV 487.

[2] The objections and answers are printed in the Weekly Edition of the Times from the 8th to the 15th May (Supp. III). Cf. A Review ib. 15th May p 313. "The importance of Lord Kelvin's opinion", concludes the latter article, "is rather enhanced than diminished by the hostile irrelevancy which some of his critics have displayed."

establishment of facts and inferences, and compress our wandering conjectures into very short and meagre hypotheses, by the aid of which we seek to forecast a goal as yet unexplored, so that we are, perhaps, too much afraid of that bolder employment of scientific data which in other circumstances may be justifiable.

Your letter seems to me to intimate a certain suspicion that I am a subscribêr to the paltry tirades of Vogt and Moleschott. Not in the least. I must also enter an energetic protest against your treating these two gentlemen as representatives of scientific research. Neither has up to the present shown by original and specialised investigation that he has acquired that respect for facts and that prudence in reaching conclusions which men learn in the school of physical research. A prudent investigator knows very well that the fact of his having penetrated a little way into the intricate process of nature gives him no more right, not a scintilla more, than any other man to pronounce dogmatically on the nature of the soul. To my mind, too, you are not right in designating the majority of prudent scientists as enemies of Philosophy. Indifferent the greater part undoubtedly are, a state of things for which the blame rests on the extravagant speculations of Hegel and Schelling, two writers who have, I grant you, been taken to represent all philosophy. . . ." [1]

Thus wrote Helmholtz on March 4th 1857, ten years after the publication of his essay "On the Conservation of Force".

On religious questions Helmholtz never made any open declaration. His biographer describes him as "in mind and conviction a religious man, in the noblest sense of the word, although not in the orthodox sense of membership of a Church" [2], and says that the famous

---

[1] L. Konigsberger, Hermann v. Helmholtz I, Braunschweig 1902, 291 f.

[2] Ib. II (1903) 75. E. Dennert (Die Religion der Naturforscher, Berlin 1901, 34) says of Von Helmholtz: "Ich erfuhr aber

scientist always regarded the philosophical views of his father Ferdinand Helmholtz "not only with pious interest, but also with the highest appreciation of their scientific value, and, as appears from later utterances, with hearty agreement"[1]. Ferdinand Helmholtz was a follower of the younger Fichte, and a convinced theist and spiritualist[2].

Mention may be made here also of the Physicist Krönig († 1879) "who has won for himself an honoured name in the field of research by his investigations into the Theory of Gases. Clausius cites him as his predecessor in this province, and corroborates his conclusions". He published in 1874 a book on "The existence of God and the happiness of man." He denies that through "blind chance, however long a period of time we assume, the atoms could by their own forces come together and form living cells. . . . Without the guidance of a purposive intelligence, organisms could never have come into existence"[3]. It is interesting to note e. g. what he has to say from the standpoint of the mathematical Theory of Probability, against those who find no difficulty in the hypothesis that in the course of endless time and after endless attempts the most complex formations may have come fortuitously into existence: "If every year for a million years, a million men were born, each of whom lived to the age of ten thousand years and every minute of his life made 20 throws with 30 dice, the mathematical probability is that amongst all these throws one of thirty aces would not have even once occurred."

aus bester Quelle, dass er Gottesdienst, ja sogar das Abendmahl hin und wieder besuchte."

[1] Königsberger, Hermann v. Helmholtz I 333.

[2] J. R(einke?) writes about an utterance of Von Helmholtz concerning the petty view that we can clear up the fundamental questions of life by scientific investigation. Deutsche Rundschau LXXXI, Berlin 1894, 131.

[3] Cf. J. Reinke, Die Welt als Tat[3], Berlin 1903, 12—14.

We here conclude our survey of the great masters to whom we owe the largest and most fruitful scientific conception of modern times. And although certain people are good enough to appeal to their authority in proof of the 'monistic' character of the 'Law of Substance', to whom are we to appeal for the deepest interpretation of their great discoveries, to the discoverers themselves, or to those who profess to be their disciples?

II. MATHEMATICS.

Mathematics is not itself a branch of Physical Science, but in many instances it is by means of Mathematics that our knowledge of nature is first raised to the status of genuine science. Astronomy and Physics are scientific precisely in so far as they deal with number and measure, in so far as they enter into alliance with Mathematics, and absorb its spirit and method.

In a work like this, then, which is concerned with the scientific conception of life, and with the essential spirit of Natural Science, some attention must be accorded to number and measure. We must not fail to examine the attitude of the leaders of Mathematics towards Christianity and religious belief in general, and to enquire whether the temper of Mathematics is reconcilable with that of religion.

To show how little we need evade the question we appeal to the most eminent authorities on the subject, the most recent writers on the History of Mathematics. "Like most other Mathematicians", says M. Cantor[1], "Euler was deeply religious without any trace of bigotry.

[1] Allg. deutsche Biographie VI 427.

He was in the habit of conducting the devotions of his family, and one of his few polemical works was a "Defence of Revelation against the Objections of the Freethinkers" the publication of which in Berlin in 1747 in the immediate neighbourhood of the Court of Frederick the Great, indicates a moral courage which lifted him far above the assaults of mere scoffers."

Leonhard Euler (born at Basle in 1707, died at St. Petersburg in 1783) does not come within the period with which this book is concerned. But even in the nineteenth century the praise which Cantor bestows on "most great mathematicians" is justified by many illustrious examples. At the beginning of this century the leaders of this department were Gauss in Germany, and Cauchy in France. In the latter half of the century two of the highest places were occupied by Hermite in France, and Riemann in Germany. If we are able to show that the relations to Christianity of these four were the reverse of hostile, we shall have refuted those writers who condemn religious belief as a kind of mysticism which cannot co-exist with the habit of exact thought inculcated by mathematics.

In the history of Astronomy the passage from the 18th to the 19th century is marked by an event of the highest importance, at once a great discovery and a great opportunity. On New Year's Night 1801, at Palermo, Piazzi discovered the first of what we now know to be a number of small planets between Mars and Jupiter. But before the observer had ascertained the positions of the planet necessary, by the methods of computation then practised, to determine accurately its path, it approached so near the sun that it was lost from sight in the sun's radiance. Thus the planet had no sooner been discovered than it was lost again, for there was no hope of locating it unless astronomers knew in what quarter of the heavens to search for it, and this could not be known without a knowledge of its path. At this juncture there came to the aid of Astronomy a young mathematician of only four and twenty: he brought a completely new method by which, from the meagre observations of Piazzi, the path of the vanished planet could be deduced. In the spot indicated by him Ceres was re-discovered by Olbers on Jan. 1st 1802.

The youthful Scientist, who thus leaped into a European reputation, was Karl Frederick Gauss, one of the foremost mathematicians of all time. It sounds incredible, but it is a well established fact that when a child of three in the workshop of his father, who was a simple artisan, he was able to detect any mistake made in the reckoning of accounts. When at nine years of age he was sent to school, the teacher of Arithmetic set as the first exercise to the class the addition of a long row of figures, each successive line of which exceeded the preceding one by a constant sum. If the first line of such a row be added to the last, the second to the second-last, and so on, the sum will always be the same; and there is consequently no need to worry oneself with a tedious addition, since the whole can be reduced to a simple exercise in multiplication. Young Gauss perceived this relation at the first glance, and while his classfellows added and added and in the end succeeded for the most part in adding wrongly, he wrote the answer on his slate and waited patiently for the termination of the affair. . . . This performance, and similar tokens of extraordinary ability decided his future career. The schoolmaster pressed Gauss's father to let his son continue his studies, and in the end managed to persuade him. He had the little spinning-wheel, on which Karl worked every evening, broken up for firewood, and the future mathematician entered on his career.

The later development of this great genius was in keeping with his first promise. His dissertation for the Doctorate on the fundamental theorem of the Theory of Equations, presented in his twenty-second year, was in itself a scientific feat. In the first part he showed that this theorem had not hitherto been really demonstrated, in the second he himself presented an unimpeachable demonstration. Two years later, appeared his epoch-making "Arithmetical Researches", and the discovery already mentioned. These were followed by a long series of other works of equal brilliancy.

In his student-days at Gottingen, Gauss was on terms of particular intimacy with a young Hungarian, Wolfgang Bolyai, who was tutor to nobleman, and in that capacity had come to the German University town. Bolyai was also a student of Mathematics. The letters which passed between the friends after their separation reveal amongst other things the attitude which Gauss maintained towards the higher problems of life. Thus, e. g. he concludes a letter to Bolyai from Brunswick, dated Dec. 3rd 1802:

"Now good-bye, my dear fellow. May the dream which we call life be for you a happy dream, a foretaste of that true life which we shall inherit in our real home, when the awakened spirit shall labour no longer under the grievous bondage of the flesh, the fetters of space, the whips of earthly pain, and the sting of our paltry needs and desires. Let us carry our burdens to the end, stoutly and uncomplainingly, never losing sight of that higher goal. Glad then shall we be to lay down our weary lives, and to see the dropping of the curtain."[1]

When Bolyai announces the birth of a son, Gauss ends his letter of congratulation (June 20th 1803) with the words[2]:

"You hold now in your hand the first links of a chain which stretches into eternity, of an everlasting life. A weighty and earnest charge, but a glorious one. May your son one day bless you as the first author of his happiness!"

When Councilor Eschenburg lost his wife in December 1798, Gauss wrote to Bolyai (Jan. 9th 1799):

"It is beyond doubt that the happiness which love can bestow on its chosen souls is the highest that can fall to mortal's lot. But when I imagine myself in the place of the man who, after twenty happy years, now in one moment loses his all, I am moved almost to say that he is the wretchedest of mortals, and that it is better never to have known such happy days. So it is on this miserable earth: 'the purest joy finds its grave in the abyss of time'. What are we without the hope of a better future? Let us keep a free heart as long as we can, and place our happiness in ourselves."[3]

In the early period of their separation the letters which passed between Gauss and Bolyai were naturally numerous. They had arranged a fixed hour at which to think of one another:

"Your letter", writes Gauss, in 1798, "reached me on the evening of the last day of last month, just when

---

[1] Briefwechsel zwischen Karl Friedrich Gauss und Wolfgang Bolyai. Herausgeg. von Fr. Schmidt und Paul Stäckel, Leipzig 1899, 47.

[2] Schmidt u. Stäckel ante 54.

[3] Ib. 16. Ludw. Hänselmann, Karl Friedrich Gauss. Zwölf Kapitel aus seinem Leben, Leipzig 1878, 92—93.

I had settled down to celebrate the anniversary of our friendship. There I sat in my armchair with a pipe filled for you, and just in the middle of my dream that you were sitting opposite in your black jacket and black cap and talking to me about old times, came your letter with its questions to show that you were actually at that moment thinking of me, and that my dream was no dream." [1]

As time went on, the two scientists, naturally enough, had not time for such poetical exercises of friendship. Their correspondence became rarer and at last altogether ceased.

Many years went by and their lives led them very far apart. The spruce Hungarian, "with his black jacket and black cap", had crusted into a peevish professor. He held a post in a college in Siebenburg, and had become a notable old crank, at feud with his wife and mother-in-law, and discontented with his son, for whose insubordination the educational theories of the pedagogue papa were not perhaps blameless.

"His cynicism", writes in 1849 a visitor of his, "passes into a sort of noble communism. Thus, for example, he keeps a servant but lets him do what he likes, for he cleans his own boots (even prepares the grease for them), makes his own bed, attends to his own cellar, and as a rule to his own meals too. . . . His room resembles in dirt and disorder the tub of Diogenes, with the sole addition of a heap of books and some blackboards. . . ." [2]

But the fame of Gauss's discoveries and researches had penetrated even to Siebenburg, and Bolyai was

[1] Schmidt u. Stäckel ante 10.

[2] Ib. 132.

moved to write once more to his old comrade. He wrote, sending news of his own fortunes, and extolling the happiness of a friend to whose lot had fallen all that the world could give of glory, all that intellect could give of knowledge, joy or consolation. This outpouring of his heart affected Gauss deeply, and in response he opened his inmost heart to the friend of his youth. He writes April 20th 1848:

"Melancholy were my feelings on receiving your letter of Jan. 18. It was as the voice of a ghost crying out of the long vanished past, or at least it cast my thoughts back to a time since which so many heavy years have passed over our heads. It is true that my life has been crowned with much of what the world thinks enviable. But believe me, my dear Bolyai, the bitterness of life, or at least of mine, which runs through it like a strand of red, and becomes less and less endurable as I grow older, is not compensated in the hundredth part by the joy of life. I will freely admit that these burdens, which to me have been so grievous, would have been lighter to many another; but our temperament is part of ourselves, given to us by the Creator with our very existence, and we have very little power to change it. I find, on the other hand, in this very consciousness of the vanity of life, which nearly all men must confess to as they draw near the end, my strongest assurance of the approach of a more beautiful metamorphosis. In this, my dear friend, let us find comfort, and endeavour to call up calmness to bear life out to the end. *Fortem facit vicina libertas senem*, says Seneca." [1]

---

[1] W. Sartorius v. Waltershausen, Gauss zum Gedächtnis, Leipzig 1856, 103. — Grunert, who quotes this passage in his Archives of Mathematik und Physik (XXVI, Greifswald 1856, Liter. Bericht CIV) remarks: "Absichtlich haben wir die religiöse Seite des grössten Mathematikers und Naturforschers der neuesten Zeit hier bestimmter hervorgehoben und stellen sie gegenüber den namentlich für die Jugend leicht so verderblich werden könnenden Ansichten einer

"Vanity of vanities, and all is vanity", one is driven to cry out over such a letter as that. So a Gauss, too, in the full possession of all that Science can procure of intellectual joy, honour and distinction comes, at the end of his days, to declare that there is no peace of spirit in it all, and that life is a riddle and a torment unless it be completed by a happy eternity. And with Gauss these are not mere passing moods but convictions which dwelt with him all his life, and formed the basis of his moral nature.

"The indestructible idea of personal survival after death", says a biographer, "the steadfast belief which he had in a Supreme Ruler, a just, eternal, omniscient, omnipotent God, formed the foundation of his religious life, and in unison with his matchless scientific achievements formed a perfect harmony."

He once expressed himself to this effect: 'There is in this world a joy of the intellect, which finds satisfaction in science, and a joy of the heart, which manifests itself above all in the aid men give one another against the troubles and trials of life. But for the Supreme Being to have created existences, and stationed them in various spheres in order to taste these joys for some 80 or 90 years — that were surely a miserable plan.' . . . 'Whether the soul were to live for 80 years or for 80 million years, if it were doomed in the end to perish, such an existence would only be a respite. In the end it would drop out of being. We are thus impelled to the conclusion to which so many things point, although they do not amount to a coercive scientific proof, that besides this material world there exists another purely spiritual order of things, with activities as various, as the present, and that this world of spirit we shall one day inherit.' This divine wisdom was the food

---

gewissen Klasse heutiger Naturforscher", that is to say of those, "die so gern das Göttliche und Geistige in den Staub ziehen und lediglich an die Materie ketten möchten."

and discipline of his soul up to that last silent midnight in which his eyes closed for ever."

Gauss gives frequent expression to his conviction of the immortality of the soul. Thus, e. g. he writes to Olbers[1]:

"I always return to the conviction that the necessary truth of Geometry cannot be demonstrated, at least by *human* reason and *for*[2] human reason. Perhaps we shall in another life attain to a deeper insight into the essence of space than is possible to us here. Till then, we must not rank Geometry with Arithmetic, which is of a purely *a priori* character, but rather with Mechanics."

Laplace is reported to have, on one occasion, described Johann Frederick Pfaff of Berlin († 1825) as the greatest mathematician of Germany. When he was reminded of Gauss, he extricated himself from the difficulty with the witty remark: "Pfaff is the greatest mathematician in Germany, Gauss the greatest in Europe."[3] Certain it is that Laplace held Pfaff in high esteem[4], and that the researches of the latter contributed greatly to

[1] Karl Friedrich Gauss, Werke VIII, Göttingen 1900, 177: Gauss an Olbers, Göttingen, 28. April 1817. — C. Vogt made a violent attack (Köhlerglaube und Wissenschaft[4], Giessen 1856, XXXIV) on Rud. Wagner, because the latter had maintained (Allg. Ztg. 1855, 1050) that Gauss entertained friendly feelings towards Christianity. Vogt adduces in proof of the contrary, that Gauss wrote under his portrait: "Thou Nature art my goddess, to thy laws my services are bound!" To write a word to refute him would be mere waste of ink.

[2] Doubly underlined by Gauss.

[3] Sammlung von Briefen, gewechselt zwischen Joh. Friedr. Pfaff und Herzog Karl von Wurttemberg, F. Bouterwek, A. v. Humboldt, A. G. Kästner u. a. Herausg. von Karl Pfaff, Leipzig 1853, Vorwort VII.

[4] Ib. 160.

the advance of his science. This "greatest mathematician in Germany" stood on very friendly relations with religion [1]. In his early letters to a "jacobinically" disposed brother he admonishes the latter: "Be a respecter of religion", "never disregard the standpoint of religion"; and in his maturer years his friends celebrate his strong "religious sense" [2].

Two years after Gauss, there died in Paris another Mathematician who had rendered to science services no less worthy, Augustin Louis Cauchy [3]. Born in 1789 at Paris, he was, at the conclusion of a brilliant course of studies, attached as engineer to the immense operations by which Napoleon undertook to elevate Cherbourg to a first-rate naval harbour confronting England. He was soon compelled by ill-health to resign this position; and he thenceforth devoted himself exclusively to scientific research, and published in rapid succession a number of brilliant works. That which attracted most attention was his demonstration of a Theory of Fermat, at which the most eminent mathematicians, including

---

[1] Ib. Brief vom 4. Jan. 1789, 89 91; cf. 114.

[2] Ib. Biograph. Einleitung 31.

[3] Cf. J. B. Biot, A.-L. Cauchy. Lettre à M. de Falloux, membre de l'Académie française, in Mélanges scientifiques et littéraires III, Paris 1858, 143—156. C. A. Valson, La vie et les travaux du Baron Cauchy (Tome I: Partie historique. Tome II: Partie scientifique), Paris 1868. Valson, Communication relative à la nouvelle édition des œuvres complètes d'Aug. Cauchy, in Congrès scientifique international des Catholiques tenu à Paris du 8 au 13 avril 1888 II, Paris 1888, 514—520. Jos. Bertrand, A.-L. Cauchy, Discours prononcé à la séance annuelle de l'Académie des sciences 1898 (reprinted in Cosmos, Revue des sciences et de leurs applications, Paris 12 févr. 1898, 211—217. Kneller in Stimmen aus Maria-Laach LXIV, Freiburg 1903, 138—148 285—298.

even Euler and Gauss, had worked in vain. Election to the Academy, and the highest educational posts in France were the reward of these first works. His subsequent achievements were no less remarkable; they are, indeed, beyond praise. Joseph Bertrand, a learned colleague of Cauchy's, but by no means a sharer of his convictions, in his discourse on Cauchy in the Academy in 1897 expressly declares his inability to render him the praise which is his due.

"For a long time now", he says, "it has been beyond the power of any eulogy to heighten the splendour of his reputation, a reputation which can never die. We come too late to say anything but what all the world knows, and yet our predecessors who spoke immediately after his death were too early. The reputation of Cauchy grew wider as years went on; his most enthusiastic admirers of half-a-century ago could not have foreseen or foretold it. He had explored new regions: the heights to which he had climbed all the world knew, but no one could then have rightly appreciated the spaciousness, the consistency, the inexhaustible fertility of his researches." [1]

Cauchy's biographer, A. Valson, joint editor of the collection of his works published at the expense of the Academy, disscussing the place which Cauchy occupies in his Science, writes:

"I confine myself to the statement that many scientific authorities consider Cauchy the first mathematician of our century: no one at any rate disputes his claim to be ranked among the greatest masters. His methods and conclusions form the point of departure of most contemporary mathe-

[1] Le rôle de Cauchy grandit chaque jour; les admirateurs les plus enthousiastes, il y a 50 ans, ne pouvaient ni le prédire ni le prévoir. Il explorait des régions nouvelles, on savait à quelle hauteur; nul n'en pouvait deviner l'étendue, la consistance et l'inépuisable fécondité. Bertrand ante 211.

maticians. Herein, above all, lies the characteristic quality of his life's work." [1]

According to O. Terquem also, the distinguishing feature of Cauchy is the creative verve of his genius; he laid new paths open whereever he went [2]. Our admiration of his extraordinary endowments is increased by the fact that his works are not limited to a single province of Mathematics, but deal with almost every part of this science. His genius for work was so amazing that at nearly every weekly meeting of the Academy he had something new to offer, and the reprint of his collected works will, according to Valson's calculation, run to 11,531 quarto pages.

At his entrance into his professorate, Cauchy had taken an oath of loyalty to the king. This oath had very serious consequences for him. When the July Revolution broke out, he considered it a breach of his bounden duty to take the oath of allegiance to Louis-Philippe also: on his refusal to do so he lost all his professional posts, and all the efforts of his friends to procure him a fresh public appointment were in vain until the Revolution of 1848. This annulled the political oath, and when the oath of personal loyalty was re-introduced, Cauchy was released from it by Napoleon III. In the first anguish of 1830, Cauchy had left France. Soon after, on the invitation of Charles X., he went to

---

[1] Congrès scientifique international des catholiques tenu à Paris 1888 II, Paris 1888, 514.

[2] Mathématicien dans le sens le plus large, l'esprit de Cauchy n'était pas cantonné dans un coin de la science. Partout il fondait, partout il créait, partout il était au premier rang. Quoted by M. Marie, Hist. des sciences mathématiques et physiques XII, Paris 1888, 166.

Prague as tutor to the Count de Chambord, and did not return to France till 1838.

This rapid sketch of Cauchy's life is sufficient to show that he was not only a man of genius, but also a man of character. And this greatness of character rested wholly and absolutely on Christian conviction and practical piety. He not merely discharged faithfully all the duties of a Catholic, but was ever foremost among those who are ready at the call of events to defend or propagate religion or to set on foot works of charity. He was a zealous member of the Conference of St. Vincent de Paul, and did all that he could do to relieve the needs of others. "Nearly every day", said the Mayor of Sceaux (where Cauchy had a country house), over his grave, "he paid me a visit. He had a poor invalid, or a foundling to recommend, a young person looking for a situation, or a soldier who was the sole support of his family and begged to be allowed to return to it."[1] Many pious and philanthropic societies were established by his efforts, as, for example, a Society to secure the universal observance of the Sunday's rest, and the still existing Society for the maintenance of schools in the East. Of other charitable enterprises he was a leading supporter as e. g. the Society of St. Francis Regis for the legitimation of irregular unions. When in 1846 Ireland was visited by a terrible famine, Cauchy succeeded in inducing the Pope to issue a Rescript on behalf of that country. In Sceaux he secured the settlement of a community of nuns, and founded a union for the protection of youth. On his deathbed he gave a touching

[1] Valson, Vie de Cauchy I 273.

manifestation of his deep piety. When the priest informed him that he was about to bring the Consecrated Host to him, he gave instructions that all the most beautiful flowers in the garden should be strewn along the stairs which were to be honoured by the passage of Our Lord. The thought which most troubled his last hours was the future of a community of the Christian Brothers which he had introduced into Sceaux.

He was very intimate with many Jesuit priests, especially with the celebrated pulpit orator P. Ravignan. When shortly before the February Revolution a violent assault was made on the Schools of the Order in France, Cauchy published two pamphlets in defence of them. In one of these we find the following explicit Confession of Faith which may well find a place here.

"I am a Christian, that is to say, I believe in the divinity of Jesus Christ as did Tycho Brahe, Copernicus, Descartes, Newton, Fermat, Leibniz, Pascal, Grimaldi, Euler, Guldin, Boscovich, Gerdil; as did all the great astronomers, physicists, and geometricians of past ages: nay more I am like the greater part of these a Catholic: and were I asked for the reasons of my faith I would willingly give them. I would show that my convictions have their source not in mere prejudice but in reason and a resolute enquiry. I am a sincere Catholic as were Corneille, Racine, La Bruyère, Bossuet, Bourdaloue, Fénelon, as were and still are so many of the most distinguished men of our time, so many of those who have done most for the honour of our science, philosophy, and literature, and have conferred such brilliant lustre on our Academies. I share the deep convictions openly manifested in word, deed, and writings by so many savants of the first rank, by a Ruffini, a Haüy, a Laënnec, an Ampère, a Pelletier, a Freycinet, a Coriolis[1] and if I avoid naming

[1] Two of those whom he here mentions, distinguished themselves in Mathematics; a brief account of them will not be out of

any of those living, for fear of paining their modesty, I may at least be allowed to say that I loved to recognise all the noble generosity of the Christian faith in my illustrious friends the creator of Cyrstallography (Haüy), the introducers of quinine and the stethoscope (Pelletier and Laënnec), the famous voyager on board the 'Urania', and the immortal founders of the theory of Dynamic Electricity[1] (Freycinet and Ampère).

These discourses were delivered by Cauchy at the *Institut Catholique* of Paris — for the establishment of which he was in part responsible — and were directed to the protection of the young students from the danger of unbelief. Many similar passages might be quoted

---

place here. Paolo Ruffini, born 1765 at Valentino in the Papal States, died 1822 at Modena, made such rapid progress in the exact sciences, that when only 23 years of age, he was elected Professor in the University of Modena in the room of his former master. He lost this position during the French invasion, because he would not take the oath of allegiance to the new government. He wrote some valuable works on the theory of Equations. He was also a doctor, and in 1817 during an epidemic, won a great deal of gratitude and praise by his courage and self-sacrifice. Among the works in which he shows his religious disposition is a pamphlet against the Encyclopedists: Dell' immortalità dell' anima, Modena 1806. Cf. Heinrich Burkhardt, Die Anfänge der Gruppentheorie und Paolo Ruffini, in the Zeitschrift für Mathematik und Physik XXXVII (Supplement), Leipzig 1892, 119—159. Gaspard Gustave de Coriolis (born in Paris 1792, died there in 1843) was from 1838 Master of Studies at the Polytechnique in Paris. Coriolis "vermochte der Wissenschaft nicht alle die Dienste zu leisten, die man bei seinen schönen geistigen Anlagen hätte erhoffen durfen; seine unglaublich zarte Gesundheit zwang ihn, vor allem jeden Tag das stets neue Problem zu lösen, wie er sein Leben weiter erhalten konne. . . . Coriolis ist mit General Poucelet einer der ersten Förderer der Reform, welche sich im Unterricht in der rationellen Mechanik vollzogen hat" (M. Marie, Hist. des sciences math. et phys. XII 191—192).

[1] Quoted by Valson, Vie de Cauchy I 173.

from them: but we shall avail ourselves here of the memorial discourse pronounced by Cauchy over a colleague.

Not long before his own death, Cauchy stood over the grave of the President of the Academy of Sciences, J. P. Maria Binet, who had died on May 12th 1856. In his funeral oration, "a discourse perfectly adequate and worthy of the occasion" he spoke "less of Binet's, great services to Science, than of the depth of his religious convictions"[1].

"Binet", said Cauchy, "was a mathematician of the first order and the finest intellect, but he was something more. With the most richly endowed minds of past centuries and also of the present century, with Descartes, Fermat, Haüy, Ampère, Laennec he ascended gladly from the knowledge of scientific truths to the eternal source of all truth. Contemplation of the sublime laws, which direct the course of the stars, and preserve order and harmony in the universe, supplied him constantly with new motives to celebrate the Architect of all these marvels with praise and prayer. The living faith of our comrade, his ardent love of God to Whom he rendered honour by his talents and his virtues, his comprehensive knowledge and his inexhaustible charity, ought to inspire us with the consoling conviction that to-day Binet is happier and wiser than any of us, that he has gone hence to find light at the source of all light, and to fathom those secret depths which we also shall one day fathom, if we hold stoutly to the road which his feet travelled. You will forgive me, gentlemen, if plunged in these sublime thoughts, I cut short my utterance of them. True grief is not a lover of words. . . . At the sight of the cross planted on this grave in token of our hope, my tongue is silent. May we all lift ourselves in thought to the other side of that tremendous gulf which separates our earthly sciences — so straitened and limited, as they are, even to the noblest

[1] Gruners Archiv XXVII 483.

intellects — from the lofty truths of that divine wisdom which shall be imparted to all in Heaven."[1]

"The life of Augustin Cauchy", wrote the celebrated J. B. Biot[2], "offers a perfect model of Christian virtue, as well as of supreme intellectual activity. He was one of the most eminent mathematicians that France has produced, and his nobility of character was not less remarkable than his genius for mathematics."

Cauchy's successor at the Sorbonne was his pupil Victor Alexander Puiseux (1820—1883) who held the position till 1882[3]. He also was a savant of the first order; according to some he was the best of all Cauchy's pupils. Bertrand says of Puiseux's masterpiece that "after 30 years it is not a single day out of date", and according to Hermite it marks an epoch in mathematical analysis. How highly Pasteur thought of Puiseux is best indicated by an anecdote related by Bertrand in his biography of the distinguished astronomer Tisserand. "About 35 years ago, I was commissioned, on what occasion I do not remember, to inspect the Third Year's Division of the *École Normale*, in which Tisserand occupied first place. Pasteur, then director of scientific studies, asked me: 'What do you think of Tisserand?' 'He is a brilliant student', I replied, 'the best of them all.' My language appeared to him much too cold. 'Tisserand', he exclaimed, 'why he is a little Puiseux.' Such praise from such a man

---

[1] Ib. [2] J. B. Biot in Mélanges III 143.

[3] Cf. Ph. Gilbert in Revue des questions scientifiques XV, Bruxelles-Paris 1884, 1—37; J. Bertrand, Éloge de M. Victor Puiseux lu dans la séance publique annuelle de l'Académie des Sciences du 5 Mai 1884; printed in the Bulletin des sciences math. et astronomiques, 2nd Series VIII, Année 1884, Paris 1884, 227—234; F. Tisserand, Notice sur V. A. Puiseux, ib. 234—245.

was very high indeed, but it will be understood by every one who knew Tisserand."

What was most admired in Puiseux as a teacher was the rare lucidity with which he handled the most intricate problems of the mechanism of the heavens. In the Bureau des Longitudes (1868—1872), and in the Astronomical Observatory (1855—1859), he displayed wonderful activity. He left it to his colleagues to select each of them whatever department of the work he specially wished to investigate, and what remained, the most arduous portions, he took upon himself. He worked out, for instance, beginning in 1869, the interminable calculations necessary for satisfactory observations of the Transits of Venus in 1874 and 1882, and revised the works of Laplace, verifying every calculation contained in them. He refused for a long time to become a candidate for the Academy, for his heart was little set on external dignities. But when in 1871 his name was proposed, his three competitors voluntarily retired, and from the fifty-five electors Puiseux received fifty-five votes. The election stands, we believe, without parallel in the whole century: there was not a single adverse vote, not a single abstention. Bertrand declared in this connection: "The election of Puiseux was due to his merit, the unanimity to his character."[1]

This high praise was repeated by Bertrand when in the Session of the Academy for the following year he pronounced a discourse on the achievements and character

[1] Seul parmi nous, seul peut-être entre tous les Académiciens de ce siècle, Puiseux a été élu à l'unanimité. . . . L'élection de Puiseux était due à son mérite, l'unanimité à son caractère (Bertrand in the Academy of Science on Puiseux' death; Comptes rendus XCVII, Paris 1883, 656.

of Puiseux. He begins with a remark of Fontenelle, who, as permanent secretary of the Academy, had been called upon to deliver memorial addresses on so many distinguished savants. He had already, said the latter in 1822, bestowed on so many dead colleagues the praise that their lives were as simple as their minds were sublime, that one might come to attribute this merit less to individual scientists than to the nature of their science itself. "Times have changed", remarks Bertrand, "The indifference towards wealth, the calm expectation of renown, the ancient Socratic contempt for everything for which the crowd so eagerly struggles, hurries, intrigues . . . are to-day neither the dowry of our science, nor the distinguishing stamp of our scientists. They are met only in exceptional cases: and such an exception was Victor Puiseux."[1]

"One of his most characteristic qualities", writes Gilbert[2], "was a complete absence of all spirit of intrigue, personal ambition, craving for pomp and dignity. His indifference to external distinctions amounted almost to antipathy. The modesty which led him, in all enterprises, to assume that part which offered the most work and the least notoriety, was perfectly sincere and without any trace of affectation. . . . The calm, simple, and regular tenor of his life impressed every one who knew him. He had no other joys than intellectual labour, contemplation of the beauty of nature, and family affection." In 1870 he was on a holiday tour in the South when the War broke out: he returned immediately to Paris to suffer siege there, and to take part in the defence of the capital. A year before his

---

[1] Ib. 227. [2] Revue des quest. scient. XV 32.

death he begged to be relieved of his professorate; "it was time to make way for younger men". It needed the unanimous and officially declared request of his colleagues to induce him to retain the title.

That his greatness of character had its source and stay in deep religious conviction Bertrand himself tells us at the close of his discourse, in a rhetorical fashion, and, as it were, against his will. Gilbert is clearer in his testimony.

"Victor Puiseux", he writes[1], "was a man of profoundly Christian convictions, loyal all his life to the duties required of him by the religion which he imbibed in youth and developed with his mature intellect. During his tenure of office in the École Normale he had ample opportunity to make manifest his belief, to anneal it in the fire of controversy, and to impart it in precious friendships. It was the time when the famous conferences of Lacordaire were ringing through France. They penetrated into the École also; teachers and students no longer confined themselves to science but engaged vigorously in philosophical and religious discussions. Puiseux took an active part in the controversy, and put at the services of his religion the prestige which his scientific distinction and his amenity of disposition had won him. But to play the part of leader consorted ill with his modesty. He preferred to efface himself behind Pierre Olivaint[2], then a student in the School of Literature. Their association was not limited to this controversy. . . . They joined in devoting a part of their holidays to works of charity, and founded a Conference of St. Vincent de Paul which is still in existence."[3]

---

[1] Ib. XV 34—36.

[2] Afterwards a Jesuit. fell a victim to the Commune 1871.

[3] Cf. Tisserand, Notice 235. On ne s'occupait pas que de science à l'École; les discussions philosophiques et religieuses y étaient fort vives: M. Puiseux y prenait une part active et mettait au service de ses convictions religieuses l'ascendant naturel que son intelligence

"Inexhaustible bounty, active charity constituted, as it were, the soul of his life. He was a loyal and zealous servant of St. Vincent, and only when struck down by fatal illness did he cease to climb the stairs of the poor. He was the stay and support of a multitude of good works which were unknown, even to his family, until his death. Side by side with the members of the Institute and of the Scientific Faculty, there walked at his funeral the outcast and disinherited children of life, come there to lament their benefactor."

With Cauchy and Weierstrass must be associated, as author of the Mathematical Theory of Functions, Bernard Riemann, Professor at Göttingen. Born on Sept. 17th 1826, at Breselenz in Hanover, where his father was a Protestant clergyman, he had not completed his fortieth year when he died of phthisis (July 20th 1866) at Selasca on Lake Maggiore. Riemann's metaphysical ideas, derived in part from Th. Fechner, are often bold even to singularity, and by times are merely fantastic, but they detract in no way from his religious fervour. His death, as related in the biographical sketch prefixed to his collected works, gives sufficient token of this. "His wife was saying to him the Our Father, he was no longer able to speak: but at the words Forgive us our trespasses, he raised his eyes aloft: she felt his hands grow cold within her own: and after two or three gasps his noble heart had ceased to beat.

---

d'élite . . . lui avaient assuré tout d'abord. . . . Toutefois, dans son domaine spécial, M. Puiseux aimait à s'effacer devant Pierre Olivaint, alors élève de la section des lettres, entré depuis dans la Compagnie de Jésus et tombé, en 1871, victime de la Commune. . . . For the religious aspect of the school and the group of Catholic students. Cf. Ch. Clair, Pierre Olivaint, prêtre de la Compagnie de Jésus, Paris 1878, 21.

The pious habits which he had learned in his childhood remained with him all his life, and he served God loyally, if not always after the orthodox forms. Daily self-examination in the presence of God he regarded, to use his own expression, as one of the elements of religion." [1]

On Jan. 14th 1901 there died at Paris "the last of the great mathematicians of the second half of the nineteenth century", a grey-haired veteran of seventy-eight, whose eminence in the history of science was proclaimed in the highest terms of praise by the highest authorities. The first of these eulogists was Fouqué, President of the Academy of Sciences of Paris.

"Hermite", he writes, "doyen of our Geometrical section, and member of the Academy since 1856, was one of our special glories. All who sit here as geometricians think it their chief honour to have been pupils of his, all are penetrated with gratitude for the generous aid which he has constantly given them. Wherever science is cultivated, the name of Hermite is spoken with veneration." [2]

To the praise of his scientific genius there was added recognition of his lovable character.

"With Hermite", wrote *La Nature*, "there disappears one of the unsullied glories of French science. Hermite not only stood among the masters of mathematics of the last

---

[1] Bernhard Riemanns Gesammelte mathematische Werke und wissenschaftlicher Nachlass. Herausgeg. unter Mitwirkung von Richard Dedekind von Heinr. Weber. Zweite Aufl., bearbeitet von Heinr. Weber, Leipzig 1892, 557.

[2] Comptes rendus hebdomadaires des séances de l'Academie des sciences CXXXII, Paris 1901, 49. We quote the following passages and Notices from the Essay in the Revue des questions scientifiques XLIX, Louvain 1901, 353—396. Cf. Naturwissenschaftliche Rundschau XV, Braunschweig 1901, 333 348.

century; his private life, also, was a model. No one ever pushed unselfish devotion to science farther than he did.

"He leaves to history an imperishable name, and to all those who had the happiness to know him, the memory of a man as great of heart as of intellect. A convinced spiritualist he believed that the soul would one day be crowned with a complete revelation of those mathematical harmonies of which only the reflex is accessible to human nature."[1]

Not very long before, on Dec. 24th 1892, France had celebrated with the greatest splendour Hermite's seventieth birthday. The Minister of Education presided at the Jubilee Assembly, the most eminent French mathematicians were present, and nearly every learned society offered an address. The King of Sweden decorated Hermite with an order, hitherto conferred on no one in France except the President of the Republic and Pasteur. And all these honours were well deserved, for, as Poincaré said in his discourses, Hermite had for fifty years laboured incessantly in all the most difficult departments of mathematics and had enriched mathematical analysis, Algebra, and the Theory of Numbers with "inestimable conquests"[2]. When only twenty years

[1] Avec M. Hermite disparaît une des gloires les plus pures qui aient jamais illustré la science française. M. Hermite ne fut pas seulement un des plus grands mathématiciens du dernier siècle, sa vie fut un exemple, personne n'a poussé plus loin l'amour désintéressé de la science etc. (Painlevé in La Nature XXXIX, 2 févr. 1901, 144—146). — Il laisse pour l'histoire un nom impérissable et pour tous ceux qui ont eu le bonheur de l'approcher le souvenir d'un homme aussi grand par le cœur que par l'intelligence. Spiritualiste convaincu, il pensait que l'âme aurait un jour la révélation complète de ces harmonies mathématiques dont le reflet seul est accessible à l'intelligence humaine (Revue des sciences pures et appliquées XII, 15 févr. 1901, 109—110).

[2] Cf. Les fêtes jubilaires des MM. Hermite et Pasteur, in Revue des quest. scient. XXXIII, Louvain 1893, 235—247.

of age he had addressed to Jacobi an essay of a very few pages which placed him at one bound on a level with the first mathematicians in Europe. After the death of Cauchy, Gauss, Jacobi and Dirichlet, he was universally regarded as the leader of his science. At the mathematical Congresses at Zurich in 1897, and at Paris in 1900, he was elected, with acclamation, Honorary President.

Of his discoveries we may mention one, which will be understood even by those who have no technical knowledge of mathematics. It was Hermite who in 1873 demonstrated for the first time that the quantity e is transcendent i. e. it cannot be the root of an algebraic equation with integral co-efficients. Hermite's line of proof was in 1881 extended by Lindemann to the quantity π, and by means of it an interesting fact was established. Inasmuch as π cannot be the root of a quadratic equation it follows that it cannot be determined with rule and compass, in other words, that the "squaring of the circle" is impossible. That π does not admit of determination with other instruments does not of course follow; in point of fact it can be determined with the help of the integraph, invented in 1880 by the Russian Abakanowicz[1]. An old problem was thus at last solved: it had taken two thousand years, and the expenditure of a vast deal of pains and penetration to discover that the attempt so often renewed was *a priori* impossible. Professor F. Klein may justly say that this discovery, suggested and made possible by Hermite, marks an epoch in the history of mathematical science[2].

Painlevé's reference to Hermite's "spiritualism" will be more clearly understood if it is stated that the great mathematician was simply a member of the Catholic

---

[1] Cf. J. G. Hagen S. J., Synopsis der hoheren Mathematik III Berlin 1900, 84

[2] The Evanston Colloquium 1893, 52.

Church. In his younger days his religious views had undergone certain variations. But "thanks to the charity of the Sisters of Mercy who nursed him through a severe illness, thanks also without doubt to the influence of Cauchy" he returned to the Faith, and, "from the day in 1856 on which he found his road to Damascus, the fervour of his religion never diminished[1]".

"From 1877 on", writes the Catholic Review from which we borrow these notes, "he took a lively interest in our review, and constantly congratulated our late-lamented general secretary and his collaborators on their articles, which he found so solid and so appropriate to the intellectual needs of the day". . . . Fifteen years later he expressed himself to the same effect, and added that he had the happiness to share the Faith professed by the writers of the Review[2]. To the Congress of Catholic Scientists, held at Brussels in 1894, he contributed a paper[3].

"Hermite", says the celebrated mathematician Émile Borel, "was deeply attached to the Catholic religion; it was the stay and the centre of his life. . . . His opinions and his works were in perfect harmony with Catholic ideas, and this is certainly no ordinary merit."[4]

Highly important contributions to the History of Mathematics were made by the Roman prince Baldassare Boncompagni Ludovisi († March 13th 1894).

---

[1] Revue des quest. scient. XLIX (1901) 364. [2] Ib.

[3] Congrès Scientifique International des Catholiques VII 5—11. He also sent contributions to the Papal Academy de' nuovi Lincei III 155—164, and to the Annales of the Société Scientifique of Brussels I (1875—1876) II (1877—1878).

[4] Laisant et Buhl, Annuaire des Mathématiciens 1901—1902, Paris 1902, XXI.

"He was", writes a well-qualified judge[1], "a man of the most extensive learning. His favourite subject of study and research was the History of Mathematics. Guido Bonati, Gerard of Cremona, Plato of Tivoli were, one may confidently assert, first brought to general knowledge by the essays devoted to them in the series of publications for which he was responsible."

It was Boncompagni, too, who by his work on Leonard of Pisa, "the teacher of the three centuries that came after him", and by the publication of his writings "evoked and made possible the first true appreciation of that genius".

"A Review well known to specialists under the name of the *Bulletino Boncompagni*" contains many works of the editor. He often bore the cost of the publication of the works of other savants. "Enormous were the sums spent by the prince in this fashion, enormous were the sums swallowed up by his library which contained 600 MSS. and 18,000 printed works. A princely fortune, and a mind in the best sense of the word princely were needed to make such things possible. And these were not his only benefactions. Whenever Boncompagni learned of a promising student, whose deve lopment was hampered by poverty, he proferred assistance in the most courteous and tactful manner. How many transcripts of MSS. has he not commissioned here, there, and everywhere, either in order to put them

[1] M. Cantor in the historical and literary department of the Zeitschrift für Mathematik und Physik XXXIX, Leipzig 1894, 201 to 203. "Alle Arbeiten des Herrn Buoncompagni sind für jeden, der dem Studium der Geschichte unserer Wissenschaft seine Zeit und seine Kräfte widmen will, ganz unentbehrlich" (Gruners Archiv 1856, Lit Bericht Nr 105).

unselfishly at the disposal of young students, or merely to give the transcribers a chance of earning something! And how many bewail in him the death of a benefactor!" He bore, amongst other charges, the expense of printing the papers of the Papal Academy.

Only a sudden death prevented Boncompagni from bequeathing his precious MSS. and books to the Vatican Library. This alone is enough to show that the Prince was "a man of both science and faith", who proved by example that "between scientist and Christian there is no opposition" [1].

To the names mentioned we might add many others. Charles Dupin (1784—1873) e. g. was during the first half of the nineteenth century one of the most eminent and best known scientists in France. Before he had reached his twentieth year he had already established several important mathematical theorems, and both as engineer and as Professor of mathematics and mechanics he made valuable contributions to every province of thought that he cultivated [2]. In time, indeed, his talent for statistical and economic research drew him away from Pure Mathematics. He made a profound study of the political and industrial resources of England and France, and displayed in the Chamber a commendable zeal for the improvement of the education and the industrial methods of the country.

---

[1] Cosmos, Paris, 30 avril 1898, 553; cf. 26 mai 1894, 223. Concerning the edifying death of the Prince and his friendship for the Society of Jesus v. Civ. catt., Ser. 15, X, Roma 1894, 361, and 12 ser. I (1883) 84. For his connection with the Papal Academy, Études XLV, Paris 1888, 134.

[2] Jos. Bertrand, Éloges académiques 221. Biographie générale par Hoefer s. v.

When he died full of years in 1873, it was recorded of him that "his convictions were always sincerely Christian and Catholic" [1].

Mention should also be made e. g. of Louis Poinsot († 1859)[2], Gergonne († 1858)[3], Michael Chasles († 1880)[4], W. M. Drobisch († 1896)[5] and Philippo Gilbert († 1892), Professor at Louvain and author of widely-used test-books on Higher Mathematics and Analytical Mechanics, as well of numerous scientific essays[6]. Amongst those recently deceased we may instance Eugène Vicaire († Jan. 18th 1901)[7], an engineer who occupied the highest positions in his profession in France, and laboured with such success in the province of pure science that he held the professorate of Astro-Mechanics in the Collège de France from 1883 to 1885, and published works of the first importance on Astronomy, Solar Physics, and Pure Mathematics. He was a practical Catholic[8], and had the happiness of giving two of his nine children to the priesthood.

---

[1] Ses convictions furent toujours sincèrement chrétiennes et catholiques. Les Mondes XXX, Paris 1873, 135.

[2] Natur und Offenbarung VI, Munster 1860, 96.

[3] Ib. V (1859) 288.

[4] Cf. Ph Gilbert in the Revue des quest. scient. IX (1881) 517—590. In concluding this Obituary Notice, he says: "Dieu a fait à Chasles la grâce d'une fin vraiment chrétienne. Dans toute la plénitude de sa volonté et de son intelligence, le grand mathématicien a reçu les consolations que l'église catholiques réserve à ceux qui meurent dans son sein; puis il s'est endormi confiant et tranquille."

[5] Allg. deutsche Biographie XLVIII, 82.

[6] Cf. Revue générale LV, Bruxelles, mars 1892, I—IV.

[7] Revue des quest. scient. XLIX (1901) 420—431.

[8] Fermement attaché à la foi catholique, il ne s'est jamais écarté des directions spirituelles qu'elle lui avait tracées (ib. 423).

Hermann Grassmann († 1877), Gymnasium professor at Stettin, is described by Cantor and Leskien as "one of the most remarkable mathematicians of our times". At first indeed his works went practically unnoticed. His "Theory of Extension" put forward in 1844 ideas on the nature of Geometry which became current many years later, but it might as well not have been printed. Two discoveries made by him in Physics met with no acceptance until they were made anew by Clausius and Helmholtz. Crushed by this ill-success he turned to the study of Sanscrit, and although he entered this province so late he nevertheless made in it important conquests. This notable man was a loyal Protestant; he was much interested in Foreign Missions, and left behind him a work which bears the title "On the Decay of Belief" [1].

But the names enumerated above are sufficient for our purpose. Instead, therefore, of extending the list we shall devote a page or two to a renowned scientist whose authority is very frequently invoked to show the irreligious character not only of mathematicians, but of mathematics and exact research in general.

No one denies the invaluable contributions made by Pierre Simon Laplace († 1827) to the theory of the motion of the heavenly bodies, as also to many other branches of Physics and Mathematics. He was commonly called the French Newton, and was brought into comparison with the great Englishman in nearly every one of the discourses pronounced over his grave.

Nowadays it is a commonplace of scepticism to invoke the authority of Laplace; and an anecdote which is told of him is supposed to afford proof of his unbelief. When he presented

[1] Allgemeine deutsche Biographie IX 595—598. Allgemeine Zeitung, Augsburg 1877, Nr. 291, Beil. p. 4371.

one of his works to Napoleon the latter is reported to have said: "Newton in his work speaks of God. I have gone through yours, but find no mention of God." To which Laplace is said to have replied: "Citizen First Consul, I found no need for that hypothesis." So runs the anecdote, and from it many writers eagerly draw the conclusion: Laplace then has declared that the existence of God is a mere hypothesis. And so, according to the greatest astronomer of modern times, the existence of the world affords no proof of the existence of God.

This anecdote had begun to circulate during Laplace's life-time. When he learned shortly before his death, that it was to appear in a sketch of his life in an Encyclopedia of Biography he commissioned Arago to demand that it should be excised by the editor. This fact was learned from Arago's own mouth by H. Faye[1]: it shows that in any event it was against Laplace's will that he was represented as an atheist. As for the story itself, its truth is established by no sufficient evidence, and it is *a priori* improbable that the accommodating Laplace would have spoken in such a fashion to the all-powerful ruler of France. For Napoleon was well known to be no friend of atheism, and to have administered a sharp reproof to the astronomer Lalande because of his profession of it[2].

But even supposing that Laplace did use the words, it does not at all follow that he wished to characterise the existence of God as an unsupported hypothesis. In the

---

[1] Sur l'origine du Monde[3], Paris 1896, 131. Cf. p. 130—132, where the alleged saying of Laplace is dealt with. Cf. J. de Joannis in Études LXXI, Paris 1897, 541 f.

[2] Moreover we may remark in passing that Lalande did not sincerely believe in Atheism. Abbé Émery, who had opportunities of speaking to him, said to a priest, a friend of his: "M. de Lalande n'est pas plus athée que vous et moi" To Émery he had expressed the wish to receive the last sacraments from his hand. The fulfilment of this wish was prevented by Lalande's friends. Vie de M. Émery II, Paris 1862, 39. E. Méric, Hist. de M. Émery II, Paris 1885, 210.

anecdote, he contrasts his theory with that of Newton: it is necessary then only to bear in mind the points on which he was at variance with the great Englishman in order to grasp the sense of the epigram. Newton had at the sight of so many planets and worlds, circling perpetually round with reciprocal influence and disturbance, given way to the fear that these countless, intricate movements must result at last in inextricable confusion, and that the intervention of God from time to time was needed to obviate this confusion. But one of the greatest achievements of Laplace was precisely his proof that such intervention is unnecessary. He showed by mathematical considerations, afterwards completed and extended by Leverrier, that such confusion can never occur. How intricate soever the paths of the planets, however numerous and continual the reciprocal disturbances, all these disturbances must in the course of time re-adjust themselves. If Laplace, then, did in fact reply to the First Consul in the manner alleged, in all probability he had before his mind merely the advance which he had made in the Theory of Planetary Motion, as compared with Newton. The hypothesis which he dismissed as unnecessary would be, in this interpretation, not the existence of God but that intervention of God in the economy of the planetary system which Newton regarded as indispensable[1]. We find in Laplace's work another criticism of Newton, expressed in another fashion. The disposition of the planets and satellites according to number, size, and relative distance could not in Newton's opinion be derived from mechanical causes, but

[1] Cf. v. Mädlers Reden und Abhandlungen uber Gegenstände der Himmelskunde, Berlin 1870, 334: Laplace's answer "ist vollkommen richtig; denn auch wir bedurften und bedurfen der Hypothese von einem einhelfenden, nachbessernden, korrigierenden Gotte nicht und werden ihrer nie bedurfen. Das Universum ist ein Uhrwerk, aber kein solches, wo man den Verfertiger zu Hilfe ruft, weil es nicht mehr recht gehen will. Unser Gott thront uber Zeit und Ewigkeit, und bei ihm ist kein Wechsel, und je tiefer wir in seinen Werken forschen, desto mehr werden wir in dieser Ansicht bestärkt".

must be regarded as the direct work of Divine Omnipotence. But Laplace has, by means of his celebrated theory of the development of the solar system from the rotating fiery nebula, exhibited it as highly probable that the disposition of the planets and satellites can be explained by natural causes, and in this regard he might also have allowed himself to criticise Newton. This does not necessarily mean that he denied the existence of God. In fact the whole duty of science is to explain the phenomena of nature by created, secondary causes [1]. The acceptance of the system of Laplace is in no way derogatory to the Wisdom and Omnipotence of the Creator. It is in no wise easier to create the egg and the acorn out of which the chicken and the oak are in due course to develop, than to create immediately on the spot the chicken or the oak. And in precisely the same way it is a no lesser manifestation of Divine Omnipotence to create the nebula, and to endow it with the capacity of developing into the planetary system than it would be to call the latter at once into existence.

That Laplace is in point of fact to be understood in this sense is shown by a passage in his "Exposition du système du monde" [2]. He there quotes the passage in which Newton ascribes the orderly arrangement of the planetary system to

---

[1] "Gott ist nicht das nächste und unmittelbare Prinzip der Naturerscheinungen. Er ist auch nicht direkt Gegenstand der Naturwissenschaften . . . und es ist, von der frivolen Deutung abgesehen, ganz berechtigt, wenn Laplace sagt: ich habe Himmel und Erde durchforscht und keinen Gott gefunden, wie es berechtigt ist, wenn Vogt erklärt, es sei ihm die Seele und Lebenskraft noch nie unter der Lupe begegnet" (P. L. Haffner, Das Ignoramus und Ignorabimus der neueren Naturforschung, in Sammlung zeitgemässer Broschüren, Frankfurt-Luzern 1887, 222). Likewise J. Reinke, Die Welt als Tat [3], Berlin 1903, 476: "In Laplaces Werke brauchte Gott so wenig vorzukommen wie im Exerzierreglement. Hätte ich ein Handbuch der Physiologie zu schreiben, so würde das Wort Gott darin gleichfalls fehlen"

[2] Livre 5, chap. 6, 6e éd., Bruxelles 1827, 522.

the immediate, creative act of God, and, to explain its immunity from confusion, has recourse to the recurrent intervention of the same creative power. In criticism of this theory Laplace says: "But may not this disposition of the planets be itself an effect of the laws of Motion: and may not the Supreme Intelligence to whose intervention Newton had recourse, have made this orderly disposition dependent on a phenomenon of a more general character?" The necessity of a supplementary intervention of God in His own Creation he repels with the words: "Leibniz, in his controversy with Newton on the discovery of the infinitesimal calculus, criticised sharply the theory of a Divine intervention as a corrective of the disturbances of the solar system. 'To suppose anything of the kind', he said, 'is to exhibit very narrow ideas of the wisdom and power of God. Newton replied with a criticism just as sharp of the Pre-Established Harmony of Leibniz which he characterised as a perpetual miracle. Posterity has not accepted these vain hypotheses, but it has rendered the most ample justice to the mathematical achievements of these two men of genius."

It is not difficult to discern in these passages the idea which lies at the root of the anecdote in question. But it will be observed that this idea has in it no leaven of Atheism. Laplace speaks in both places of "empty hypotheses". But what is it that he designates by these words? Obviously not the existence of God, but the Theory of Pre-Established Harmony, and the assumption that an intervention of God is necessary from time to time in order to supply the imperfections of the natural order.

On the other hand it is admitted that Laplace cannot be held up as a model of loyalty to religion. In his writings, e. g. in the *Essai philosophique sur la probabilité* there are to be found many turns of thought which show the influence of the philosophy of the eighteenth century. But there are two facts which cannot be disputed. In the first place the great mathematician was never in his own estimate a materialist. In proof of this we have the evidence of one who stood on the most intimate terms with Laplace, J. B. Dumas the chemist [1]. And if during his life he made only too many concessions to the dominant spirit of the time, this is only another example of that pliancy of character which even Laplace's greatest admirers constantly deplored. When he came to die and had nothing further to hope for from the world, he sent for a priest and devoted himself to settling his account with heaven [2].

III. ASTRONOMY.

A religious of the Catholic Church stands by a twofold right at the head of the Astronomy of the 19th Century, in virtue both of a brilliant discovery and of the enterprise which led up to it.

---

[1] Discours et Éloges Académiques II 255 Laplace "fournit aux matérialistes leurs plus spécieux arguments, sans partager leurs convictions".

[2] Nr. 66, March 7th 1827, of La Quotidienne contains the following: "Paris, 6 mars. M. le marquis de Laplace, pair de France, membre de l'Institut, auteur de la Mécanique Céleste et de plusieurs autres ouvrages qui l'ont fait placer parmi les plus grands géomètres de ces derniers temps, est mort hier dans son hôtel Rue du Bac, entre les bras de ses deux pasteurs, M. le curé des Missions Étrangères et M. le curé d'Arceuil, qu'il avait fait appeler pour en recevoir les derniers secours de la religion. Nous aurons à publier une notice sur la vie de ce savant célèbre; mais nous devons dès ce moment faire remarquer ce que sa mort a présenté d'édifiant à sa famille, à ses amis et à ses admirateurs. C'est un contraste que nous aimons à opposer au récit de morts scandaleuses qui font la joie des ennemis de la religion. Ses obsèques auront lieu demain mercredi, 7, en l'église des Missions Étrangères. . . The same information is found in the paper, L'ami de la Religion et du Roi LI, Paris 1827, 107 126 (cf. J. de Joannis in Études LXXI 655). M. Marie (Hist. des sciences math. et phys. X, Paris 1887, 70) calls the wavering Laplace "réactionnaire et ultra-royaliste", assumes him to "afficher des sentiments religieux outrés qu'il ne partageait pas" and ascribes to him "Palinodes", which however would not have been able to retard the progress for which his Cosmogony had cleared the way.

"The first day of the century", says the celebrated astronomer Frederick William Bessel[1], "was marked by a brilliant discovery: Piazzi of Palermo on the first day of January 1801 found a new planet, 'Ceres'. His discovery was a by-product of a great and admirable undertaking, the determination, namely, by a long series of observations, of the positions of some 7 000 fixed stars." Bessel proceeds to explain the significance for astronomical science of this determination of the latitude and longitude of so many stars with the greatest possible accuracy, and recounts the laborious efforts of Tycho Brahe and his successors to arrive at the same result. "Piazzi", he continues, "had striven strenuously to secure the erection of an observatory at Palermo, and to equip it with splendid instruments, the work of the never-to-be-forgotten Ramsden; and when he had succeeded in this he stepped at once to the head of astronomical science. He published in 1803 after incalculable labour a catalogue of the positions of some 7 000 stars, and so resolute was his determination to secure the most accurate results attainable with his instruments that he repeated all his observations, and in 1814 was able to publish a second and much improved edition of his catalogue. Here was in truth a worthy beginning of the century. The appetite for thorough observation was roused from the slumber in which it had lain since the death of Bradley."

At first sight the figures mentioned by Bessel may not seem very formidable. Some may not consider it a colossal undertaking to direct a telescope on one after another of 7000 stars, and read off their positions on the graduated circle. But the life of Piazzi supplies an effective reply to such a criticism. During the course of the observations he believed that he had found the long-sought parallax of certain fixed stars that is, the dis-

---

[1] Populäre Vorlesungen über wissenschaftliche Gegenstände von F. W. Bessel. Nach dem Tode des Verfassers herausgegeben von H. C. Schumacher, Hamburg 1848, 21—23; cf. 239 538.

placement which the position of the stars must undergo from the fact that in the course of the earth's annual movement they are observed from widely separated points of observation. On closer examination, however, he discovered that it was not the stars but his telescope that had suffered displacement, in all probability from the fact that the tower on which the telescope rested received more heat from the sun on one side that on the other. This will give a hint of the minute accuracy requisite in astronomical observations. Further, every instrument has its trifling defects, which import an element of error into all observations, and is further liable to disturbance by the most trivial occurrences, so that to arrive at practically useful results there is needed not only inexhaustible patience and persistence, but also acute insight, so as to discover the various sources of error and either devise a telescope that will make them inoperative, or correct the results mathematically. After the practical work of observation the astronomer must be prepared for weary hours at his desk. Every star must be observed several times, for no one observation ever corresponds precisely with another: and to the list of figures thus obtained, the Calculus of Probabilities must be applied so as to arrive at the closest possible approximation to the truth.

No one could appreciate better than Bessel the difficulty of compiling such a catalogue, for he himself stood in the first rank of observers, and had reduced to workable form Bradley's essay in the same direction, which contained only single observations.

"Nearly all the Flamsteed stars", he writes, "were observed five times, so that I had to reduce to shape a total of more than 25000 observations. . . . On Piazzi's catalogue which contains still more observations than Bradley's two astronomers were engaged and the task occupied many years: I am now convinced that that gigantic work has been estimated rather below than above its value."[1]

Bessel drew a rich yield from the works of Piazzi and Bradley. When he had resolved on his plan for the revision of Bradley's catalogue he wrote to Olbers:

"Thanks to the known dexterity of Bradley, and the excellent instruments of the Greenwich Observatory, Bradley's catalogue yields little in point of accuracy to Piazzi's. An interesting feat, surely, to attain the same accuracy in 1750 as in 1800!"[2]

The collation and revision of the two catalogues helped, in the event, to bring to light a very interesting fact: the self-movement of the fixed stars. It showed "that nearly one half of the stars contained in both catalogues (numbering 2959) possess a self-movement amounting to the tenth of a second annually, or, in certain cases to more"[3]. The greatest movement was that exhibited by a star of the fifth magnitude Nr. 61 of the Swan: it was as considerable as five seconds a year. Bessel selected this double star on which to renew the search for the long-sought parallax. His labours were successful. He determined the parallax, about the third of a second, and with it the distance of one of the nearest fixed stars. "Nearest" is, however, hardly a word to accentuate in this connection. Its distance from the sun is according to Bessel about 657,700 times the radius of the earth's orbit. Light takes ten years

---

[1] Bessel an Olbers, 26th February 1809: Briefwechsel, herausgegeben von Erman, I 205.

[2] 10th May 1807: ib. I 97—98.

[3] Bessel, Populäre Vorlesungen 248.

to travel that distance: a train covering 200 miles a day would take two hundred million years[1].

These discoveries count, it is true, to the credit of Bessel, not of Piazzi, but it is clear that but for Piazzi's work they could never have been made. Bessel himself speaks elsewhere of the "invaluable services"[2] of the Italian astronomer, and always mentions his name with the most marked respect. And a greater than Bessel, Gauss himself, honoured Piazzi so far as to call him his first-born son Joseph[3].

It was his practice of observing each star more than once that led up to the significant discovery of the first asteroid, Ceres. On January 1st he noted down the position of a small star, on January 2nd he made a second observation of it but found figures different from the first. Either then, one of the observations was incorrect, or the star possessed a movement of its own. Further investigation decided in favour of the latter alternative.

Piazzi was a member of the Order of Theatines founded by St. Cajetan of Thiene. Born in 1746 at Veltlin, he made his first studies at Milan and there entered the Order. He received a decisive impulse towards the cultivation of science from the two editors and expounders of Newton, Thomas Leseur[4] († 1770),

---

[1] Bessel, Vorlesungen 261. [2] Ib. 239.

[3] Cf. his Briefwechsel mit Bolyai 184.

[4] Philosophiae naturalis principia mathematica; auctore Isaaco Newtono, Eq. Aurato; Perpetuis Commentariis illustrata, communi studio PP. Thomae Le Seur et Francisci Jacquier, ex Gallicana Minimorum Familia, Matheseos Professorum. 4 vols. Genevae 1739—1742. It was due in a great measure to this essay that Newton's work, the style of which was very involved, became generally

Professor at the Sapienza, and Francis Jacquier († 1788), Professor at the Roman College, both of whom belonged to the Order of the Minims of St. Francis of Paula. Having completed his course in Philosophy at Genoa and Ravenna, and in Mathematics at Malta, he was appointed Professor of Dogmatic Theology at Rome where he formed a lifelong friendship with his colleague Barnabas Chiaramonti, afterwards Pope Pius VII. On the advice of Jacquier, Piazzi in 1780 accepted the post of Mathematical Professor at Palermo, and thus made his entry into the field in which he was to attain such distinction. He at once bestirred himself to give the scientific Faculty an impulse in a new direction. He was supported by the Government in his efforts, and especially in his project of erecting at Palermo an Observatory of the first class. Journeys to France and England brought him into association with the first scientists of the 18th century, and gave him an opportunity of appreciating the scientific needs of the day. After his return the Observatory was erected in 1786, and Piazzi entered into occupation of it. Under the rule of the Bourbons he received a call to Naples where he died in 1826[1].

The "Columbus of the lesser planets" is not the only Catholic priest who during the 19th century rendered notable service to astronomical science. We enumerate here, in accordance with our general plan, the names of the more notable.

One of the foremost, a co-discoverer of the new planet, was Count Barnabas Oriani († 1832), Director of the Milan

intelligible, and that Newton's teaching gained ground. R. Wolf, Gesch. der Astronomie 439—470.

[1] For Piazzi cf. Cosmos 2 mars and 15 juin 1901, 269 f 748 f.

Observatory, like Piazzi a priest and a successful astronomer. Born of a poor family he began life as a mason: his education was taken in hands first by some Carthusians who recognised his great ability, and later by the Barnabites. His work won him the rank of Count, and his reputation stood so high that under Napoleon I. he might have become a Bishop or Minister of Education if he had not declined both dignities [1].

Another name of European note is that of Giovanni Inghirami († 1851). Born in 1779 at Volterra, he entered the Piarists at an early age. He studied Mathematics and Philosophy in his native town, and afterwards Mathematics and Astronomy at Florence, where he became Director of the Observatory founded by the Jesuit L. Ximenez († 1786). He published in 1830, as the result of fourteen years trigonometrical mensuration, a map of Tuscany. When the Academy of Berlin undertook the preparation of the chart of the celestial equator, which was to contain all stars down to the ninth magnitude, a section of this work was entrusted to Inghirami. Although this section, that of the aggregate nebulous stars, presented great difficulties, Encke, in his speech at the celebration of the King's birthday in 1850, characterised Inghirami's performance as amongst the most remarkable in the whole enterprise. Equally high was the estimate of Inghirami formed by Murchison, the well-known geologist. Murchison praises in particular "the excellent map of Tuscany which I found of great service in the geological exploration of the Apennines" [2]. Inghirami attained in his Order the positions of Provincial and General. He lies buried in a chapel erected by him for the younger students, and the inscription on the tomb asks them to pray for him to the Blessed Virgin [3].

---

[1] Nouv. Biographie générale par Hoefer XXXVIII 786.

[2] Journal of the R. Geographical Society of London XXII, London 1852, LXX.

[3] A. v. Reumont, Beiträge zur italienischen Geschichte VI, Berlin 1857, 472—478. Antonelli, Sulla vita e sulle opere di Giov. Inghirami, Firenze 1854. Allgemeine Zeitung, Augsburg 1851,

Filippo Cecchi († May 2nd 1887), who came next but one after Inghirami at Florence, belonged also to the Piarist Order [1]. He specialised chiefly in Meteorology, and enjoyed a great reputation in that department. The Meteorological Observatory at Urbino was established in 1850 by the Prior of the Piarist College there, Alessandro Serpieri († 1885). His researches were directed mainly to the storms of Italy, shooting-stars and above all to the zodiacal light which he sought to exhibit as a terrestrial phenomenon. He was awarded a gold medal in recognition of his works on seismic disturbances; and on the suppression of the Orders he received special permission to select a Chair in whatever Italian University he liked best [2].

Francesco Denza († 1894) was a Barnabite. At the Congress of Meteorologists held at Paris in 1878 he was elected President: for he had won a leading place in the science not only by a series of valuable observations of his own, but by his success in establishing all over Italy, "by private persuasion, and by extensive correspondence" a network of more than 200 meteorological stations. In addition to this he made many contributions to the photography of the heavens. The Vatican Observatory was rebuilt by him for this purpose, and had the honour of being included among the eighteen observatories to which was entrusted the preparation of an international photographic chart of the heavens [3].

Nr. 246, p. 3929. Zach writes on 21 August 1830. "Mr. Inghirami est un homme extrêmement actif." His Observatory is in better order than the one in Florence in which Pons worked. Vierteljahrsschrift der naturforschenden Gesellschaft in Zurich XXXI (1886) 237.

[1] Civiltà cattolica, Ser. 13, VI, Roma 1887, 484—485. T. Martini, Intorno alla vita ed ai lavori di Filippo Cecchi, delle scuole pie, Venezia 1888.

[2] Fed. Mici, Al. Serpieri, scienziato ed educatore. Discorso letto nell' inaugurazione dell' anno scolastico 1885—1886 nell' università d' Urbino, Urbino 1886.

[3] J. Pl(assmann) in Jahresbericht der Görres-Gesellschaft fur das Jahr 1894, Köln 1895, 20—22. Civiltà cattolica, Ser. 16, I,

The Jesuit Francesco de Vico, Director of the Observatory of the Roman College, won a European reputation by his laborious observations of Saturn and the comets. Driven from Rome by the Revolution of 1848 he had an honourable reception in France and England, but died suddenly at London on October 15th 1848 [1]. The Observatory of the Roman College showed energies in other directions too, so long as it remained in the hands of the Order [2]. At the Jesuit's English College at Stonyhurst worked Joseph Perry a "distinguished astronomer" universally known by his publications on solar physics and earth-magnetism. . . . The best proof of his ability is to be found in the numerous scientific commissions with which he was entrusted by the English Government [3]. Thus he was sent to make observations of the Transits of Venus in 1874 and in 1882 in the island of Kerguelen and in Madagascar respectively, and in 1886, 1887, and 1889 to the West Indies, Russia, and an island near Cayenne to study eclipses of the sun. The last expedition (in 1889) cost him his life.

Great scientific activity was shown also by the "historic" Observatory of the Benedictines at Kremsmünster. Marian

---

Roma 1895, 93—94. Annuaire pour l'an 1890 publié par le Bureau des longitudes 696.

[1] A. Secchi, Ragguaglio intorno alla vita ed ai lavori del P. F. de Vico, Roma 1850. Ami de la religion CXL, Paris 1849, 239—242. Ib. Civiltà cattolica, Ser. 1, VI, Roma 1851, 493.

[2] Among the active members were C. Dumouchel († 1840) who was the first to rediscover the Halley Comet, which had returned, and P. Rosa († 1874), who in 1881 instituted observations of the sun, comets, eclipses, and the passage of Mercury. When Doppler in Vienna had drawn attention to the colour-phenomena of the double-stars, B. Sestini († 1890), who was soon afterwards driven to America by the Revolution, taking up the study of these phenomena, devoted himself to it for several years (Sitzungsberichte der Wiener Akademie VIII [1852] 91).

[3] Wildermann in Jahrbuch der Naturwissenschaften VI, Freiburg 1891, 498. The particulars in The Month LXVIII, London 1890, 305—323 474—488.

Koller († 1866), Director of this Observatory, celebrated for "his genius of observation" and his "perfect mastery of the Calculus" published between 1830 and 1847 numerous accounts of investigations made in Astronomy, Meteorology, and Earth-Magnetism. "A worker of rare assiduity" was the characterization of his successor Augustin Reslhuber († 1875). He was the author of many essays and treatises on Meteorology, Terrestrial Physics, and observations of comets, asteroids, etc.[1] Sigmund Fellöcker was a collaborator in the Berlin Chart of the celestial equator, completing in 1848 the portion (Hora VII.) assigned to him[2].

Mention should also be made of Canon A. Stark of Augsburg († 1839) whose observations of sun-spots were of great value to R. Wolfe in his determination of the well-known eleven years period: of the Jesuit Francis Paula von Triesnecker († 1817) remarkable for his extreme industry in astronomical calculations[3]: and of the Benedictine Placidus (Joseph) Heinrich († 1825) of St. Emmeram, whose contributions to the climatology of the Danube Valley are "of the highest value"[4]. Halma († 1828) and Bossut († 1814), two secular priests, published volumes on the History of Astronomy[5].

---

[1] Allgemeine deutsche Biographie XVI 478 f; XXVIII 247 f. S. Fellöcker, Geschichte der Sternwarte Kremsmunster, Linz 1864. A. Reslhuber, Über das magnetische Observatorium zu Kremsmünster, Wien 1854. For Koller cf. Almanach der k. Akademie der Wissenschaften XVII, Wien 1867, 201—239. Vierteljahrsschrift der deutschen astronomischen Gesellschaft II, Leipzig 1867, 149—153.

[2] C. Bruhns, Joh. Franz Encke, sein Leben und Wirken, Leipzig 1869, 123.

[3] Günther in Allgemeine deutsche Biographie XXXV 488.

[4] Günther ib. XXXII 52. F. v. Schmöger, Erinnerungen an Pl. Heinrich, Regensburg 1825. Katholische Literaturzeitung von v. Kerz 1825, II Intelligenzblatt 75; Verzeichnis der Schriften ib. 85.

[5] Cf. for those named above R. Wolf, Geschichte der Astronomie.

The name of P. Angelo Secchi († 1878) is so well-known and so fresh in the general memory that it is unnecessary for us to deal with him here at any length. Even the Piedmontese Government did not venture, after the seizure of Rome in 1870, to remove the world-renowned astronomer from his Observatory, although he resisted all inducements to betray his fidelity to Pope Pius IX. and the Society of Jesus. Secchi's chief work was done in the province of meteorology, his special achievement being an apparatus for the automatic registration of meteorological phenomena. In speculative physics too, he held a high position. His ideas on the subject are to be found in his work on the "Unity of the Forces of Nature". But nowhere does he appear as the pioneer of so many new tendencies as in his works on the physical constitution of the sun and stars. He applied the methods of spectral analysis as created by Bunsen and Kirchhoff to the investigation of the stellar light, und in this way studied some 6000 fixed stars. To this must be added his observations of spots and protuberances on the sun, and exact measurements of 1324 double stars. His papers on this subject are so numerous that, as Respighi says, they seem "to represent the labours of a scientific association rather than of a single individual". Moigno is of opinion that Secchi single-handed did more work of this kind than the ten collaborators of Arago. The catalogue of his writings enumerates in addition to 65 separately published books and papers, 42 reviews which contain contributions of his, and in many cases very frequent contributions. Thus, for instance, we find in the index of the Reports of the Paris Academy of Science 182 papers and notes by Secchi, in the Astronomical News of Schumacher 132, in the Transactions of the Roman Academy de' Nuovi Lincei 81, in those of the Italian Spectroscopists' Association 46, and so on[1].

One can thus stand at the head of modern astronomy without necessarily being an adherent of materialism and atheism. This was the thesis which we wished to establish as against the assertions of certain writers, and we think that the names to which we have made appeal justify our contention. Piazzi and Secchi at least will be conceded places in the first rank of astronomers, and they were not merely believers in God but Catholic priests. But let us inquire into this subject a little further, and see whether among lay or Protestant leaders of Astronomy the representations of our adversaries find any better verification.

According to Mädler, it is admitted on all hands that Bessel and Gauss stand pre-eminent among the re-organisers of Astronomy. They differed indeed in the nature of their contributions, for "Gauss's activity, fruitful in the highest degree, was confined almost exclusively to the theoretical side, while Bessel, on the contrary leaves us in doubt whether to admire most the number and excellence of his theoretical works or the acuteness of his observations, and the vast fields over which they are scattered"[2]. With Gauss we have already dealt in

[1] Cf. Jos. Pohle, P. Angelo Secchi. Ein Lebens- und Kulturbild, Köln 1883. C. Bricarelli S. J., A. Secchi in Memorie della Pont. Accademia dei Nuovi Lincei IV, Roma 1888. C. Sommervogel mentions other biographies and Secchi's own works: Bibliothèque de la Compagnie de Jésus, 1e partie: Bibliographie VII, Bruxelles-Paris 1896, 993—1031. For the celebration of the 25the Anniversary of his death v. Civ. catt, Ser. 18, IX, Roma 1903, 614; X 349 and the Works of B. Carrara (Padua 1903) and E. Millosevich (Rome 1903).

[2] Cf. R. Wolf, Gesch. der Astronomie 525.

the section devoted to Mathematics, and we purpose here to bring Bessel within the scope of our inquiry.

Born at Minden in 1784 Frederick William Bessel had little opportunity of cultivating a taste for humanistic studies. In mature life he set little store by them, and held in all seriousness the opinion that no one could be accounted an educated man who had not studied Laplace's astronomical works. His father, an official with a large family and mediocre resources, took him away early from school, where indeed he had shown no great promise, and apprenticed him to a merchant at Bremen. Here Bessel had an exacting time of it; his hours of business were from eight o'clock in the morning till eight o'clock in the evening, but from the first he was loyal and assiduous in his work. With the design of qualifying himself to fill the position of "Cargador" or agent for over-sea trade he studied at night Geography and Commerce, English and Spanish. He determined to master also the Art of Navigation, as likely to be very useful in his profession: this led him into Astronomy, and Astronomy into Mathematics. The field, into which he was thus introduced, took his mind completely captive. From half past eight in the evening till two o'clock he toiled at Mathematics and astronomical calculations, but eight o'clock saw him once again in his office.

In Bremen at that time lived Olbers, a physician and celebrated astronomer, already known as the discoverer of several of the smaller planets. One day the young clerk plucked up courage to accost him in the street, begging him to verify the computation of a comet. Olbers consented, and recognising the rare ability of Bessel, persuaded him to make Astronomy his profession, and helped him to prosecute his studies. In 1810 Bessel became Professor in Königsberg, where an Observatory was erected after his plans, and equipped with the most perfect instruments of the day.

His relations with Olbers were always up to the death of the latter of the most intimate kind; Bessel honoured him as a father. Numerous letters of both are preserved[1], a glance through which will be sufficient to show the advocates of materialism that they can no more rely on the authority of these two coryphaei, than on that of Gauss.

It was assuredly no materialist who wrote the name of God so often and so reverently as we find it in Olbers' letters.

"God be thanked, a thousand times over, that your wound had no further evil consequences!" he writes, when Bessel had been bitten by a dog supposed to be mad[2]. "Most gratefully must I celebrate the tender care of my good son. ... May God reward him for the love he shows towards his old father."[3] "God keep you hale and happy!"[4] "Heaven preserve you and yours in unclouded health and prosperity!"[5] "Heaven grant you, my dear Bessel, health to follow on to the end your great and brilliant discoveries!"[6] Similar phrases are to be found many times repeated[7] especially in the letter written by Olbers on August 14th 1832. He had just had a stroke of apoplexy and believed that he was sending his friend a last farewell. "May Heaven bestow on you, my dear, dear friend, many a long year of health, strength, happiness and good fortune, so that your labours

---

[1] Briefwechsel zwischen W. Olbers und F. W. Bessel, herausgeg. von Erman.

[2] Ib. II 76: 16. Februar 1818.

[3] Ib. II 140: 20. April 1820. [4] Ib. II 198: 21. Mai 1821.

[5] Ib. II 269: 25. Januar 1825. [6] Ib. II 280: 3. August 1825.

[7] Cf. ib. I 257 383 399; II 228 252 285 296 435 438.

may develop still more fully a science which already owes to you its complete re-organisation. God bless you and yours! My hand trembles and my head grows heavy." [1] . . .

Not long before his death he sent (July 5th 1838) to Bessel a letter in which he declares his belief in Providence and in the immortality of the soul. "He is, indeed", he writes, "troubled with the inevitable ailments of old age."

"But all this has got to be borne, and no one can hope for perfect health at such an advanced age. I am grateful for the easy circumstances with which Providence has blessed me, which permit me to spend my last years *in otio cum dignitate.* I am still able to rejoice in life. But in another respect I am a *conviva satur* who has tasted and enjoyed to satiety all of good that this earthly life has to offer and is now able to take his departure without reluctance. And this departure is made easier by the feeling that I am become a wholly useless and dispensable member of human society, and by my curiosity to learn in my own person the experience which awaits man after bodily death. I pray only that my leave-taking may be brief, without any long and weary illness." [2]

---

[1] Briefwechsel II 364.

[2] Ib. II 427. Similarly he writes to Gruithausen on 17. Nov. 1839: "Meine Gesundheit und meine Kräfte nehmen jetzt stark ab, und aller Wahrscheinlichkeit nach werde ich nicht lange mehr hienieden weilen. Nun, wie Gott will! Ich bin zum Abschiede aus dieser Zeitlichkeit ebenso bereit als willig" (Wilhelm Olbers. Sein Leben und seine Werke. Im Auftrage der Nachkommen herausgeg. von Dr. C. Schilling I, Berlin 1894, 672). In his treatise on Die Moglichkeit, daß ein Komet mit der Erde zusammenstoßen (und sie zerstören) könne, Olbers writes: "Ist es nicht vermessen von einem eingeschränkten Verstand, daß er entscheiden will, nur der Plan des Weltgebäudes, der alle solche Katastrophen ausschließt, sei der unendlichen Weisheit des Schöpfers angemessen? Kann es nicht mit seinen unerforschlichen Absichten vielleicht ebensogut bestehen,

Bessel replies to this letter on October 28th:

"Your last letter, my dear and venerated friend, gave me such a shock that it took me a long time to recover my self-possession. Everything we treasure on earth drops away from us, or we drop away from it. . . . But I continue to hope, notwithstanding your last letter, that we may be left together for a long time yet. . . . I should be so lonely if you left me, so lonely to be compelled so late in life to learn to stand alone. God grant that we may remain unseparated for many a year to come, and that he who lives the longer may find strength and calmness in his sorrow. You know how closely I am knitted to you: I have never been able and am not yet able, to think of a separation as possible. Several years ago you regarded your condition as hopeless, but Heaven averted what you then feared was the end." [1]

In other passages also, the great astronomer speaks of God and Providence in language which is far from being merely formal.

When in 1808 it was feared that Bessel would be called away on military service, and Olbers offered, if the worst came to the worst, to provide the 800 or 1000 thalers necessary to pay a substitute, Bessel replied (Aug. 5th).

"I am learning to know more and more that the true darlings of fortune are those whom Heaven has blessed with a friend who accepts that name as something more than a mere commonplace." [2] In the severe season of 1811, he writes to Olbers: "Let us enjoy what God, Whose goodness is so infinitely beyond that of man, has given

daß ein Planet, wenn nun die große Erziehung seiner vernunftigen Bewohner gänzlich vollendet ist, wenn alle physischen und moralischen Kräfte und Vollkommenheiten, deren seine Einrichtung fähig war, sich nun völlig entwickelt und gleichsam abgebluht haben, daß, sage ich, dann ein Planet eine große Veränderung erleide, die seine bisherige Organisation zerstört, um einer neuen, vielleicht vollkommeneren wieder Platz zu machen?" (Ib. I 106.)

[1] Briefwechsel II 364—365. [2] Ib. I 184.

us."[1] On occasions of rejoicing he does not fail to express his gratitude to Heaven, to wish his friend the blessing of Heaven[2], and he employs many other expressions native to the Christian mind, which certainly would not have flowed without protest from the pen of an enemy of religion. "But this business must be completed", he writes in 1815 of a scientific work, "and so it shall be, God willing, in the Spring."[3] . . . "Would to God, dear Olbers, that you found in science . . . consolation for the sorrow that has fallen upon you."[4] "God knows how hard it is for me to be so near you and yet not able to visit you."[5] In writing of the difficulties that were thrown in his way at the time of his settlement in Königsberg, he says[6]: "The whole affair is an intrigue on the part of the old staff, who treat us new men in a most unchristian way."[7]

When after the death of Laplace, Biot was asked by Professor Pritchard whom he regarded as his worthiest successor he answered: "Were it not for my strong personal attachment to him I would say without hesitation: John Herschel."[8]

---

[1] Briefwechsel I 260: 3. März 1811.

[2] Ib. I 234 250 281 359; II 116 152 323 332.

[3] Ib. II 5: 24. Dezember 1815.

[4] Ib. II 115: 15. April 1819.

[5] Ib. II 275: 18. April 1825.

[6] Ib. I 231: 8. Juli 1810.

[7] H. W. Brandes († 1834), Professor at Leipzig, who discovered the periodicity of the movements of the shooting stars in August, concludes his popular Vorlesungen über die Astronomie (II, Leipzig 1827, 273) with the thought that the sight of the heaven may just as well fill the spectator "mit Demut vor dem, der unzählbare Welten in den Ozean der Unendlichkeit aussäte, als es ihn mit Freude erfüllt, zu bekennen, dass die Himmel die Ehre Gottes erzählen und die Erde voll ist von seiner Güte".

[8] Dictionary of National Biography, ed. by Leslie Stephen and Sidney Lee XXVI, London 1891, 267. Cf. besides the biographical article ib. 263—268. Ad. Quetelet in Annuaire de l'Académie roy. des sciences de Belgique XXXVIII, Bruxelles 1872.

The name of Herschel has twice been borne by Astronomers of the first rank; by William Herschel (1738—1822) the greatest discoverer of the 18th century and one of the greatest discoverers of all time, and by his son John Frederick William Herschel (1792—1871) who attained almost equal distinction. Biot's high opinion of the younger Herschel was shared by others competent to judge. R. Wolf[1] says that "in the province of optics, mathematics, and astronomy he won before long a name no less distinguished than that which he had inherited", that "his father had in him a capable successor, hardly inferior even to himself". Quetelet[2] declared that he stood among the masters of Astronomy and the declaration was echoed by Arago. John Herschel compiled a catalogue of the stars of the southern hemisphere, and continued the researches of his father into the structure of the stellar system, the constitution of variable and double stars, the Milky Way and so on.

In regard to religion Herschel was not only a firm believer but also a man of great personal piety[3]. Materialistic writers found no mercy at his hands, even though they made a great parade of science. Buckle's "History of Civilisation in England" angered him extremely. In the book Buckle had employed the statistical works of Herschel's correspondent Quetelet as evidence against Free Will, and this fact, together with the favourable way in which Buckle spoke of Quetelet, brought the latter also under suspicion of atheism. Herschel immediately wrote an urgent letter to Quetelet praying

---

[1] Gesch. der Astronomie 505. [2] Ante.

[3] His private life was one unbroken tenour of domestic affection and unostentatious piety (Dict. of Nat. Biogr. 276).

for re-assurance on the point. Quetelet does not print this letter in his biographical sketch of Herschel, but nevertheless conveys clearly Herschel's detestation of atheism, and his religious habit of mind[1]. Nor does Herschel himself in his writings miss any opportunity of declaring against materialism. Two of his lectures "On Atoms", and "On the Origin of Force"[2] are directed to prove that an explanation of the world by means of atoms and motion alone is impossible, and that we must of necessity call in the ideas of thought, reason, will, motive, power, and design.

"Constituted as the human mind is, if nature be *not* interpretable through these conceptions, it is not interpretable at all; and the only reason we can have for troubling ourselves about it is the utilitarian one of bettering our condition by subduing nature to use . . ., or the satisfaction of that sort of curiosity which can find its gratification in scrutinising everything and comprehending nothing. But if these attributes of mind are not consentaneous, they are useless in the way of explanation. Will without motive, Power without Design, Thought opposed to Reason, would be admirable in explaining a chaos, but would render little aid in accounting for anything else."[3]

[1] Chez des personnes religieuses, la crainte de voir leurs croyances se mêler aux discussions scientifiques, et d'entendre contester des points considérés comme solidement établis, fait qu'elles jugent avec une certaine défiance les ouvrages qui donnent lieu à ces craintes. Les doctrines défendues par Buckle, dans son grand ouvrage "History of civilisation in England", avaient un peu effarouché le bon et savant Herschel, qui avait cru, d'après la manière favorable dont Buckle m'avait jugé, que je partageais ses opinions sur l'athéisme (Quetelet ante XXXVIII 189).

[2] John F. W. Herschel, Familiar lectures on Scientific Subjects, London 1867, 452—459: on Atoms; 460—475: on the Origin of Force.

[3] Herschel, Familiar lectures 474—475.

Materialistic theories can tell us nothing more definite than that in the beginning there were atoms, and that these atoms "in obedience to the laws of their nature" began to act one upon another, and thus produced the world as we know it. According to Herschel, these are mere phrases, the emptiness of which appears on serious examination, and the world-conception to which they lead is no better than that which he ridicules in the following words:

"In the beginning was nebulous matter or *Akasch.* Its boundless and tumultuous waves heaved in chaotic wildness, and all was oxygen, and hydrogen, and electricity. Such a state of things could not possibly continue; and as it could not possibly be worse, alteration was here synonymous with improvement."[1]

Unfortunately, says Herschel, the phenomena of nature are a little too complicated for such hypotheses.

"The relations in which atoms stand to one another are anything but simple ones. They involve all the 'ologies and all the 'ometries, and in these days we know something of what that implies. Their movements and interchanges, their hates and loves, their attractions and repulsions, their correlations, their what not, are all determined on the very instant. There is no hesitation, no blundering, no trial and error. A problem of dynamics that would drive Lagrange mad is solved *instanter*. *Solvitur ambulando.* A differential equation which, algebraically written out, would cover the earth, is integrated in an eye-twinkle: and all the numerical calculation worked out in a way to frighten Zerah Colburn, George Bidder, or Jedediah Buxton. In short, these atoms are most wonderful little creatures."

Only one explanation is adequate, that which Anaxagoras opposed to the dreams of the old Greek atomists:

---

[1] Ib. 456 f.

"The presence of mind is what solves the whole difficulty." [1]

A name known even to those who are not specialists in science is that of the great master of the theory of the planets, Urbain Jean Joseph Leverrier (born 1811 at Saint-Lô, died 1877 at Paris, where he was Director of the Observatory). Who indeed could fail to have heard of the discovery of Neptune, the existence and the location of which Leverrier demonstrated mathematically, and which was thereupon actually discovered by Galle of Berlin in the place indicated? The achievement compelled the admiration of all Europe. "It was a discovery", said Piazzi Smith on the death of Leverrier, "which almost took men's breath away for the moment in astonishment and admiration: and showed that the age of intellectual giants cast in the mould of Newton and Laplace was not yet closed." [2] The name of Leverrier was in every mouth, and honours and distinctions were showered on him from every quarter.

And yet the discovery of Neptune is not perhaps Leverrier's greatest service to Astronomy. Even without his famous computation, Neptune must have been before long discovered. But what science might not yet have attained, were it not for Leverrier's mathematical genius, his masterly grasp of every intricacy of celestial mechanics, and his iron industry and perseverance, is the exact determination of the theory of the planetary system as

---

[1] "The presence of MIND is what solves the whole difficulty; so far at least as it brings it within the sphere of our own consciousness and into conformity with our own experience of what action is" (Herschel ante 458).

[2] Proceedings of the Royal Society of Edinburgh IX (1877 to 1878) 489.

a whole. For it was this that Leverrier chose as the main business of his life[1].

The great Astronomer had begun his career in 1836 with some theses in chemistry. But three years later we find him busy with astronomical calculations, a field which he was not to abandon till death. In 1839 he published a mathematical calculation of the variations of the planets during the period 100 000 B. C. to 100 000 A. D., in which he perfected Laplace's imperfect proof that despite the disturbing influence of the planets on one another, the planetary system can never of its own intrinsic forces fall into disorder. In 1843 he worked out the path of Mercury: in 1845 Arago, then Director of the Observatory, recommended him to study the path of Uranus, the most distant of the planets at that time known. By November of this latter year he had worked out a full computation of the path of that planet on the assumption that no influence was operative save that of the planets already known. In June 1846 there followed an essay in which the path thus computed was compared with actual observations, and it was shown that in order to explain the divergences from the path it was necessary to posit the existence of another planet lying outside Uranus. On August 31st 1846 Leverrier published a computation of

---

[1] J. Bertrand, Éloge historique d'Urbain-Jean-Joseph Leverrier lu dans la séance publique annuelle de l'Académie des sciences du 10 mars 1879: Annales de l'observatoire de Paris. Mémoires XV, Paris 1880, 3—22. F. Tisserand, Les travaux de Leverrier. ib. 23—43. Discours prononcés à l'inauguration de la statue de Leverrier, à l'observatoire de Paris, le jeudi, 27 juin 1889. Annuaire pour l'an 1890 publié par le Bureau des longitudes, Paris: Discours de M. Fizeau 637—645, de M. le contre-amiral E. Mouchez 645 to 656, de M. Tisserand 657—667.

the path of this new body, the existence of which he had thus deductively established. Subsequent observations proved that he was not deceived, and led to the most remarkable of all the discoveries of Astronomy.

In the years 1844—1847 there appeared exhaustive studies of certain of the comets which revolve about the sun, those, namely, which are called after Lexell, Faye, and De Vico. Leverrier traced up the history of these comets, showed by colossal calculations how their paths must have been, and must in the future be, determined by the influence of the planets, especially of Jupiter, and sought to ascertain when these comets became associated with the solar system, and when they will once again pass out of the sphere of influence of the sun.

The planet tables then employed were not in complete agreement with actual observations; the divergences were slight, but still large enough to indicate some mistake in the assumptions on which they were founded. On July 2nd 1849 Leverrier laid before the Academy the "gigantic plan" of a new computation of these tables. "This Herculean labour", as Tisserand calls it, "he continued down to his death, and he had the fortune and glory to bring it by his sole efforts to a consummation." Mercury, Venus, the Earth, and Mars occupied twenty years: the other planets which presented still greater difficulties were computed in a shorter space.

Amongst the honours bestowed on Leverrier for these brilliant achievements were the dignity of Senator of the Empire, and the Directorate of the Paris Observatory (1854). It may be doubted, however, whether Leverrier was precisely the man for this latter position.

He worked, throughout the night "and grudged even a few hours rest to his body, exhausted by continuous labours of this kind. The result was a severe and tedious illness, which had an unfavourable influence on his character"[1]. Thus his subordinates found him a hard taskmaker, and the exacting demands he made on them were not mitigated by any courtesy or consideration of manner. Under his Directorate the Observatory exhibited great activity, the results of which are to be found in its publications, but the discontent with Leverrier became so acute that in the year 1870 the Government removed him from his position. Three years later he was, however, restored, for Leverrier was one of those men who cannot be dispensed with. Nor was it his staff alone that had experience of the great savant's ability to make himself unpleasant. When under the Third Republic orders were issued that the motto "Liberté, Fraternité, Egalité" should be inscribed on all public buildings, and even on churches, Leverrier refused to allow any other inscription over the door of the Observatory except the single word *Observatoire*, and the Government had to give him his way[2].

Leverrier was known in France as a "Clerical". "Under the Empire", complained a Paris newspaper, on his re-appointment, "he was a clericalising senator, pledged no less deeply to the interests of the altar than to those

---

[1] Mouchez. Discours prononcés à l'inauguration de la statue de Leverrier 654.

[2] Mac Mahon caused him one day to be requested to prepare the observatory for the visit of the Shah of Persia. "Maréchal, la science n'illumine pas les sauvages", was his answer.

of the throne."[1] In a discourse pronounced at his funeral, Tresca declared that the study of the heavens had only confirmed and deepened his lively faith in Christianity[2]. It was given to him, said Dumas on the same occasion, to write the last word of the last page of his immortal work in the last hour of his life, murmuring as he concluded: Nunc dimittis servum tuum, Domine[3]. On June 5th 1876 Leverrier laid before the Academy the last instalment of his great work, containing the tables of Jupiter and Saturn. Referring to the speech in which J. B. Dumas had a few days before declared against materialism, he said:

"Throughout this protracted undertaking, lasting over thirty years, we have had need to draw support from the spectacle of one of the glories of creation, and from the thought that our study tended to confirm us in the imperishable truths of the spiritualistic philosophy. It was then with profound emotion that I heard at the last meeting of the Academy, our illustrious permanent Secretary re-affirm those great principles which are the very source of the purest science. That declaration will remain as an honour

---

[1] Quoted from the République française by Pierre Larousse, Grand dictionnaire universel du XIXe siècle X, Paris 1873, 445: Sous l'Empire, il fut sénateur cléricalisant et non moins inféodé aux intérêts de l'autel qu'à ceux de la dynastie.

[2] La fin de ce savant, qui fut illustre avant l'âge, et par laquelle on n'apprendra pas sans émotion, peut-être, que l'étude du ciel et la foi scientifique n'avaient fait que consolider en lui la foi vive du chrétien, c'est là un exemple qui sera donné de bien haut à la conscience publique et à la moralité de notre époque (Comptes rendus hebdomadaires des séances de l'Académie des sciences LXXXV [1877] 589).

[3] . . . écrivant le dernier mot de la dernière page de son œuvre immortelle à la dernière heure de sa vie et murmurant pieusement alors. Nunc dimittis servum tuum, Domine (ib. 582).

and an inspiration to French science: and I esteem it a great happiness to have this opportunity of rising in the midst of our Academy, and proclaiming my cordial adhesion to his principles."[1]

Among the foremost of contemporary French Astronomers stood Hervé Faye († July 7th 1902). In 1897 he celebrated his golden Jubilee as Member of the Academy, and Professor of the Polytechnic School: and his scientific works are held in the highest esteem. In his volume "On the Origin of the World" he sets forth his ideas on the history of the solar system, and in the spirit of a thorough believer expounds the relation which exists between the narrative of creation given in the Old Testament, and the cosmogonic conceptions of modern science. The introductory chapter, "Science and the Idea of God", shows how the study of nature must lead up to a recognition of the existence of God.

Faye takes as his point of departure the feeling of wonder and admiration which the starry heavens evoke in every mind capable of any high emotion. No insight into the mechanism of the stellar systems is needed to produce such a feeling. "This impression vague though it appears to me in my dull attempt to analyse it, has in it a deep satisfaction. We feel exalted in mind, as it were, to a world

[1] Durant cette longue entreprise, poursuivie pendant trente-cinq années, nous avons eu besoin d'être soutenu par le spectacle d'une des plus grandes œuvres de la création, et par la pensée qu'elle affermissait en nous les vérités impérissables de la Philosophie spiritualiste. C'est donc avec émotion que nous avons entendu dans la dernière séance de l'Académie française, notre illustre Sécrétaire perpétuel affirmer ces grands principes qui sont la source même de la science la plus pure. Cette haute manifestation restera un honneur et une force pour la science française. Je m'estime heureux que l'occasion se soit présentée de la relever au sein de notre Académie, et de lui donner une cordiale adhésion (Comptes rendus LXXXII [1876] 1280).

raised far above the paltry things by which we are surrounded on earth. We contemplate, we come to understand, in so far at least as it falls within the scope of our senses, this world which of itself does not understand anything. For there are realities other than the body, other than material things, other than this glittering world of stars. There is thought, there is intellect. And as our human intellect has not created itself, there must be in existence a higher intellect from which ours derives. The nobler the conception we frame of this higher intellect the nearer we approach the truth. We run no risk of deceiving ourselves in regarding it as the source of all existence, we trace back to it all these celestial splendours which have stirred our imaginations, and we find ourselves at last able to understand and ready to accept the traditional formula: Almighty God, Creator of Heaven and Earth." [1]

In an earlier part of this book we have treated at length of eminent Italian astronomers who belonged to various religious orders. We subjoin the names of two eminent laymen.

Giovanni Sante Gasparo Santini, born in 1787, and occupied in astronomical research at Padua from 1806 till his death in 1877, made important contributions to science in the course of his long life. He published a catalogue of the stars between the tenth degree North and the tenth degree South latitude, and

---

[1] . . . Et comme notre intelligence ne s'est faite elle-même, il doit exister dans le monde une intelligence supérieure d'où la nôtre dérive. Dès lors, plus l'idée qu'on se fera de cette intelligence supérieure sera grande, plus elle approchera de la vérité. Nous ne risquons pas de nous tromper en la considérant comme l'auteur de toute choses, en reportant à elle ces splendeurs des cieux qui ont éveillé notre pensée, et finalement nous voilà tout préparés à comprendre et à accepter la formule traditionnelle: Dieu, Père tout-puissant, Créateur du ciel et de la terre (H. Faye, Sur l'origine du monde. Théories cosmogoniques des anciens et des modernes[3], Paris 1896, 3).

computed the paths of no less than seventeen comets. His name became widely known when his calculation of the time of return of the Bialasch comet was verified by the event. In many works of reference we find him wrongly described as a priest. But although not a priest, Santini was a deeply religious man, who all through life preserved the faith of his childhood [1].

A contemporary of Secchi's at Rome, Lorenzo Respighi [2], attained almost equal distinction in the field of solar physics and on many questions even surpassed Secchi. Born at Corte Maggiore (in the province of Piacenza) on October 7th 1824, he lost his parents when very young, but his education was taken in hands by an elder brother, who lived at Parma, and after his death by a cousin at Bologna. In Bologna University, he was appointed (as early as 1851) to the Chair of Optics and Astronomy, and in 1855 to the Directorate of the Observatory. He discovered three comets (in 1862 and 1863), reduced to systematic form the meteorological notes of the Observatory staff during

---

[1] Cf. Giovanni Santini, La sua vita e le sue opere. Discorso letto nella chiesa di s. Sofia in Padova dal Prof. Giuseppe Lorenzoni nel dì trigesimo dalla morte dell' illustre astronomo, Padova 1877, 5: Nessuna meraviglia pertanto, che il nostro Santini, d'indole buona per natura, abbia poi ritenuto quella morale (that of the Gospel) per norma costante della sua vita ed abbia sempre nutrito e coltivato nell' intimo del suo cuore quel profondo sentimento religioso, che ne addolcì di tante consolazioni le traversie della vita e che, sopravvissuto aggli splendori della sublime intelligenza, rischiarò di un melanconico e tranquillo lume gli ultimi e vacillanti passi della sua mortale carriera.

[2] Lorenzo Respighi. Suo elogio pel P. G. St. Ferrari d. C. d. G. Nell' anniversario della sua morte letto nella Pontificia Accademia Tiberina il 6 dic. 1890. Roma 1891.

the period 1814—1858, and published studies on the phenomenon of irradiation in the human eye and the eye's power of accommodation. His investigation of the declination of the magnetic needle in Bologna were rudely interrupted, when in 1864 the Piedmontese Government demanded of him an oath of allegiance. Respighi declared that he could not conscientiously subscribe to the oath proposed, and as a result he was "relieved" of his professorate and his post in the Observatory. Pius IX., by way of compensation placed him in charge of the Observatory on the Capitol, but here too he came, in 1871, under the menace of the fatal oath. Respighi again refused to take it[1]: but no one capable of filling his position being forthcoming, the Government restored him in 1872 without exacting any oath. In the interval he had, at the instance of the British authorities, proceeded to India and made observations of a total eclipse of the sun. At Rome he devoted himself mainly to spectroscopic research: and his works on the solar protuberances, and the constitution of the sun generally, attracted attention throughout Europe[2]. In addition to these he explained with the aid of the spectroscope the luminosity of the stars, investigated the causes of the variation in the sun's diameter, made many meteorological studies, and in 1870 co-operated in the measurement of a degree of latitude at Rome. Another very valuable work of Respighi's was his accurate catalogue of the declination of 2534 stars of the northern hemisphere published in 1880 and 1885. The corresponding right ascensions he did not live to complete, for on

---

[1] Civiltà catt., Ser. 8, IV, Roma 1871, 487; cf. 236.

[2] Encyclopaedia Britannica II, Edinburgh 1875, 788.

December 10th 1889 death cut short the labours of a savant, as rare in character as in intellect, and a Christian of the highest type.

In the year 1819 an envoy of the Scottish Monastery of Regensburg visited the fatherland of the Order in search of talented lads for the seminary which had been long attached to the Monastery of Regensburg. Since the days of the Reformation the education of Catholic priests in Scotland had been impossible, and many such journeys had been taken by the Regensburg Benedictines, but that of 1818 was especially notable for of the two boys whom Prior Robertson in that year brought back with him to Regensburg, one was destined to find in Bavaria a new home, and to become one of the most active and celebrated of Bavarian astronomers of modern times.

Johannes Von Lamont was born in 1805 at Braemar, not far from the Castle of Balmoral. His father, a not over-rich tax-collector, died young, and the talented boy would have been compelled to give up his studies, had not a happy chance introduced him to the envoy of Regensburg. Under the direction of the Benedictines he completed his gymnasium course, and then took up philosophy and theology. But he did not become a priest. His prior, Dom Benedict Deasson († 1855), a distinguished mathematician and physicist, soon discovered his pupil's extraordinary aptitude for science, and sent him to the newly established Observatory at Munich to push his studies deeper. Here Lamont so distinguished himself that in 1835 he was appointed Director of the Observatory. In this post, which he occupied till his death, he did an enormous amount of work. He investigated constellations and nebulae, calculated the mass of Uranus, and catalogued after repeated observations 80000 stars of the 7th to the 10th magnitude. He also made important contributions to the geodesy of his adopted country. But these difficult and tedious labours hardly hold the first place in Lamont's achievements. "Although enough of themselves", writes Professor Gunther, "to make a famous man these achievements fall below his invaluable contributions to terrestrial physics." He founded a society, with many branches, for meteorological research, and its Journal, although short-lived, is "an inexhaustible quarry for the specialist". He invented apparatus which automatically registered meteorological phenomena, investigated the temperature of the earth, atmospheric electricity, and above all the magnetism of the earth, in the study of which he made extensive journeys with the portable theodolite invented by himself[1].

Lamont's religious opinions were well-known in Munich. "He was", writes Professor Von Schafhautl, "in this, as in every other respect, for all his mildness a man of the firmest character, and his Catholicity was firm and unwavering. When a clouded sky drove him from his Observatory he loved to pass his evenings at the lately founded Catholic Casino, and liked best the company of simple intelligent business people. Their ways of thinking and feeling the savant found completely to his mind, and he became a great favourite with the towns-people and all the members of the Casino. At about ten o'clock he usually took his leave and returned through the dark and lonely English Garden to

[1] Cf. Gunther in Allgemeine deutsche Biographie XVII 570.

his home at the Observatory, a walk of more than an hour. . . ."

In this lonely Observatory where he had spent so great a part of his life, he was also to die. "He suffered no pain, and was so little conscious of declining strength that till almost the last moment he had no suspicion that his life was in danger. He however received the last Sacraments at the instance of his friends, and for his own spiritual consolation. 'Now I am content', he said stretching out his icy hand in a last farewell."

"In the frantic witches' dance of our time, Lamont stands apart, a spectacle of peace — a keen observer, a deep thinker, and, what is still more, a man of character, a brave, thorough, Christian man."[1] "He possessed", remarks another writer[2] who lays special emphasis on Lamont's charitable disposition, "that calm and cheerful manner, which proceeds from spiritual peace, and he had the secret of keeping it unclouded. Love of truth and moral stability were the essence of his character."

Another astronomer who distinguished himself in the field of earth-magnetism was the Austrian Karl Kreil[3] (1798—1862). A pupil, like Lamont, of the Benedictines, he received his first lessons in science at Kremsmunster under Dom Bonifaz Schwarzenbrunner, and showing himself apt and enthusiastic, he was set to work at meteorology. In 1827 he held a post at Vienna and later at Milan, in 1845 he became Director at Prague, and in 1850 Director of the Meteorological Observatory at

---

[1] v. Schafhäutl in Historisch-politische Blätter LXXXV 78 80 82. Cf. E. Ringseis, Erinnerungen IV 154—156.

[2] C. v. Orff in Leopoldina XVIII, Halle 1882, 55.

[3] C. v. Wurzbach, Biograph. Lexikon des Kaisertums Österreich XIII, Wien 1865, 179—187.

Vienna. A happy chance turned his attention to the study of earth-magnetism, and he became the pioneer of this branch of science in Austria. "He was one of the most active members of the International Magnetic Society founded by Gauss, the observations and communications of which furnished Gauss and Weber with invaluable material for the development of the theory of earth-magnetism. The work of Kreil is, for versatility and accuracy, unequalled in its kind, and it won the warm recognition of the first of contemporary specialists, among others of Gauss, Sir John Herschel, Sartorius Von Waltershausen, and Humboldt." Kreil was the first scientist on the Continent to undertake extensive journeys for the study of earth-magnetism. In 1843—1844 he toured Bohemia, under a commission from the Bohemian Scientific Association; in 1846—1848 the other provinces of the Empire; in 1854 the coast-lands of the Adriatic; in 1858 the Danubian Principalities. His enterprise found many imitators in other countries.

Kreil's achievements are to be ascribed solely to his enthusiastic love of science, and to his personal sacrifices in its service. To the favour of circumstances, or the support of powerful patrons he owed very little. The praise is his alone; he chose a subject of investigation that came within the range of his resources, and pushed on his inquiries in spite of every obstacle. And the obstacles were great. At Prague he found the Observatory in a state of extreme dilapidation. "With the savings that he was able, by a life of unexampled simplicity, to scrape together out of his salary — 800 gulden, a stipend utterly unworthy of such a savant — he purchased for his own use scientific instruments, and these were, necessarily of the cheapest kind." Lacking the means to erect for magnetic observation a hut, free from iron, he made his observations in an ordinary building, and corrected the consequent inaccuracy of his results by protracted calculations. His journeys "were attended in some cases with actual danger, in all with severe labour, which on one occasion brought on an illness of considerable duration".

Kreil's "simple and lovable character, his benevolence free from all stain of affectation, his great modesty were the happiness of his family, and of his small circle of intimate friends. His religious convictions were fervent and deep-rooted, and far from interfering with his researches in science were a powerful ally, and a continual source of strength"[1].

The same zeal for science, which, despite the scantiness of resources, finds a sphere of fruitful activity, manifests itself in the North-German astronomer Edward Heis[2] (born 1806 at Cologne, died 1872 at Münster in Westphalia). The Münster Observatory not possessing any of the larger astronomical instruments, Heis devoted himself to investigations for which such instruments were not needed; he studied shooting stars, zodiacal light,

---

[1] Kreil, une des gloires scientifiques les plus pures de l'Autriche, n'avait encore que 54 ans; son caractère doux et aimant, sa bienfaissance éloignée de toute ostentation, son extrême modestie faisaient le bonheur de sa famille et du petit nombre de ceux qu'il admettait dans son intimité. Ses convictions religieuses, intimes et profondes, loin de se heurter contre ses occupations scientifiques, leur ont prêté un puissant appui et y puisaient au contraire une force toujours nouvelle (Paper of Count Marschal in Les Mondes I, Paris 1863, 403).

[2] Natur und Offenbarung XXIII, Münster 1877, 508—511. Deutscher Hausschatz III, Regensburg 1876—1877, 807—810. Leopoldina XIII, Halle 1877, 178—180.

variable stars, sun spots and the polar lights. He succeeded also in interesting others in the same line of research so that the same meteor or Northern light might be observed from as many stations as possible: the various observations were then compared and the determination (e. g. of the path of the meteor in question, its distance or that of the polar light from the earth, or the relations existing between the lights of the North and those of the South), was effected. In 1858 the "Journal of Astronomy, Meteorology, and Geography" was established by Heis to serve as a common centre for the scientists associated with him. A paper published after his death gives particulars of 15 000 observations of shooting-stars made by him in 37 years. As early as 1849 he had determined for the first time the point of the heavens from which meteors seem to take their departure.

His chief work is however his atlas of stars visible from Central Europe with the naked eye[1]. The earlier charts were very defective: they gave the relative degrees of brightness incorrectly, marked dimmer stars while they omitted brighter ones, and in other respects also presented a false picture of reality. The first who sought to make the necessary corrections was Argelander, and the important work begun by him was completed by Heis. The gradation of the stars in the latter's atlas is quoted in the famous Harvard Photometry[2] as possessing an authority comparable to that of Argelander's Uranometry, of the Bonn catalogue, and of

---

[1] Cf. Heis himself in Natur und Offenbarung XVIII, Münster 1872, 518—532.

[2] Annals of the Astronomical Observatory of Harvard College XIV.

Gould's Uranometry. Heis was occupied on this work not less than twenty seven years — the number of stars marked is 5421 — for these stars are "innumerable" only in the sense that as one continues to gaze steadily at the heavens fresh stars continually become visible. A further merit of Heis' atlas is that it contains the first trustworthy chart of the Milky Way. This had not been included in Argelander's work: and, incredible as it may seem, in older charts the treatment of the Milky Way had been founded not on observation but on the description of it given by Ptolemy. The Munster astronomer was the first to present an exact delimitation of the boundaries of the Milky Way, and a reliable account of the gradation of brightness among the stars of which it is composed.

Next in importance to this Atlas come his studies of the variable stars. These were first published in 1903 (together with Krueger's observations) by his pupil and friend J. G. Hagen S. J. Heis' notes extending over 37 years, exhibit, as his editor remarks, extraordinary tenacity of purpose and rare precision. Two Latin essays of Heis rank among the earliest contributions to Photometry[1]. Heis as a teacher was interesting and stimulating: his activities in this direction produced some very valuable text-books. One of these, "A Collection of Examples", had before his death reached a fiftieth edition.

Heis was a perfect type of the fervent and zealous Catholic who finds his greatest joy in his faith, and in the practical discipline prescribed by his faith. He went

[1] De magnitudine relativa numeroque accurato stellarum quae solis oculis conspiciuntur fixarum. Munster 1852. Beobachtungen uber Mira Ceti von 1840—1859, in the Vorlesungsverzeichnis der Munsterer Akademie 1859—1860.

to Mass every day, unless prevented by illness, received the Sacraments regularly, said the Rosary every night with his family, and was an honorary member of the Academic Congregation of Mary. He made it a rule to forego his lecture on the feast of St. Aloysius, the patron of youth, and took part with the greatest pride and devotion in every ceremony of the Church. Nor did he make any attempt to conceal his faith when, as in the Kulturkampf, to profess it openly meant to sacrifice one's interests. One of the first copies of his Atlas he sent to Pius IX: and the letter of thanks, signed by the Pope's own hand, was one of his proudest possessions. It was his desire that his tombstone should bear the symbol of the dove with the olive-branch such as we find it in the Catacombs.

Heis had no lack of the critical faculty. When A. Von Humboldt was commissioned by the Prussian Government to investigate the alleged visions of the battle at Birkenbäumchen, and was prevented by illness from discharging his commission, he appointed Heis as his substitute. Heis summoned before him all who had claimed to have seen the visions, but it proved on examination that nobody had seen anything definite. "It is a cloud battle", said Heis at the end of his judgment[1].

Johann Franz Encke († 1865) is known chiefly through the comet called after him. He did not actually discover it, but proved mathematically that it travels round the sun in a closed elliptical path, and so, like the planets, belongs to our solar system. Encke was also director of the great undertaking which had for its

[1] Cf. F. Zurbonsen, Die Sage von der Völkerschlacht der Zukunft 'am Birkenbaume', Köln 1897, 73 f 78 f.

object to produce charts of the whole celestial equator. The work stretched over the years 1826—1859. One amongst its many good results was to make possible the discovery of new planets: and to the accuracy of this Berlin Atlas is to be ascribed e. g. the prompt discovery of Neptune, the location of which had been mathematically determined by Leverrier[1]. In Encke's writings and lectures we find numerous references to a ruling Providence: and although he was not an exemplary church-goer there was never any doubt as to his religious convictions[2].

Among more recent German astronomers the name of E. L. A. Von Rebeur-Paschwitz († 1895) stands very high. "Dying at the age of thirty four he had done work which most men of twice his age might regard with satisfaction as the fruits of time wellspent." To him is due above all the employment of the horizontal pendulum. "He was as distinguished for depth of religious feeling", writes a biographer, "as for keenness of scientific insight."[3]

To this long list of Italian, German, and French savants we may add the names of two leaders of astronomy in Switzerland who also were fervent Christians. We refer to Rudolf Wolf (1816—1893) of Zurich, and Alfred Gautier (1793—1881) of Geneva, the two discoverers of the relations between sun-spots and terrestrial magnetism. The former left instructions in his will that "his grave should be marked with a cross

[1] E. g. Monatsberichte der Berliner Akademie 1861, 506; 1869, 173.

[2] C. Bruhns, Joh. Franz Encke, sein Leben und Wirken, Leipzig 1869, 321.

[3] Leopoldina XXXII, Halle 1896, 14.

similar to that which he had erected over his mother and sister"[1]. And that the Cross was for him no empty symbol is shown by numerous passages in his writings. As to the relations of science and religion he was of the same mind with Secchi[2]. Gautier's adherence to the Christian belief is clearly affirmed in a memorial article in the Review edited by Wolf[3].

We may then conclude our inquiry among the leaders of Astronomy with the words of J. H. Von Mädler of Dorpater († 1874), himself an adept in the science:

"No! Science and its true and genuine champions do not merit the censures and contempt which have been heaped on them by certain writers, who accuse them of hiding away from view the things of God, and degrading men to atheism. Such charges are absolutely groundless: of astronomy in particular we hope to show that exactly the opposite is true, and that appeal should be made to it to restore and confirm those beliefs which are rightly esteemed the noblest possession of mankind."

"If science is to take up arms against materialism, it must rely strictly on observed facts, all the more as it is from these that materialists profess to derive their conclusions. Were we to be silent as to the implications of these facts, it would amount — *qui tacet consentit*, says the proverb — to a confession that our views are at variance with them."

"But to this it must not and cannot come. Spirit as such . . . is no obstacle to our research and cannot be, for otherwise it would not be spirit at all. From the fact

---

[1] Mitteilungen der naturforschenden Gesellschaft in Bern aus dem Jahr 1893, Bern 1894, Nr. 1305—1334, p. 214.

[2] V. infra in the Section VIII.

[3] "Pratiquant sans bruit les vertus chrétiennes, il est mort comme il avait vécu, au milieu de ses livres et de ses œuvres pieuses" (Vierteljahrsschrift der naturforschenden Gesellschaft in Zurich XXVI, Zurich 1881, 398).

that we abstain from transgressing the necessary limits of our science, and trespassing on other provinces of thought, it must not be inferred that we deny the principles established in those other provinces. . . ." [1]

IV. PHYSICS.

1. THEORY OF ELECTRICITY.

In three directions, especially, Physics has brilliant conquests to record during the 19th century — in the fields, namely, of electricity, light, and heat. While as regards light and heat the advance made has consisted, not so much in the discovery of new facts as in the deeper and more systematic interpretation of those already known, the reverse has been the case with electricity. The nature of electricity remains as before an enigma; but the immense body of new facts discovered in the first half of the century, the wonderful applications of this knowledge in the second half, have outshone nearly every other achievement of Physics. The 19th century is the age of electricity. At its opening the discoveries of Volta, at its close the discoveries of Röntgen held all eyes fixed in admiration: and the interval is filled with the illustrious names of Faraday, Oersted, Ampère and the long list of inventors who translated the accumulated stores of discovery into practical appliances the value of which is beyond estimation. Our survey of the leaders of Physics may, therefore, appropriately begin with the pioneers of Electricity.

As to who these pioneers really were, we find official testimony in the very terminology of the science.

[1] J. H. v. Mädler, Reden und Abhandlungen uber Gegenstände der Himmelskunde, Berlin 1870, 326 328.

The units in which electricity is measured bear the names of distinguished investigators, and the names so honoured are naturally those with which the progress of the science is chiefly associated. We find among them Volta, Ampère, Faraday, Ohm, Coulomb. The reason for selecting two of these names is obvious: Coulomb was the first to make experiments in the quantitative determination of electricity, Ohm discovered the law on which such determination is nowadays invariably based. There remain the names of Volta, Ampère, and Faraday. We proceed to glance at the achievements of these masters, and to inquire what attitude they assumed towards Christianity and religion in general.

Alessandro Volta († 1827), the discoverer of current electricity, was a man about whose religious position there is no room for doubt [1]. "He was", writes a biographer, "much given to investigation of the grounds on which Catholicity is based, and had a wide and comprehensive grasp of them. Every utterance of his gave evidence of unusual lucidity of mind and large erudition. But in every matter affecting the dogmatic substance of faith, or the observation of prescribed religious duties, he was, for all his learning, as teachable as a child." Throughout his professorate at Como he was in the habit of devoting academic holidays to religious studies, and he made constant use of the Monastery libraries, especially of that of the college for-

---

[1] C. Grandi, Alessandro Volta, Milano 1899. Cf. Stimmen aus Maria-Laach LIV, Freiburg 1900, 1—25 138—156. As well as the books mentioned on page 4 of the latter cf. P. Riccardi, Sulle opere di A. Volta. Note bibliografiche, in Memorie della regia Accademia di scienze, lettere ed arti in Modena XVII, Modena 1877, 159—196.

merly occupied by the Jesuits. But in spite of his extensive acquaintance with these matters, perhaps because of it, he never set out to teach theologians or to reform theology in the name of scientific progress. "Modern discovery", he once wrote, "the laws which we have brought to light, the paths which we have opened, ought not to excite any prejudice against the older truth, nor ought it presume to obstruct or draw men away from the one way, trodden by so many feet."

Volta suffered no human respect to estrange him from the exercises of religion. During his visit to Paris he was scrupulous never to miss Mass, and it was the same during his presence at the Assembly of Notables at Lyons, although in this latter place (as his letters inform us) he had great difficulty in finding an "unsworn" priest. When at home he went daily to Mass, and received the Sacraments on all Feast-days. On Corpus Christi he decorated his house and street for the passing of the procession, took part in the public devotions offered before an ancient Crucifix which stood in the Church of the Annunciation, and in all those testimonies of love and veneration practised by pious Catholics towards the Mother of God, showed himself as ardent as the humblest of his townsmen. He had over his door a picture of the Blessed Virgin, and, when entering, invariably raised his hat in salutation. Every Saturday a lamp was lighted before it, and if the servant forgot to light it, Volta himself repaired the omission. From his father and mother he had learned to recite the Rosary every evening, and this practice he continued throughout life.

We find still stronger evidence of his love for the Christian belief in his earnest endeavours to implant and confirm it in the hearts of others. Anyone visiting the parish Church, San Donnino, on the afternoon of a Feast-day would have found Volta in the midst of a group of children to whom he was explaining the Catechism. Precisely the same desire to do something for the salvation of others gave birth to the remarkable document in which he makes an express and solemn Confession of Faith. Early in 1815 Canon Giacomo Ciceri had in his care a dying man whom he vainly sought to convert. Every appeal was met with the reply that religion was only for the vulgar and the rabble, and that men of science, among whom the speaker counted himself, no longer concerned themselves with it. Ciceri instanced in disproof the name of Volta, a man who certainly knew something about science and yet was an exemplary Christian. The name made an impression on the freethinker; he replied that if Volta's religion was not a mere external show, but a reality, he would be willing to make profession of it. The Canon, who was acquainted with Volta, appealed to the latter to send a few lines to the poor sinner and received the following response[1]:

[1] "Non so chi mai possa dubitare della mia sincerità e costanza in questa Religione che professo, che è la Cattolica, Apostolica, Romana, nella quale sono nato ed allevato, ed a cui mi sono attenuto sempre sì interiormente, che esteriormente. Ho ben mancato, pur troppo, riguardo alle buone opere di Cristiano cattolico, e mi sono fatto reo di molte colpe: ma per grazia speziale del Signore, non ho mancato mai, per quanto mi dice la coscienza, di fede. Che se quelle colpe e disordini miei hanno per avventura dato luogo ed occasione a taluno di sospettare in me qualche incredulità, a titolo di reparazione e ad ogni buon fine dichiaro a quel tale e ad ogni altra persona, e sono pronto a dichiarare in ogni incontro ed a qualunque costo, che ho sempre tenuto e tengo per unica, vera ed

"I do not understand how anyone can doubt the sincerity and constancy of my attachment to the religion which I profess, the Roman, Catholic and Apostolic religion in which I was born and brought up, and of which I have always made confession, externally and internally. I have, indeed, and only too often, failed in the performance of those good works which are the mark of a Catholic Christian, and I have been guilty of many sins: but through the special mercy of God I have never, as far as I know, wavered in my faith. If my offences and transgressions have given occasion to anyone to suspect me of disbelief, I here, by way of reparation and for any other good purpose that may be served, assure such or any other persons, and am prepared to maintain this declaration in any circumstances, cost what it may, that I have always believed and still belive the Holy Catholic faith to be the one true and infallible religion: and I constantly give thanks to God, Who has infused into me this belief in which I desire to live and die, with the firm hope of eternal life.

In this faith I recognise a pure gift of God, a supernatural grace; but I have not neglected those human means

infallibile questa Santa Religione Cattolica, ringraziando senza fine il buon Dio d'avermi infusa una tale fede, in cui mi propongo fermamente di voler vivere e morire con viva speranza di conseguire la vita eterna. La riconosco sì per un dono di Dio, per una fede soprannaturale· non ho però tralasciato i mezzi anchi umani di vieppiù confermarmi in essa, sgombrare qualunque dubbio potesse sorgere a tentarmi, studiandola attentamente nei suoi fondamenti, rintracciando colla lettura di libri sì apologetici che contrarî le ragioni pro e contra, onde emergono gli argomenti più validi, che la rendono anche alla ragione naturale credibilissima, e tale che ogni animo non pervertito da vizî, e da passioni, ogni animo ben fatto non può non abbracciarla ed amarla. — Possa questa protesta, che mi viene ricercata, e che io di buon grado rilascio scritta e sottoscritta di mio mano, ostensibile come si vuole ed a chiunque, giacchè non erubesco Evangelium, possa produrre qualche buon frutto." This confession of faith was printed during Volta's life. The autographic copy was extant until the burning of the Volta-exhibition at Como, 8th July 1899. Cf. Grandi ante 575 f.

which confirm belief, and overthrow the doubts which at times arise. I studied attentively the grounds and basis of religion, the works of apologists and assailants, the reasons for and against, and I can say that the result of such study is to clothe religion with such a degree of probability, even for the merely natural reason, that every spirit unperverted by sin and passion, every naturally noble spirit must love and accept it.

May this confession which has been asked from me and which I willingly give, written and subscribed by my own hand, with authority to show it to whomsoever you will, for I am not ashamed of the Gospel, may it produce some good fruit!

Milan, Jan. 6., 1815. Alexander Volta.

Such was the judgment of Christianity formed by a man of whose intellectual greatness an eloquent token is furnished in his discovery of the voltaic pile. In this discovery nothing is to be assigned to chance, it was wholly the outcome of piercing, logical, and patient reflection. When, after years of study, Volta stepped into his laboratory one day and built up his pile out of pieces of silver, zinc and moistened cloth no other physicist save himself could have foretold what would result. But Volta was sure of his ground, and this knowledge he owed to a supreme intellect and patient inquiry. Starting from Galvini's more or less accidental discovery of the twitching of a frog's muscle he had been the only scientist to furnish a valid explanation of the phenomenon. From this he had moved on step by step, conquering one difficulty after another, till at least "the most wonderful instrument of man's device" stood out before his mental vision. This same piercing vision was directed, as his Confession tells us, to a scrutiny of the reasons for and against Christianity, and his conclusion was that from precisely such an examination the strongest arguments for Christianity are to be derived. The lesson from Volta's life is that there is no mind so rich and lofty but can find perfect content within the Christian dispensation.

Of the great Ampère, who, taking up Volta's work in electricity, developed it in many directions, the same is to be recorded. André Marie Ampère[1] was, according to the judgment of all who knew him and as his discoveries show, a man remarkable alike for acuteness and width of mind, a many-sided genius. His point of departure in science was Oerstedt's accidental discovery of the influence of a galvanic current on a magnetised needle. This at once suggested to Ampère a truth of much larger scope, namely, that magnetism could be transformed into electricity, and that electric currents in general exercised an influence on one another. He devised apparatus for the investigation of this hypothesis, and in a short time had established its truth, and formulated the laws according to which currents attract and repel one another, and cause deflections of magnetic needles. These discoveries have proved inexhaustible in their consequences, and mark the first step towards a true understanding of earth-magnetism and of magnetism in general. While the general course of scientific discovery is the establishment of the facts by one investigator, a general explanation of them by a second, and an exact formulation of the laws governing them by a third, in the case of electro-dynamics the three

[1] For Ampère cf. our article in the Stimmen aus Maria-Laach LXI (1901) 20—36 151—165. Cf. also two letters of Ampère's in the Comptes rendus of the Academy of Science 92, Paris 1881, 398 954.

stages were performed by the single mind of Ampère. "A man who possessed all the characteristics of scientific genius, spacious vision, acuteness, and infallible accuracy in deduction", is the estimate of Ampère given by Clausius[1], surely a competent judge. And Bertrand says: "Ampère's essay is one of the most wonderful productions of modern science, and forms the foundation of the vastest and most perfect construction erected by natural philosophy since the time of Newton."[2]

Science owes to Ampère other discoveries in addition to those which have made his name immortal. He opened his career with mathematical works of great brilliancy, and it was, indeed, through these that he obtained his position in Paris and Membership of the Academy of Sciences. In Chemistry he had independently re-established the important law discovered by Avogadro[3] in 1811 but since then completely forgotten: and in the controversy on the nature of chlorine he was a vigorous upholder of the true view at a time when the greatest specialists in Chemistry confessed themselves puzzled[4]. In Zoology and Botany he was also thoroughly grounded. But it was philosophy proper that interested him most, and his last work was an essay in the classification of the sciences.

Ampère's religious experience included an early period of indifference, and after his return to Christianity a

---

[1] Über den Zusammenhang zwischen den großen Agentien der Natur, Bonn 1885, 18.

[2] Éloges académiques, Paris 1890, 56.

[3] H. Kopp, Die Entwicklung der Chemie in der neueren Zeit, Munchen 1873, 354—357.

[4] Ib. 473. A.-M. Ampère et J.-J. Ampère, Correspondance et Souvenirs I, Paris 1875, 87.

period of great doubt and distress. These were however merely stages in his development. At the time of his great discoveries he was once more a zealous and convinced Christian, and in this faith he remained to the end. Ozanam, who lived for some time in Ampère's household expresses himself unmistakably on this point.

"But over and above his scientific achievements there is something more to be said: for us Catholics, this rare genius has other titles to our veneration and love. He was a brother in the Faith. . . . Religion presided over the labours of his mind, shed its light over every field of his thought: and it was from this sublime point of view that he judged all things, even science itself. . . . This venerable head, with all its wisdom and glory, bowed unreservedly before the mysteries of the Divine Teaching. He knelt at the same altar as Descartes and Pascal, side by side with poor women and children, humbler in soul than the least of them. No one could have observed more scrupulously the austere, and yet sweet discipline of the Church. . . . But most beautiful of all was the operation of Christianity in the interior of his noble soul: that admirable simplicity, the modesty of a genius which, knowing everything, was content to be ignorant of its own greatness: that high scientific probity, eager not after glory, but after truth alone, nowadays so rare: that affable and communicative temper, pouring out in familiar conversation treasures beyond count, so communicative indeed that its ideas lay at the mercy of the plagiarist; finally that benevolence towards all he met but especially the young. . . . We know more than one, towards whom he showed the care and affection of a father. I say emphatically that those who knew only his intellect knew the less perfect part of him. For if he thought deeply, he loved more deeply still."[1]

Ampère's discussions with Ozanam hardly ever concluded without some mention of the name of God.

---

[1] Oeuvres complètes de A.-F. Ozanam VIII[4], Paris 1872, 89.

"Then Ampère took his broad brow between his hands and cried out: 'How great God is, Ozanam, how great God is! All our knowledge is absolutely nothing.'"[1]

We add to Ozanam's testimony that of Sainte-Beuve, a witness certainly not open to the charge of prejudice:

"The religious doubts and struggles of his early life had ceased: or at least his trouble of mind was no longer so acute. For years many things had been leading him back to the faith and submission of mind which he had so well expressed in 1803, in an affecting document which no doubt he had often re-read in the interval. Interior sorrows, his instinct for the infinite, active correspondence with his old friend Father Barret[2], the very atmosphere of the Restoration, all drew him back. Throughout all the years that followed down to the very end, we saw him effecting without effort and in a fashion to arouse admiration and respect, a reconciliation and alliance of faith and science, of belief and hope in human thought and adoration before the Revealed Word."[3]

In Ampère's own writings we find many passages in which he speaks of Nature as leading up to God:

"We can see only the works of the Creator but through them we rise to a knowledge of the Creator Himself. Just as the real movements of the stars are hidden by their apparent movements, and yet it is by observation of the

---

[1] Oeuvres complètes de A.-F. Ozanam X 37.

[2] Klemens Barret, one of Ampère's friends in Lyons, entered the Society of Jesus in 1814, died 1848.

[3] Les anciens doutes et les combats religieux avaient cessé. . . . Jusqu'à la fin, et pendant les années qui suivirent, nous l'avons toujours vu allier et concilier sans plus d'effort et de manière à frapper d'étonnement et de respect, la foi et la science, la croyance et l'espoir en la pensée humaine et l'adoration envers la parole révélée (Sainte-Beuve in his Introduction to Ampère's Essai sur la philosophie des sciences II, Paris 1843, L).

one that we determine the other: so God is in some sort hidden by His works, and yet it is through them that we discern Him and catch a hint of the Divine attributes."

One of the most striking evidences of the existence of God is the wonderful harmony by which the universe is preserved and living beings are furnished in their organization with everything necessary to life, multiplication, and the enjoyment of all their powers, physical and intellectual." [1]

The third of the great founders of the Theory of Electricity was Michael Faraday[2]. His pre-eminence in the science is certified by every authority. "Taking him for all in all", says Tyndall, "I think it will be conceded that Michael Faraday was the greatest experimental philosopher the world has ever seen." Du Bois-Reymond echoes these words almost literally. He describes Faraday as "the greatest experimental philosopher of all time". J. B. Dumas the famous chemist, in his memorial speech to the French Academy of Science on May 18th 1868 characterised Faraday as "the greatest scientist the Academy had ever counted among its members"[3].

---

[1] Essai sur la philosophie des sciences II, Paris 1843, 24 f

[2] Bence Jones, The Life and Letters of Faraday[2], 2 vols, London 1870. John Tyndall, Faraday as a Discoverer, London 1868; Fragments of Science[5], London 1876, 246—267. J.-B Dumas, Discours et Éloges Académiques I, Paris 1885, 51—124. Silvanus P. Thompson, Michael Faradays Leben und Wirken. Autorisierte Übersetzung von Agathe Schütte und Dr Heinrich Danneel, Halle a. S 1900.

[3] Tyndall, Faraday as a Discoverer 147. E. Du Bois-Reymond, Reden, Zweite Folge, Leipzig 1887, 389 502. Dumas, Discours I 53. Cf. v. Martius in the Sitzungsberichten der Munchener Akademie 1868, I 440: "Man hat Faraday den größten Experimentator seiner Epoche genannt, und wohl mit Recht."

These estimates were more than justified, for at his death (Aug. 25th 1867), Faraday could look back on a long series of discoveries any one of which was almost enough to immortalize his name. It is impossible here to give so much as a summary of them. To give an idea of his work in Electricity it would, as Dumas says, "be necessary to write a complete manual on the subject". "There is nothing in this department of science that Faraday did not investigate, complete, or recast: there is a great deal of which he is the sole and absolute creator." Tyndall arranges these discoveries in four groups, the first of which relates to induction and outer currents, the second to the chemical action of electricity and the theory of the voltaic pile, the third to the influence of the magnet on light-rays, and the fourth to the phenomena of diamagnetism[1].

Faraday as a worker in science was equally distinguished by supreme ability and steady perseverance. Born at Newington Butts on Sept. 22th 1791 of a poor family of Irish origin, he was at the age of thirteen put to work with a bookseller who employed him to deliver newspapers, and taught him bookbinding. But he had no taste for this occupation: wide and eager reading among the books which came to him for binding aroused in him a passion for science, and when in 1812 business of his masters gave him an opportunity of hearing (from the gallery) some lectures of the celebrated Sir Humphry Davy his mind was definitely determined. In his simplicity and inexperience he wrote straightway to the President of the Royal Institute of Sciences at London explaining his wish to be a scientist. Naturally enough

[1] Dumas, Discours I 75. Tyndall, Faraday as a Discoverer 145.

he received no reply. He had, however, better success with Davy to whom he submitted notes of the lectures he had heard. He wished, he told Davy, to get out of business because it is "a source of vice and self-seeking" and to devote himself to the service of science because "it makes men large-hearted and sympathetic". The great scientist could not but laugh a little at the naiveté of the young book-binder, but he perceived his rare intellectual power, and took him under his protection. In March 1813 he procured him the position of Laboratory Assistant in the Royal Institute, and in October of the same year took Faraday with him on a long journey through France and Italy. After his return in the April of 1815 Faraday continued his studies in Physics and Chemistry, and won his way step by step to the topmost heights of honour and fame.

Faraday was a thorough and convinced Christian. Like his father he belonged to the Glassites or Sandemanians, a sect which, opposed alike to Anglicans and Presbyterians, held that Christianity consists simply in belief in the Divinity of Christ, that this belief is a gift from God, and that it has for fruit and token obedience to the law of Christ. A month after his marriage in the year 1821 Faraday formally professed adherence to this sect, appearing before the congregation and making confession both of his sins and of his belief. In 1840 he attained the dignity of Elder, and in this capacity preached a series of sermons, rough notes of which are still extant [1].

Faraday did not, as far as is known, engage in any philosophic or apologetic studies on the foundations of

[1] Jones, The Life and Letters of Faraday I 5 297; II 99 ff.

Christianity. Neither did he seek to gain over converts to his particular belief; indeed, it was only in reply to questions on the subject that he spoke of religion in ordinary conversation.

"There is no philosophy", he wrote on October 24th 1844, "in my religion. I am of a very small and despised sect of Christians known as, if at all known, Sandemanians, and our hope is founded on the faith that is in Christ. . . . But though the natural works of God can never by any possibility come in contradiction with the higher things that belong to our future existence, and must with everything concerning Him ever glorify Him, still I do not think it at all necessary to tie the study of the natural sciences and religion together, and in my intercourse with my fellows creatures, that which is religious, and that which is philosophical have ever been two distinct things." [1]

What makes these expressions invaluable in the present connection is not the positive evidence they give of the great scientist's attachment to Christianity. That we must seek in other passages of his writings. The point to be observed in the present passage is Faraday's unambiguous statement that he never was able to perceive any opposition between science and religion. We find many other passages to the same effect in his works; occasionally he pushes his thought further and speaks of nature as necessarily leading up to God. A few of these passages may be quoted here.

In a lecture on Magnetism, delivered before Prince Albert on February 26th 1849, he concludes with a rapid sketch of the wonderful diffusion of magnetic energy throughout the universe [2]:

---

[1] Jones, The Life and Letters of Faraday II 191.

[2] Ib. 239.

"What its great purpose is, seems to be looming in the distance before us; the clouds which obscure our mental sight are daily thinning, and I cannot doubt that a glorious discovery in natural knowledge, and of the wisdom and power of God in the creation, is awaiting our age, and that we may not only hope to see it, but even be honoured to help in obtaining the victory over present ignorance and future knowledge."

In the year 1847 he concluded a series of lectures at the Royal Institution in the following words:

"Our philosophy, feeble as it is, gives us to see in every particle of matter, a centre of force reaching to an infinite distance, binding worlds and suns together, and unchangeable in its permanency. Around this same particle we see grouped the powers of all the various phenomena of nature; the heat, the cold, the wind, the storm, the awful conflagration, the vivid lightning flash, the stability of the rock and the mountain, the grand mobility of the ocean, with its mighty tidal wave sweeping round the globe in its diurnal journey, the dancing of the stream and the torrent, the glorious cloud, the soft dew, the rain dropping fatness, the harmonious working of all these forces in nature, until at last the molecule rises up in accordance with the almighty purpose ordained for it, and plays its part in the gift of life itself. And therefore our philosophy, whilst it shows us these things should lead us to think of Him Who hath wrought them; for it is said by an authority far above even that which these works present, that 'the invisible things of Him from the creation of the world are clearly seen, being understood by the things that are made, even his eternal power and God-head'."[1]

Seven years later he repeats the same views in his lecture on "Mental Education":

"High as man is placed above the creatures around him, there is a higher and far more exalted position within his

---

[1] Ib. 224—225.

view; and the ways are infinite in which he occupies his thoughts about the fears, or hopes, or expectations of a future life. I believe that the truth of that future cannot be brought to his knowledge by any exertion of his mental powers, however exalted they may be, that it is made known to him by other teaching than his own, and is received through simple belief of the testimony given. Let no one suppose for a moment that the self-education I am about to commend in respect of the things of this life, extends to any consideration of the hope set before us, as if man by reasoning could find out God. It would be improper here to enter upon the subject further than to claim an absolute distinction between religious and ordinary belief. I shall be reproached with the weakness of refusing to apply those mental operations which I think good in respect of high things to the very highest. I am content to bear the reproach; yet, even in earthly matters, I believe that the invisible things of Him from the creation of the world are clearly seen, being understood by the things that are made, even His eternal power and Godhead; and I have never seen anything incompatible between those things of man which are within him, and those higher things concerning his future, which he cannot know by that spirit." [1]

In his private notes also, as for example in his diaries of travel, religious reflections come spontaneously to his pen. During his Swiss tour of 1841 he finds in a country churchyard a grave of extreme poverty: marked only by a wooden cross, furnished with a sort of roof, and under this, written on a plain sheet of paper the date of birth and death. The survivors were too poor to erect any more elaborate memorial, but Faraday thinks it compensation that beneath the roof there hangs the empty chrysalis of a now matured butterfly. He writes: "How old and how beautiful is this figure of the Re-

[1] Jones, The Life and Letters of Faraday I 298.

surrection! Surely it can never appear before our eyes without touching the heart."[1]

At Coblentz he reads the celebrated inscription set up by the general of the French on his march to Russia, and the note added by the general of the Russians when passing through the town in pursuit of the defeated French. "A striking illustration of the saying that all is vanity and vexation of spirit", remarks Faraday in his diary[2]. The more he came to know of nature, the more fully did he recognise the power of God. "To all the objections of Colenso or to any scepticism as to the Mosaic theory of the origin of the world", writes his nephew Francis Bernard to Dr. Gladstone, "he would have simply answered in the words of the Apostle: 'Is anything too difficult for God?'"[3]

In spite of these declarations we find to our amazement that Faraday also was in his day represented as an enemy of Christianity. It was during the heat of the Darwin discussions that a letter dated July 6th 1860 apprised the unsuspecting Faraday of the fact, and begged for an explanation. In an attack on the Biblical story of the creation of man, some popular lecturer or other had alleged that in discourses at Oxford, Cambridge, and London, Faraday had declared life to be mere electricity, had produced worms and other little animals manufactured by electricity, and had expressly stated that man had come into existence in the same way. In fact the whole drift of his discourses was said to have been so unorthodox that he was compelled to bring then to an abrupt conclusion. In reply Faraday was of course able to say that there was not a single word of truth in the allegation.

He had never lectured at Cambridge, he had never been compelled to cut short any course of lectures elsewhere, and

---

[1] Ib. II 133. [2] Ib. II 128.

[3] Thompson, M. Faraday's Leben und Wirken 223.

if he had provoked opposition it was "because I was supposed to pay too much respect to the Bible, which I believe to be the word of God" [1].

We see than, that the three great pioneers of electrical science were, all their lives, faithful to Christ, and to the Christian revelation. The fact is beyond dispute, and its significance is obviously very great.

When the half-educated man of the world glides in an electric car through the streets, under the golden glow of electric lamps; when he converses with friends hundred of miles away, and even recognises their voices; when he commits to express train or steamer a message for America or Australia, how often pride in these marvellous inventions brings to his lips a curl of contempt for the old woman telling her Rosary beside him, or for those others who are gabbling of religion and churches! How apt he is to dismiss the past with all its beliefs and achievements, Christianity included, as obsolete and exploded! And yet his contempt is itself contemptible, and is merely a token of ignorance and shallowness. The intellects that laid the foundation of all these marvels, bowed in acceptance before the truths of Christianity; the skilful hands that were the first to unveil on the laboratory-table the secret laws of electricity did not scorn to be folded in prayer, and Volta and Ampère told their Rosary beads as humbly as any poor woman. Let unbelief seek what capital it can find in other fields of science; in the field of electricity, which, more than any other, attracts and dazzles the masses, it will certainly find no authoritative name to serve as a weapon against Christianity. There is a further point that should be

---

[1] Jones, The Life and Letters of Faraday II 436 f.

emphasized. Ampère and Volta made special study of the grounds of Christian belief. Both were men of supreme intellect, thoroughly acquainted with all that has been said on each side of the controversy between faith and scepticism; and inquiry led both to complete acceptance of the Christian dispensation. If then authority is to decide the question, must not one man of the stamp of Volta or Ampère outweigh a thousand who may indeed know their Physics or Chemistry but as regards higher questions are obliged to confess with Darwin that they had never found time to investigate them? And must not such a man outweigh ten thousand of the type of Haeckel, who give themselves out with the loudest assurance as the champions of science, and when they come to discuss points of Christian history and belief display an ignorance that absolutely stupefies one into silence?

Volta, Ampère, Faraday stand at the head of the science of electricity, but there are also other great discoverers of whom we must take account. We have already mentioned Coulomb and Ohm. There is also Galvani, a precursor of Volta, and Oersted, a precursor of Ampère. Maxwell in England, and Hertz in Germany led the way in the interpretation of electrical phenomena, and the establishment of a theory of its inner nature[1].

A brief study of these six will only serve to confirm the results already arrived at. L. Galvani († 1798) was a deeply religious man, and indeed a Member of

[1] If we go back to earlier times we must before all name B. Franklin. He openly acknowledged the existence and the providence of God; his position as regards Christianity is not clear. Cf. Correspondance de B. Franklin (1757—1790), trad. de l'anglais et annotée par E. Laboulaye, 2 vols, Paris 1866.

the Third Order of St. Francis[1]. Coulomb was noted for his firm and upright character, and the fact that at the outbreak of the Revolution he resigned his offices shows that his civil and domestic virtues rested on a basis other than that of "Liberalism"[2].

An amiable and friendly nature was that of George Simon Ohm († at Munich July 6th 1854), discoverer of the law called by his name.

"Nature", said Lamont[3], "had given him in liberal measure good nature and modesty, and these rare qualities appeared in all his intercourse with the world. In matters of merely personal concern he yielded to the tide of fortune readily and without bitterness. The mishap which at the outset of his career deprived him of an advantageous post did not leave in him a trace of misanthropy, and when his abilities at last received due and brilliant recognition, success in no way altered his simplicity of character and bearing."

That Ohm had as little sympathy with the campaign of destruction as the others cited here is shown by many passing remarks in the introductions and notes to his works. In the preface of the first volume of his Molecular Physics he promises a second and third volume and "if God gives me length of days for it, a fourth". On finding after the publication of his book that a discovery recorded in it as original had been

---

[1] Stimmen aus Maria-Laach LIX (1900) 18.

[2] J.-B. Biot in his Mélanges scientifiques et littéraires III, Paris 1858, 104, compares Coulomb with Clouet, a disciple of Rousseau's, and is of opinion that a greater contrast than that between these two is inconceivable. "Coulomb", he continues, "a vécu avec patience parmi les hommes de son temps, ne se séparant que de leurs passions et de leurs erreurs, se maintenant toujours juste, calme, ferme, et digne, in se totus, teres atque rotundus, comme le sage Horace."

[3] Denkrede auf die Akademiker Dr. Thaddäus Siber und Dr. Georg Simon Ohm, München 1855, 35.

anticipated by a Swedish scientist he consoles himself with the remark: "The episode has given a fresh and deep sense for my mind to the saying 'Man proposes, and God disposes'. The project that gave the first impetus to my inquiry has been dissipated into mist, and a new one, undesigned by me, has been accomplished in its place."[1]

The campaign against Christianity will derive no more support from Hans Christian Oersted[2] († 1851) than from Ohm. At the millenial celebration of the introduction of Christianity into Denmark, Oersted chose as the subject of his address the influence of Christianity on Science.

"I shall be permitted", run his opening words[3], "as speaking in the name of our University to present to your attention the favourable influence exercised by Christianity on science and on intellectual development generally, and the advantage that it has itself derived from that development. This mutually helpful relation has been misrepresented, now by the enemies of religion, now by those of enlightenment; but convinced as I am that the kingdom of truth can never be divided against itself, I believe that it is our highest duty to demonstrate again and again its absolute concord, so that honest but unfortified friends of the truth may not be seduced from the true path by the clamour and confusion of merely partisan polemics."[4]

"No religion", he says further, "can in this respect compare with ours"; for most other religions "have shown them-

---

[1] Lamont ante 23 26.

[2] Cf. C. Hauch und G. Forchhammer, H. C. Ørsteds Leben. Zwei Denkschriften. Aus dem Dänischen von Dr. H. Sebald. Spandau 1853.

[3] Hans Christian Örsted, Der Geist in der Natur. Deutsch von Prof. Dr. K. L. Kannegießer, II, Leipzig 1854, 142.

[4] Ib. 143.

selves on the whole inimical to the intellectual progress of humanity. Ours, on the contrary, has always been intimately associated with that progress."

"In most instances the struggle which was supposed to have been one between Christianity and enlightenment was really one between merely human opinions which were mistaken for Christianity, on the one side, and shallow licence, which was mistaken for enlightenment, on the other."[1]

Oersted loves to speak of nature as a way leading up to God. He maintains that "every fundamental investigation into nature must issue in a recognition of the existence of God"[2]; and he planned a special work to be devoted to the development of this thesis. "All reality", he says, "is a product of the incessant activity of God and bears in every part the stamp of infinite and immutable reason." For us this continuous operation of Divine Reason and its perpetual accord with itself are manifested as 'Laws of Nature'. From the contemplation of the stars we learn that "man is nothing as against God, but that through God he becomes something". In a note made originally for his private use we read:

"Make your conception as living as possible! The better you succeed in this, the more joy will you feel in communion with Him. Your soul will acclaim Him as the source of all good; you will be able to say 'I love God', in so far, at least, as the name of earthly passion can be applied to so sublime a motion of the spirit."[3]

While these citations show what a gulf there is between Oersted and the enemies of religion, it must be admitted that in his positive exposition of the nature of God and of Christianity he was far from happy. His differences with the Danish theologians of his day are indeed easy to under-

---

[1] Orsted, Der Geist in der Natur 148. [2] Ib. II 227.
[3] Ib. 173 175 280.

stand. They maintained that inanimate nature had been altered by the Fall — a contention refuted six hundred years before by St. Thomas Aquinas — and Oersted can hardly be blamed for opposing such a view. And since it was still necessary in the Denmark of 1837 to defend the Copernican system against objections drawn from the Bible we should feel grateful to Oersted for undertaking the defence.[1] But his teaching as to the nature of God is practically Pantheism, and he does not sufficiently recognise the supernatural character of Christianity.

Many theories have been advanced to account for the phenomena of electricity, but to-day only those are entertained which move in the paths opened in 1855 by James Clerk Maxwell[2]. (Born June 13th 1831, died November 5th 1879 at Cambridge, where from 1871 he had been Professor of Experimental Physics.) Maxwell was in religious questions a life-long ally of Faraday[3]. He was a professed and practical Christian. He read the evening prayers in his family every evening[4]; "he was a constant regular attendant at church, and seldom, if ever, failed to join in our monthly celebration of Holy Communion, and he was a generous contributor to all our parish charitable institutions. But his illness drew out the whole heart and soul and spirit of the man: his firm and undoubting faith in the Incarnation and all its results; in the full sufficing of the

---

[1] Ib. 151.

[2] L. Dressel, Elementares Lehrbuch der Physik II, Freiburg 1900, 757.

[3] The Life of James Clerk Maxwell. With a selection from his correspondence and occasional writings and a sketch of his contributions to science. By Lewis Campbell and William Garnett. London 1882.

[4] Ib. 507.

Atonement; in the work of the Holy Spirit"[1]. On his death-bed he frequently repeated the lines of Richard Baxter:

> Lord, it belongs not to my care
> Whether I die or live;
> To love and serve Thee is my share,
> And that Thy grace must give[2].

"Mr. Colin Mackenzie repeated to me two sayings of his during those last days which may be repeated here: 'Old chap! I have read up many queer religions: there is nothing like the old thing after all', and 'I have looked into most philosophical systems, and I have seen that none will work without a God'."[3] These sayings carry all the more weight inasmuch as Maxwell, like Volta and Ampère, was widely read in Philosophy and even in Theology. On Sundays after his return from church, he "buried himself"[4] in the study of the old English theologians. He did not, however, take sides in the controversy between Anglicans and Calvinists.

In his discussions on the atomic theory Maxwell never fails to raise the question of the origin of the atoms. On at least three occasions he develops his own views in detail, and he regards it as an established conclusion of pure science that the atoms do not present or possess in themselves the ground of their existence.

The first place in which we find an expression of this view is towards the end of his book on Heat. Maxwell there gives a bird's-eye view of the molecular theory in its application to Physics generally. According to this theory every body is made up of a determinate number

---

[1] The Life of J. C. Maxwell, by Campbell and Garnett 416.
[2] Ib. 409. [3] Ib. 426. [4] Ib. 321; cf. 415.

of minute particles, each possessing a definite mass and definite properties. The molecules of the same substance are all alike, but they differ from those of any other substance. Moreover there is no gradual passage from the molecules of one element to those of another. Every molecule belongs to a definite class; and there are no intermediate connecting links between the various classes. Single atoms are immutable and indestructible.

We have here the main lines of the atomic theory as it had been accepted by the physicists. Maxwell raises many further questions. How does it come that only atoms of absolutely fixed properties exist, and that there are no connecting-links between two classes? This cannot be the outcome of a process of development since they are insusceptible of change. Neither can we postulate, to explain it, a process of elimination, by which atoms intermediate between the existent classes would have been expelled. For if that were the case, whither have these eliminated atoms been driven? The fixed stars are composed of just the same elements as earth and sun. There remains for Maxwell only the hypothesis that the atoms were created by God, and that He in the beginning created them alike. This theory solves all difficulties.

"But", he writes, "if we suppose the molecules to be made at all, or if we suppose them to consist of something previously made, why should we expect any irregularity to exist among them? If they are, as we believe, the only material things which still remain in the precise condition, in which they first began to exist, why should we not rather look for some indication of that spirit of order, our scientific confidence in which is never shaken by the difficulty which we experience in tracing it in the complex arrangements of visible things, and of which our moral estimation is shown in all our attempts to think and speak the truth, and to ascertain the exact principles of distributive justice?"[1]

This line of reasoning is to be found more fully developed in a paper "On Molecules" read by Maxwell at the meeting of the British Association at Bradford[2].

The complete similarity of the atoms is according to him assured by spectrum analysis. Analysis of the light which comes to us from Sirius and Arcturus shows that hydrogen atoms in these distant bodies transmit the same rays and consequently possess the same properties as hydrogen atoms in our laboratories. This similarity and unity cannot be the outcome of a process of development. "None of the processes of nature, since the time when nature began, have produced the slightest difference in the properties of any molecule. We are, therefore, unable to ascribe either the existence of the molecules or the identity of their properties to the operation of any of the causes which we call natural."

On the other hand the similarity of constitution in molecules of the same class gives them the character of "manufactured articles"[3], and precludes the hypothesis that they

[1] J. Clerk Maxwell, Theory of Heat[3], London 1872, 312.

[2] Printed in Nature VIII, May 1873 to October 1873, London and New York 1873, 437—441. Cf. the article Atom in the Encyclopaedia Britannica III[9], Edinburgh 1875, 36—48.

[3] For this comparison (which had been used by Herschel in his Preliminary Discourse on the Study of Natural Philosophy, London 1851, 38) Maxwell was attacked in Nature (X, 15. October 1874, 481). The conclusion of his article Atoms in the Encyclopaedia Britannica is, as Maxwell himself says in a letter (Campbell and Garnett, The life of J. C. Maxwell 393), expressly intended as an answer to this criticism. In this document he writes: "What I thought of was not so much that uniformity of result which is due to uniformity in the process of formation, as a uniformity intended and accomplished by the same wisdom and power of which uniformity, accuracy, symmetry, consistency, and continuity of plan are as important attributes as the contrivance of the special utility of each individual thing."

are eternal and self-existent. "We are thus led back along a strictly scientific path very near to the point at which science must stop.

But in tracing back the history of matter science is arrested when she assures herself, on the one hand, that the molecule has been made, and on the other, that it has not been made by any of the processes which we call natural."

In further explanation of his theory, Maxwell remarks that an atom in its concrete form cannot be described as necessary.

"That matter as such should have certain fundamental properties — that it should exist in space and be capable of motion, that its motion should be persistent, and so on, are truths which may, for anything we know, be of the kind which metaphysicians call necessary. We may use our knowledge of such truths for purposes of deduction, but we have no data for speculating as to their origin.

But that there should be so much matter and not more in every molecule of hydrogen is a fact of a very different order. We have here a particular distribution of matter which we have no difficulty in imagining to have been arranged otherwise."

At the conclusion of his address Maxwell speaks of the immutability of atoms, a quality which makes them "the true foundation stones of the material universe". The solar system is constantly changing, but, though everything else alters, the atoms remain the same as ever.

"They continue this day as they were created, perfect in number and measure and weight, and from the ineffaceable characters impressed on them we may learn that those aspirations after accuracy, measurement, truth in statement, and justice in action, which we reckon among our noblest attributes as men, are ours because they are essential constituents of the image of Him who in the beginning created, not only the heaven and earth, but the materials of which heaven and earth consist."

On other philosophico-religious questions also Maxwell expresses himself with equal clearness. Thus he writes on "Natural Science and the Immortality of the Soul"[1]:

"The progress of science, therefore, as far as we have been able to follow it, has added nothing of importance to what has already been known about the physical consequences of death, but has rather tended to deepen the distinction between the visible part, which perishes before our eyes, and that which we are ourselves, and to show that this personality, with respect to its nature as well as to its destiny, lies quite beyond the range of science."

Maxwell belonged to a philosophical club which included among its members Lightfoot, Hort, Westcott and others, and he read before it on February 11th 1873 a paper dealing with the question whether the progress of natural science has been unfavourable to the doctrine of free-will[2]. His answer is in the negative. We may fitly conclude our study of Clerk Maxwell with a fragment found among his papers after his death. It is the true prayer of the man of science[3]:

"Almighty God, who hast created man in Thine own image, and made him a living soul that he might seek after Thee, and have dominion over Thy creatures, teach us to study the work of Thy hands that we may subdue the earth to our use, and strengthen our reason for Thy service; and so to receive Thy blessed Word, that we may believe in Him whom Thou hast sent to give us the knowledge of salvation and the remission of our sins. All which we ask in the name of the same Jesus Christ our Lord."

All who knew Maxwell intimately describe him as one of the noblest men it had ever been their fortune

---

[1] Nature XIX, London, 19th December 1878, 142.

[2] Reprinted in The Life of J. C. Maxwell, by Campbell and Garnett 434—444.

[3] Ib. 323.

to meet. His doctor, and those who nursed him in his last illness tell us that no suffering could alter or embitter the sweetness of his character[1].

J.-B. Dumas in one of his brilliant discourses before the Academy adds to the names we have mentioned still another. "Ampère, Faraday, Auguste De la Rive", he says, "made electricity the study of their lives, and enriched the science with great discoveries; they were all three deeply religious."[2]

The authority of a man like Dumas is not to be ignored, and his praise of De la Rive is in no way exaggerated. Both as a discoverer and as a student of contemporary science, the latter was a man of the highest distinction. In questions of religion he was of one mind with his friend Faraday, as is shown by the correspondence which passed between them.

"He believed", said Dumas, "that human personality has its seat elsewhere than in the dust of which our bodies are composed. Is it to be supposed that matter, which obeys, is imperishable, while spirit, which commands, is perishable? 'I prefer to believe', said De la Rive, that the reasoning soul is immortal and that unreasoning matter is doomed to destruction.' He regarded the universe as having come into existence through an act of creation. For he was able to demonstrate, as a truth of the purely scientific order and by arguments which were more fully developed by Clausius, that the world did not always exist and that it cannot for ever continue in existence."[3]

"A devoted adherent of the Protestant Church of Geneva he none the less profoundly venerated the Catholic Church, in which he had many friends and relatives, and to which belonged the majority of the population of Présinge, his place of residence. Universally respected by his Catholic

[1] Ib. 412. [2] Discours I 277.

[3] Dumas, Discours I 277.

neighbours he sympathised with all their undertakings, moral and religious, and even contributed on occasion to the repair of their Church. The spirit of religious tolerance was so native to the mind of our colleague that he made it a law to himself to avoid everything that could give the slightest offence to the convictions of others. But there are times when to be silent is to be false to one's faith, and De la Rive was unwilling that it should be supposed that those who preached materialism in the name of science enjoyed the sanction and support of all men of science. 'That is not true', he said, 'and it is our duty to proclaim its untruth.'"[1]

If De la Rive was inclined to believe in the final complete destruction of unreasoning matter, the theologian will observe that the teaching of Christianity does not include any such destruction. The 'destruction' foretold in the Apocalypse is limited to a breaking-up of the present form of the universe; it does not go so far as complete annihilation. St. Thomas Aquinas expressly proposes it as a question whether any created thing will be annihilated and replies in the negative[2]. His reasons for ascribing even to the material world, or at all events to its fundamental constituents, eternal duration are derived from a consideration of the nature of God and of the matter which He has created. The whole form and fashion, in which the latter exists, implies a destiny other than that of annihilation. We thus find "mediæval" theology more modern in this point than the modern savant De la Rive[3].

---

[1] "Cela n'est pas, disait-il avec fermeté, et notre devoir est de le proclamer" (ib. 299).

[2] Unde dicendum est, quod nihil omnino in nihilum redigetur (S. Thom. 1, q. 104, a. 4).

[3] From the theological point of view, explanations and qualifications like those which we have appended to De la Rive's words, might be added to many of the passages quoted from the scientists. However when the passages cited were on the whole correct, we have refrained from remarks, which might perhaps earn for us the reputation of fault finding. Meanwhile we must defend ourselves from the supposition

We have dealt with those pioneers of electrical science who have given their names to the standard electrical units; we may add two others: Von Siemens and W. Weber.

The resistance of substances is at present calculated in ohms. Before the adoption of this unit, that associated with the name of Von Siemens was widely employed; but Wilhelm Weber's services in the measurement of electricity gave him at least an equal claim to be so honoured. To these two scientists we shall devote just a few words.

Werner Von Siemens († 1892) was scientific adviser to the famous firm of Siemens and Halske, and in his day stood at the head of electro-technicians. This position he owed to the fact that he possessed not merely a technical but also a profound scientific knowledge of his subject: and when the perfecting of electrical apparatus necessitated the solution of problems hitherto unfaced, he was equal to the task. Siemens in 1867 formulated the principle of the dynamo, made valuable contributions to the theory of the submarine cable, and, especially after 1874 (when he became a member of the Berlin Academy of Science) published a long series of works on theoretical physics[1].

---

that we are in entire agreement with every word and thought which we shall quote.

[1] Hovestadt in Natur und Offenbarung XXXIX, Munster 1893, 167—171. A brother of Werner v. Siemens, William Siemens († 1883), settled down in England and distinguished himself by his achievements in science as well as in technology (W. Pole and E. F. Bamber, Life and scientific works of the late Sir W. Siemens. London 1891, 4 vols). He concluded his opening address to the British Association 1882 as follows: "We shall thus find that in

The "Naturanschauung' to which he was led by deep and laborious study finds expression in his Address to the Association of Physicists in 1886: "The deeper we penetrate into the harmonious and immutable order of nature, and unveil her hidden forces, the more modestly do we come to think of the little compass of our knowledge, and the more intense is our admiration of the supreme ordering Wisdom which pervades the whole created world." [1]

Wilhelm Weber († 1891), one of the celebrated Seven of Göttingen, who in 1837 surrendered their posts rather than swear allegiance to the new government, stands in the first rank of German physicists. He worked at the theory of wave-motion, and acoustics, but above all at electricity. His celebrated electro-dynamic law is indeed no longer accepted, but even his critics admit that Weber's conception bears the stamp of genius, and it held the allegiance of scientists for a long time [2]. Weber is also remembered for his contributions to the measurement of electricity, and he was, with Gauss, the first to apply (in 1833) the galvanic current to telegraphy.

Reinke includes Weber in his list of great scientists who were also believers [3]. A somewhat longer biography [4] which we have seen, although entering as little as possible

---

the great workshop of Nature, there are no lines of demarcation to be drawn between the most exalted speculation and commonplace practice, and that all knowledge must lead up to one great result, that of an intelligent recognition of the Creator through his works" (Report of the 52nd meeting of the British Association for the Advancement of Science, held at Southampton in August 1882 [London 1883]. President's Address p. 33)

[1] Ib. 170.

[2] H. Hertz, Über die Beziehungen zwischen Licht und Elektrizität, Bonn 1889, 7.

[3] J. Reinke, Die Welt als Tat, Berlin 1903, 468.

[4] Leopoldina XXVIII, Halle 1892, 147 169 178 185 201.

into religious questions testifies that he "preserved all his life the heart and faith of a child"[1]. We find in it the following account of his death: "At midday he fell asleep, seated in an arm-chair. As the sun was sinking in the West he awoke again, and his eyes, bright and eager, strained out into the distance; their gaze was no longer fixed on the things of earth but uplifted to that sublimer reality for which his heart had so long hungered."[2] We have in this passage, despite the somewhat rhetorical style, clear evidence of Weber's belief in the immortality of the soul.

William Robert Grove († 1896), who also took electricity for his province, says at the close of his celebrated book "On the Correlation of Physical Forces":

"It is a great assistance in such investigations to be intimately convinced that no physical phenomenon can stand alone: each is inevitably connected with anterior changes, and is inevitably productive of consequential changes, each with the other, and all with time and space; and, either in tracing back these antecedents, or following up their consequents, many new phenomena hitherto believed distinct will be connected and explained: explanation is, indeed, only relative to something more familiar, not more known, i. e. known as to causative or creative agencies.

In all phenomena the more closely they are investigated, the more are we convinced that, humanly speaking neither matter nor force can be created, and that an essential cause is unattainable. — Causation is the will, Creation, the act, of God."[3]

---

[1] Ib. 201.

[2] Ib. 204.

[3] W. R. Grove, On the Correlation of Physical Forces: being the substance of a course of lectures delivered in the London Institution in the year 1843, London 1846, 48 50.

2. THE THEORY OF LIGHT.

To the second half of the 19th century belong the development of the theory of electricity, and the establishment of the mechanical theory of heat. The first half saw, indeed, the discovery of many fundamental laws of electricity, but it is significant in the history of science mainly for the formulation of the modern theory of light. Fresnel, Fraunhofer, Fizeau, Foucault are the names that come to everyone's lips in this connection; it is to their labours that we owe the current conception which regards light, not as a substance, but as a wave-motion in the ether.

The external life of the great Augustin Fresnel[1] is soon told. Born on May 10th 1788 at Broglie in the Department of Eure, he received his early education at home, and subsequently went to the Central School in Caen, to the Polytechnic, and to the School of Engineering in Paris. He then obtained a post as engineer in the North of France. When Napoleon returned from Elba, Fresnel considered himself bound as a good Royalist to take service in the army of the South. The outcome was that he secured leisure for scientific studies; for after the triumph of Napoleon he was deprived of his position as engineer and placed under police supervision. Fresnel now began his investigations into the nature of light; and, thanks to the kindness of his superiors, he was able to continue them after his resto-

[1] Œuvres Complètes d'Augustin Fresnel, publiées par MM. Henri de Senarmont, Émile Verdet et Léonor Fresnel, 3 vols, Paris 1866 f. Duleau, Notice sur A. Fresnel, printed in the Rev. Encyclopédique XXXIX, livr. 117, Paris, Septembre 1828, 558—567.

ration to office. The essays published by him during 1819—1827 on refraction, interference, and related subjects are few in number, but every one of them is a masterpiece. He also made many improvements in the apparatus used in lighthouses. He died young, not yet forty, on July 14th 1827, at Ville d'Avray near Paris.

The famous physicist came of a deeply religious family. Thus his mother writes in 1802 in reply to a letter from his elder brother asking news of Augustin, then at college: "I pray God to give my son the grace to employ the great talents, which he has received, for his own benefit, and for the God of all. Much will be asked from him to whom much has been given, and most will be required of him who has received most." [1] Augustin inherited this religious habit of mind. During the early years of his life as an engineer he was almost friendless, and was cast wholly on his own resources. He sought distraction in study, and with all the greater ardour inasmuch as he had never any taste for the practical life. "But the first inclination of his life was by no means to optics. Under the influence of a home education in which religion had held the first place he began to reflect on philosophical problems, and endeavoured to reach a rigorously scientific proof of certain of those doctrines to which he adhered with an ardent belief. But he never opened his mind on these questions save to members of his family or to his most intimate friends." [2]

---

[1] Œuvres Complètes I, Paris 1866, XCVIII.

[2] Sous l'influence des souvenirs d'une éducation de famille où la religion avait tenu la première place, il commença à méditer sur les questions philosophiques et s'efforça de trouver une démonstration

The editor of Fresnel's scientific works shows little inclination to dwell on the religious side of his character, but in spite of this we find many proofs that the great scientist remained all his life an adherent of the "Spiritual School"[1]. We find notes for instance of an essay in defence of the doctrine of immortality forwarded by Fresnel to a sceptical uncle of his.

Fresnel's piety of disposition remained unaltered down to the last moment of his life. His friend, the engineer Duleau, who nursed him in his last illness, tells us that the constant theme of his conversation was the greatness of God, Whose power and wisdom he saw manifested in every part of nature. He always regarded his own intellectual endowments as a gift from God, and held it a duty to employ them for the advance of knowledge and the benefit of his fellow men. The thought of his untimely death and of the works he was compelled to leave unfinished, in no way troubled his devotion; there was something higher, he said, for mankind than science and genius[2].

---

scientifique et rigoureuse de la vérité de quelques-unes des croyances qui avaient été jadis pour lui l'objet de la foi la plus ardente; mais il ne communiqua jamais ses pensées qu'aux membres de sa famille et à ses plus intimes amis (Œuvres Complètes I XXVIII).

[1] On August 5th 1811, Léonor Mérimée writes to his nephew Aug. Fresnel: "J'ai serré dans mon tiroir ta lettre philosophique, pour la reprendre quand j'aurai le loisir de débrouiller ma case de métaphysique." Here Léonor Fresnel makes the marginal note: "Il s'agit sans doute d'un essai psychologique, où A. Fresnel développe les principaux arguments sur lesquels se fonde la doctrine spiritualiste, dont il fut toujours défenseur" (Ib. II [1868] 811).

[2] "Il a vu approcher sa fin avec les sentiments religieux d'un homme qui, ayant été initié plus avant que ses semblables dans le secret des merveilles de la nature, était profondément pénétré de la puissance

Such is the testimony of Duleau, and if his words are in certain respects a little vague, they are, as regards the aim of this book, clear and unmistakable. Unbelief can make no appeal to the authority of Augustin Fresnel.

The same can be said of our great countryman Joseph Fraunhofer (born about a year earlier than Fresnel, March 6th 1787, died a little less than a year before him, June 7th 1826)[1]. The story of his life and labours

---

et de la bonté infinies de leur auteur. Les services qu'il rendait aux sciences par ses méditations, les applications utiles qu'il en a faites, n'étaient à ses yeux que l'accomplissement d'une mission pour lui obligatoire. C'était surtout par la pratique des vertus les plus touchantes qu'il croyait pouvoir s'acquitter envers l'humanité et qu'il satisfaisait sa conscience. C'est à moi . . . qui ai assisté à ses derniers moments, qui ai recueilli ses dernières paroles, de dire quels étaient ses principes sévères et invariables; son adoration pour la vertu, qu'il plaçait bien au-dessus de la science et du génie; sa force d'âme, je ne dirai pas contre la mort seulement, mais contre l'interruption des découvertes, qu'il avait préparées et ébauchées, et dont il espérait tirer des applications utiles . . ." (Duleau, Notice, in Revue encycl. XXXIX 566 567). Arago says in his Éloge on Fresnel, referring to his frame of mind during the last days of his life · "Toutes ses pensées s'étaient tournées vers sa fin prochaine, tout l'y ramenait." Not even the presentation of the Rumford medal, one of the highest honours which England has to give, made any impression on him (Œuvres complètes III 525 526).

[1] F. Thiersch in Bulletin der königl. Akademie der Wissenschaften, München 1852, 126—143. Ph. Jolly in Allg. deutsche Biographie VII 323—325. Cf. (Utzschneider) Kurzer Abriß der Lebensgeschichte des Herrrn Dr Joseph v. Fraunhofer, in Kunst- und Gewerbeblatt für Bayern vom Jahre 1826. Ph. Jolly, Das Leben Fraunhofers. Rede an die Studierenden der k. Ludwig-Maximilians-Universität zu Munchen, gehalten am 2. Dezember 1865, München 1866. C. M. v. Bauernfeind, Gedächtnisrede auf Joseph v. Fraunhofer zur Feier seines 100. Geburtstages. München 1887. Jos. von Fraunhofers Gesammelte Schriften, herausgeg. von E. Lommel, München 1888.

is well known; it exhibits the spectacle of a man of supreme intellect and iron industry, stubbornly battling with obstacles that all but succeeded in overwhelming him. As an orphan of eleven, he came from his native Straubing to Munich, and was there apprenticed to a maker of mirrors, who undertook to teach the delicate lad on condition that he worked for six years without pay. Some diagrams that he saw on the walls of the Sunday School made him aware of the existence of a science of Geometry. He bought a text-book for a couple of kreutzers, and set to work to master its contents. But everything was against him. His companions ridiculed him; his master did everything he could to stifle this itch for useless learning; others, whose advice he sought, told him that his project was hopeless. An accident helped him on. His master's house toppled down, imprisoning him in the ruins; and his rescue after four hours' excavation made him an object of public notice. The Elector, Max Joseph, and Utzschneider interested themselves in him and helped him in his studies with money and advice. After six years' hard work he was so far advanced that he obtained an appointment as optician in the Institute of Reichenbach and Utzschneider, and was set to work at the erection of geodetic and astronomical instruments [1].

[1] The Institute was situated within the walls of a former Benedictine Monastery. The Benedictines, Ulrich Schiegg and Niggl, deserved well of it, aiding it with scientific advice. For the astronomer Schiegg (1752—1810) cf. A. Lindner, Die Schriftsteller und die um Wissenschaft und Kunst verdienten Mitglieder des Benediktinerordens im heutigen Königreich Bayern II, Regensburg 1880, 98—101. Bauernfeind in Allg. deutsche Biogr. XXXI 180.

This marked the beginning of a new life for Fraunhofer. The telescopes made by him, were perfect in every respect, as well in their measuring apparatus as in their lenses, and inaugurated a new epoch in observational astronomy. "A striking proof of their excellence, almost to our day, is afforded by the fact that members of the Astronomical Commission, appointed by the German authorities to observe the transits of Venus in 1874 and 1882, employed instruments which had been made in Fraunhofer's workshops and under his personal direction. With the single exception of apparatus for photographing the transit — a process undiscovered in Fraunhofer's time — there was nothing that had not proceeded from the hands of the great scientist."[1] His brilliant achievements are to be ascribed, however, not so much to mere manual skill, as to his firm grasp and vast knowledge of the scientific side of his subject. To grapple with the practical problems, encountered in the construction of achromatic lenses, a perfect mastery of methods hitherto in use was not enough; there was needed also a genius for independent research in theoretical optics. Fraunhofer possessed such genius, and he "enriched the physics of Light with epoch-making discoveries". The so-called Fraunhofer lines of the sun's sceptrum bear witness to one sphere of his activity; his works on the diffraction and refraction of light are held in high estimation; and his determination of the wave-lengths of light of various colours is remarkable not only for its wonderful accuracy, but for the part it played in establishing the undulatory theory of light.

[1] Bauernfeind, Gedächtnisrede 15.

Unfortunately, at the early age of forty, Fraunhofer was snatched away by a painful and incurable disease. "His demeanour under acute suffering was that of a sterling Christian. He showed no impatience and uttered no complaint, but resigned all hope of recovery to the Divine Will which had brought him forth into life from the night of nothingness."

"Fraunhofer was a man of disciplined and benevolent temper, occasionally clouded, it is true, by outbursts of his natural irritability. He was a loyal adherent of his religion, so thorough in his obedience that even those invited to his house were obliged to observe the prescribed fasts and abstinences, a remarkable contrast, surely, to the licence of his day." [1]

On many essential points of the Theory of Light Fresnel had been able to advance only conjectures, and on many others he accepted, as proved, certain laws which demanded further investigation. Much remained for his successors in the development of the new theory, and men of genius were found for the task. "No physicist of our time", says Cornu [2], "has contributed more to the final formulation of the wonderful wave-theory than Fizeau." This was an invaluable service to science, and it bore fruit in other departments than that to which it was first applied.

[1] Historisch-politische Blätter XI, München 1843, 485. — That Fraunhofer was a sincere Catholic is also testified by J. N. von Ringseis in his speech as rector, 11th December 1855; v. E. v. Ringseis, Erinnerungen an J. N. v. Ringseis IV 322 331.

[2] Cornu, L'œuvre scientifique de M. Fizeau, in the Annuaire pour l'an 1898, publié par le Bureau des longitudes, Notice C, reprinted in Cosmos, 17 et 26 sept. 1898, 374—379 400—405.

Armand Hippolyte Louis Fizeau, born 1819, was the son of a Professor of Medicine at Paris, and was originally intended to follow in the footsteps of his father. His medical studies were however interrupted by illness, and this gave him an opportunity of cultivating his taste for physics. Before long he engaged in independent experiment and research. He first turned his attention to the recently invented Art of Photography, and in the year 1841 he introduced many improvements. The daguerrotypes of the time were faint, impermanent, and very slow in developing. Fizeau expedited the process of development a hundredfold by the use of bromides, and by the application of certain salts of gold produced pictures at once vivid and lasting. The first discovery was made in conjunction with another scientist who was to be one day famous, Léon Foucault. They also investigated the photographic activity of various sources of light, and produced successful photographs of the sun and its spots. The conclusion of their paper on these latter, laid before the Academy in 1845, marks "a new epoch in the history of optics". Sound-waves grow weaker as they diffuse themselves over a wider area, but in all other respects remain unaltered. Does the same hold good of light-waves? There were reasons to doubt it, and the lack of certainty on the point involved the theory of light in some obscurity. Fizeau and Foucault now showed that even after thousands of vibrations there is no change either in the shape or form of individual waves, or in their relation one to another. Fresnel had assumed that this was the case, but his assumption had not been raised to the plane of an established fact.

These triumphs were followed by another still more notable. However strong had been the grounds for accepting the new undulatory theory, nobody had yet brought forward a phenomenon which was not explicable by the old emanation-theory. Arago had indeed observed that if this latter were true, light should travel faster in water than in air; if the wave-theory were true the relative velocities should be reversed. But the matter had never been put to the test, the necessary measuring apparatus not being at hand. Foucault and Fizeau showed themselves equal to the task, and after the dissolution of their partnership, each of the two published (in 1850) an account of experiments proving that light travels faster in air than in water. This gave its death-blow to the emanation-theory.

It yet remained to determine the absolute velocity of light in atmospheric air. Fizeau took up the problem, and struck out a brilliant idea; he measured the velocity of light by the passage of a slender ray between the teeth of a rapidly revolving toothed-wheel. Mathematically regarded, the experiment is a very simple one. The great practical difficulty was the conduct of a slender ray of light along a path of several kilometres in such a way as to prevent diffusion or diffraction. "The skill with which this was effected", says Cornu [1], "ranks among the most notable triumphs of Physics. One hardly knows which to admire the more, the boldness of the idea or the splendid simplicity of the means taken to realise it."

Fizeau now projected a measurement of the velocity of electricity by a somewhat similar method. But his

---

[1] Cornu in Annuaire pour l'an 1898, publié par le Bureau des longitudes C 14.

work on the subject published in 1880 in conjunction with Gounelle had a very cold reception. Neither Fizeau's results, nor his treatment of electricity as a wave-motion fitted in with the scientific conceptions then current. To-day the case is different, and opinion is much more favourable to Fizeau [1].

"A real discovery" was also the great improvement which he introduced into induction apparatus, the condenser in which still bears his name. As regards the Physics of the ether, Fizeau "was far in advance of the science of the day" [2]. Having ascertained the velocity of light in air and in water, he asked himself the question whether in disturbed air or in disturbed water the respective velocities were in any way altered; in other words, whether or not the particles of light-ether are carried along by the moving particles of air or water. The query had been started by Fresnel. He had been obliged to assume, in order to explain observed phenomena, that in a certain measure, determined by the refraction-exponent, the light-ether is undoubtedly affected by the movement of the surrounding medium. Fizeau, displaying his usual ingenuity in the invention of apparatus, proved experimentally the correctness of Fresnel's assumption. The measurement of the velocity of light in disturbed water is described as "the most difficult in modern optics". It was not till near the end of the 19th century that any scientist ventured to repeat it. The result was to confirm Fizeau's conclusions.

Inasmuch as the earth's atmosphere revolves together with the earth itself at a great velocity, this cannot fail to affect the light which streams across the atmo-

---

[1] Cornu, Annuaire C 16. [2] Ib. C 21.

sphere. Not even Fizeau succeeded in demonstrating the fact by experiment, but his attempts to do so led him to an important discovery. Christian Doppler had suggested in 1842 that approach to the source of sound or light must produce a change of pitch or colour; Fizeau developed this suggestion to the exact formula, known as the law of Doppler and Fizeau, which has borne such fruit in astronomy, enabling us, as it does, to calculate the rate at which a star is approaching us.

In addition to these "works of the first importance[1] which set Fizeau at the head of the physicists of his day", he also published many others, e. g. those on the application of monochromatic light.

After this chronicle of scientific triumphs readers will be astounded to learn that Fizeau's death (September 18th 1896) attracted practically no notice. He received no funeral honours; and, save Cornu, not a single scientist raised his voice in praise or commemoration[2]. We may, perhaps, furnish an explanation of the riddle.

Fizeau's general philosophy of life, apart from his triumphs in his special province, receive but scant treatment at the hands of Cornu. He had an unshakable confidence in everything that he believed to be soundly established by "tradition or evidence"; his admiration for the great laws of science and their discoverers "had a tinge of mysticism"[3]. These expressions rather deepen

---

[1] Cornu, Annuaire C 33.

[2] The obituary notices in the Comptes rendus CXXIII (1896) 471 in La Nature LIV, Paris 1896, 523—524, and in Leopoldina XXXII, Halle 1896, 182.

[3] "Sa parole, ordinairement si calme, s'animait d'une vivacité singulière, lorsqu'il exprimait son admiration un peu mystique pour les grandes choses ou pour les grands génies qui les ont accomplies.

the mystery. Let us turn for an explanation to Fizeau's own works.

At the Public Session of the Academy of Sciences on March 10th 1879, he delivered, in his capacity as President, a discourse on the departed year. He expressed himself as follows concerning the relations between the philosophy of the day and natural science:

"But even in the flush of these great successes, Science, anxious above all to retain her dignity and independence, wisely refuses to ally herself with philosophic systems which in their ardent enthusiasm might come to dominate her, and seduce her from her proper path. She has always shown herself able to repel what might have become an enslaving yoke; on her part she limits her ambition to the diffusion of knowledge, and does not intrude inopportunely on philosophical or social questions nor set herself in hostility to the noble promptings of the heart, or the pure voice of conscience." [1]

In these words we have a clear condemnation of the misuse of science to propagate materialism. Elsewhere we find positive expression of Fizeau's veneration for religion; as, for example, in his speech at the unveiling of the statue to Leverrier. The French Republic had

---

Il avait une confiance inébranlable dans ce qu'il considérait comme solidement établi par tradition ou par évidence" (Cornu ante C 38).

[1] Cependant, au milieu de ces grands succès, toujours attentive à conserver intactes sa dignité et son indépendance, la science évite avec sagesse de se mêler aux ardeurs et aux entraînements des systèmes qui pourraient, en la dominant, la détourner de sa route; ayant montré, en toute occasion, qu'elle sait repousser tout ce qui ressemble à un joug destiné à l'asservir, elle borne à son tour son ambition à répandre au loin sa lumière, sans vouloir entrevenir, hors de propos, dans les questions philosophiques ou sociales, ni se mettre en opposition avec les nobles accents du cœur ou la voix pure de la conscience (Comptes rendus LXXXVIII [1879] 447).

not looked favourably on the project of honouring a man of Leverrier's principles with a memorial in a place so public and so impressive, as that which his friends had chosen. At the unveiling Fizeau expressed his amazement at the action of the Government:

"Without inquiring here into the probable motives behind such a decision, let me remind you that under the Empire, Leverrier was appointed Director of the Observatory; he was also a Senator. But under the Empire also he was disgraced and degraded; and it was the Republic that restored him to the Observatory, there to die. We know indeed that Leverrier was a deeply religious man. Is that a subject of reproach? We know that he was a man of haughty temper, master of a severe eloquence which made him formidable in argument: whose is the grievance? I can then only give expression to the amazement with which this decision has been received by all the friends of Science."[1]

In his memorial discourse on Desains, Fizeau praises his piety of character; in his speech on Becquerel he also renders homage to religion[2].

All this may suggest to the reader the explanation which we are about to offer. We have, through the medium of a friend in Paris, information of the most trustworthy kind that Fizeau was all his life a loyal, open, and practical Christian. It was for this reason his name was struck out of the list of those presented for the Cross of the Legion of Honour at the Centenary celebration of the Academy. Were scientific merit regarded, what dignity could have been too high for him?

---

[1] . . . On sait encore que Leverrier était religieux; et qui aurait qualité pour le lui reprocher . . . (Annuaire pour l'an 1890, publié par le Bureau des longitudes 643).

[2] V. the passages in the following extract p. 171 172.

Cornu's was the only voice raised in protest against the "odious and revolting intrigue"[1].

We have already made mention of the name of Léon Foucault[2], collaborator of Fizeau in his earlier work. It is often the case that men of genius excel in only one province, not rising in others above the level of mediocrity, and Foucault is a striking example of this. A delicate and timid lad, he had the greatest difficult in completing the ordinary course of studies. He then proceeded to medicine, but found himself unable to bear the sight of blood, and was forced to relinquish all thoughts of this career. The professor of Microscopy, however, discerned something of Foucault's qualities, and entrusted him with the preparation of experiments. This brought into play that unique combination of skill and inventiveness which he was before long to apply to the most complicated problems of Mechanics and Optics. He began his career with certain improvements in the process of photography; then followed his collaboration with Fizeau, and in 1850 his famous apparatus for comparing the velocity of light in air with its velocity in water. He attained a European reputation through the well-known pendulum-proof of the rotation of the earth on its axis; and in 1852 he published an

[1] "Il était Chrétien convaincu et pratiquant, et ne s'en cachait nullement du reste; c'est même pour cette raison, qu'il a été lors du centenaire de l'institut l'objet d'une mesure absolument odieuse et révoltante" etc.

[2] Recueil des Travaux Scientifiques de L. Foucault . . . mis en ordre par C. M. Gariel, Paris 1878 (vol. II contains a sketch from life drawn by Lissajous). Ph. Gilbert in Revue des questions scientifiques V (1879) 108—155 516—564. Jos. Bertrand, Éloges académiques, Paris 1890, 247.

account of another apparatus, the gyroscope, designed for the same end. In 1854 he became Physicist to the Observatory of Paris, and during his tenure of this post introduced many improvements in the construction of telescopes and microscopes. "I have matter for another twenty years", he said about 1866, after his reception into the Academy. But the twenty years were not to be vouchsafed him. He was occupied in the construction of a regulator for the Paris Exhibition, and had spent infinite labour on it; overwork brought on a stroke of apoplexy on July 10th 1867; he sank slowly, and died on February 13th 1868 at the age of forty-nine.

Foucault, during the period of his feverish scientific activity, had given little thought to religious questions. But this attitude of mind changed as sickness overwhelmed him, and all earthly hope vanished. The name of God was constantly on his lips. Step by step he returned to his childhood's faith in a Creator and a Redeemer, and found in it strength and consolation. Although the apoplectic fit had all but deprived him of the power of speech "it was extraordinary to observe the facility with which he spoke of God and Jesus Christ, scarcely any trace of impediment appearing". He died peacefully in communion with the Church [1].

The name of Edward Ketteler stands high among the leaders of Optics (born in 1836 at Bocholt, died December 10th 1900, a Professor at Münster) [2]. He was a fervent and outspoken Catholic.

Two Catholic priests also deserve a brief mention. Abbé Laborde, in a communication to the Paris

---

[1] Moigno in Les Mondes XVI, Paris 1868, 344; cf. 337.

[2] Leopoldina XXXVII, Halle 1901, 35—36.

Academy of Science, anticipated to some extent Fizeau's determination of the velocity of light[1]. And it seems to be beyond doubt that Foucault's famous pendulum-experiment was suggested long before by Canon Augustin Stark († 1839) of Augsburg[2].

On February 2th 1903, there died at Cambridge a savant "known to every student of Physics, held in the highest esteem by all specialists in his particular province". This was Sir George Gabriel Stokes[3] (born in 1819 at Screen in Ireland, Lucasian Professor at Cambridge from the year 1849). In addition to this, he was member of Parliament for the University and President of the Royal Society of Science, two positions that had been filled by no one man since Newton. He was in 1899 created a Baronet, and he also held the German Order *Pour le Mérite.*

Stokes is perhaps best known for his researches into the phenomenon of fluorescence. But his real strength lay rather in mathematical than in experimental Physics. He published works on the problems of Optics, on the wave-theory, but more particularly on Hydro-dynamics, his contribution to this latter being of fundamental importance. It was Stokes who with Maxwell and Lord Kelvin won for the Cambridge School of Physics the reputation which it still enjoys. Stokes had the greater part of his scientific achievements behind him when occasion called him to speak out his mind on the existence of God, and more specifically on natural religion and

---

[1] Cosmos-Les Mondes, 3e sér. V, mai-août 1883, 164 166.

[2] Gunther in Allg. deutsche Biographie XXXV 488.

[3] Obituary Notice in Naturwissenschaftl. Rundschau XVIII, Braunschweig 1903, 217, cf. Encyclopaedia Britannica XXXII[10] 867 ff.

morality. He received an invitation from the University of Edinburgh to deliver the Gifford Lectures for 1891[1]. The terms of the foundation of this Lectureship prescribed for subjects the existence and nature of God, and the precepts of the moral law, but without any reference to a positive revelation.

Stokes intimates clearly in his lectures that this limitation does not meet with his approval. He expresses doubts whether a tenable theology and ethics can be developed on any other basis than that of Christianity. Hints and suggestions, at least, must be constantly adopted from the Christian system even if the principles in question are provable by pure reason. And this being so, is it not a curiously unnatural proceeding to ignore the sources from which we are drawing? Stokes confesses frankly that for a task such as that prescribed for the Gifford Lectures he is ill-prepared[2]:

"What I have previously written has been mainly scientific memoirs; as to theology, I have merely written a few short articles, and in those, though I did not scruple to employ natural reason, I have gone on the basis of accepting a supernatural revelation, more especially on that of accepting the Resurrection of Jesus of Nazareth as a supernatural historical fact."

Subsequent statements are even more to our purpose; and we subjoin some extracts from the course, published later under the title of "Natural Theology". What a man like Stokes has to say e. g. on the order and majesty of nature cannot fail to be interesting,

---

[1] Natural Theology. The Gifford Lectures, delivered before the University of Edinburgh in 1891, by Prof. Sir G. G. Stokes, Bart., M. P., London and Edinburgh 1891.

[2] Ib. 270.

although these are questions by no means exclusively scientific:

"It will be absurd to deny to the creating will powers which the created being is found to possess. Now there is one of these possessions of which we are innately conscious; I refer to free will. I feel that I have the option of moving my hand to the right or the left, and similarly with regard to innumerable other actions. The words of every language testify to the consciousness of such a power. Of course I may wish to do a thing which I have not the power to do; but that is a different matter altogether. A thief might wish to carry away on his shoulders an ingot of gold worth £50000 but he would not be able. Such an ability does not in the least degree militate against our consciousness of free will. We cannot deny man's Maker this power which we find man himself possesses. . . .

"Now we know very well that a man may in general act uniformly according to a certain rule, and yet for a special reason may on a particular occasion act quite differently. We cannot refuse to admit the possibility of something analogous taking place as regards the actions of the Supreme Being. If we think of the laws of nature as self-existent and uncaused, then we cannot admit any deviation from them. But if we think of them as designed by a Supreme Will, then we must allow the possibility of their being on some particular occasion suspended. Nor is it even necessary that some results out of the ordinary course of nature should be brought about, that they should even be suspended; it may be that some different law is brought into action whereby the result in question is brought about without any suspension whatsoever of the laws by which the ordinary course of nature is regulated. I will endeavour to illustrate my meaning by reference to something with which we are familiar. Suppose that a clock with an iron pendulum had long been observed and noted. Its rate we know is determined by the laws of motion and gravitation. Suppose that on one occasion it went much faster for an hour or two, and then resumed its usual rate. It may have been that some one designedly put a powerful magnet under it, which after a time was taken away again. The acceleration of rate was here produced not by any suspension of the laws of motion or of gravitation, but by bringing into play for a time a special force which left the laws of motion and of gravitation perfectly intact, and yet brought about the result that we have supposed to have been observed.

"It will probably have been perceived that in what I have just been saying I have had in view the question of the abstract possibility of what are called miracles. Admit the Existence of God, of a personal God, and the possibility of miracles follows at once; if the laws of nature are carried on in accordance with His will He Who willed them may will their suspension. And if any difficulty should be felt as to their suspension, we are not even obliged to suppose that they have been suspended." [1]

Of the proofs of the existence of God, Stokes lays most stress on that derived from design; for, that nature does manifest design, he considers undeniable. Having, for instance, concluded a description of the eye, he writes: "I think the evidence of design which it affords must be to most minds well nigh overwhelming, though at the same time, I grant that it requires some knowledge of the laws of light, and also of the structure of the eye itself to feel the full force of the argument." [2]

Inasmuch as Darwin's theory is by many supposed to invalidate the argument from design, Stokes examines in some detail the doctrine of evolution. He begins by pointing out that Darwin, before he can speak of the struggle for life or the survival of the fittest has to assume certain postulates, "the existence of life; the power possessed by living things, whether animal or vegetable, of reproducing their kind; the general similarity of offspring to parents, combined with small variations of detail" [3]. But if these are the indispensable postulates of the theory then, according to Stokes, the

---

[1] Natural Theology 22—25. [2] Ib. 41. [3] Ib.

principle of the survival of the fittest by no means supplants and makes superfluous a purposive Creator. For if we do not accept His existence whence are we to derive life, the power of reproduction, the transmission of qualities once acquired?

"It seems to me likely enough that this principle may really operate to a certain extent, and so far as it does, it points out a sort of self-acting mechanism, founded in its action on the postulates with which we started, for adapting the structure of the living thing to the requirements of its environment. This however does not destroy, but only alters the argument of design. If, indeed, the postulates of the theory were taken as self-existent and uncaused, then I grant the argument would fall to the ground. But I have heard on good authority that Darwin himself regarded the argument from design as rather elevated than destroyed by the adoption of his theory." [1]

"But even supposing the theory to be accepted as accounting for the permanence of more or less neighbouring species, it seems to me inconceivable that it should be competent to bridge over the interval which separates remote forms. There are structures so complex, so artificial, so eminently (to all appearance at least) having a purpose to serve, that it seems inconceivable that they could have been built by a mere selection of haphazard variations from a type which in consequence of this selection undergoes a slow secular change. Take, for example, that exquisitely contrived organ, the eye.... It seems to me well-nigh inconceivable how any one who studies these various arrangements, so far as man has been able to follow them, can imagine them to be merely the cumulative effect of casual variations selected in the manner supposed, or can fail to be impressed, perhaps if he does so regard them, with the idea that they were designed for the office which we find them to fulfil." [2]

A writer in the Encyclopaedia Britannica of 1902 ranked Lord Rayleigh, Lord Kelvin, and Sir George Stokes

[1] Ib. 42 f. [2] Ib. 43 f.

as the three greatest physicists of the day[1]. We have seen the views of all three as to the relation between science and religion.

3. SUPPLEMENTARY.

We have now dealt at some length with the pioneers in Heat, Light and Electricity, and the reader will have perceived how very far they are from declaring unanimously against Christianity. Before leaving this branch of our subject we desire to add one or two distinguished names, which for various reasons have not been included in the preceding two sections.

"For many years, longer indeed than an average lifetime, there was to be met in the Academy of Sciences in Paris a venerable figure, no less remarkable for his lively interest and constant interventions in the discussions of that learned and brilliant body, than for the universal honour and respect which he received from his colleagues. Tall and powerfully built, he retained beneath the snow of years the vigour and resolution of youth; his pale face mobile and clear-cut, was the mirror of a subtle and rapid mind; his voice, although thin with age, was firm and impressive, and in the unconscious modulation of the moment gave token of unwavering conviction. . . . The whole presence and bearing of this remarkable man was that of a cosmopolitan savant, who found the only content worth having in the propagation of those scientific and moral principles to which he was so ardently attached."

The scientist of whom these glowing words were spoken by Von Martius, the botanist, at a meeting of

[1] Encyclopaedia Britannica XXXII[10] 184.

the Bavarian Academy was J. B. Biot[1] (1774—1862). He was one of the most celebrated men of his day, a leader in Physics, a historian of the science, and a brilliant stylist. He enjoyed membership of three of the five French Academies, and it is impossible to-day to read a text-book of Physics without finding honourable mention of his name. His original research-work was done mainly in the field of Optics; but he was also engaged for several years in Spain and the North of England as a member of the French Commission for the measurement of the degrees of longitude, and as a teacher of Mathematics and Physics he exercised a wide influence. He possessed, says Von Martius, "a rare lucidity of intellect, which, unaccompanied by any great imaginative power, found its real attraction in the nobility of justice, moral worth, and absolute truth". "Biot was an austere, independent, inexorable critic who believed exclusively in pure reason. In accordance with its dictates he ordered his life, ambitions, and studies, and no other consideration had any weight with him."

As for his religious opinions, Biot was not always a believing Christian. For many years the recollection of his First Communion was the only relic left to him of a pious boyhood. Under the influence of the circle that gathered round Laplace his indifference developed into a vague Deism. But his experience of Deists and Atheists and of the practical fruits of Christian belief, as he saw them in the lives of some of his nearest relatives, led him back to the faith of his childhood.

---

[1] Gedächtnisrede on March 28th 1862 in v. Martius, Akademische Denkreden, München 1866, 456.

For the last thirty years of his life he was a fervent Catholic, and he so continued to the end. His friend and confessor, Père Ravignan, could justly characterise him as a true Christian savant, as he does in a letter acknowledging the receipt of Biot's memoir of the mathematician Cauchy: "That is Cauchy to the life, and you yourself to the life! You manifest to all in the noblest language an intimate alliance between true science and true faith."[1] But this memoir was by no means Biot's only confession of faith. "He had", as Abbé Moigno[2] tells us, "shown the liveliest joy at the entrance of his grand-son M. Millière into the priesthood, and it was an affecting sight to see the august old savant receiving Holy Communion in the Basilica of Saint-Étienne-du-Mont from the hands of the young priest who called him grandfather."

Biot's return to the Church was not regarded by all with favourable eyes. If Sainte-Beuve sought to depreciate his reputation as a scientist, and others busied themselves in exaggerating the blemishes of his life, we must ascribe this in part to anti-Christian feeling. This feeling found further expression in the attempt to fill the chair in the Academy left vacant by Biot's death, by the election of an atheist. The candidate

[1] A. de Ponlevoy, Vie du R. P. Xavier de Ravignan de la Comp. de Jésus II[15], Paris 1900, chap. 27, 387. For de Ravignan's relations to Biot cf. chap. 19, 131—133.

[2] In his newspaper Cosmos XX, Paris 1862, 203. Moigno characterizes the same Biot as a "chrétien convaincu, sincère et pratiquant. Son retour à la foi datait de près de trente ans; un des premiers nous en reçûmes la confidence". — Cf. Lefort, Un savant chrétien, J.-B. Biot, in Le Correspondant déc. 1867; U. Maynard in Bibliographie catholique XL, Paris 1868, 93.

put forward was Littré, a materialist, socialist, and atheist. He succumbed however, to the vigorous opposition of Lacordaire, and did not till a later date obtain a place among the immortals. Littré himself, it is worthy of remark, did not remain a materialist till death. He wrote many articles in his Revue Positiviste of a Christian tendency, as if to prepare his friends for a change, and in his last illness he asked for baptism and died in the faith[1].

Many important contributions were made to Optics by Jacques Babinet († 1872) whose name is perpetuated by various physical apparatus. His loyalty to the Christian belief was shown strikingly in his last painful illness, which he endured with exemplary patience and resignation. He was all his life charitable almost to a fault. He gave without stint, and the number of his beneficiaries was countless[2].

---

[1] Allgemeine Zeitung, Augsburg 1881, 2301 2310. For Littré's earlier relations to Christianity cf. Ch. Clair, Le R. P. Milleriot de la Compagnie de Jésus[24], Paris-Bruxelles-Genève 1881, 179 f. Littré's Article is reprinted from the Revue posit. in Les Mondes LV, Paris 1881, 2, 224: "Certaines âmes pieuses se sont intéressées à mes dispositions intimes. Il leur a semblé que, n'étant un contempteur absolu du christianisme et lui reconnaissant avec insistance des grandeurs et des bienfaits, il y avait en mon cœur des cordes qui pourraient vibrer. . . . Comme je n'ai éprouvé ni exprimé de la répulsion ou du malaise en me sentant l'objet des sentiments dont je viens d'esquisser les nuances etc. — In a letter of 14. April 1878, which has been published lately, Littré writes to a person who wished to dedicate a book to him: Je ne puis accepter la dédicace de votre livre. Il est d'une polémique trop aggressive à l'égard des idées théologiques et du catholicisme, pour qu'il convienne à la position que j'occupe dans l'école de la philosophie positiviste (L'intermédiaire des chercheurs et curieux XLVII, Paris 20 mars 1903. Quest. n. 386).

[2] Moigno writes of him in Les Mondes XXIX, Paris 1872, 293: Cette mort précédée d'une longue et cruelle infirmité, supportée avec une patience incomparable, rompt pour nous les liens d'une

The discoverer of fluorescence, David Brewster († 1861), was also a fervent Christian. He was a Protestant of the older school and found prophecies of the Pope in many passages in the Old Testament (Dan. 7)[1]. But he was a firm, practical Christian, and he enriched Optics with many acquisitions. He invented the kaleidoscope and the lensed spectroscope, and wrote a biography of Newton[2].

During the middle years of the 19th century, perhaps the greatest living physicist was Victor Regnault (born 1810 at Aix-la-Chapelle, died 1878 at Paris).

"It was in the year 1849", writes Berthelot[3], "that I first came to know him, and received from him advice and inspiration not easily to be forgotten. Science was then full of his glory, his name was cited by all our teachers in the company of the greatest physicists of all time. The genius of precision seemed to have taken flesh in his person. The celebrity of Gay-Lussac, of Dulong, of Faraday built up by so many magnificent discoveries seemed to pale before that of Victor Regnault; and the glory he enjoyed was spotless, earned by the sheer force of hard work, without the aid of intrigue or self-advertisement, political or literary."

---

amitié étroite de plus de 35 ans. Nous avons eu du moins la consolation de voir notre illustre savant dans les sentiments d'une foi sincère et d'une résignation vraiment touchante. . . . Notre ami avait une qualité bien rare, poussée chez lui jusqu'à l'excès, il donnait tout ce qu'il avait; le nombre des infortunés qu'il soulageait est incommensurable. — Faye says in his funeral oration: Réconcilié avec tous et par-dessus tout avec Dieu, vous avez révélé dans cette longue agonie la force de votre âme (ib. 338).

[1] J.-B. Biot, Mélanges I 407 415. The life of Sir J. Newton by D. Brewster, London 1831, 227 272.

[2] Il s'est endormi dans une profonde paix et dans l'espérance ferme du salut parfait en Jésus-Christ, wrote his son to the Academy of Munich. V. its Sitzungsberichte, München 1868, I 469.

[3] Science et philosophie, Paris 1886, 218.

How highly Regnault was esteemed throughout Europe was shown on the occasion of an accident which befell him, Aug. 9th 1856. His condition from hour to hour was everywhere the subject of conversation, and the newspapers published as full and frequent bulletins as if he had been a prince[1].

Regnault's fame is not perhaps quite so brilliant to-day. But he remains one of the first experimenters of the century, and his investigations, especially into the expansion of gases, are classical in point of accuracy and skill in detecting possible sources of error. He had toiled his way up from the humblest origin to the proudest heights of science and glory when trial after trial began to oppress and all but overwhelm him. In 1856 he had lost his wife and her mother; in 1871, during the Franco-Prussian war, his laboratory was reduced to ruins, his instruments destroyed, and his notes, representing the work of years, were burned. His son, who had already had some success as a painter, was killed in battle, and in 1873 Regnault himself had a stroke which although it did not cloud his intellect, left him in many other respects weak and helpless. "Few men", said Daubrée, "have in their declining years been more sorely tried. . . . His religious faith alone was capable of consoling him, and it was a source of consolation that never failed."[2]

---

[1] Allgemeine Zeitung 1856, 3581 3672 3693 3709 3725.

[2] Peu d'hommes ont été, comme on le sait, plus cruellement frappés, pendant les dernières années de sa vie. Quel douloureux contraste, si nous nous reportons à trente-cinq années en arrière lorsque nous le rappelons, ayant vaincu toutes les difficultés de son adolescence, avec tous les charmes séduisants de la jeunesse et de l'esprit, entouré d'une charmante famille dont il était l'idole, au

"Worthy rivals of Regnault in elegance of method and accuracy of measurement" is the description given by Troost of the physicists Paul Desains and De La Provostaye. Their elaborate researches prove that as regards emission, absorption, reflection, refraction, and polarization, radiant heat possesses all the qualities of light. The universal theme of the memorial speeches pronounced over Desains († May 3th 1885) was the upright character of the dead scientist. Fizeau praised his benevolence and rectitude, his loyalty to his friends, his untiring devotion to duty, and his religious habit of mind. A personal friend of his, the Academician Mezières, said that to him death was "the day-spring of realisation for those immortal hopes to which he had always clung with robust belief" [1].

César Mansuète Despretz († March 15th 1867) laboured for forty years in the investigation of heat, sound, and electricity. He inaugurated no new theories, but his industrious researches established a mass of important facts, and we find him, on that account, frequently cited in text-books of Physics. Despretz was a believing Catholic. He defended the Church and clergy from various attacks with courage and effect. Nevertheless he so far gave way to the

---

milieu des succès les plus brillants, recevant de toute part les honneurs les mieux mérités. Sa foi religieuse pouvait seule le consoler, et cette consolation ne lui a pas manqué (Comptes rendus LXXXVI, Paris 1878, 141).

[1] Après avoir rappelé les titres qui honorent le savant, dans M. Desains, nous ne ferons qu'exprimer le sentiment de tous ceux qui l'ont connu, en rendant hommage aux rares qualités de son coeur. Si sa droiture, sa bonté, son esprit de justice, sa fidélité à ses amis, son infatigable dévouement à ses devoirs, ses sentiments religieux, la dignité de sa vie, en un mot, lui ont toujours mérité les respects de tous pendant sa vie, le souvenir des qualités et des vertus dont il a donné l'exemple ne peut manquer de rester attaché à sa mémoire (Fizeau in Comptes rendus C, Paris 1885, 1259). — Tu as vu venir la mort avec calme; elle était pour toi le commencement d'une vie nouvelle, l'aurore des immortelles espérances dont ta foi robuste n'a jamais douté (Mézières ante 1266).

influence of the age that not till his death-bed did he return to the practical exercise of his religion [1].

César Antoine Becquerel († 1878) is a name familiar to every student of science. His line of research is well known. "For more than fifty years", he himself writes, "I have been engaged in physico-chemical research, working mainly at the question of the relations existing between electricity and attraction at greater or less distances, and between electricity, light, and heat."

Becquerel was a convinced Christian. In the memorial speech pronounced at his grave-side Fizeau declared that he had died "with the serenity of a philosopher, the tranquility of soul of a good man, the trust in God and immortal hope of a Christian" [2]. Becquerel himself had spoken out unmistakably his verdict on materialism. In his work on physico-chemical forces, and the part they play in the production of natural phenomena he expressly declares that it is impossible to explain the origin of life on earth apart from the conception of a Creator.

Every thinker who accepts the modern theory of the formation of the earth, is constrained to hold that in the beginning it was without vegetation. Organic life could only have begun in the soil deposited as sediment. But how was the passage from inorganic to organic effected? That is the secret of the Creator.

---

[1] Moigno in Les Mondes I, Paris 1863, 141 143. Cf. Sitzungsberichte der k. bayr. Akad., Munchen 1863, II 385—388.

[2] M. Becquerel touchait à la fin de sa quatre-vingt-dixième année, lorsqu'il s'est éteint doucement, au milieu des siens, avec la sérénité du sage, la tranquillité d'âme de l'homme de bien, la confiance en Dieu et les immortelles espérances du chrétien (Comptes rendus LXXXVI, Paris 1878, 128).

"Geology tells us that nature has followed a progressive plan in the creation of organised beings, beginning with the simplest and gradually rising to the most complex forms as atmospheric conditions changed. But what are the forces that went to the formation of all these organised bodies? Our ignorance in this regard is such that, while we know that if the organic bodies and other various substances of the earth were to be suddenly volatilised by excessive heat, and if this were followed, as in the first ages of the earth, by a gradual cooling down, our inorganic compounds would be reconstitued according to known laws, we are quite unable to conceive in what fashion vegetable and animal life could be reproduced. We must then postulate the existence of a creative power which has manifested itself at certain epochs, but whose sole operation at present is to conserve those living species actually in existence."

Becquerel then quotes a passage from Berzelius in which the great chemist argues in favour of the existence of God and against materialism, and continues [1]:

"We have cited these sublime words in order to show that, in the opinion of the most gifted minds, matter is incapable of ascending to the stage of organic life by the sole agency of the forces which govern inorganic nature." [2]

---

[1] It will be given in an extract, v. p. 180.

[2] . . . Ce n'est que dans les terrains de sédiment que la vie organique a dû commencer; mais comment s'est opérée la transition de la vie inorganique à la vie organique? Là est le secret du Créateur. . . . Il faut donc admettre l'existence d'une puissance créatrice qui s'est manifestée à certaines époques, et qui ne semble plus agir aujourd'hui que pour perpétuer les espèces actuellement vivantes. Berzelius s'exprime à cet égard en ces termes: . . . Nous avons cru devoir rapporter ces paroles sublimes, pour montrer que les esprits les plus élevés ne pensent pas que la matière puisse s'organiser elle-même par le concours seul des forces qui régissent la nature inorganique (Des forces physico-chimiques et de leur intervention dans la production des phénomènes naturels. Par M. Becquerel, Paris 1873, 4—5).

The name of Luigi Palmieri († 1896) was first introduced to the scientific world in 1843 by the invention of an electro-magnetic apparatus designed to show the existence of earth-magnetism. In 1856 he became director of the Observatory which King Ferdinand II. had built in 1841 on Vesuvius to facilitate the study of the volcano. Palmieri filled this post for forty years with tireless industry, and made many valuable contributions to Meteorology, and to the study of volcanoes. He invented many instruments for the measurement of tellural disturbances, of the velocity of wind, and of atmospheric electricity. His work on the latter is very celebrated. He made observations of an outbreak of Vesuvius under most dangerous conditions [1].

Palmieri was a thorough going Catholic. "He heard Mass not only on the prescribed Feast Days but also on those in regard to which there was no obligation, and till his death at the age of 89 his piety continued unabated. . . . We can repeat of Palmieri, what he himself said of Galluppi: 'The Catholic religion was the inspirer of his studies, and, fortified by its unspeakable consolations, he passed from earth to eternal peace.'" [2]

Everyone who has studied in any detail the theory of Laplace as to the origin of the planetary system has also heard of the Belgian physicist, Plateau. J. A. F. Plateau (born at Brussels 1801, died at Ghent 1883) had in 1843 the misfortune to be blinded in the course of his researches into sense-illusions, but in spite of this he continued his scientific career, and established many laws of the first importance regarding the conditions of equilibrium [3]. He too is to

---

[1] L. Palmieri, Die atmosphärische Elektrizität. Ubersetzt von Heinr. Discher, Wien 1884. Der Ausbruch des Vesuv vom 26. April 1872. Deutsch von C. Rammelsberg, Berlin 1872.

[2] Civiltà cattolica, Ser. 16, XI, Roma 9 agosto 1897, 470.

[3] Sketch from life in the Annuaire de l'Académie royale des sciences, des lettres et des beaux-arts de Belgique LI, Bruxelles 1885, 389 to

be counted with those scientists whom widening knowledge of nature only confirmed in their veneration of religion. "Plateau", says his son-in-law, Van Der Mensbrugghe, "was a convinced Christian; it always pained him to hear scientists speak of the wonderful scientific achievements of our century as making in favour of materialism, and against the religious conception of life. Religion, he said, is a heavenly balsam for all our sorrows of soul and body; and it is high treason against humanity to seek to deprive poor sufferers of this consolation. As for himself, the deeper he penetrated into the secrets of nature the more humbly he bowed before the mysteries of the supernatural order." [1]

Peter Guthrie Tait († July 4th 1901) is a name famous far beyond the shores of his native land, although less for his original research than for his textbooks and popular scientific writings. In collaboration with Sir W. Thomson he began a manual of Theoretical Physics, the single completed volume of which was translated into German by Von Helmholtz. His books on thermo-dynamics, light, heat, and cognate subjects

---

486. Cf. Faye in the Comptes rendus of the Academy of Paris XCVII (1883) 687—689.

[1] Plateau était un chrétien convaincu; il se désolait chaque fois qu'un savant se prévalait des progrès merveilleux de ce siècle pour avancer des doctrines matérialistes ou antireligieuses; la religion, disait-il, est un baume céleste pour toutes les souffrances morales ou physiques, et c'est un crime de lèse-humanité que de chercher à en priver les malheureux ici-bas. Quant à lui, plus il avait approfondi les secrets de la nature, plus il s'inclinait devant les mystères de l'ordre surnaturel (Sketch of his life in the Annuaire de l'Académie royale des sciences etc. LI 460).

went into numerous editions and translations[1]. He was a man who had a comprehensive grasp of Physics, as a whole, without being a mere superficial dabbler. For this reason his views on the limits of science, and its relations with philosophy are likely to be more valuable than those of a specialist, who never emerges from his particular province nor troubles his head about even his next door neighbour in the city of science. In an address delivered before the British Association at Edinburgh Tait sets out to determine the frontier line between the realities which can be reached, and the realities which cannot be reached, by the methods of Physics. He describes two classes of writers on the subject.

On the one side there is "a crowd of ignorant persons whose sole recommendation is their rapidly increasing number, and the adhesion of a few fanatical deserters from the ranks of science. They refuse to admit that all phenomena of dead matter belong essentially and exclusively to physical science. On the other hand, there is a numerous group, not in the slightest degree entitled to rank as Physicists (though in general they assume the proud title of Philosophers), who assert that not merely life, but even Volition and Consciousness, are mere physical manifestations. These opposite errors, into neither of which is it possible for a genuine scientific man to fall, so long at least as he retains his reason, are easily seen to be very closely allied. They are both to be attributed to that credulity which is characteristic alike of ignorance and incapacity. Unfortunately there is no cure; the case is hopeless, for great ignorance

---

[1] Vorlesungen uber einige neuere Fortschritte der Physik, deutsch von G. Wertheim, Braunschweig 1877; Wärmelehre, deutsch von E. Lecher, Wien 1885; Die Eigenschaften der Materie, deutsch von G. Siebert, Wien 1888; Elementares Handbuch der Quaternionen, deutsch von G. v. Scherff, Leipzig 1880.

almost necessarily presumes incapacity, whether it shows itself in the comparatively harmless folly of the Spiritualist or in the pernicious nonsense of the Materialist" [1].

Tait deals in the same address with the chemico-physical interpretation of vital processes:

Even if we had wholly unveiled the secret of life, he says, it must not be imagined that we should be able to produce the simplest living being except from already existing life. "Our President's (Sir W. Thomson) brilliant idea of the vortex ring will enable us, if it rests on truth, to understand matter completely, and to investigate all its properties mathematically. Yet its very basis implies the absolute necessity of an intervention of Creative Power to form or destroy one atom even of dead matter." [2]

We may conclude this section with the opinion of still another German scientist on the philosophical import of the conclusions of science. Philip Jolly († 1885) worked with much success at the determination of the mass of the earth, the theory of heat, etc. "He never failed", says a biographer, "to add at the conclusion of his earlier lectures that all science is only piece-work, and is incapable of making any pronouncement as to the ultimate ground or end of existence." [3] If Physics is incompetent to reach any conclusion in this regard, then it is incompetent to find arguments against the teaching of Christianity.

---

[1] Report of the 41st Meeting of the British Association for the Advancement of Science, held at Edinburgh in August 1871, Transactions of the sections: Mathematics and Physics. Address by Professor P. G. Tait, London 1872, 7.

[2] Ib. 6.

[3] Allgemeine Zeitung 1885, Nr. 80, Beil. p. 1179.

V. CHEMISTRY.

The modern science of Chemistry is, comparatively speaking, of very recent growth. It begins with Lavoisier († 1794) who was the first to lay proper stress on accurate measuring and weighing, and whose analysis of the process of combustion gave the first insight into the nature of chemical union.

A theory of fundamental importance is that which conceives the elements as composed of atoms. This atomic theory was established by Dalton († 1844). The two laws on which it rests, that of gravity and that of multiple proportions received their full experimental proof in the innumerable analyses and calculations of Berzelius († 1848)[1].

Of the various theories of the nature of chemical combination the so-called dualistic hypothesis of Berzelius held the field during the first half of the 19th century. It has given way however to the substitution-theory of the French chemist Dumas († 1884).

Organic chemistry is also practically a creation of the 19th century. Amongst the most brilliant pioneers of the science were Dumas, Chevreul († 1889), and Liebig († 1873).

We do not propose to give here even the most cursory sketch of the history of Chemistry in the last

[1] We can get no precise information about the discoverer of the fundamental law named after Avogadro († July 9th 1856). However an Obituary Notice which appeared in the Gazzetta Piemontese, the official organ of the Government of Sardinia, nine days after his death, says he was "religioso senza intolleranza dotto senza pedanteria" etc. Alfonso Cossa, Il conte Amedeo Avogadro di Quaregna, Milano 1898, 5.

century: we merely adduce the names of a few of the most brilliant workers in this province, and shall proceed to inquire what they had to say as to the philosophical significance of their discoveries. The witness of Berzelius, Liebig and Dumas would of itself be ample; for if these great intellects were unable to discern any hostility between science and religion, why should we pay any heed to the clamour of lesser men? We shall not however confine ourselves to the names cited.

Antoine Laurent Lavoisier does not fall within the scope of this book, inasmuch as he died under the guillotine of the Revolution before the beginning of the 19th century. We content ourselves with remarking that he died in the Christian faith[1]. Dalton's religious sincerity was never a matter of doubt[2]. And, as for Berzelius, his belief in God and his dislike for atheistical systems find expression in his great treatise.

"An incomprehensible force, foreign to those of dead matter, has introduced the principle (of life) into the inorganic world. This has been effected, not by chance, but with the striking variety and supreme wisdom of a plan designed to produce definite results, and to maintain an unbroken succession of transient individuals which are born one from another, and which at their death bequeath their

[1] Ce grand nom de Lavoisier doit être particulièrement rappelé dans notre Société, car l'illustre chimiste était resté un croyant. C'est ce qui ressort de tous les documents retrouvés sur sa vie dans ces dernières anées, et particulièrement du témoignage, certes non suspect, de Grimaux, qui avait eu entre les mains beaucoup de papiers de ce grand homme (M. G. Lemoine, Revue des questions scientifiques L 78—79).

[2] Chez Dalton le caractère de l'homme égalait la supériorité des lumières: il fut un modèle de vertus sans ostentation, et de religion sans fanatisme (Nouv. biographie générale XII, Paris 1866, 830).

decomposed constituents to the formation of new organisms. Every process of organic nature proclaims a wise purpose, and bears the stamp of a guiding mind; and man, comparing the calculations he makes to attain certain ends with those which he finds in organic nature, has been led to regard his faculty of thought and calculation as a reflection of the Being to whom he owes his existence. And yet it has happened more than once that a philosophy, proud all the while of its own profundity, has maintained that all this was the work of chance, and that such organisms only held their ground as had accidentally acquired the power of self-preservation and reproduction. But the advocates of such systems do not perceive that the element in nature which they call 'chance' is a thing physically impossible. Everything that exists springs from a cause, an operative force, this latter tending (like desire) to break into activity and secure for itself satisfaction so as to arrive in the end at a state of untroubled repose, a process which in no degree corresponds to our idea of 'chance'. It will always be more honourable for man to admire the wisdom, which he cannot rival, than to puff himself up with philosophical arrogance, and attempt with his paltry reasonings to penetrate mysteries which will probably remain for ever beyond the scope of human reason." [1]

---

[1] Tout ce qui tient à la nature organique annonce un but sage et se distingue comme production d'un entendement supérieur; et l'homme, en comparant les calculs qu'il fait, pour atteindre un certain but, avec ceux qu'il trouve dans la composition de la nature organique, a été conduit à regarder sa puissance de penser et de calculer comme une image de cet être à qui il doit son existence . . . (Traité de Chimie par J. J. Berzelius, traduit par M. Esslinger, V, Bruxelles 1833, 2e partie, Chimie organique, 3—4). That Berzelius was "ein Mann von umfassender Bildung und von liebenswurdigstem Charakter" is testified e. g. by K. C. v. Leonhard, Aus unserer Zeit in meinem Leben II, Stuttgart 1856, 130, G. H. Rose, who has been already quoted, and others. Cf. G. W. A. Kahlbaum, Monogr. a. d. Gesch. der Chemie VII, Leipzig 1903 (Auto-biographical Notices of Berzelius).

Among the most eminent predecessors of Berzelius are the German Klaproth († 1817), the discoverer of uranium, and the French Louis Nicolas Vauquelin († 1829) to whom chemistry owes its first knowledge of chromium and glucinium. Klaproth is characterised by Von Leonhard, on the authority of his friends, as a "profoundly religious man"[1]. Vauquelin died a faithful Catholic, striken down during a visit to his native place[2].

There presented himself one day to Vauquelin a youth, some sixteen years of age, of countrified aspect and an accent far from Parisian. He came to beg the chemist to engage him as his servant asking no salary save to be present at his laboratory experiments. The old savant was far from rich, and, being loth to add a fresh burden to the 20 francs a month which he spent on his laboratory, refused the lad's request. Vauquelin's sister however interposed; he was a promising boy, she said, and would not, like the other assistants, "let the pots boil over". Vauquelin at last gave way, and the young peasant not only took excellent care of the "pots", but grounded himself profoundly in Chemistry, and came in time to be a famous teacher and discoverer. In 1804 he succeeded Vauquelin at the Collège de France, and in 1810 he was elected to the Academy of Sciences. He celebrated his election by a visit to his mother, to whom he brought an edition of Thomas à Kempis in the large print which her old eyes had

[1] Aus unserer Zeit in meinem Leben I, Stuttgart 1854, 595.

[2] Étant allé passer quelque temps dans son pays, il a été surpris par la maladie au château de M. Duhamel, maire du lieu. Il a rendu hommage à la religion en recourant aux sacrements et aux prières de l'église etc. (Ami de la religion et du roi LXII, Paris 1830, 79).

long desired. He rose higher, becoming in 1814 a Knight, in 1842 Grand Officer of the Legion of Honour, in 1825 Baron, in 1827 Deputy, and in 1832 a Peer of France; in 1861 a statue was erected to him at Sens, and in 1865 the people of his native place La Louptière asked and obtained permission to call their town La Louptière-Thenard in his honour. For the peasant lad was no other than Louis Jacques Thenard († 1857), discoverer of the superoxide of hydrogen, of the blue dye called after him, and now so widely used in the manufacture of porcelain, and of many other chemical facts. He contributed to the progress of Chemistry not only as a discoverer but also as a teacher, and his text-book, although of such an immense range, reached ten editions in six years[1]. He could without any exaggeration boast that during his thirty years at the Sorbonne, the College of France, and the Polytechnic School, 40000 students had passed through his hands. In matters of education he was among the first authorities of his day, a veritable "Marshal of Science"[2].

Thenard was an unwavering Catholic, loyal and punctilious all through life in the discharge of his religious duties. Some extracts from the funeral sermon preached over him by the rector of St. Sulpice may aptly be quoted[3]:

"Religion and gratitude alike constrain me to say that there was in Baron Thenard something greater still than that sublime intellect and boundless knowledge which shed such lustre on the Academy. There was a heart, profoundly

---

[1] P. M. Flourens, Recueil des éloges historiques III, Paris 1862, 201—248.

[2] R. Vallery-Radot, La vie de Pasteur, Paris 1901, 51.

[3] Ami de la religion CLXXVI, Paris 1857, 747 f.

Christian, armed alike against that disregard of God and eternity . . . against that vague religiosity which is in essence a mere chimera, and against the allurement of fame which, as he said, had once held him captive but now showed itself to his disillusioned mind as a vain and baseless dream. . . . He submitted his intellect to the dogmas of the Church, as he submitted his will to her precepts; every Sunday he came here, a simple unit of the congregation, and on all our great feasts he reverently communicated. . . . Never did I make an appeal to him on behalf of the poor and miserable but he responded, graciously and generously; many a time, indeed, he did not wait for my appeal, his delicacy anticipated it. . . . Never did a Sister of St. Vincent de Paul, a Sister of Charity knock at his door in vain. . . . Many were the poor whom he secretly succoured. . . . In losing Baron Thenard, I say once again, I have lost one of the best friends of my poor."

In a still fuller sense than inorganic, organic chemistry is a creation of the 19th century, and owes to it the lucid and systematic form in which it at present exists. This is how one of the pioneers describes the colonisation of this rich province:

"Into this still virgin territory, Liebig and I plunged with the greatest ardour. . . . To travel and preserve communication across these unexplored tracts we had neither compass nor guides, methods nor laws. We had been led to form ideas and to fix on doctrines which were absolutely individual to us, and we defended them with warmth and passion but without any trace of envy or jealousy. The discoveries, yet to be made, seemed to us inexhaustible, and the harvest ample for both. The task on which we were both engaged was the establishment of central stations, the opening up of roads; and I am sure that Liebig experienced as much pleasure in reading my writings as I experienced in reading his."

It was Jean Baptiste André Dumas († 1884) who, in his old age, spoke thus of the deeds of his youth[1]. Had he the right to use such language? An answer may be gather from the somewhat florid exordium to the memorial speech on Dumas by A. W. Von Hoffmann, the famous Berlin chemist[2].

Having dealt with Dumas' original researches, confined as they were to a single department of science, he continues:

"We turn however with even greater interest to the study of the man himself who, from the height to which his mastery of so vast an area of science elevated him, made a survey of so many fields of human effort. And if this man, who had scaled the heights of knowledge, retained in his heart a warm enthusiasm for the welfare of his countrymen; if he did not disdain the business of everyday life, but laid his time and strength and rich experience at the service of the common weal, this can but increase our admiration for him. . . .

"Such was Dumas. . . . Beginning at pharmacy he was luckily drawn to physiological research, and his work, done in this department even during his student days, is a model of accuracy and acuteness. But he soon turned to Chemistry, enriching it with the discovery of laws of fundamental importance, of wonderful methods of research which to-day are practised in every laboratory, and opening up paths which have never been forsaken. For more than thirty years he was the leader of French Chemistry.

"This multifarious activity in science did not however prevent him from filling an important rôle in politics and administration. Successively deputy in the Legislative Chamber, Minister of Agriculture and Commerce, Senator, President of the Municipal Council of Paris, and Master of the Mint,

---

[1] Discours et Éloges Académiques I, Paris 1885, 186 f. The complete absence of envy, of which Dumas speaks, did not prevent him from entering energetically into a competition with Liebig.

[2] A. W. v. Hofmann, Zur Erinnerung an vorangegangene Freunde. Gesammelte Gedächtnisreden II, Braunschweig 1889, 209—397.

he served his country in many directions. He was a member of the Institute, and afterwards Permanent Secretary, he was also a member of the French Academy, and in these positions he kept pace for more than half a century with every development of science, and published a mass of the most varied and valuable original works such as few of his contemporaries could rival." [1]

"The name of Dumas", concludes Von Hoffmann, "is written imperishably in the annals of science", and for Dumas as a man, he has praise no less ardent:

"If you review in imagination the whole of his career you will find in every word and work of the man, whether in the field of science, in his official positions, or in his everyday intercourse with the world, tokens of a pure and noble character. No one could have brought to the service of his fellows a more enlightened benevolence, a greater faculty of self-sacrifice; no one could, while conscious of his own genius, have given readier recognition to the achievements of others; no one could have been more scrupulously fair with tongue and pen towards even his bitterest opponents. It is easy to understand how a man in whom so fine an intellect was joined with so fine a character, attracted the respect and confidence of his countrymen, the loyal affection of his friends, the enthusiastic veneration of his pupils. These feelings found expression in many forms and fashions. . . ." [2]

A student of Dumas', the great Pasteur, writes:

"I had just come up from the remotest corner of my province, and I was hearing him for the first time. He was then 43 years old; I was a student at the École Normale, and we attended his lectures at the Sorbonne. Long before his arrival the lecture room was full; the galleries were packed with crowds of students, and late comers were able to find room nowhere except on the stairs. At the stroke of the bell he entered and was greeted with a storm of ap-

[1] v. Hofmann, Zur Erinnerung etc. 210—211.

[2] Ib. 390—391.

plause — such a welcome as only youth can give." "The greatness of his discoveries, his genius for original interpretation and large generalization, in short that combination of qualities which proclaim a master, justified us in setting his name, as we did set it, beside that of Lavoisier. It was the opinion of the pupils of the Sorbonne; it will be the verdict of history." [1]

There is no doubt about the importance of the name; what we have to determine here is the attitude towards religion and philosophy of this great leader of Chemistry and Physiology, this "first chemist of France" as Von Hoffmann calls him. The answer can be given in a very few words: Dumas was a loyal Catholic [2]. Whether he possessed the piety of an Ampère we do not know, and we may well doubt. But he remained loyal to the faith; and in many public utterances defended Christianity and condemned materialism.

At his reception into the Academy on June 1st 1876 he had to deliver a discourse on his predecessor, Guizot. He said amongst other things:

"Guizot defended Christianity against an intellectual and militant scepticism; to others of this august body, who will certainly not fail in their mission, he left it to defend the personality of the human soul against the rising tide of a purely naturalistic philosophy. The materialism of Empe-

[1] Discourse of 10. December on the Reception of J. Bertrand into the French Academy (printed in the Bibliographie cath. LXXIII [1886] 83 84). Cf. Bertrand ib. LXXII (1885) 513, also J. Bertrand, Éloges académiques, Paris 1890, 1 ff 19 ff.

[2] M. Dumas était catholique (it had been given out that he was a Calvinist). Il a reçu les derniers sacrements en parfaite connaissance de cause, et ses funérailles ont été religieuses (Tison in Revue du monde cath. LXXVIII, Paris 1884, 445. Cf. Cosmos-les-Mondes, janv.-avr. 1884, 610).

docles had, despite the brilliant verse of Lucretius, lost its beauty under the scrutiny of Christian Ethics; now after 2000 years it returns, and seeks to renew itself by a wholly fallacious reading of the discoveries of modern science. As the body comes into being through the transformation of matter, so, say our new materialists, do life and consciousness arise through the transformation of natural forces. And as at death the body returns to the earth from which it sprang, so do life and consciousness fall back into the ocean of invisible, atomic vibrations which fills and governs the universe. An entrance into life, devoid of all rights, a life devoid of goal; a death devoid of hope — this is the philosophy proposed to us. But although a few rare minds may find peace in it, and may be upheld in their journey through life by curiosity and the joy of solving difficulties, it will never content the generality of mankind.

"Advancing through victory and defeat, through triumph and disappointment, helped on by marvellous virtues and hampered by great vices, Christian Europe has made current for sixteen centuries past what was before its advent recognised in no age and no country, the right of all men to justice, sympathy, and freedom. That is what Guizot would have us remember. And assuredly we should not forget it. Under the new dispensation, right no longer bows before might; justice takes all nationalities under its sceptre; fraternal affection is not limited by the colour of men's skins; freedom raises to their feet the most oppressed races and castes; the humblest finds a shield of defence in his divine origin, and the most powerful recognises that he is answerable before the eternal tribunal. The religion, the morality, the civilisation of Europe rest on this as a foundation, on the right of all men to justice, sympathy, and freedom. The formulation of this right is the work of Christianity; those who to-day exercise it will defend it at any cost, those who are shut out from it, will by the progress of true political ideas, one day acquire it. And the passing fever of scientific thought, which, in the throes of a new birth, assails these mighty doctrines without being able to find a substitute for them, will diminish and disappear.

"In a moment of enthusiasm Virgil cried out — Virgil whose mild temper led him to an eclecticism in which all systems were charitably construed and in part accepted:

Felix qui potuit rerum cognoscere causas . . .

'Happy was he who knew the causes of things, and trod underfoot the empty terrors of inexorable fate. Happy is he also who knows the gods.' The poet of the Georgics does not decide between the materialism of Lucretius and belief in the gods of Olympus; he leaves the question in suspense. To-day science has gone deeper, and knows at least that she is ignorant of the first cause of things. Nor does it seem so far that it is part of her mission to reveal the gods or to weigh the human soul in her clumsy balance, or that she possesses the power to guarantee to men their right to justice, sympathy, and freedom." [1]

Dumas often spoke in this strain. Thus e. g. in his speech on Bérard:

"The immortal, immaterial, free soul of man; the incalculable forces of which it disposes; the organised material elements which its breath moulds and governs; the mineral elements which it absorbs into the bodily fibres; these are the four chief aspects under which life presents itself to study, the four great problems set us by death."

---

[1] M. Guizot a défendu le christianisme contre un scepticisme spirituel et frondeur; il a laissé à d'autres parmi vous, qui ne failliront pas à la tâche, le soin de défendre la personnalité de l'âme humaine contre le flot grossissant de la philosophie de la nature. . . . La religion, la morale, la civilisation de l'Europe reposent sur cette base ferme du droit de tous les hommes à la justice, à la sympathie, à la liberté, œuvre du christianisme. . . . Aujourd'hui la science humaine, plus avancée, sait du moins qu'elle ignore le principe des choses, et il ne semble pas jusqu'ici qu'elle ait reçu mission de révéler des dieux ou de peser l'âme humaine à sa grossière balance, ni qu'elle ait reçu pouvoir de garantir aux peuples leurs droits à la justice, à la sympathie et à la liberté (J.-B. Dumas, Discours I, Paris 1885, XXXV—XXXVIII).

"The Church has set and solved the last of them in that sublime and terrible sentence which she inscribes on our foreheads every year when, signing us with ashes for a symbol, she says: Memento quia pulvis es et in pulverem reverteris." [1]

In his memorial speech on Faraday, May 18th 1868, Dumas says:

"God established all things according to number, measure, and weight. These words from the Book of Wisdom date back more than two thousand years, and Chemistry finds in them and will always find a faithful expression of the harmonies it observes in the number of particles contained in bodies, in their volume and their weight." [2]

A passage may also be quoted from his speech at the reception of Taine into the Academy:

"Philosophy, as we all know, runs easily into extremes. To-day an attempt is made to exhibit thought as a mere secretion of the brain, a chemical product. But chemistry knows its limits, and it is not true chemistry that will seek to transgress these limits. There was a time when philosophy was dominated by a mysticism which denied that the mind has any sort of connection with the organism in which it manifests itself.

"That was an exaggeration, and your studies have established the function and rôle alike of the directive intellect, and of the body which serves as its instrument without rudely

---

[1] L'église a posé et résolu le dernier d'entre eux dans cette phrase terrible et sublime qu'elle inscrit sur nos fronts, chaque année, quand elle y dépose une cendre symbolique, et qu'elle répète le "Memento quia pulvis es et in pulverem reverteris" (Dumas, Discours I 33).

[2] Dieu a tout fait avec nombre, mesure et poids. Ces paroles du livre de la Sagesse datent de deux mille ans, et les chimistes y trouvent toujours l'expression fidèle des harmonies observées de nos jours, dans le nombre des particules qui composent les corps, dans leur volume et dans leur poids (ib. 82).

separating the two. The conclusions to which you have been led by a long and scientific study of human personality, at the end of which the source of it and that of the universe disclose themselves, differ only very slightly from those of the humblest, from those who find within themselves the conception of the human soul and of God and accept them as axioms which cannot be proved, and which do not stand in need of proof. Modest disciples of the faith of the unlettered (foi de charbonnier), they climb up to heaven perpendicularly, as one of our old geometers says, while the doctors are busy disputing, and is it not they who are right? Do not these two axiomatic ideas of theirs contain, as necessary implications, the ideas of moral freedom, duty, justice, and responsibility, and what egoistic system is able to create and justify such ideas? Man is made for society, and certain philosophers, viewing him as a mere animal, have called him by way of compliment the tool-making animal; but Goethe has described him as a being capable of religion. And does he not in fact seem to have been created for the apprehension of what we call, in the widest sense, the Divine?

"If the faces of our first ancestors were turned towards the heavens — the secret depths of which were yet unknown — as towards a lost fatherland, will not the last of our children lift their eyes, too, to the starry firmament as to a fatherland found again?" [1]

---

[1] . . . Vos conclusions, résultat d'une longue investigation scientifique de la personnalité humaine, au terme de laquelle apparaissent sa cause et la cause de l'Univers, diffèrent peu de celles des plus humbles créatures, trouvant sans étude au fond de leur cœur la notion de l'âme et celle de Dieu, comme des axiomes qui ne sont pas susceptibles de démonstration et qui n'en ont pas besoin. Ces modestes disciples de la foi du charbonnier, cherchant à gagner le paradis par voie perpendiculaire, pendant que les docteurs disputent, comme le disait un de nos anciens géomètres, n'ont-ils pas raison? Les deux axiomes, auxquels ils confient, n'entraînent-ils pas avec eux cette notion de la liberté morale, du devoir, de la justice et de la responsabilité, qu'on n'a jamais pu faire sortir des théories

At the funeral of Dumas, Count D'Haussonville said:

"It was Dumas himself who, speaking of his own works, declared: 'Above the sphere of the phenomena which we investigate, and about which we have so much to learn, there is a higher sphere which is beyond the reach of our methods. We are beginning to understand the life of the body; the life of the soul is in another order.' Many a time did he affirm his religious belief; he now contemplates, face to face, that reality to which he clung with such steadfast hope."[1]

Although not so distinguished as Dumas, Théophile Juste Pelouze († 1866) is well known in the history of Chemistry; his reputation is founded on analyses of various

---

fondées sur l'égoisme? Fait pour vivre en société, l'homme, dont on se plaît à faire un animal, qu'on croit complimenter en l'appelant animal inventeur d'outils . . ., ne semble-t-il pas créé, en effet, pour avoir le sentiment du divin pris dans son sens le plus large? Si la face de nos premiers ancêtres s'est tournée vers le firmament, dont ils ignoraient encore les profondeurs, comme vers une patrie perdue, les derniers de nos fils, après en avoir sondé les mystères accessibles, n'élèveront-ils pas, à leur tour, le front vers le ciel étoilé, comme vers un patrie retrouvée? (Dumas, Discours II 129 f.) The "old Mathematician" quoted is Jacques Ozanam († 1717), who referring to the theological disputes of his time said: "qu'il appartient aux docteurs de Sorbonne de disputer, au Pape de prononcer, et aux mathématiciens d'aller en paradis en ligne perpendiculaire". The definition: "Homo est animal inerme sed instrumentificum", is ascribed to Franklin. Cf. Thom. Aq., S. th. 1, q. 76, a. 5 ad 4, where the same thought is found.

[1] C'est lui-même qui, parlant de ses propres travaux, disait: "Au dessus de la sphère des phénomènes que nous étudions et où nous avons tant de découvertes à poursuivre, il y a une sphère supérieure que nos méthodes ne peuvent atteindre. Nous commençons à comprendre la vie des corps; la vie de l'âme est d'un autre ordre" (Comptes rendus XCVIII, Paris 1884, 935). Maintes fois, vous avez affirmé vos convictions religieuses: vous contemplez maintenant face à face les réalités que vous avez espérées si fermement (ib. 944).

organic combinations and a comprehensive text-book of his science. He died, as his friend, Abbé Moigno, testifies, a "Christian and edifying death"[1]. Pierre Joseph Pelletier († 1842) also devoted himself to Organic Chemistry, and by his discovery of quinine rendered an invaluable service to medicine. He was, Cauchy tells us, a man thoroughly Christian in his convictions and conceptions of life.

Dumas described as his great fellow-worker and rival Justus Von Liebig († 1873), and in Germany there is certainly no name more widely known and honoured. His strength lay not so much in pure science and speculation as in the practical application of scientific discoveries; he effected great improvements in certain articles of food, and helped to lay the foundations of a rational system of agriculture.

His efforts in this latter direction were for a long time unsuccessful. He had studied the various field-plants, and ascertained the food of which they stood in need; and had analysed portions of the soil, and determined what elements it was necessary to add to it in the form of manures in order to furnish the various crops with the requisite nourishment. There remained one difficulty. The salts to be introduced into the soil were highly soluble, and consequently liable to be washed away by the rain. Liebig bent his mind to the problem of combining these salts into compounds, more difficult of solution; his efforts were successful, the manures were manufactured after his formulae and adapted to the soil. They were wholly useless, and the inventor gained nothing but the contempt of practical farmers. The disappointment was all the sorer to Liebig inasmuch as he was for a long time unable to determine the cause. But

[1] Les Mondes XIV, Paris 1867, 261. Cf. 222.

he hit on it at last, and it became plain to him that his attempt to make the salts in the manure insoluble had frustrated everything. He had been anticipated by nature which had endowed the soil with a remarkable power of retaining undissolved the nutritive materials. These cannot be washed away by the rain; but the roots of the plants extract them from the soil. Let us record what Liebig himself had to say regarding his mistake, and the anticipating wisdom of the Creator. For, as is said by his biographer in the Encyclopedia of German Biography[1], "Liebig's scientific standpoint was indeed very far from that of materialism; he even admitted, like his predecessors in physiology, the operation of vital force, and was a zealous deist and a thorough believer."

"What gave me such real and persistent trouble was my inability to understand why the manures worked so slowly; in thousands of cases which I observed, my ingredients worked admirably when alone, but when I brought them together they did not work.

"At last I discovered three years ago, after a fresh and searching examination of all the facts, the cause. I had been criminally forgetful of the wisdom of the Creator, and had received my due punishment; I was attempting to improve His work, and in my blindness I imagined that there was a link missing from the marvellous chain of laws which preserve life on the surface of the earth, and this link I sought to make good — weak and impotent worm that I am. It was already provided for, and in such a wonderful fashion that the human mind could hardly imagine the possibility of such a law, howsoever the facts pointed to its existence. For facts are dumb, or at least they speak to deaf ears when they tell against our preconceived ideas! So it was

[1] XVIII, Leipzig 1883, 603. The "indeed" ("zwar") in the passage quoted has no logical justification in this connection.

with me. I thought it necessary to make the alkalies insoluble lest they should be washed away by the rain! I did not know then that, as far as solution goes, the earth itself holds them fast, for the law to which my study of soil had led me is: 'It is in the outer crust of the earth, and under the influence of the sun that organic life develops.' The great Architect has endowed the particles of this crust with the property of assimilating and holding fast all those elements which are necessary to the life of plants, as a magnet attracts and holds fast pieces of iron; with this law the Creator conjoined another, to the effect that the plant-bearing soil is an immense purifying apparatus for the water, and removes from it all substances injurious to man and beast, all products of the corruption and decomposition of the departed generations of plants and animals." [1]

With the noteworthy relation here described we must associate another contrivance no less wonderful.

Liebig had laid it down as the basis of practical agriculture "that the air and the rain contribute every year more nitrogenous food to the plants and the soil than the plants need for their complete development". The fact is beyond dispute, but "it became puzzling and inexplicable from the moment that we came to know that the soil holds fast the products of decomposition, among which ammonia finds a place, and does not give off any of them through evaporation. No other source was known, from which ammonia could be derived except decomposition; there was no recorded fact to suggest that it was possible for the nitrogen of the atmosphere to assume a form in which it could supply nutriment to plants". The origin of the ammonia to be found in the soil remained quite unknown.

"I regard it then as a piece of great good fortune to have come to know of Schönbein's latest discoveries which explain this riddle, and put the mind in possession of a

[1] J. v. Liebig, Die Chemie in ihrer Anwendung auf Agrikultur und Physiologie. Erster Teil: Der chemische Prozeß der Ernährung der Vegetabilien [8], Braunschweig 1865, Einleitung 69 f.

new, and till then, inconceivable wonder. No chemist could ever have been led by the facts as then known to suppose that it was possible for the nitrogen of the atmosphere to pass over into nitrate or nitrite of ammonia; now the simplest experiment shows that every light, burning in the air, transforms a certain amount of its nitrogen into nitrite of ammonia, and that every process of rotting is a source both of nitric acid and of ammonia, and that the mere evaporation of water is enough to produce both classes of plant food. The magnitude of the fact will be appreciated if we bear in mind that the burning of a pound of coal or wood not only restores to the atmosphere the elements necessary to reconstitute this pound of wood, or in certain circumstances this pound of coal, but that the process of combustion also transforms a certain quantity of atmospheric nitrogen into a food indispensable for the production of bread and meat!

"Truly he alone recognises the power and wisdom of the Creator who tries to follow out His thought in the great book of nature, and everything else that men know or say of him seems in comparison but an empty and idle speech." [1]

In 1856 Liebig delivered a public lecture "On Inorganic Nature and Organic Life" [2], in which he broke a lance with those who attempt to exhibit physical science as the stay and support of materialism. It is not, he said, the true savants and discoverers who hold up materialism as the necessary conclusion of their researches. "Such assertions come from the dilettantes, who, fresh from a stroll along the outer fringe of science, take it upon themselves to inform the ignorant and credulous masses how the world and how life came into existence and how thoroughly man has unveiled

[1] J. v. Liebig, Die Chemie 71—73.

[2] Allgemeine Zeitung, Augsburg 1856, Nr. 24 25, p. 369 ff; Wiener Kirchenzeitung 1856, 100 f 106 f.

the highest mysteries; and these same ignorant and credulous masses believe them and not the real scientists, just as they believed in the tables that walked, talked, and wrote, and ascribed a special power to old wood."

Of all the centenary feasts of the century, that which took place on August 31st 1886 at Paris was among the most remarkable. The hero of it, the great chemist Michel Eugène Chevreul (1786—1889), attended in person, and despite his great age he continued to enjoy such excellent health that he was able to sit out twenty-four eulogies in prose, and two in verse without being any the worse for it! His popularity was so great as to make the affair practically a national festival; every political party sent its chiefs; the first congratulatory message was presented by the director of the Chinese Education Commission on behalf of the mandarins, and every country in Europe was represented.

Chevreul had won his reputation mainly by his analyses of fatty substances, and the importance of his work for industry and commerce may be gathered from two facts. He made possible the present wholesale production of soap, and he replaced the filthy tallow-candle of former days, the wick of which had to be continually snuffed, by our present stearine candle. But Chevreul's services were not limited to practical and utilitarian objects; in Theoretical Chemistry also he was a pioneer of the first importance.

"It is not without difficulty", wrote the Berlin Academy to him on his hundredth birthday [1], "that we carry our imagination back to the time when, an almost isolated pioneer,

[1] Sitzungsberichte 1886, 949—954.

with no other ally save courage and knowledge, you struck into the unknown province of Organic Chemistry, and sought and found paths through its immensity. . . . Your first care was turned to the fuller development of elemental analysis. Equipped with this powerful weapon, so greatly improved by your efforts, you began your memorable study of fatty bodies of animal origin. . . . It is with the keenest interest that we still read this classical work, uncertain whether to admire more warmly the steady perseverance which established one by one this endless series of facts, or the insight which, gathering them all under one binding idea, reduced them to a scientific whole."

Many discoveries of other famous chemists are spoken of in the Berlin Address as direct results of Chevreul's.

"They are", runs the document, "fruits of the tree planted by you. Nor is it a mere accident that France was the scene and the author of these brilliant achievements; her scientists had you before their eyes as a great exemplar. Our Academy, on this your day of honour, has felt impelled to call up in review your scientific career; but we have been able merely to glance at a few of its most brilliant moments. To form an adequate idea of your rich and crowded life it would be necessary to trace the stream of your creative activity along its whole course, as it flowed, refreshing and fruitful, through every province of Chemistry and the neighbouring sciences; it would be necessary to recapitulate the innumerable investigations by which you determined the nature of various minerals and salts, and the composition of countless organic substances; it would be necessary to read through your chemico-physiological works . . . and your many contributions to the science of public health, it would be necessary to follow your expeditions into the borderland between Chemistry and Physics, and gain from them an insight into the laws of the contrast of colours and the systematic determination and naming of colours. . . . It would be necessary to call back the days when a cloud of fantastic delusions, whirled along by fashion, threatened to enwrap the minds of men but was quickly dissipated when you, holding up the book of history in your hand, showed your contemporaries the errors of the present in the mirrors of the past[1]. With such a picture of your achievements in his mind, the student of your career would set you in the first rank of those who have spread the fame of France in science to the most distant quarters of the universe."

The admiration and respect of Chevreul, conveyed in these words and echoed on all sides, was manifested anew three years later when on April 13th 1889, his funeral took place. It was a State ceremony at the cost of the State. Followed by innumerable representatives of academies and learned societies it proceeded under military escort to Notre Dame, the portico and interior of which were draped in black. Archbishop Richard, himself, conducted the funeral service[2].

A savant who laboured beyond the years of man in the service of science has certainly a right to be heard when he speaks of the philosophico-religious bearings of modern discoveries. Happily Chevreul has spoken his mind out expressly on the question of materialism.

"In an age when we hear it asserted more loudly than ever that modern science leads to materialism, I have asked myself whether a man who has lived in the midst of books, and in his chemical laboratory, and has devoted his days to the pursuit of truth, is not in duty bound to raise a protest against such assertions, diametrically opposed as they are to true science. That is the motive which impels me to declare that I have never been either a materialist or a sceptic, and to state my reasons.

---

[1] Refers to Chevreul's: De la baguette divinatoire, du pendule dit explorateur et des tables tournantes, au point de vue de l'histoire, de la critique et de la méthode expérimentale, Paris 1854.

[2] Cf. for example Allgemeine Zeitung, München 1889, 1573 1586. Ib. (1886) for the birthday celebrations 3557 3573 3605.

"My first conviction is that of the existence, outside myself, of matter. Of this I have full certainty, and have therefore never been a sceptic.

"My second conviction is that of the existence of a Divine Being, creator of a double harmony, the harmony which governs the inanimate world and which is revealed by the science of Celestial Mechanics, and that of molecular phenomena, and the harmony which governs the organic living world.

"I have therefore never been a materialist, during any portion of my life, my mind having never been able to regard this double harmony as the product of chance. . . ."

Chevreul develops his thought in greater detail. The "harmony of the heavens" and the "harmony of molecular changes" convince him of the existence of objective reality; for it is absurd to regard the recurrent phenomena of which Astronomy and Chemistry take cognizance as processes going forward merely in the observing subject. As to the "harmony of organic life" he expresses himself as follows:

"The first fact that strikes me in the history of organic life is the transmission by living beings to their descendants of their specific form. Monuments, hundreds of years older than our Christian era, furnish us with pictures of many of these forms and show that they were precisely what they are now, and that in organ and function they have not changed. . . .

"If we now turn from plants and animals to man, what profound differences we find! Instinct is with him limited to the first few years of life; as he grows up his rational faculties develop, and he alone is capable of perfection. The young absorb and make use of the knowledge won by their parents, enlarge it in their own time, and transmit it to their successors. Man, I repeat, is alone among living beings perfectible; thanks to his intellectual faculties which are so superior to those of even the best organised brute, thanks to the consciousness which he possesses of his own existence, his own ego, thanks to the moral sense by which he distinguishes right from wrong, thanks above all to his faculty of free-will.

"I recapitulate what I have been saying.

"The continuance of species in time and space; the uniformity of organisms, as to structure and function, among the individual members of each species; the perpetuation of the wonderful instinctive faculties of animals, faculties which faithfully direct and never deceive them — these cannot be the products of chance, and still less can the existence of man be a product of chance.

"But when we contemplate the wisdom and foresight which have presided over the constitution of the world, and are made manifest in the mechanics of the heavens, in molecular action, in the mutual dependence of the two organic kingdoms, in the working of animal instinct, are we not led to ask ourselves whether, at certain epochs of human society, the marvellous spectacle of the non-living world and of the living world outside man should not be to us less an incentive to pride than a humiliating contrast to what I will not describe in detail: namely that societies of the only full-facultied being on earth, endowed with free-will, reason and moral perception, should live in a state of perpetual war with one another, and that this should continue from the lowest grade of savagery up to the highest grade of civilization, so that the greatest enemy of man is man? How charged with bitter derision is, then, the teaching of that Positivist school which employs the name of Humanity in the sense in which the older systems employed that of Divinity!" [1]

[1] . . . Tel est le motif pour lequel, en disant qu'il n'a jamais été ni sceptique ni matérialiste, il en expose les raisons.

La première opinion concerne la certitude que j'ai de l'existence de la matière hors de moi-même.

Je n'ai donc jamais été sceptique.

La seconde est une conviction de l'existence d'un être divin, créateur d'une double harmonie: l'harmonie qui régit le monde inanimé et que révèlent d'abord la science de la Mécanique céleste

Chevreul's jubilee had a somewhat remarkable epilogue. The claims of religion to be represented at it had been totally ignored by the promoters, and the purely secular character of the celebration had been dwelt on by a certain section of the press as a proof that Chevreul was an unbeliever.

The allegation was warmly contested by the friends of the savant. It was, said an article in the "Univers", a direct contradiction of Chevreul's declared convictions. In the course of the discussion an interesting incident

---

et la science des phénomènes moléculaires, puis l'harmonie qui régit le monde organisé vivant.

Je n'ai donc jamais été matérialiste, à aucune époque de ma vie, mon esprit n'ayant pu concevoir que cette double harmonie ainsi que la pensée humaine ait été le produit du hasard. . . .

L'homme, je le répète, est donc perfectible, et l'est seul parmi les êtres vivants, grâce à ses facultés intellectuelles, si supérieures à celles de la brute la mieux organisée, grâce à la conscience qu'il a de son existence propre, de son moi, enfin grâce au sens moral d'après lequel il discerne le bien du mal, grâce enfin à son libre arbitre.

Je me résume:

La perpétuité des espèces dans l'espace et le temps;

La conservation des organes quant à leur structure et à leurs fonctions dans les individus de chaque espèce;

La perpétuité des admirables facultés instinctives des brutes, facultés qui les dirigent toujours, sans les tromper jamais;

Ne peuvent être le produit du hasard, pas plus que l'existence de l'homme.

Mais en voyant cette sagesse prévoyante qui a présidé à la constitution du monde, sagesse que proclament la Mécanique céleste, les actions moléculaires, la dépendance mutuelle des deux règnes organiques, les animaux et leurs instincts . . . et pourtant par une amère dérision, certaines bouches disent humanité, comme d'autres disent divinité (Comptes rendus LXXIX, Paris 1874, 631 ff).

was recalled. Three or four years before, Chevreul, while on a trip in Dourdan, had missed his train; and the local priest, to whom he had introduced himself, wrote to say that the great chemist had spent the time of his enforced wait, in the Catholic Church, and had recited the Rosary before the Virgin's Altar[1].

The outcome of the controversy was that Chevreul himself made public declaration of his attitude towards religion. In a letter to the Comte de Montravel who had defended him in the *Salut Public* he proclaimed his adherence to the faith. "I am no more than a scientist; and those who know me, know that, born a Catholic and of Christian parents, I live and wish to die a Catholic."[2]

Berzelius, Dumas, Liebig, Chevreul will remain for ever the most brilliant names in the Chemistry of the nineteenth century. One and all they opposed materialism, a fact sufficient in itself to redeem their science from the reproach of atheism. We shall find their contention amply corroborated if we turn to other leaders of chemical advance.

---

[1] Cf. the daily papers, for example, Le Bien public, Lundi, 13 septembre 1886.

[2] Paris, le 5 septembre. Monsieur. J'ai l'honneur de répondre à la lettre excellente que vous avez bien voulu m'adresser. Vous avez parfaitement deviné mes sentiments. Nous vivons dans un temps et je suis à un âge où l'on se mêle souvent, à mon insu, de me faire parler et écrire. Je ne suis qu'un savant; ceux qui me connaissent savent que, né Catholique et de parents chrétiens, je vis et je veux mourir en Catholique. Recevez, monsieur, mes remerciements et l'assurance de ma considération la plus distinguée. E. Chevreul (printed in the Le Bien public of September 17th 1886. Cf. for instance The Tablet LXVIII, London, 25th September 1886, 495; Civiltà cattolica, Ser. 14, IX, Roma 1891, 292 etc.).

Liebig's attempts to make his science practically fruitful recall the work of a forerunner, not indeed Liebig's equal in the field of pure science. Jean Antoine Chaptal (1756—1832) had as a private citizen done much to promote the industrial advance of his country. Raised by Napoleon I. — as Dumas by Napoleon III. — to the post of Minister of the Interior, he found still wider scope for his activity. The great development of industry and commerce in the France of that day, the superb Alpine roads over the Simplon, Mont-Cenis, and Mont-Genèvre were Chaptal's work, and carried his name over Europe.

Born in a village of Southern France, and educated by religious, he preserved all his life the faith of his boyhood.

"I maintain then, for a thorough study of his works has convinced me of it", writes one of his successors in the Chemistry Chair at Montpellier, "that Chaptal's greatness of character sprang from the Christian principles in which he was educated. His incessant labour, his ardent charity of which I have cited instances, had their inspiration in a living Christian faith. It was his conviction that nothing great and enduring can be created save by men who accept the spiritual interpretation of life, and that doubt, unless it be the merely methodic doubt of Descartes, is a force that disintegrates and dissolves. . . . He had observed that at the head of every department of knowledge there stand believers —, Socrates, Plato, Aristotle, Thomas Aquinas; Copernicus, Galilei, Kepler, Newton; Descartes, Pascal, Leibniz, Euler; Lavoisier, Ampère, Biot." [1]

[1] A. Béchamp, Éloge hist. de J.-A. Chaptal, prononcé à la séance de rentrée des facultés et de l'école supérieure de pharmacie le 15 novembre 1866, Paris-Montpellier 1866, 51. For Chaptal cf. Flourens, Recueil des Éloges III, Paris 1862, 159 ff.

Towards the end of his life Chaptal was reduced to the brink of poverty by the extravagance of his son, whose debts he considered himself morally bound to discharge. In spite of this he presented to the parish church of his native place a picture for the Altar of the Blessed Virgin, and a silver monstrance.

"I have", he wrote to the parish priest, "a great affection for the place in which I was born, and for the church in which I was baptised." Chaptal's old servant remained faithful to him in his days of trial, and after the death of his master had the funeral orations and reviews of his life collected and published at his own cost — a fact as honourable to the one as it is suggestive of the lovable character of the other[1].

On Liebig's pronouncement[2] against materialism a friend of his wrote to him as follows (Feb. 17th 1856):

"As you can imagine, I was more than a little interested in what you had to say lately on contemporary materialism. It is a word spoken in its hour, and it gives me all the greater satisfaction inasmuch as I have the utmost detestation of that crude and mindless theory, and have on occasion publicly opposed it. Little as I relish Hegelianism, I had rather a thousand times accept it than the philosophy of Vogt. For I had rather regard myself as a particle of God, than as a bundle of filth."[3]

The writer, who thus declared his agreement with Liebig, was the celebrated chemist Christian Friedrich Schonbein of Basle (1799—1868). Sprung from a

[1] Ib. 49 54. [2] Ante p. 196.

[3] "Denn lieber will ich mich fur ein Stuck Gott als fur einen Dreckklumpen angesehen wissen" (Justus v. Liebig und Christian Friedrich Schönbein. Briefwechsel 1853—1868. Herausgeg. von Georg W. A. Kahlbaum und Eduard Thon, Leipzig 1900, 47—48).

deeply religious family of Pietists who lived at Metzingen in Württemberg, he entered a chemical factory as apprentice at the age of fourteen, gave himself up with the greatest zeal to the study of theoretical science, during his spare time, and in 1822 proceeded to the University of Tübingen and later to that of Erlangen. During his professorate at Basle (1828—1868) he distinguished himself not so much by quantitative analysis or by the broaching of new theories as mainly by the discovery of a long series of remarkable facts. We may instance e. g. the transformation of ordinary cotton into gun-cotton and collodion, the transformation of oxygen into ozone, the transformation of iron in the so-called passive condition [1].

There is an interesting story told of Schönbein's early years. It seems that in the ballot for military service he drew an unfavourable number, and was obliged to take his place in the ranks. When the military oath was tendered to him he refused to take it. "Let your speech be always Yea, Yea, Nay, Nay", it was written; and he would be loyal without any oath. The attention of the king was drawn to Schönbein by this incident; he summoned the young man to his presence, and gave him help in the prosecution of his studies.

Whether the story is true or not [2], it is certainly in

---

[1] On this account people called him in jest a kind of magician. The enthusiastic sportsman Fr. v. Kobell once wrote to him: "Sie verwandeln mit ihren faustischen Kunsten so vieles; könnten Sie doch auch die Engländer in Gemsen verwandeln, da wäre die Schweiz ein anderes Land" (Kahlbaum und Thon, Briefwechsel 100).

[2] It is denied in the pamphlet: Christian Friedrich Schönbein. Ein Blatt zur Geschichte des 19. Jahrhunderts von Georg W. A. Kahlbaum und Ed. Schaer, Leipzig 1899, 20.

accord with Schönbein's character and principles. There is no difficulty in finding expressions of his attitude towards Christianity and materialism. Thus he writes during his student years from Erlangen:

"Professor Schubert is kindness itself — oh! how thoroughly at home I feel in this society — he unites the profoundest erudition with the liveliest attachment to Christianity; he would certainly win your heart. I will only say that in a word we live like brothers." [1]

Another letter of Schönbein's written about this time may also be cited. He wrote in 1820 to an old friend of his:

"He is guilty of idolatry who in the strict sense of the words lives only for science. How often I myself have committed this frightful crime, how many commit it without recognising its vileness and the punishment it deserves!"

A contemporary of Schönbein's, author of a biographical sketch of his career, comments on this passage [2]: "This conviction, although expressed in a form which in later years he would scarcely have employed, he preserved in essence all his life." For although in his latter years he broke with the Pietists he remained a believer till the last.

"With great firmness", continues the writer, "and on many occasions — more especially in an academic publication of

---

[1] Verhandlungen der Schweizerischen Naturforschenden Gesellschaft in Einsiedeln am 24., 25. und 26. August 1868. 52. Jahresversammlung. Jahresbericht 1868, Einsiedeln, 209. — G. H. v. Schubert (1780—1860), Professor of Science in Erlangen from 1819, and in Munich from 1827. His chief work is Geschichte der Seele, Stuttgart 1830, 5. ed. 1878.

[2] Verhandlungen der Schweizerischen Naturforschenden Gesellschaft ante 217.

the year 1853: 'On the Significance and Aim of Natural Science' —, he opposed that theory which attempts to derive the endless variety of the world, living and non-living, from the blind sport, which a blinder chance wages with a sea of atoms. He maintained that the world is the admirable and purposive creation of a God, infinite at once in power and in wisdom; and despite the popularity of materialistic systems, and the evil odour into which teleology had fallen, he held to his convictions unwaveringly. Conceiving, as he did, that science consists essentially in a knowledge of the relations of purpose and mutual adaptation existing between the different elements of nature, he came quite naturally to conclude a purely scientific paper on Hydrogen with a discussion of the teleological significance of the properties of that gas. . . . Schönbein's philosophy led him to approach science with the greatest modesty and reverence. 'However splendid', he wrote, 'the fabric of human science may seem to be, no one realises so well as the real scientist how incomplete and fragmentary it is, and how inadequate it must always remain in comparison with the actual process of reality.'"[1]

These convictions remained with Schönbein all his life. Scoutetten records a meeting with the Basle savant at Schinznach in June 1867:

"In the course of a walk along the Aar, we reached a point from which a beautiful view was to be seen. Schönbein came to a sudden stop like one transported out of himself, and raising his hand to heaven he exclaimed: How beautiful it is! How could anyone look without delight on the snowy summits of those mountains, on that river which issues from their flank to carry life far and wide, and in the end to be caught up in vapour to the clouds from which it has come? Such life and movement, such interweaving and concatenation of phenomena must evoke our admiration. Yes! everything in nature reveals a God, Whose wisdom

[1] Verhandlungen der Schweizerischen Naturforschenden Gesellschaft 218—219.

and power humble our pride and urge us on to labour and study; for, in his works, we have learned to know and to worship him."[1]

Schönbein published in 1855 a diary of a journey through Germany and Austria[2], some passages of which may appropriately be quoted. The opinions of so lucid and independent a mind on science, politics, religion and creeds cannot but be interesting.

"But who, then, can doubt that nature which floods our minds with the conception of a supreme Intelligence is really the manifestation of such an Intelligence? But if nature really is what we maintain it to be, if in it, and through it, the kingdom, power and wisdom of God are revealed, then it assumes for man an incomparably nobler significance as leading him to that knowledge in which he finds his greatest and purest joy, and the richest element of his existence. This is the knowledge of the first and final cause of all things, of the source and root of all life, Whose will and good pleasure have called man into being.

"There are, indeed, men who think in their narrow-mindedness that the deeper the human mind has penetrated into the secrets of nature, the more comprehensive its grasp and mastery of the outer world, the more oblivious it becomes of the source of all things. Many have gone so far as to say that the pursuit of science necessarily leads to atheism. The assertion is absolutely groundless. He, who lives in daily and hourly contemplation of the processes of nature, will not merely believe, he will see and come to be profoundly convinced that there is no corner of reality,

[1] . . . tout dans la nature nous révèle un Dieu dont la sagesse et la puissance humilient notre orgueil et commandent l'étude et le travail, car c'est dans ses œuvres que nous apprenons à le connaître et à l'honorer (Les Mondes XVIII 764).

[2] Menschen und Dinge. Mitteilungen aus dem Reisetagebuch eines deutschen Naturforschers, Stuttgart 1855. (Appeared anonymously.)

however insignificant, but manifests in glorious and wonderful wise the Divine life."[1] . . .

On the dignity of man he writes[2]:

"Although man is not indeed the centre of the universe, he is assuredly the noblest of the inhabitants of the earth. If nature has energised through immeasurable spaces, has called into operation the mightiest forces, has created and destroyed innumerable living beings, has made whole worlds and again unmade them, in order that, at the end of the process, man might appear on the earth, it cannot but be that such a being possesses a significance and a mission of supreme importance. And although the earth itself be, as it undoubtedly is, no more than a pin-point in the universe, its physical insignificance in no way lessens the greatness of its noblest inhabitant: for the true worth and dignity of things depend, not on their extension through time and space, but on their essential nature, the character of their activity, the degree of life and mind manifested by them."

Towards the Catholic Church Schönbein was not unfriendly.

"I do not conceal the fact", he writes[3], "that I envy the oldest of the Churches many superiorities which she possesses over her younger rivals. She has preserved institutions, customs, and forms which are not only admirable in themselves, and founded on the deep needs of humanity, but possess also the dignity of age, a title to veneration which cannot be estimated too highly.

"There could not be an opinion narrower or more groundless than that which regards the Catholic Church as an institution built up by the avarice and love of domination of crafty priests. That their conduct was often determined by motives of self-aggrandisement, that they did many things absolutely un-Christian and indefensible, we freely admit, and we certainly do not seek to represent here black as white.

[1] Menschen und Dinge 26—29. [2] Ib. 96.
[3] Ib. 186—188.

But, despite these blots, the Catholic Church remains one of the most wonderful phenomena of human history, a marvellous marriage of the genius of the East with that of the West, a joint organism whose various points are adjusted and unified with incomparable insight.

"To understand and appreciate at its full worth an institution of such power and antiquity is not easy. It is impossible to anyone who approaches the task in the temper of a bigot, whether his bigotry be on the side of belief or on that of disbelief. For it demands a knowledge of fact, an insight into the whole nature of man, a freedom of mind, which are but seldom found combined in one man; and the majority of writers on the subject show themselves at every step the slaves of office, interest, party-spirit, and prejudice.

"What I find most admirable in the Catholic Church, what is indeed unique in it, is its antiquity. What human institution is there, as vast as this Church, that could have maintained itself so long? The Roman Empire, like the other World-Empires, has fallen; revolution has shaken Europe, again and again, to its bases; systems of philosophy have followed one another to oblivion; tempests of hostility have broken over the Church itself, and threatened it with destruction. The Church has survived them all, and stands today impregnable as of old.

"This activity and stability must have a still firmer basis than Peter, the rock; this Church of nearly two thousand years must have something in it which is independent of the passing hour, and in deep harmony with the needs of human nature, above all with its weakness and imperfection; for how else, with all its hostilities to what we count reason and intellect, could it have endured for so long? Its strength must be drawn from some deep lying source, the discovery of which is eminently an object for philosophic research."

Much of Schönbein's criticism indicates that he knew Catholicism only from the outside, but the above passage shows how deep an impression even this external view must make on a mind that is capable of independent thought. The Catholic religious orders also provoke Schönbein's admiration. He makes a long detour in order to visit Kremsmünster, and gives a very friendly description of the Monastery [1]. The sight of the great buildings of the Benedictines draws from his pen many a word of spontaneous admiration [2].

Our account of Schönbein may fitly conclude with a criticism passed by the great chemist on the science of the 19th century [3].

"This corruption in the minds of the peoples, from what does it spring? From this above all, that man has severed the bond which must unite temporal with eternal, if human relations are to remain loyal and stable; from this, that man has become too external and sensual in his views, has turned his eyes away from the world of spirit, and sought to make his home in the world of matter, and to that end has endeavoured to shake off the dominion of religion and morality. And this profound sensuality, this defection from spiritual things, this sceptical indifference towards the supreme laws and forces of reality have taken possession not of a mind here and there, but of millions in all classes of society."

We quoted above a speech made at the funeral of Dumas, in which praise was given to Dumas for his religious habit of mind, and in which the speaker declared his own belief in those eternal realities which to his dead friend had become truths of sight. The orator was the Alsatian, Karl Adolf Wurtz, one of the great chemists of France, who followed Dumas to the grave in the same year, 1884. Wurtz was a Protestant of the Liberal school, and it is consequently not

---

[1] Menschen und Dinge 191—203. [2] Ib. 142 208.
[3] Ib. 288.

easy to arrive at a precise account of his religious tenets. The speech in question is however enough in itself to show that the study of chemistry had not overthrown his belief in the spirituality and immortality of the soul.

"Wurtz", writes A. W. Von Hofmann [1], "remained all his life a loyal adherent of the Augsburg Confession in which he was educated. The practical good sense, which he showed in all the affairs of the Protestant congregation to which he belonged, secured his election to the Consistory as well as to various Synods, and in these his vote was always cast in favour of free inquiry. No wonder, then, that it was considered a piece of great good fortune, to have secured the co-operation of the eminent scientist in the organisation of the Protestant Faculty (on its transfer after the war from Strassburg to Paris). And although his life's work had been done in a very different field, he helped on the new corporation with no less ability than enthusiasm, and the governing body had no hesitation in making him president of a section for the advancement of theological studies. Wurtz afforded a fresh proof, although the example of Faraday had been proof enough, that science and religion are not, as certain writers pretend, irreconcilable enemies."

In the sketch which the chemist and mineralogist Charles Friedel gives of the life of Wurtz he celebrates his sincere patriotism. His whole life was given for the advancement of his country; the measures which he advocated as making for that end were civil freedom, universal education, the cultivation of the scientific spirit, and moral progress "which latter he held to be safe only in the hands of Christianity". A Christian patriot, he was also a Christian scientist.

---

[1] Zur Erinnerung an vorangegangene Freunde. Gesammelte Gedächtnisreden III 304.

"As a savant and thinker Wurtz had not, in minutely specialised research, lost the faculty of viewing things as a whole; the great discoveries he had seen streaming out of his retort did not bring him to believe that everything could be explained by chemical or physical changes, and that there is no reality other than that which impinges on our senses." [1] . . .

"The alliance of science and religion which is so often treated as a chimera he knew by personal experience to be possible; he had seen it realised in many eminent fellow-workers, and he appreciated it both for religion, which it renders more human, and for science, to which it gives wings and an impulse towards the ideal." [2]

Wurtz himself had publicly declared his views concerning the relation of science to religious belief. At the meeting of French Scientists held at Lyons in 1874, he delivered the opening speech on the atomic structure of the universe. The last words contain a confession of faith.

"Such is the order of nature; and as science more and more penetrates it, we come to appreciate at once the simplicity of the means employed, and the infinite diversity of the results. Thus beneath the corner of the veil, which it permits us to raise, we catch a hint of the profound harmony of the plan of the world. As to first causes they remain inaccessible. They lie in a sphere which is not that of science, but which the human mind will always be eager to enter and explore. For so the human mind is made, and

---

[1] Bulletin de la Société chimique de Paris XLIII, Paris 1885, LXXI.

[2] L'alliance de la science et de la religion qu'on traite souvent de chimère, il la savait possible par son expérience personnelle, il l'avait vue réalisée chez bien des hommes éminents, et il en sentait tout le prix, à la fois pour la religion qu'elle rend plus humaine, et pour la science à laquelle elle donne des ailes pour s'élever vers l'idéal (Ib. XXV. Quoted in the Revue des quest. scient. L, Louvain 1901, 94).

you will not succeed in altering it. In vain will science expound the structure of the world, and the order of phenomena; the mind aspires higher, and in its instinctive belief that things do not contain in themselves their origin, continuance, and purpose, is led to subordinate them to a First Cause, a unique and universal cause, God." [1]

Charles Friedel (1832—1899), from 1876 Professor at the Sorbonne, whose account of his teacher and countryman Wurtz we have just quoted, was himself "a man of much eminence in chemistry" [2]. Friedel was a loyal Protestant. The Louvain chemist, Louis Henry, who, as he tells us, enjoyed his friendship for forty years, says that Wurtz's declaration at Lyons in 1874 represented Friedel's philosophy also [3].

---

[1] Tel est l'ordre de la nature, et à mesure que la science y pénètre davantage, elle met à jour, en même temps que la simplicité des moyens mis en œuvre, la diversité infinie des résultats. Ainsi, à travers ce coin du voile qu'elle nous permet de soulever, elle nous laisse entrevoir tout ensemble l'harmonie et la profondeur du plan de l'univers. Quant aux causes premières, elles demeurent inaccessibles. Là commence un autre domaine que l'esprit humain sera toujours empressé d'aborder et de parcourir. Il est ainsi fait, et vous ne le changerez pas. C'est en vain que la science lui aura révélé la structure du monde et l'ordre de tous les phénomènes: il veut remonter plus haut, et dans la conviction instinctive que les choses n'ont pas en elles-mêmes leur raison d'être, leur support et leur origine, il est conduit à les subordonner à une cause première, unique, universelle, Dieu (quoted by M. Sepet in Revue des quest. hist. XVI 2, Paris 1874, 602; by L. Henry in the Académie R. de Belgique, Bulletin de la classe des sciences 1899, Bruxelles 1899, 336).

[2] Thus the obituary notice in the Zentralblatt fur Mineralogie, Geologie und Paläontologie, Jahrgang 1900, Stuttgart 1900, 53.

[3] L. Henry, Notice sur Charles Friedel, ante. After quoting the words p. 214, ed. 2, selected from Wurtz's discourse, Henry p. 336, says: J'ose affirmer que cette philosophie si fortement et si

Louis Henry himself, who celebrated his jubilee at Louvain in 1900, declared himself a "Christian who knew how to rise above nature and render honour to the Author of nature"[1].

"A man of a profoundly religious disposition" is also the account given of Karl Remigius Fresenius who died in 1897[2]. "And this did not abandon him in his days of trial", we read, "but kept him constant and loyal to his faith."[3] Although his religious enthusiasm may seem to Catholics in some respects misdirected — he was a member of the Protestant Union and leader of the Church Liberals in Nassau — it shows at all events how little atheism and materialism can appeal to the authority of the most famous of the younger chemists of Germany. For Fresenius was a master; his hand-book of quantitative analysis ran to sixteen editions in Germany, and was translated into every European language and into Chinese.

We may add yet another name here, that of Henri Sainte-Claire Deville[4]. He began his career with Organic Chemistry and contributed to the discovery of aniline dyes, but his chief work was done in Inorganic Chemistry. His labours were of great practical fruitfulness.

éloquemment exprimée était celle que professait Friedel lui-même. Cf Revue des quest. scient. L, Louvain 1901, 95: Le double charactère d'éminent chimiste et de chrétien sincère se retrouve dans Friedel comme dans Wurtz son maître.

[1] Revue des quest. scient. XLVIII, Louvain 1900, 223.

[2] Bericht der Deutschen chemischen Gesellschaft, XXX. Jahrg., Bd. II, Berlin 1897, 1355.

[3] Allgemeine deutsche Biographie XLVIII, Leipzig 1904, 742.

[4] Jules Gay, Henri Sainte-Claire Deville. Sa vie et ses travaux, Paris 1889 (Reprinted separately from Cosmos 1886). D. Gernez, Notice sur Henri Sainte-Claire Deville, in Annales scientifiques de l'École normale supérieure, 3e série, XI, Paris 1894, Supplément 1—70. Tison, Henri Sainte-Claire Deville et son œuvre scientifique, in Revue du monde catholique LXIII 488—503.

"If aluminium is to-day an industrial product, this is due to the French chemist Henri Sainte-Claire Deville (1818 to 1881), who has left a name famous in nearly every department of Chemistry and Metallurgy"[1]. Of his other works — e. g. those on boron, silicon, the density of gases at very high temperature — we have space here to mention only his discovery of what is called the dissociation by heat of chemical combinations, "one of the greatest conquests not only of Chemistry but also of Philosophy, regarded as an interpretation of nature" (Dumas). This discovery enables us to understand the constancy of the sun's heat, and affords the first explanation of the noteworthy fact that in spite of the innumerable chimneys that send up their smoke into the air, there is no increase of carbonic acid gas in the latter.

Like his brother Charles, the geologist, Henri Sainte-Claire Deville "remained faithful all his life to the religion of his boyhood, and died in its bosom"[2]. Many

---

[1] F. X. Rüf in Stimmen aus Maria-Laach XLIV, Freiburg 1893, 51 ff.

[2] Cet éminent chimiste qui est resté toute sa vie fidèle à la religion qu'il avait appris à aimer dans son enfance, et dans le sein de laquelle il a voulu mourir (Tison ante 489). Plusieurs jours avant sa mort il demanda lui-même les secours de la religion (ib. 503). — Of the brothers Charles and Henry Deville, J. Gay (ante 21) says: Unis dans la vie, ils le furent dans la mort. Ils la virent venir sans défaillance, et, après avoir appelé eux-mêmes le prêtre à leur chevet, ils firent leurs adieux à leur famille; ils laissaient à ceux qui les avaient aimés, avec le souvenir d'une vie sans défaillance, la suprême consolation, la seule efficace en une pareille douleur, d'une fin chrétienne, et l'espérance d'un revoir dans une autre région. — Ib.: Les frères Sainte-Claire Deville appartenaient par eux-mêmes et par leurs alliances à ces vieilles familles françaises et catholiques, . . . où les croyances les plus nobles et les plus élevées s'allient tout

years before his death he had expressed a desire that his funeral discourse might be pronounced by his friend Louis Pasteur. It is said that the expression was used in a bantering way to cheer up Pasteur who was at the time very ill. But however this be there is no doubt, says a biographer of Pasteur, "that he felt that nobody else could understand him so well. Both alike pursued science with a passionate love; both alike were ardent patriots. And they were at one also in their confidence in the future evolution of the human spirit, and in the religious system from which they learned the secrets of eternity"[1].

VI. GEOGRAPHY.

The recognised founder of General Comparative Geography was Karl Ritter (born at Quedlinburg in 1779, appointed Professor at Berlin 1820, died 1859). It was the labours of Ritter, and the application of his methods that raised Geography to the status of a science.

Johannes Janssen[2] has given us a masterly picture of the life and character of Ritter, in which we find a clear statement of the great savant's attitude towards religion. "It is a matter for rejoicing that Ritter, unlike Alexander von Humboldt, never either in his life or in his writings paid homage to the sceptical idols of his day, but was always a resolute upholder of the Christian Revelation. Steadfast in his faith in the living God, and in His incarnate Son, our Redeemer, he is a

---

naturellement à une fière indépendance et à un ardent amour du travail.

[1] R. Vallery-Radot, La vie de Pasteur, Paris 1901, 462.

[2] Zeit- und Lebensbilder I[4], Freiburg 1889, 113—179.

shining proof that such faith, far from being hostile to scientific progress . . . is the greatest stimulus that the mind can receive towards a profound, all-embracing, and living knowledge of nature." [1]

"Ritter", says Janssen elsewhere [2], "undertook all these journeys" — to France, Austria, Greece, England and Italy — "in the cause of science, and all his labours were directed to the honour of God."

---

[1] Ib. 179. Cf. Ratzel in Allg. deutsche Biographie XXVIII 688: "Je tiefer Ritter in die Wissenschaften eindrang, desto wahrer und wärmer wurde sein Glaube." — Side by side with Janssen's severe sentence as to Humboldt, a milder one, that of the botanist v. Martius, may find place. When v. Martius treats of Humboldt's views on vitality, he says: "Man hat aus diesen Äußerungen, und daß er es in seinen Werken mit einer gewissen Absichtlichkeit vermieden, die Gebiete der Idealität zu beschreiten, auf seinen Unglauben schließen wollen. Trotzdem spreche ich es mit Zuversicht aus, daß das stolze Schiff seines Wissens an einer sicheren, aber tiefverborgenen Überzeugung vor Anker gelegen sey. . . . Seine Jugend fiel in jene Periode, da es in gewissen Kreisen zum guten Ton gehörte, nicht von Religion zu sprechen. Die Denker bewahrten ihre Überzeugungen im Schrein des Herzens. Als später, bei kirchlicher Bewegung, sich unter redlichen Bekennern auch Sophisten zur Schau trugen, gelobten jene sich ein Schweigen, das nicht selten gemißdeutet wurde. Unter den in der Wissenschaft und im Leben ehrwürdigen Männern habe ich solcher Schweigsamen mehrere kennen gelernt. Zu ihnen rechne ich auch Alexander v. Humboldt. Wenn er sich durch seine Begabung aus dem Kreis der spekulativen Philosophen ausgeschlossen fühlte und sich selbst beschränkte, so berechtigt dies nicht, an einer geheimen Welt seiner höchsten Gedanken zu zweifeln. . . ." Akademische Denkreden, Leipzig 1866, 395—396. When the Journal hist. et litt. XXIV, Liége 1857, 493 f, had defended Humboldt against the reproach of never having mentioned God in his Kosmos, he sent an autograph to be placed under his portrait of 1856, in which he characterizes Nature as "Gottes erhabenes Reich" (ib. 541 f).

[2] Ante 163—164.

"We are", he wrote to his wife from Trieste, "both in the hands of God, Whose Majesty encompasses land and sea and extends to all the ends of the earth. There is only one thing greater, and that is His Mercy and Love, which watch over body and soul and preserve them from the destruction which might any hour befall them. At home or away from home He guards us; or rather His presence makes everywhere home. Not a hair can fall from our heads, not a sparrow from a house-top, unless He so wills it. How then can man but dedicate all his labours to the honour of Him without Whose sustaining presence the universe had long ago fallen into ruin with every creature it contains? This consideration, and the belief I have that my vocation casts on me the duty of seeking out the truths of my science not only in that home which He has so filled with rich and pleasant things for me, but also in more difficult places, inspire me in my work; and I continue my researches into what seems to me one of the most important elements of the history of humanity; and so far at least as my poor abilities and resources and my somewhat limited and partial points of view permit me, I continue to spread the light of science. And I am full of confidence in my undertaking, for I rely only on God."

Ritter was a Protestant, and rather bigoted in his attitude towards Catholicity. His books are full of disparaging allusions to the Church. It is for this reason all the more remarkable that in his correspondence he refers again and again to Catholic priests as among his most valued fellow-workers, e. g. Father Wimmer of Madern, Father Mayer of Klagenfurt and others. "He stands", he wrote of Father Mayer, "in the first rank of those, who occupy themselves with the natural features and the geography of our country; he received me with the utmost heartiness and geniality, and did everything possible to assist me. I spent all day yesterday with him, and that is the reason I have been unable to write till this moment, an hour before I leave; he stayed till 12 o'clock last night and could hardly tear himself away, for he was enchanted to find that I knew his dear Carinthia, his fatherland, and wanted to hear all about everything that had been happening in it. He overwhelmed me with stores of information, and we made a most interesting excursion together." . . . Wherever he came in contact with Catholic priests, secular or religious, he was favourably impressed by their good scientific education as e. g. in the Monastery of Einsiedeln, and among the Mechitarists in Venice [1].

If modern Geography, understood in the largest and most usual sense of the word, begins with Ritter, the Physical Geography and Meteorology of the sea are in in a still higher degree bound up with a single name, that of an officer of the American marine Matthew Fontaine Maury († 1873) [2]. Born in 1807 in County Spottsylvania in Virginia, he entered the marine as a cadet in 1825, and made many voyages. A fracture of his leg in 1839 incapacitated him for further service, but the long list of works issued by him from the Hydrographic Bureau at Washington were of far more value to seamanship than any voyage he could have made. He became the lawgiver of all the navies of the world.

Maury had remarked that the routes followed at sea had not been fixed upon by reflection and con-

---

[1] Janssen, Zeit- und Lebensbilder I 172.

[2] Cf. A life of M. F. Maury, U. S. N. and C. S. N Compiled by his daughter Diana Fontaine Maury Corbin, London 1888. Ad. Quetelet in the Annuaire de l'Académie de Belgique XL, Bruxelles 1874, 291—341. E. du Hailly in Revue des deux mondes mars 1858, Paris, 33—56 414—444.

sideration, but by usage. The first captain had, somehow or other, found a route and reached his goal; others followed the same route, and by the usage of long years it became fixed and settled as the proper one. But nobody had examined for himself whether it was in fact the shortest. Now the route chosen at sea is by no means a matter of indifference, and it is far from universally true that the most direct is the most rapid. There are certain constant currents of wind and water, which may accelerate or delay a voyage. These currents had never been systematically studied until Maury laid the project before the American Government.

The source from which data were to be drawn was obvious; the log-books of all vessels would contain notes of those areas of the ocean in which an acceleration or diminution of speed had been experienced, with all necessary details. But at first Maury's appeal to the seafaring community to submit their log-books to him met with very little response. He was restricted to the scanty material afforded by the logs of the Navy proper. But when in 1828 a trip from Baltimore to South America, which had hitherto taken 41 days, was performed, thanks to a chart of Maury's, in 24 the ice was broken. After the International Congress at Brussels in 1853 nearly every fleet in the world was co-operating in Maury's great project. Observations reached him from every quarter of the globe, and in ten years 140,000 copies of his chart had been issued. The scientific material accumulated through long years of labour was wrought up by Maury into a great and striking work: "The Physical Geography of the Sea". The tone of the book is identical with that of Ritter's.

"Another characteristic of Maury is the essentially religious temper of all his work. I do not refer to the frequent allusions to texts of Scripture, nor to the curious interpretations he gives of them; that is, as we know, distinctive of the genius of Protestantism. . . . His assiduous study of the phenomena of nature is in effect a continuous expression of gratitude towards the Supreme Wisdom which reveals itself in nature, and every new fact is to him a new revelation of the eternal harmony. Not indeed that Maury ever sets himself to the deliberate propagation or advancement of the faith; in his eyes science and religion are united by indissoluble bonds, and neither can be developed without throwing fresh light on the other."[1] "Maury's early religious training and temperament", writes E. Douglas Archibald[2], "appear to have exercised a large influence on his public and private life. His Physical Geography is illustrated by frequent extracts from the Book of Job, and is instinct with the same spirit which prompted and pervaded the memorable Bridgewater Treatises. The following extract from his address to the University of the South will indicate this phase of his mind: 'Astronomy is grand and sublime, but Astronomy overpowers with its infinities and overwhelms with its immensities. Physical Geography charms with its wonders, and delights with the benignity of its economy. Astronomy ignores the existence of man; Physical Geography confesses that it is based on the Biblical doctrine that the earth was made for man. Upon no other theory can it be studied — upon no other theory can its phenomena be reconciled.'"

The character of the "Bridgewater Treatises" may be gathered from their title, "Bridgewater Treatises on the Power, Wisdom, and Goodness of God, as manifested in the Creation"[3].

---

[1] E. du Hailly in Revue des deux mondes 15 mars 1858, Paris, 443.

[2] Nature, 9. August 1888, London and New York 1888, 340. The University of the South is in Tennessee.

[3] Bridgewater Treatises on the Power, Wisdom, and Goodness of God, as manifested in the Creation. London 1833—1840. Francis

Maury continued steadfast in his faith to the end. "With his last breath . . . he offered up his soul to Jesus Christ, and prayed God to take him out of this world to Himself."[1]

The names of Ritter and Maury serve to impress on us anew a fact to which we have so many times drawn attention. It is the smatterers in science that have so much contempt for religion; the true masters and pioneers, as a rule, regard it with favour. We do not seek to explain this fact fully, it is enough for our purpose to record it. To give science a new direction, to open out to it new paths, demands not only width and depth of vision but also a rare independence of mind, for one must break with the views of the majority of one's contemporaries. And that minds of this stamp should so often be thoroughly Christian, but never in any event so sceptical as the popularizers and pamphleteers, is a fact of deep significance.

Henry Egerton, Earl of Bridgewater († 1829), left in his will £ 8000 to be expended on a work, the aim of which is sufficiently evident from the title, which we have just given. The President of the Royal Academy of Science, who was commissioned to carry out of the design, entrusted its execution to eight men of learning. Thomas Chalmers wrote on the Moral and Intellectual Condition of Man; John Kidd on the Adaptation of External Nature to the Physical Condition of Man; Charles Bell on the Hand; William Kirby the Habits of Animals; William Whewell on Astronomy and General Physics, P. W. Roget on Animal and Vegetable Physiology; W. Buckland on Geology and Mineralogy; W. Prout on Chemistry, Meteorology and the Functions of Digestion. Bell, Buckland, and to a certain extent, Whewell and Kirby were men of an European reputation.

[1] Il a rendu le dernier soupir . . . en confiant son âme à Jésus-Christ et priant Dieu de le retirer de ce monde (Quetelet in Annuaire de l'Académie de Belgique XL, Bruxelles 1874, 337)

We will not devote much further space to the science of Geography. It does not bring us into such intimate connection with the fundamental problems of religion as other branches of science. Whether a great geographer be like Elisée Reclus, an Anarchist, or like Wappaus[1] or H. A. Daniel[2] a deeply religious man, is not a circumstance on which we can decisively rely. Still less do we propose to examine the attitude towards Christianity of the great discoverers. We should find many of them who like Cameron[3] or Sven Hedin[4] called on God in their hour of danger, but such data would be more illustrative of the moral value than of the intellectual validity, of religion. We shall then simply select out of the great multitude of discoverers two names which could not well be ignored. One of these has already been mentioned. The other occupies a position of eminence in the science of Astronomy, but his greatest work was done in Geography. They are Claude Desaulses De Freycinet († 1842), and Antoine Thomson D'Abbadie († 1897).

---

[1] See below p. 244.

[2] Only an untimely death prevented him from becoming a member of the Catholic Church. Hulskamp in Liter. Handweiser Nr. 108 and 109, Munster 1871, 453.

[3] He landed in his native country "voll Dank im Herzen gegen Gott, dessen Gute mich durch so viele Gefahren beschirmt hat". Verney Lovett Cameron, Quer durch Afrika. Deutsche Ausgabe II, Leipzig 1877, 240.

[4] "Schon der Gedanke, den Aufstieg heute fortzusetzen, hätte geheißen Gott versuchen." Sven Hedin, Durch Asiens Wusten I, Leipzig 1899, 233. He will mildly treat one who has wrong acted towards him "Denn hatte nicht der Allmächtige seine Hand uber mich gestreckt, als ich damals in Lebensgefahr war?" Ib. II 191.

Freycinet was a colleague of Cauchy's, and we have spoken of him on an earlier page[1]. We treat here of his contributions to Geography.

As recently as the end of the 18th century the continent of Australia was very imperfectly known. The geographers of that day were doubtful, for example, whether or not the Gulf of Carpentaria stretched all the way from North to South and divided the Continent into separated parts. In order to determine this question the French Government in 1800 despatched an expedition under Baudin; and Freycinet, then a young man of twenty-one, formed one of the crew. He distinguished himself so much in what was otherwise a rather disappointing voyage that he not merely became an officer, but was given charge of some explorations undertaken by the way e. g. that of the Hunter Islands. On the return of the expedition it was Freycinet who prepared for publication the materials collected[2]. He had barely completed this work when he was given the command of another scientific expedition. Its object was, by means of pendulum observations in different latitudes, to throw some light on the shape of the earth, to obtain data regarding earth-magnetism, and to collect plants, animals, and minerals hitherto unknown. Freycinet left Toulon, on board the corvette Urania, on September 17th 1817. At Rio Janeiro, the Cape of Good Hope, and the Island of Mauritius observations were made, and the voyage

[1] Cf. ante p. 56. For biographical details of Friedr. Embacher cf. Lexikon der Reisen und Entdeckungen, Leipzig 1882, 121. Nouv. biographie générale XVIII, Paris 1885, 843—852. Fr. Grille, L. de Freycinet, Paris 1853.

[2] Voyage de découverte aux terres australes pendant les années 1800 à 1804 [2], 4 vols, Paris 1824.

was thence continued to a quarter already known to Freycinet, the south-west of Australia. The expedition from this point made a wide sweep of the continent, passing by way of the Marian and the Sandwich Islands, and after a stoppage at Sydney, made for Cape Horn. In the neighbourhood of the Falkland Islands the Urania was so badly damaged that she had to be abandoned. But the mass of her valuable carge was fortunately saved, and, purchasing a new vessel, Freycinet reached Le Havre on November 13th 1820 after an absence of three years. He had sailed 18,862 naval miles; the observations made by him filled 31 quarto volumes; he brought home specimens of 4 new species of mammals, 45 new species of birds, 49 of reptiles, and an invaluable collection of minor animals and plants. In their published form the results occupied 13 quarto volumes, with four atlases. They were of course edited and arranged by Freycinet, but he died before the appearance of the last three volumes. Two of these, dealing with magnetism and mineralogy, were subsequently issued, but the last, which treated of the languages of Oceania, although in many respects the best, never saw the light.

The other discoverer, of whom we speak, won his laurels in a very different field. He had to contend not with cliff and rock, wind and wave, but with the ignorance and superstitions of a half-savage people, with political distrust and suspicion, and he fought his battle with wonderful strength and stubbornness.

Antoine Thomson D'Abbadie[1], a scion of an old French family, was born in 1810 in Dublin, whither

[1] Revue des quest. scient. XLI, Louvain 1897, 598 ff. Radau in Revue des deux mondes, 1. févr. 1867, Paris, 722—736. Hatt

his father had fled at the time of the Revolution. In 1813, however, his parents returned to France, bringing Antoine with him. From his youth he showed a passion for observation; and, as the wealth of his family assured him a competence, the young man was free to devote himself to study and travel in distant lands, where new and rare things were to be discovered, adventures to be encountered, Christianity to be introduced or revived. The little-known home of the dark race early attracted his attention, and Bruce's Travels in Abyssinia fixed his choice on this latter region. According to report there were to be found on the banks of Lake Tana, palaces, ruins, books, savants, a literature, everything in fact that we understand by the word culture, and this attracted him more than the prospect of travel among utter savages. He anticipated no opposition from the fanaticism of Islam for, as he himself says: "I knew that with time the Abyssinians had altered their religion, and I even proposed to work for its restoration. I also entertained the hope of discovering the cradle and home of the negro races, seeking it as I did in the region to which their own tradition points. I hoped also to throw some light on the sources of the Blue Nile." All this he expected to be able to accomplish in two or three years.

D'Abbadie spent six years in preparation for his expedition, studying all the necessary sciences; before undertaking it he even went, on the advice of Arago, to the equatorial region of Brazil to ground himself in earth-magnetism.

---

in Comptes rendus of the Parisian Academy of Science CXXVI, Paris 1898, 173—181, reprinted in Cosmos 5 févr. 1898, Paris, 182—186.

He devoted ten years to the trigonometrical measurement of Abyssinia, and published a map inclusive of the southern province previously almost unknown. The area mapped out by him is as large as France; its most northerly point is as far from its most southerly as Calais from Saragossa. In this area D'Abbadie determined the altitude and relative situation of about 900 different points; he worked quite alone, and employed a method invented by himself; and he completed his task "in spite of the climate, in spite of privation and sickness, in spite of the wild animals, the impassable ways, and, worst of all, the hostile natives"[1].

We shall give just one example of his almost superhuman courage. When in 1838 he had reached Abyssinia from Massava and begun his work, he found that his methods and instruments were inadequate. He, thereupon, resolved to return to France, to procure fresh instruments, devise a new method, and begin his whole task anew. In the beginning of 1839 he was back in Paris; by the end of January 1840 he had reached Massava, and attempted to re-enter Abyssinia. But the native ruler refused him permission, and to make his calamities complete he was attacked by a disease of the eyes. He went to Aden to look for medical assistance, but the English governor of the island refused him admittance. He returned to Africa, endeavoured to penetrate Abyssinia from the south, and failed at two points. But even these accumulated misfortunes could not break the spirit of D'Abbadie. He made a fresh attempt from the north, and was at last successful.

"One can but marvel", says Hatt[2], "at the sight of such strength and self-denial which led a man, out of pure love for science, to devote the best years of his life to such terrible labour. D'Abbadie was of so strenuously moral a

[1] Revue des deux mondes 724.

[2] Comptes rendus CXXVI 176.

character that he was regarded by the Abyssinians as a monk. They received with incredulity the news that he had married in Europe." [1]

D'Abbadie's work is a marvel of accuracy. His topographical details were for a time suspected, but they have been cleared from that suspicion, as the words of one of the most judicious geographers of Germany will testify.

Petermann who, before the appearance of D'Abbadie's maps, had prepared a map of North East Africa, and was advised to revise his work in view of the French explorer's discoveries, was in a unique position to appreciate "the extraordinary conscientiousness of his work, and the accuracy and infinite pains which the measurements and calculations required". "It gives us the greatest pleasure to say that in our opinion the travels and works of D'Abbadie are among the most brilliant and fruitful of which the whole continent of Africa can boast. There is no other part of Africa in which the observations of the original explorers were so strikingly thorough, and it is only of places where the general staffs and scientific expeditions of European governments have been at work that we possess information of greater or even equal accuracy." [2]

In addition to his geographical material, D'Abbadie brought home 234 Ethiopian manuscripts, the richest

---

[1] D'Abbadie has himself given his opinion as to where the power of Will is situated, in a letter to Lord Clifford on 1. August 1852 (Annales de la Propagation de la foi XXIV, Lyon 1852, 444—454). Of the climate of Massava, he says: L'activité morale doit s'y affaiblir chez ceux qui ne retrempent pas leur âme aux sources élevées de la prière et de l'espérance (ib. 446).

[2] A. Petermann, Mitteilungen, Gotha 1864, 38 116. Also Embacher says (Lexikon der Reisen und Entdeckungen, Leipzig 1882, 1), suspicion unjustly (ungerechterweise) has been thrown on D'Abbadie's researches. Later travellers have removed all taint of disbelief.

collection in Europe, and a dictionary of the Amarhasa language, extending to 15,000 words. All his material was in due time published. A Catholic missionary named Sapeto had accompanied D'Abbadie on his first expedition to Abyssinia, and two missions were established by him.

D'Abbadie contributed in many other ways to the advance of science. He effected improvements in the instruments used for earth-measurement; mooted the idea, carried out in 1882, of applying photography to the observation of the Transit of Venus; and endeavoured to elucidate the remarkable phenomenon of the variation of the vertical line, ascribing it to the impact of the tidal wave on the elastic crust of the earth.

But he was not the man to shut himself up in his study. In July 1851 we find him in Norway, in July 1860 in Spain studying solar eclipses. In 1882 he was in San Domingo observing the Transit of Venus, and three years latter he made an extended journey to obtain observations of telluric magnetism. He went by way of Athens, Alexandria, Cairo, and Suez to Aden, and back by way of Suakim and the Nile Valley Jerusalem, Constantinople, and the Piraeus, Naples, and Rome. As he had no children, he presented (in 1895) to the Academy of Sciences his property of Abbadia in Southern France, the income of which is 20,000 francs a year, and added to it the capital sum of 400,000 francs. This is to be spent on the construction of laboratories, but more particularly in building an Observatory, which is to be used for the compilation of a catalogue of 500,000 stars. The work is to be completed by 1950, and is to be assigned to a religious order.

D'Abbadie was well known as a zealous Catholic. This circumstance was in the eyes of some an obstacle to his admission to the Academy, but Arago[1] — as D'Abbadie related at the unveiling of a statue to the great astronomer — although himself a sceptic, opposed and defeated the unworthy intrigue.

About a year before D'Abbadie's expedition, another savant had entered Abyssinia in order to study the Botany of that region. This was Wilhelm Schimper, brother of the celebrated botanist who discovered the law of the leaf-formation of plants. Schimper became a Catholic in 1843[2], married a native of Abyssinia, and remained there till his death in 1878.

D'Abbadie's work in Abyssinia bore fruit in other parts of the African continent. Before starting for Madagascar in 1888 to establish an astronomical observatory there, the Jesuit missionary Elie Colin came to consult D'Abbadie, and to the latter's advice is to be ascribed the valuable geodetic work done by Colin in collaboration with D. Roblet[3]. The latter had in 1888

[1] A propos d'une candidature à l'Académie des sciences, un membre objecta que le candidat était un ardent catholique. Nous n'avons pas, dit Arago, à disséquer ce qu'il y a de plus intime dans l'homme, ce qu'il a de régler à sa guise; nous n'avons à examiner que les travaux de M. d'Abbadie; ses opinions religieuses ne sont pas de notre domaine. Quant à moi, ajouta le secrétaire perpétuel, je porte envie à ceux qui croient (Revue des quest. scient. XLI, Louvain 1897, 604).

[2] The Journal of the R. Geographical Society of London XIV, London 1844, CXL. Annales de la Propagation de la Foi XVII, Lyon 1845, 274.

[3] Cf. Colin's Rechenschaftsberichte in the Comptes rendus CXVIII, Paris 1894, 510—514 570—573; CXXVII (1898) 708—711; CXXVIII (1899) 716—718; CXXXVI (1903) 1298 s. Les études géographiques

published a map, founded, as far as the centre of the Island was concerned, on his own measurements. It will be interesting to cite a specialist's estimate of this map.

"The map before us has already received the best recommendation that can be given to a map of Madagascar; it has received the praise of A. Grandidier who knows the island better than any other living man. And Grandidier expressed his opinion so warmly in a communication to the geographical society of Paris that they awarded their gold medal to the author of the map." [1]

Equal praise is extended to the detailed maps of the two provinces of Madagascar, prepared by Grandidier from the data of Roblet and Colin.

"The maps fill one with amazement at the activity of these three men who have given us more accurate knowledge of Madagascar than we possess of many parts of Europe, and whose work is worthy to stand by the side of that of the governmental survey department of any country." [2]

In December 1903 Colin received the prize of the Academy of Sciences for Physical Geography. The area surveyed by him ran to 31,000 kilometers [3].

à Madagascar in La Géographie, Bulletin de la soc. de Géographie II, Paris 1900, 183—198. Roblet tells us about the labour which the construction of his map entailed, in Études religieuses LIII, Paris 1891, 482—492; cf. XLV (1888) 450—452.

[1] A. Supan, Geograph. Literatur-Bericht fur 1889. Beilage zum 35. Band von Dr. A. Petermann's Mitteilungen, Gotha 1889, 73.

[2] Ib. Literatur-Bericht fur 1895. Beilage zum 41. Band, 117.

[3] Comptes rendus CXXXVII, Paris 1903, 1118 f.

VII. MINERALOGY.

We learned from Bessel that a Catholic priest stands at the head of 19th century Astronomy. This is true in a still larger sense of scientific Crystallography. Its founder was a simple professor in a school at Paris, conducted by priests.

René Juste Haüy[1] was born on Febr. 28th 1743 in a little village of the Departement of Oise. His father was a poor linenweaver, who found it very hard to earn his bread; and, despite the talent shown by his eldest son, there seemed to be no other prospect before the boy except to earn his bread by the work of his hands.

Happily there was in Hauy's native place a house of the Premonstratensians, and the lad early gave tokens of a vocation to the religious life. His devout demeanour brought him under the notice of the Prior, and the latter, discovering his remarkable talents, undertook to procure him a place at Paris. This proved somewhat difficult, and young Haüy was for some time employed as a choir boy, but he eventually secured a place at the College of Navarra. Here he showed such ability that on the completion of his course he was appointed on the teaching staff. He taught for many years at the College of Navarra, and afterwards at the College of Cardinal Lemoine, absolutely content with his humble position, careless of advancement, and so far very superficially versed in physical science.

---

[1] Cuvier, Recueil des éloges historiques, lus dans les séances publiques de l'Institut royal de France III, Paris 1827, 123—175.

It was solely to oblige a fellow-professor that he began to study Botany. In the College Lemoine there was a Father Lhomond, a very learned man and capable writer, who, however, devoted his brilliant powers solely to the education of the young, and wrote elementary books which enjoyed a wide circulation. Haüy chose Lhomond as his confessor, accompanied him on excursions, and cared for him when he was ill. Lhomond studied Botany in his walks, and Hauy during his vacation determined to master at home enough of the science to surprise and delight his friend on his return. He carried out his plan, and on his first walk with Lhomond was able to give the Linnaean names of nearly all the plants they met with.

This was his first step in a field which was soon to become more and more attractive. He began to frequent eagerly the botanical gardens which lay near his college; but one day, seeing the mineralogist Daubenton enter with his class, he joined them and discovered a subject which ousted even Botany from his affections.

He was already a mature man when he took up this study, but in a short time he showed himself as thoroughly at home with it as if he had been a mineralogist all his life. One property of minerals struck and surprised him particularly. While in plants every single part however complicated, always appears of identically the same character, in minerals this constancy seems to be absent. The same mineral appears now in one, now in another crystal-form. One day as Hauy was meditating on this peculiarity he had the misfortune to let fall a beautiful group of prismatic crystals of calcareous spar and a crystal was broken off.

The fracture exhibited surfaces as smooth as the outside of the prism, and a new crystal emerged as it were from the broken one, the conformation of which was not prismatic. Haüy examined it and found to his surprise that it was the same crystal-formation as island spar, that is to say, it was rhomboidal. An idea flashed across his mind. Had he not here the solution of the problem which had so long perplexed him? Might it not be that the various crystal formations in which the same mineral appeared were simply different arrangements of the same ultimate crystal? Haüy was by this happy accident put on the right track; he followed up his idea resolutely, and laid the foundation of the modern science of Crystallography.

Although his discoveries gave him a European reputation Hauy remained always an humble and faithful priest. When he first began to attend the sittings of the Academy, he appeared in a clerical dress of somewhat antiquated cut. His friends fearing that invincible prejudices might be aroused aginst him, tried to persuade him to lay aside his clerical costume on these occasions, but Hauy refused to do so until the opinion of a Doctor of the Sorbonne had been taken on the matter. When in 1792 those religious who refused allegiance to the Revolution were thrown into prison, Haüy was among the number. His papers were seized, his crystals bundled away, and he himself, with his fellow-professors, was confined in the Seminary of Saint-Firmin which had been turned into a prison.

Influential friends interested themselves on his behalf, and secured an order for his release. Haüy at first refused to accept his liberty. His crystals and instruments had been brought to his cell, and he was working away at them as contentedly as if he were in his own laboratory. It was only with difficulty that he was persuaded to leave on the following day[1].

He suffered no more under the Revolution. "While Lavoisier was under arrest, and Borda and Delambre were dismissed, it is a remarkable fact that Haüy, a priest who had refused the oath and who continued to exercise the religious duties of his office, was actually presenting memorials for the release of his lay colleagues. This he did without hesitation, and without incurring any penalty for it."[2] It was during the Revolution that he finished his great work:

"Possessed of a vast collection", says Cuvier, "which constantly received fresh accessions of all known minerals and aided by the co-operation of those ardent and capable students whom the École Polytechnique placed at his disposition, many of whom stand to-day in the front rank of mineralogists, he soon made up for the time which he had spent on less valuable work, and raised in a few years that striking monument which we may say has done for France what the peculiar circumstances of his life did for M. Hauy, and has lifted her, after centuries of neglect, to the head of this department of natural history. This book possesses in effect two qualities rarely found in union: on the one hand it is founded on a discovery completely original and due solely to the genius of its author; on the other this discovery is applied with inconceivable minuteness and perseve-

[1] According to Cuvier he left the prison exactly a day before the Massacre in September. But Isidore Geoffroy Saint-Hilaire says in the Life of his father, who was chiefly instrumental in securing Hauy's liberation, that the latter had informed Hauy of his liberation at 10 p. m. 14th August, and that Hauy left the prison on the following day (Vie, travaux et doctrine scientifique d'Étienne Geoffroy Saint-Hilaire, Paris 1847, 14).

[2] Cuvier, Recueil des éloges historiques III 153.

rance to every known species of mineral. The plan of the book is spacious, the detail rigorously accurate; the whole is as perfect as the theory of which it is the formulation."[1]

On the death of Dolomieu, Haüy was appointed Professor of Mineralogy at the Museum of Natural History. His appointment infused new life into the place. The collections increased fourfold, and "Europe, or at least that part of it which was interested in mineralogy, streamed thither, partly to study so exhaustive and well-ordered a collection, partly to hear a lecturer so lucid, elegant and courteous"[2]. The most noticeable trait of Hauy's character was his courtesy and willingness to oblige. "The most ordinary students were received as amiably as the most distinguished savants; for he had pupils of all classes. . . . He brought his École-Normale classes to his own house, and initiated them in all his secrets. He was on these occasions the old college-professor, he took part in all the fun of the young people, and never let them go without a merry meal."

Amid all the honours that were showered on him Haüy preserved the simplicity of life which had marked his earlier days. He made no alteration in his hours of dining or of rising; and he continued his walk, employing it as in old times as much for the pleasure of others as for his own. He showed strangers the way, procured them tickets of admission to his museum, explained the collections and rendered all sorts of services; and few indeed, of those whom he was so ready to oblige, recognised the great savant. He was hidden away under old fashioned clothes, and an almost exaggerated

[1] Recueil des éloges historiques III 153.
[2] Ib. 165.

modesty of speech and manner. One day he encountered two ex-soldiers, who were preparing to fight a duel. He ascertained the cause of the quarrel, reconciled them, and brought them into a café to seal the peace with a bottle of wine. On external splendour he set no value. He had free access to the finest collections of precious stones in Europe, he wrote a memoir on jewels, but to him they were no more than interesting crystals. A variation of half a degree in the angle of a familiar crystal would have stirred his attention more acutely than all the treasures of India.

In his declining years Haüy had reason to congratulate himself on the modest habits of life which he had cultivated. Circumstances led to a considerable reduction of his salary, and he had to live out his days on crippled resources. He lived to the ripe age of seventy-nine. A fracture of the knee, resulting from a fall in his room, marked the beginning of the end. Throughout the whole course of his illness he never altered in benevolence towards others, in cheerful submission to Providence, or in zeal for science. He divided his time between prayer, supervision of the new edition of his book, and labour to secure the future of the students who had worked in collaboration with him. He died on June 3rd 1822. He had been a living proof that a man may be the pioneer of a new era in science, without for that reason contemning God and His Church. "As loyal to his religion as to his science", says Cuvier[1], "he never suffered the loftiest speculations to draw him away from the minutest discharge of the observances prescribed by his Church."

---

[1] Ante 168.

An opponent of Haüy in several scientific questions, but united with him in religious sentiment was a German savant who has deserved well of Mineralogy.

After the break-up of the Scientific Conference of Naples in 1845, Leopold Von Buch after taking leave of the Munich professor Von Thiersch called after him: "Present my respects to Fuchs in Munich! He is a man to whom I have never spoken without learning some valuable new thing." [1]

Such praise from such an authority is high indeed, but not too high for Fuchs. He is described by Von Gümbel, also, as one of the foremost and most original mineralogists of the nineteenth century.

"In that head of his", writes Von Martius [2], "there was a whole universe of clearly apprehended facts, reduced to coherence and unity, not by fantastic combinations and intuitions, but by the operations of pure intellect. Fuchs was the personification of reason. Logical, almost to a fault, he was fore-armed against all the prejudices of the schools. It would be difficult to find in his writings a single passage showing any trace of a 'Philosophy of Nature', although to such a philosophy he made invaluable contributions. He concentrated his mind solely on his special subject and buried himself in its depths, preserving all the while, however, that wise scepticism, that prudence and foresight without which an inquirer is apt to lose sight of his goal and stray from his proper path. The laws which he formulated were put to the test not only of experiment but of counter-experiment. He was as original in the objections which he advanced against his own conclusions as in the conclusions themselves, and he never regarded an investigation as complete until he had determined the relation of

---

[1] Bulletin der k. Akademie der Wissenschaften, Munchen, 18. Mai 1853, 214.

[2] Akademische Denkreden, Leipzig 1866, 592.

his subject to other known facts, and either subsumed it under or distinguished it from them."

Johann Nepomuk Von Fuchs († 1856)[1] was born of an humble peasant family in Mattenzell near Regensburg, and received his early education from the friars of Frauenzell. Subsequently he studied at the gymnasium at Regensburg managed by the ex-Jesuits of St. Paul. He began with medicine, but although he duly obtained his degree he never practised, but devoted himself entirely to Chemistry and Mineralogy, securing a chair in these sciences at Landshut in 1805, and at Munich in 1823.

His work at Landshut and Munich covers a wide area of subjects. Beginning with certain improvements in the spirit-lamp and the blow-pipe of the laboratory, he advanced to investigations of the first importance. He turned his attention to mineral analysis, and with apparatus of the poorest kind obtained the most excellent results. The reputation which these brought him was greatly heightened by a successful controversy with Haüy. He made contributions not only to Chemistry and Mineralogy but also to technical industrial processes. Under the first head, as being mainly of theoretical value, we may mention his discovery of the amorphous character of many substances, and of the fact that in minerals certain chemical combinations can appear as substitutes of one another. Turning his attention to industries he led the

[1] v. Gumbel in the Allg. deutsche Biographie VIII 165—168. Gesammelte Schriften des Joh. Nep. v. Fuchs. Zum ehrenden Andenken herausgeg. von dem Zentral-Verwaltungs-Ausschusse des polytechnischen Vereins fur das Königreich Bayern. Redigiert und mit einem Nekrologe versehen von Dr. Kajetan Georg Kaiser, München 1856.

way in the artificial production of ultra-marine, and effected many improvements in the processes of dyeing, in the manufacture of sugar from beetroot, and in the brewing of beer. He was also a pioneer in the manufacture of cement, and of hydraulic lime. A discovery which he himself valued highly was that of water-glass and its application to wall-painting, or as it is called, "stereochrome". He was working at this in the last year of his life, noting down his investigations with a hand tremulous with old age[1]. At the close of his paper on the subject he takes his leave of the world.

"Here I conclude my notes on stereochrome, and bring to its end an inquiry which has cost me more trouble and time, not to speak of the great expense, than half the rest of my works put together, a fact to which many of my friends can bear witness, for many of them gave me their co-operation in the task. To them I offer my sincere thanks. But above all I give thanks to God that He has allowed me, old and feeble as I am, to complete this work on water-glass and its practical uses in such detail that it can without much labour be applied and extended by others.

"To the Giver of all good gifts I offer up my work, and the labours I have endured in preparing it. May He vouchsafe to bless it!

"Omnia ad maiorem Dei honorem et gloriam."

These were his last published words. "Towards the middle of February 1856 he fell ill of a complaint that for many years had been troubling him at ever shorter intervals. His physical exhaustion was such that he knew death to be at hand, and he prepared to meet it with a resolution and piety which edified all about him. 'Christ lead us to the light!' he said with his

[1] Bereitung, Eigenschaften und Nutzanwendung des Wasserglases mit Einschluß der Stereochromie, in Gesammelte Schriften 260—285.

dying breath."[1] . . . During the last ten years of his life he had laboured "with ever increasing zeal to establish and assimilate the religious truths, which he had always clung to", and his conversations on the subject showed "the same lucidity as his scientific treatises". We may quote Von Ringseis in this connection:

"Fuchs lived and died in the fullest assurance of the truth of the Christian Revelation. I feel it a special duty to bear this witness to his memory; for from 1805 to 1812 I lived continuously with him at Landshut, and for nearly four years attended his lectures on Chemistry and Mineralogy. From 1826 till his death, and especially towards the end, I was constantly with him, and I can testify to the exact fervour with which he took part in the exercises of his religion. His life and death are in themselves a complete refutation of the assertion that the physical sciences, especially Geology, have destroyed the foundations of the ancient faith."[2]

François Sulpice Beudant († 1852) was another who combined a fervent faith with the greatest distinction in Crystallography. He delivered many lectures at the

[1] Ib. Nekrolog XXVIII. — An obituary notice of the editor of the works of Von Fuchs, Kajetan Georg Von Kaiser († 1871), Professor of Chemistry at the Polytechnic at Munich, says: "Er ertrug die ihm auferlegten Leiden (in seiner Todeskrankheit) mit der freudigen Geduld, wie sie einem vom wahren Christentum erfullten Gemute gewährt wird. Sein katholischer Glaube war der gefeite Platz seines Herzens, an welchem er unter allen Prufungen sein eigenstes Selbst wiederfand." His life-long belief is mirrored in the short remark in one of his diaries, where he says referring to a serious misfortune, which happened to him: "Gott hat noch andere Prufungen mit mir vor" (Berichte der deutschen chemischen Gesellschaft IV, Berlin 1871, 897 899).

[2] Ringseis, Nekrolog auf Fuchs, reprinted in Wiener Kirchenzeitung, 18. Juli 1856, 459.

Institut Catholique, an institution founded for the defence of religion [1].

J. F. L. Hausmann († 1859) was an orthodox Protestant. Wappäus writes of him [2]:

"His philosophic principles were in perfect harmony with his religious belief. Although he was never in the mid-current of the more strenuous religious movement of his later years he was always, like so many other scientists of his period, a man of genuine piety, and in every vicissitude of life he showed himself firm and steadfast in his religion. His researches in his special branches of science never led him beyond the frontiers of religious belief; he was unable to understand the supposed conflict between science and faith, and treated it as ridiculous rather than terrible. He was an enquirer not only with his head but also with his heart, and it was with good warrant that his old and intimate friend Karl Ritter said of him: His writings were a hymn of praise to God."

"On July 6th 1894, there died at Paris suddenly and prematurely, a scientist who was the pride of the Department of Mines and one of the glories of French science. What Fresnel was in the history of Physical Optics, Maxwell in that of Magnetism and Electricity, Edward Suess in that of Geology, this man had in less that twenty years come to be in Crystallography and Mineralogy. He had renewed the face of these two allied sciences, and added to their domain vast provinces hitherto unknown or but dimly guessed at. When on the morrow of his death the French Mineralogical Society had engraved in letters of gold on its ceiling

---

[1] Valson, La vie et les travaux du baron Cauchy, Paris 1868, 205.

[2] Sitzungsberichte der k. bayr. Akademie der Wissenschaften, München 1860, 61.

the name of Ernest Mallard, in company with the ever-famous names of Haüy, of Romé-de-l'Isle and of Bravais, no one thought the honour too great for him, nor could anybody think of a savant worthier to be associated with the three illustrious founders of Crystallography." [1]

Other French Reviews spoke in the same strain, and to their praise was added that of the leaders of science in every other country of Europe [2]. Lord Kelvin had described Mallard as "one of the ablest minds of the century"; Fletcher declared at the Oxford meeting of the British Association after his death that Mineralogy had to lament "its greatest Philosopher" [3]. In Germany he was characterised as "one of the finest mineralogists of France whose works have done more than anything else to raise Crystallography to its present undisputed position among the exact sciences" [4].

Much of Mallard's work was devoted to an attempt to determine the constitution of the molecule of the crystal, and it is unique for the penetration with which he deduces the inner structure of crystalline bodies from their external properties.

Mallard wrote on Geology as well as on Mineralogy, and also did good service to miners by his investi-

---

[1] P. Termier in Bulletin de la Société géologique de France, 3me série, XXIII, Paris 1895, 179.

[2] De Lapparent in Annales des mines, 9me série, Memoires VII, Paris 1895, 267—303. Wyrouboff in Bulletin de la Société franç. de minéralogie, Paris 1894, 248 f.

[3] Cf. Lapparent ante 297. Lord Kelvin himself at Lapparent's request confirmed the genuineness of the utterance.

[4] Wildermann's Jahrbuch der Naturwissenschaften, Freiburg 1895, 438.

gations concerning safety-lamps and the use of blasting materials in mines.

In 1872 Mallard delivered a discourse at Rive-de-Gier on the "History of the Earth". The manuscript of the lecture, published after his death, contains the following passage:

"Man should not be too exalted; he should continually remind himself that he is a little flickering light of ephemeral duration, which the least breath may extinguish. Still less should he hold too low an opinion of himself. He is truly a creature made in the image of God, and, on this account, he is permitted by means of his reason to enter into the plans and thought of the Creator of all things. This ought to be his highest ambition here below, and it is this ambition that science helps him to realize. . . .

"In my eyes, our true greatness, our real superiority consists not in the fact that we possess better heating apparatus, better clothes and better vehicles than our forefathers, but in the fact that we know more than they did. We are not in this world merely to enjoy ourselves, and to find here the final purpose for which we were created. That would be a sad goal if it were the end of man. No, we are here, religion tells us, to love and serve God; we are here, science tells us, to try to understand and to admire the Will and the Ideas of God; properly understood these two answers are but one." [1]

---

[1] Il ne faut pas que l'homme s'exalte trop; il faut qu'il se rappelle sans cesse qu'il est une petite lumière vacillante, d'une éphémère durée, que le moindre souffle éteint. Mais il faut encore bien moins qu'il arrive à se trop mépriser. Il est vraiment une créature faite à l'image de Dieu, et, à ce titre, il lui est permis d'entrer par sa raison dans les desseins et la pensée du Créateur de toutes choses. Ce doit être ici-bas sa plus haute ambition, et c'est cette ambition que la science lui permet de réaliser. . . . Nous ne sommes point ici-bas pour jouir et pour consommer. Triste fin que celle-là, si c'était la fin de l'homme. Non, nous sommes ici-bas, nous dit la

Other scientists, who distinguished themselves in Mineralogy, will be mentioned in another chapter.

VIII. GEOLOGY.

When the discussion turns on the relations between Geology and Christianity we must first of all consider the Mosaic account of the Creation, and its relation to modern researches concerning the history of the earth. If we wished to enter on the question we could name a series of honoured geologists of the 19th century who sought to show the agreement between science and the Holy Writ in this connection. For example, De Luc († 1817), G. Cuvier († 1813), Mac Culloch († 1835), Von Fuchs († 1856), Buckland († 1856), Hugh Miller († 1856), De Serres († 1862), Hitchcock († 1864), F. Pfaff († 1886), Dana († 1895), Dawson († 1899), W. Waagen († 1900).

We here disclaim any intention of seeking to strengthen the agreement between the Bible and Nature by the testimony of naturalists. It is not necessary to lay any weight on the proof of the agreement under consideration.

A thousand years before the dawn of geological research, St. Augustine put forward the view that the whole world was made at one time and in the same instant, and that the six days of the Mosaic account of Creation were only a narration of the different classes and orders

---

religion, pour aimer et servir Dieu; nous sommes ici-bas, nous dit la science, pour tâcher de comprendre et pour admirer la volonté et la pensée divines· à bien les prendre, ces réponses n'en font qu'une. Quoted from Termier ante 190.

of creatures so that each and every thing created might be pointed out with greater clearness as the work of the Almighty power[1]. This interpretation has never been condemned by the Church. Hence if Geology could prove that the literal interpretation of the Biblical account of creation is untenable, it would only be proved thereby that the correct explanation of that part of Holy Writ in terms of natural history was to be sought for on the lines pointed out by St. Augustine. Of course there can be no contradiction between the trustworthy results of science, and the properly interpreted word of God.

But what are the trustworthy results of Geology, and what is the correct interpretation of the revealed word of God looked at from the point of view of natural history? Holy Writ usually speaks of natural processes in popular terms, derived from the external appearance of things, which make no attempt to explain their essence. From the trustworthy results of science we must find out how the realities which underlie these terms are to be understood. Accordingly, there can be no question of any contradiction between Biblical expressions and scientific knowledge. On the other hand it is extremely difficult, when treating of Geology, to separate trustworthy results from hypotheses more or less probable. What is the accepted view to-day may in twenty years time be recognised as an error. Therefore caution is necessary in investigating the agreement between the Bible and Nature. Scholars have often read their favourite geological opinions into Holy Writ, and

---

[1] Deum ab exordio saeculi primum omnia creavisse, quaedam conditis iam ipsis naturis, quaedam praeconditis causis (Aug., De Genesi ad litt. 7, 28). — Concerning the history of the work of the six days v. F. de Hummelauer, In Genesim, Parisiis 1895, 49 ff.

then defended them as revealed dogmas. Some have tried to bring the text of Holy Writ into harmony with what were apparently results of science, but which in reality were not scientific results [1].

So, when we draw attention below to investigators who believed in the Bible, or bring forward statements made by them concerning the Mosaic account of Creation, it is not because of those statements themselves, nor is it in order to recommend in detail the methods by which these scholars sought to reconcile science and Holy Writ. Such statements, or the mere fact that a famous geologist accepted the Biblical account, are valuable to us merely in so far as they are proof that the scholars referred to found nothing in the trustworthy results of their science which stood in clear contradiction with Holy Writ, or with the other essential foundations of Christianity. In this way we shall of course bring forward as proof the belief in the Bible entertained by famous geologists. As an instance we shall take the first of the scientists mentioned above, as he was the first of the investigators whose activity falls at least partly into the 19th century. Jean André De Luc, born at Geneva in 1727, died at Windsor in 1817, a highly respected geologist in his day, was a zealous defender of Christianity. "Is it not touching", writes Abbé Emery to Cardinal Fesch [2] in 1803, "to find in a Protestant such zeal for the defence of Revelation. He said to Barruel that he would be grieved if there were a single quarter of an hour in his life which was

---

[1] Cf. J. Knabenbauer in Stimmen aus Maria-Laach XLVI (1894) 140—143.

[2] Vie de M. Émery II, Paris 1862, 31.

not utilised in defence of the Christian Revelation." It is perhaps still more surprising that De Luc saw in the Catholic Church the only bulwark against unbelief. "I am convinced", said De Luc[1], "that Revelation can be guarded only by the Catholic Church, that all Protestant churches lead to Deism. Should I meet anyone who was unhappy I would advise him to enter the Catholic Church."

To-day De Luc's writings are out of date, but his scientific works certainly show a marked superiority to those of the Encyclopaedists. For this we have the testimony of a witness of whose competence there can be no question.

G. Cuvier ranks him several times with the first geologists of his day[2]; in one passage with Pallas, Saussure, and the school of Werner, in another with the same and with Dolomieu, and Ramond.

In other places, too, he speaks of his works with marked respect[3]. In K. C. Von Leonhard's eyes De Luc was "one of the acutest minds amongst the geologists of his time — whose services to our science stand in need of no exposition"[4].

George Cuvier († 1832), the great zoologist and geologist, was, as is well-known, a believing Christian and often expressed himself to that effect.

---

[1] Vie de M. Émery II 32. Cf. Élie Méric, Hist. de M. Émery II, Paris 1885, 217 219.

[2] Rapport hist. sur les progrès des sciences naturelles et physiques depuis 1789 et sur leur état actuel, présenté au gouvernement le 6 févr. 1808, Paris 1827, 161 166.

[3] Ib. 168 169 171 173.

[4] Aus unserer Zeit in meinem Leben I, Stuttgart 1854, 138. Leonhard censures (ante) De Luc's excessive predilection for certain daring opinions.

"Our sacred books", he says in one place in recommending the study of natural history, "bring before our eyes at the very outset the Creator bidding his creatures pass under the gaze of the first man and commanding him to give them names." Cuvier discerns in this a deep allegorical meaning. "It teaches us clearly that one of our first duties is to cultivate a sense of the goodness and wisdom of the Author of Nature by a continuous study of the works of His power."[1] Pasquier, who was chosen to deliver the eulogy on him in the Chamber of Peers on 17th December 1833, says of Cuvier's famous Treatise on Fossils: "These researches rest on a deeply moral and religious foundation. Cuvier, like all masters of thought, believed in a first cause, which directs the destinies of all creatures, and which has foreseen and ordered all. From this point of view there could be no doubt that the existence of organised beings proceeds from a supreme intelligence which has fitted them all with organs suited for the purpose for which they were created. This necessary interdependence put into his hands the means of determining with certainty the remaining undiscovered parts of an organism from parts already known."[2]

Cuvier was a Protestant, but in the Education Department and in the Council of State of which he was a

[1] Nos livres saints, à leur début, nous représentent le Créateur faisant passer ses ouvrages sous les yeux du premier homme, et lui ordonnant de leur imposer des noms: heureuse allégorie qui nous enseigne assez clairement que l'un de nos premiers devoirs est de nous pénétrer de la bonté et de la sagesse de l'auteur de la nature, par une étude suivie des œuvres de sa puissance (Cuvier, Rapport sur l'état de l'hist. nat.: Éloges III 450).

[2] Reprinted in the Ami de la religion 74, Paris 1833, 622.

member, "he never showed himself hostile to the Catholic religion or to the Catholic clergy. On the contrary he was more favourable to them than many of his fellow members who were supposed to be Catholics. We have several times heard this testimony given by a prelate and ecclesiastic who had experience of him in numerous connections and who praised his judgment, his justice and his moderation" [1].

Cuvier was unable to discover any contradiction between geological facts and the Biblical account of Creation.

At a later date Marcel De Serres († 1862) dealt in many works with the agreement of the Biblical cosmogony with the facts of Geology [2]. He was a first rate expert in his special branch. The "extraordinarily active and productive" De Serres, says Von Zittel [3], has done a giant's work in many departments of Geology. In France, especially, he, with his two assistants Dubreuil and Jeanjean, "was one of the great pioneers of cave research".

For the theory of the formation of mountains modern science is deeply indebted to the "epoch-making works of a French geologist", Léonce Élie De Beaumont († 1874) [4]. Born in 1798 of an old and noble family

---

[1] Ami de la religion 72 (1832), 160.

[2] La cosmographie de Moïse comparée aux faits géologiques I, Paris 1838; II, Paris 1841, deutsch von Steck, Tübingen 1841; Les connaissances consignées dans la Bible mises en rapport avec les découvertes modernes, Paris 1844.

[3] Geschichte der Geologie und Paläontologie bis Ende des 19. Jahrhunderts, München und Leipzig 1899, 311.

[4] Cf. for him Jos. Bertrand, Éloges académiques, Paris 1890, 77—103.

of Normandy, Elie De Beaumont, after a highly distinguished course of study at the Paris Polytechnic School, devoted himself to Mining Engineering, and by indefatigable observations and surveys in the Cantal and Mont d'Or Mountains, in the Alps, on Etna, in the Vosges, in the Ardennes, in Dauphiné, on Mont-blanc, and by the exhaustive work in which he recorded his observations, rose to be the leader of his science in France. His masterpiece is a geological map of France which was begun by him in conjunction with Dufrenoy in 1825, and which occupied eighteen years in completion. "This great work exercised a powerful influence on the entire development of French Geology, and gave both authors a well-earned place amongst the leading scientists of France." De Beaumont filled positions of the first importance. He became Professor in the École des Mines and in the Collège de France, and was Chief Inspector of Mines from 1835. "In this capacity, and further as Grand Officer of the Legion of Honour, as Senator of the Empire, Permanent Secretary of the Institut de France, and from 1861 Vice-President of the Council General of Mines, Élie De Beaumont exercised a wide and weighty influence which was employed with great unselfishness and impartiality in the interests of his colleagues. After the conclusion of his general survey, De Beaumont conducted many special surveys in France. He died on September 21st 1874. He gained for himself an imperishable name by his brilliant and indeed epoch-making works on the age and origin of mountain systems."

After this glowing eulogy of the great scientist by the German geologist Von Zittel[1], it is hardly necessary to

[1] Gesch. der Geologie 451 ff.

set down the opinions of his own compatriots. Still a few extracts from the funeral oration pronounced over him may be quoted. Laboulaye declared:

"For more than twenty years there has not been in all Europe a geologist or mineralogist but betook himself to Élie De Beaumont to learn his science from him. He was the head of a school. His ideas, his methods, were carried over the whole world by his pupils, and they bore with them also the renown of his great name." [1]

Even more enthusiastic was the praise which J. B. Dumas lavished on his dead friend. We may quote it here because the orator dwelt among other things on the religious beliefs of De Beaumont:

"The great scientist whom we have accompanied to his last resting-place, one of the most learned men of the century, belonged not only to our association (The Academy of Science), not only to France. His glorious name was in every civilised country and in every nation, the personification of Geology itself, taking the word in its most scientific and its highest meaning." [2]

Then follows a short characteristic passage from the first notable work of the deceased (published in 1829), which closes with the words of the 113th Psalm "The earth trembled before the countenance of the Lord, the sea saw it and fled, the mountains leapt like the rams and the hills like the lambs."

"Élie De Beaumont's method of work, and the turn of his genius stand completely revealed in these three circumstances. The materials on which his theory is founded were collected with endless patience, and tested with rigorous accuracy. His piercing imagination drew from them sublime conclusions. His piety interwove them without effort into one texture with the sacred writings. An indefatigable observer, persevering and precise; a poet after his fashion, a

---

[1] Comptes rendus LXXIX, Paris 1874, 722. [2] Ib. 710.

poet inspired with all the passion of lofty ideas; a Christian always, and a convinced Christian; such does Élie de Beaumont show himself in this admirable work of his youth: such he remained all his life."[1]

The great scientist was snatched away by a sudden but not unexpected death. "Élie De Beaumont understood all his duties and neglected none of them: he was ever ready, and if the angel of death touched him with his wing without warning he did not surprise him. He was one of those men whose debts are always paid. His pure and immortal spirit, was able without anguish or dismay to take its leave of the world, the splendours and harmonies of which he had wrought so nobly to reveal. It was able to ascend in peace to those regions of light, the fixed object of the aspirations of our venerated comrade, and to appear with confidence before that sovereign judge in whom he had always placed his hopes and his faith."[2]

---

[1] La manière de travailler de M. Élie de Beaumont et le tour de son génie se révèlent tout entiers dans ces trois circonstances. Les matériaux sur lesquels va se fonder sa doctrine, sont recueillis avec patience et contrôlés avec une rigoureuse exactitude. Sa vive imagination en tire des conséquences sublimes. Sa piété les rattache, sans effort, aux textes sacrés. Observateur infatigable, persévérant et sûr; poete à sa maniere, et poète passionné pour toutes les idées élevées; chrétien toujours, et chrétien convaincu: tel se montrait M. Élie de Beaumont dans cette œuvre admirable de sa jeunesse; tel il est resté toute sa vie (Comptes rendus LXXIX, Paris 1874, 712).

[2] Mais M. Élie de Beaumont comprenait tous ses devoirs; il n'en négligeait aucun. il était toujours prêt, et si l'ange de la mort l'a touché de son aile sans l'avertir, il ne l'a point surpris. Il était de ceux dont les dettes sont toujours payées. Son âme immortelle et pure a dû quitter sans trouble et sans effroi cette terre, dont il a tant contribué à révéler les splendeurs ou à faire admirer les harmonies. Elle pouvait remonter calme vers les régions sereines, objet constant des aspirations de notre vénéré confrère, et se présenter confiante devant le souverain Juge en qui il avait toujours placé ses espérances et sa foi (ib. 714). Also Jos. Bertrand (Éloges académiques 102) says: Pieusement fidèle aux enseignements de son

Another speaker praised in particular De Beaumont's benevolence to the poor: —

"What a chorus of praise and gratitude would arise here, if I could assemble around this grave all whom your benevolent hand succoured in their distress. You yourself were the first to forget the innumerable instances of generosity of which we have heard only from those whom you helped. I will respect, even at this final moment, your noble reticence. It is not we on this earth who can give you the reward of such deeds. They have already found their worthy and true reward in a better world, in the bosom of Him Who gave you your inspiration, to the teachings of Whom you ever lent a submissive ear." [1]

The speaker of these words was himself a famous scholar, and had behind him an active life, rich in scientific achievements, Ch. Sainte-Claire Deville († 1876)[2]. He chose as the object of his studies the Southern Antilles, more especially Guadeloupe, a district the geology of which had scarcely been investigated at all.

---

enfance, la foi éclairée d'Élie de Beaumont les conciliait avec la hardiesse de ses études. Les pratiques commandées étaient accomplies avec l'assiduité tranquille qu'il apportait à tous ses devoirs. . . .

[1] Mais quel serait le concours d'éloges et de reconnaissance qu'on entendrait ici, si je pouvais rassembler autour de cette tombe tous ceux que votre main bienveillante a secourus dans la détresse. Vous oubliiez vous-même le premier ces traits innombrables de générosité, dont la connaissance ne nous est parvenue que par ceux que vous aviez obligés. Je veux respecter, encore á ces derniers moments, votre noble susceptibilité. Ce n'est pas nous, d'ailleurs, sur cette terre, qui pouvions vous donner le prix de telles œuvres. Elles ont déjà trouvé dans un monde meilleur leur digne et véritable récompense dans le sein de celui qui vous les a inspirées, et dont vous écoutiez ainsi vous-même les enseignements (ib. 719).

[2] Vom Rath in Verhandlungen des naturhistorischen Vereins fur Rheinland-Westfalen XXXIII, Bonn 1876, Sitzungsberichte 235.

He published in 1841 a map of the last named island, and, seizing a favourable opportunity, made in 1842 an excursion to Teneriffe, the geological investigation of which was materially furthered by him in spite of the shortness of his stay. On February 18th 1843 he witnessed from a neighbouring island the earthquake which devastated Guadeloupe. "From the elevated point on which I stood I could observe the huge clouds of dust, which, spreading over the island, announced that a terrible disaster had fallen upon it." The towns were laid in ruins, 2000 persons being engulfed in the catastrophe. Deville's scientific collections and papers were destroyed. At the instance of the French government he published, after five months' study, a monograph on the disaster. After his return to France, which was necessitated by the uncongenial climate, he set to work to record the results of his investigations in a great work. However he did not get much further than the first volume, for he soon became convinced that he could not restore from memory the lost notes of his diary. He published many works on the mineral springs of France and other scientific subjects; he was drawn to Naples by the eruption of Vesuvius in 1855, and began there his epoch-making work on the Funnels of Volcanoes, by which earlier views were materially modified and the laws of volcanic outbreaks definitely formulated. He pursued his investigations on volcanoes in the Lipari Islands and in Sicily. The last decade of his life was devoted more particularly to meteorological research. He founded numerous weather-stations in Algiers and elsewhere.

An expression of Deville's religious feeling has already been given in the words quoted from his discourse on

Élie de Beaumont. Another testimony to it had already appeared elsewhere [1].

On the 5th October 1883 there died at Frohsdorf near Vienna, far from his native France from which he had voluntarily exiled himself, one of the most distinguished palæontologists of the nineteenth century, Joachim Barrande [2]. All over the learned world the death of this man was felt to be a heavy loss to science.

"In every land in which Palæontology has a place", writes Ferdinand Roemer [3], "the announcement of this death will be received with sympathy and sorrow. For who is there to whom his name is unknown? Who is there but has contemplated with a mixture of admiration and astonishment the long row of mighty quartos that bear his name, marvelling, even though he be ignorant of their contents, that such a mass of work could proceed from a single pen? But what student of palæontological remains is there that has not occasion, almost every day of his life, to consult Barrande's works, and to thank him for the almost inexhaustible ocean of information which he has brought together in them?"

The investigator who is praised in this wise was born on his father's estate near Sangues, in the department of Haute-Loire. A strong Legitimist, he left France in 1830 with the banished royal family, and settled in Bohemia as tutor to Count Chambord. From 1833 he devoted himself to the investigation of the geological and palæontological conditions of that country. Supported

[1] P. 217. Cf. Revue des quest. scient. L, Louvain 1901, 100.

[2] F. Roemer in Neues Jahrbuch fur Mineralogie, Geologie und Paläontologie, Stuttgart 1884. I. C. de la Vallée-Poussin in Revue des quest. scient. XVI, Bruxelles-Paris 1884, 5—71.

[3] Ante 1.

by the kingly generosity of his former pupil he achieved wonderful results.

"By the epoch-making work of Joachim Barrande", says Von Zittel[1], "Bohemia became a classic ground of the oldest fossil-bearing formations." A preliminary sketch of the Bohemian silurian basin, issued in 1846, was followed in 1852 by the first volume of his great work on the silurian system in Bohemia. There is practically nothing that can bear comparison with it in the whole literature of Palæontology. In 22 mighty quarto volumes, with 1160 wonderfully executed tables, Barrande from 1852 to his death in 1883 described the trilobites and other crustaceans, molluscs and brachiopoda, to be found in the Bohemian silurian basin."

Barrande investigated in the first place the geological formation of the Bohemian silurian district. He recognised it as a tolerably regularly formed basin of elliptical shape, consisting of several successive layers and veins. The earliest layers appeared on the outer circumference, the latest in the middle.

"He next sought to investigate with the greatest zeal the organic contents of the different veins, and their subdivisions. He collected fossils as no one ever did either before or after him. He kept in his pay all the year round an army of collectors and labourers; he worked numerous quarries for no other purpose. He thus brought together a collection of fossils the like of which has not been gathered from any other area of palæozoic strata. It contains some 5000 species, and numerous examples of almost every one of these."[2]

After years of preparation he began the publication of his work. "Its appearance", says Roemer, "was received by his colleagues with amazed admiration. It was difficult to know what to admire most, the fulness of the new ma-

---

[1] Gesch. der Geologie und Paläontologie 598.

[2] Roemer ante 3.

terials, the keen observation, the careful description, the comprehensive knowledge of all relevant literature or, finally, the unsurpassed fidelity to nature and the clearness of the drawings. The volume not merely gives a description of the Bohemian trilobites, but brings forward for comparison everything that was previously known from other countries concerning these remarkable animals. The description thus assumes the proportion of a great monograph on trilobites."

When Barrande began his work in Geology there were 13 species of trilobites known; at his death he bequeathed to the Bohemian museum 5000 species, 3060 of which he had himself examined and described. In order to attain such results he had to exercise an indomitable patience and pertinacity, for the trilobites break up very easily after the death of the animal. You may find thousands of fragments before you meet a specimen in which the parts preserve their original arrangement. To attain certainty in respect of one particular kind of trilobite (Dalmanites socialis) took a ten years' search although traces of it were to be found at every step. Occasionally in his excavations he would encounter for years only the same types at the place of his search and then there suddenly would come to light a quite new and important fossil.

Barrande was a fervent and practical Catholic. His religious temper of mind finds frequent expression in his great work. We take as an instance a passage in which he is writing of instinct and intelligence as they present themselves in the animal kingdom. In the contrivances which enable the nautilus to swim, he contends, we discern clear tokens of a shaping intelligence, an intelligence which does not reside in the tiny creature itself.

"We are forced then to the conclusion that the marvellous structure and organs of the cephalopoda are the work of a Mind superior not only to them but to man. This great Mind, author not only of these but of all the other wonders of life, can be no other than the Creator and Sovereign Lord of all things. . . . Man, created in the image of God, possesses moral freedom and an intellect to which we find no parallel among the lower animals. He can show works of his mind and hand which almost justify his assumption of the proud title, King of Nature. But in all his creations in science or art he is confined within the limits of his finite nature. The devices in which he seeks to embody his thought, bear tokens of their limited and imperfect author, fail to attain their purpose at one effort, and often demand — as in the case of the steam-engine — a long course of modification and development before reaching even a moderate degree of effectiveness.

"By contrast the lower animals may be compared to slaves, set by the Creator to do a day's work, which is in all its details mapped out and prescribed. They possess only a sufficient endowment of intelligence to enable them to perform the tasks assigned them. But, as it were by way of compensation, their faculties go out directly to the ends prescribed them without any preliminary feeling and fumbling. Such an order of things, so simple and at the same time infallible, can proceed only from an infinite Intelligence. We have already observed that in many instances the human mind cannot reach so far even as to understand it, although perceiving its results so clearly." [1]

In the dedication of a later volume Barrande observes that "from the point of view of our religious belief" Astronomy, the sublimest of the natural sciences, con-

---

[1] De tels procédés, à la fois simples et infaillibles, ne peuvent dériver que d'une intelligence infinie. Nous venons de constater que, dans certains cas, l'homme n'est pas en état de les comprendre, même en voyant leurs effets (Barrande, Système Silurien II, texte 5e partie, chap. 19 E, Prague-Paris 1877, 1495).

fesses sisterhood with Palæontology. "Both reveal to us, each in its manner and measure, the power and glory of the Creator."[1]

The dedication in question bears the date Dec. 8th 1881, the Feast of the Immaculate Conception. A friend of Barrande's, observing this, concluded that it had been his wish to complete his great work under the protection of the Mother of God. He asked Barrande if this was the case, and was told that his inference was perfectly just[2].

Almost all of Barrande's works bear the dates of great Catholic feasts. Thus the various sectional parts of Vol. II are dated: September 15th 1852 (Octave of

[1] La Paléontologie de récente origine est humblement placée vers le bas de l'échelle des connaissances humaines, dont le sommet est couronné par l'antique et noble Astronomie. Mais, au point de vue de nos croyances, ces deux sciences sont rapprochées et liées par une intime connexion. Tandis que l'Astronomie nous expose les splendeurs de la Création, dans l'immensité des Cieux, la Paléontologie nous révèle modestement d'autres merveilles, non moins admirables, dans l'apparition et la succession progressive des formes de la vie, sur notre globe terrestre. L'une et l'autre de ces sciences nous raconte donc à sa manière, suivant ses attributions, la puissance et la gloire du Créateur (ib. VI, 1e partie [1881], Dédication).

[2] Comme j'entretenais alors une correspondance avec le vénérable savant, je lui écrivis que cette date du 8 décembre par lui choisie me faisait entendre son intention de placer l'achèvement de ses travaux sous l'égide de l'Immaculée Conception. Quelques jours plus tard il me répondait sur ce point par ces mots qui sont une profession de foi: "Monsieur, vous m'avez bien compris" (de la Vallée-Poussin in Revue des quest. scient. XVI, Bruxelles-Paris 1884, 9). — Charles de la Vallée-Poussin († 1903) was for almost forty years Professor of Mineralogy and Geology in the University of Lyons He also composed valuable treatises on geological subjects. Cf. L. Henry, who was likewise a zealous Catholic, in the Revue générale XXXIX, Bruxelles 1903, 681—700.

the Nativity of the Blessed Virgin); "Easter Day, April 1st 1877." Vol. III is dated May 30th 1867 (Ascension Day), Vol. V July 1st 1879. This last is the Octave of John the Baptist and, at Paris, a Feast of the Blessed Virgin which had a special significance for the exiled savant: Notre Dame de Bonne Délivrance. Other sections exhibit September 28th 1877: Feast of Venceslas, patron-saint of Bohemia, March 25th 1871 (Feast of the Annunciation); December 8th 1881 (Feast of the Immaculate Conception).

"We mourn in Joachim Barrande", says H. B. Geinitz, "a man, venerable for his noble struggle to attain truth and justice, for the self-sacrifice with which he laboured for the advancement of science; a master of all humanistic and realistic culture, a loyal colleague, and a generous friend" [1] — and let us add, in the interest of historical fact, a fervent Catholic.

---

[1] Sitzungsberichte und Abhandlungen der naturwissenschaftlichen Gesellschaft Isis in Dresden, Jahrgang 1883, II, Dresden 1883, 67. — In his memorial speech on Barrande, Geinitz (ib. 65) lays particular stress on his teaching as to evolution: "Im allgemeinen stehen die aus Barrandes gewissenhaften Untersuchungen sämtlicher silurischen Faunen gewonnenen Resultate im Gegensatz zu der Evolutionstheorie, und folgende Sätze können als augenscheinlich nachgewiesen betrachtet werden: 1. Die generischen Typen und spezifischen Formen der silurischen Faunen sind in den Hauptgegenden in großer Anzahl erschienen, ohne daß man ihren Ursprung auf eine präexistierende Form zurückzuführen vermöchte, weil eine solche dort nirgends bekannt ist. 2. Beim Erscheinen derselben nach vollständigen Unterbrechungen sind fast alle auftretenden Arten neu, und man kann nirgends in den neuen Faunen eine Lücke erkennen, welche sich der Abwesenheit derjenigen Arten zuschreiben ließe, die einem örtlichen Abstammungszusammenhange entsprächen. 3. Im Gegenteil hat sich ein Maximum der Formen in gewissen Gegenden unmittelbar nach einer vollständigen Unterbrechung gezeigt. 4. In andern

A name of high eminence among more recent geologists is that of Gabriel Auguste Daubrée († 1896)[1]. "Not often", says Lapparent, "has a life consecrated exclusively to science been so rich in honour and recognition. No mark of public respect was lacking to it. In complete possession of his faculties, full of years and of honours, he quitted the world with the calm resignation of a true Christian. "He was President of the Academy of Sciences, Director of the Higher School for Mining, Professor in the Jardin des Plantes, and Grand Officer of the Legion of Honour. At the outset of his career he was commissioned to visit England, Sweden, and Norway. A study of the metalliferous strata of Scandinavia, which he published at this time, won warm praise from Berzelius, the first of all authorities on that subject. During his Professorate at Strassburg he produced a very exhaustive study of the geology of Lower Alsasce, and in 1841 a masterly study of tin-bearing formations. He had remarked that in the neighbourhood of tin-deposits fluoric minerals are always to be found, from which he inferred that fluorspar plays a part in the formation of tinstone veins. He proceeded with his investigations from this point of view, and succeeded in producing artificially various mineral substances. He showed by examples that in order to the formation of minerals it is not necessary to postulate forces and circumstances no longer to be met

Gegenden ist ein relatives Maximum auf ein absolutes Minimum gefolgt 5. In andern Fällen endlich folgt auf ein sehr entwickeltes Maximum ein Minimum ohne eine Spur von Filiation."

[1] A. de Lapparent in Bulletin de la Société géologique de France 3e série, XXV, Paris 1897, 245—284; also in the Revue des quest. scient. XL, Louvain 1896, 89—102.

with in nature. During a visit to the Baths of Plombières, a place in which Roman remains are to be found, he discovered in cracks in the walls crystalline minerals which for the most part exhibited all the properties of zeolites. The gradual operation of the luke-warm and slightly mineral water had in process of time produced this formation. Daubrée also won great distinction by his studies of meteorites.

"His career was in every respect a fortunate one", alike through his achievements in science, his independence of life, and his domestic happiness. "He himself gave expression to fervent gratitude for his lot in a fragment which was discovered among his papers, and which exhibits great elevation and at the same time a profoundly Christian turn of thought."[1]

The name of a still living French geologist, who has of late years attained a wide reputation in Germany, calls for a passing mention. Albert De Lapparent, President of the last Assembly of Catholic Scientists at Munich, and Professor of the Catholic Institute at Paris, stands among the leaders of his science. His Traité de Géologie, published in 1883, not merely superseded all other French manuals, but gained a European reputation and circulation. It would be discourteous to pry into his intimate life, but the part he has taken

[1] La carrière de Daubrée a été favorisée de toutes façons. . . . Lui-même s'est plu à le reconnaître dans des pages d'une grande élévation, que ses enfants ont retrouvées parmi ses papiers, et où le Chrétien confiant se révèle d'une manière explicite (Revue des quest. scient. XL 99—100). Cf. Bulletin de la Société géologique de France 3e série, XXV 258: Sa fin a été douce . . ., ses facultés étaient demeurées intactes, et le sentiment chrétien, très nettement exprimé, lui adoucissait le grand passage.

in the foundation of Conferences of St. Vincent de Paul is a matter of public knowledge[1].

If we turn from France to take a glance at her neighbours we find that the first, or at all events one of the first geologists of Italy, Antonio Stoppani, was a priest[2].

In Belgium the great pioneer of Geology is on all hands admitted to have been Jean Baptiste Julien D'Omalius D'Halloy[3] († 1875), a highly interesting figure. "If we glance back to the beginning of the career of the man who is honoured to-day", says Dupont[4], "we come upon one of the finest passages in the history of science. It was the period when the lines of positive Geology were being laid, and the part filled by D'Omalius in the work of initiation was a very remarkable one. To him belongs the honour of having co-ordinated all the geological elements of Western Europe in a unified scheme. He was engaged on the work from 1804 to 1814. His first publication, a description of the district between the Rhine and Pas de Calais, laid the foundations of our national Geology.

---

[1] He composed the Rapport sur l'histoire de la Conférence de Saint-Médard 1868, Ch. Clair, Pierre Olivaint, prêtre de la Comp. de Jésus, Paris-Bruxelles 1878, 81. — Cf. Natur und Offenbarung XLV, Munster 1899, 34 ff.

[2] Sansoni in R. Istituto Lombardo di scienze e lettere. Rendiconti Ser. II, vol. XXVI, Milano 1893, 98—127. A. M. Cornelio, Vita di A. Stoppani, Torino 1898.

[3] E. Dupont in the Annuaire of the Belgian Academy XLII, Bruxelles 1876, 181 ff. Bulletin de la Société géologique de France 3ᵉ série, VI, Paris 1877—1878, 453—467. — The family originally came from the village of Omal (Hesbaye); Halloy is a village in which one branch of the family resided.

[4] Ante 181.

He next turned his attention to that classic ground of his science, the Paris Basin, and put the crown on his work by the issue, at the age of thirty-one, of a geological chart of the French Empire."

Von Zittel[1] adds his word of corroboration to this estimate:

"The Belgian scientist supplemented in a striking fashion the work of Cuvier and of Brongniart. The outcome of his incessant scientific 'tramps' in all directions between 1804 and 1814 was a geological chart of France and of the neighbouring districts of Belgium, Germany, and Switzerland. It was an invaluable basis for the more detailed special surveys of Dufrenoy and De Beaumont. . . ."

D'Omalius was born on February 6th 1783. He was of noble family, and, after the fashion of his day and station, was sent to Paris in 1801 to finish his education, his parents desiring that by intercourse with the best society, study of French literature and frequentation of the theatre he should acquire that polish and distinction of manner on which the aristocratic classes set a perhaps extravagant value. But the son's natural bent carried him in a very different direction. He had read Buffon, and was all aflame with enthusiasm for scientific research. The first visit he paid was not to the theatre but to the Jardin des Plantes where Fourcroy was lecturing on Chemistry, and "Citizen" Lacépède on Geology. "What a delight it is", he wrote home, "to see and hear this master of the secrets of nature, the friend and the continuator of Buffon! How lucidly and beautifully he handles his subjects! If I can manage it, I will not miss a single lecture."[2] He kept

[1] Geschichte der Geologie und Paläontologie 152.

[2] Dupont ante 186.

his vow, and neither tragedies nor comedies could allure him away from science. His parents however were not at all pleased. They were afraid that he would return to them with his head full of unpractical learning, and they wrote him continual letters of remonstrance and rebuke. D'Omalius would reply that he was all good will to follow their advice, but of what avail was good will! As for literature, it was so hard in Paris to find what one wanted! Let his father and mother pronounce on the business themselves! He had most conscientiously attended a lecture on literature although it clashed with Fourcroy's course. But he "soon found that literature was not for him". He then determined to make a trial of the courses at St. Antoine. But there the Professor "talked the whole time, if you please, about poetry!" How could all the good will in the world sacrifice Fourcroy to poetry? In short, despite all the remonstrances from home he could not tear himself away from "Fourcroy and Company" as his mother angrily termed them, either during his first visit, or again during his second in 1803, and his third in 1805. The young noble lived in Paris in the simplest manner, made all his journeys and excursions on foot, and paid no more than six francs a month for his room, and thirty-three for his pension. He was caught in the wave of enthusiasm aroused by Napoleon Bonaparte, and to the grave displeasure of his father sent him letters addressed "To Citizen D'Omalius at Halloy".

His journeys home were always slow and circuitous; he transformed them into a geological survey of Northern France. His first publications on the subject attracted considerable notice, and confirmed D'Omalius in his project of extending his survey and researches over the whole of France. His family began to think more kindly of Geology when D'Omalius was commissioned to execute a geological map of France, and was on that ground dispensed from service in the army. He continued his labours, and by 1813 had travelled more than 25 000 kilometres in France and Italy, when, owing to the disturbed state of affairs on the Continent, his father insisted that these dangerous expeditions should be abandoned. D'Omalius obeyed, and, as it were, turned down the last page of this phase of his career.

In the next phase he would seem to have utterly forgotten science. The great map of France slumbered in oblivion in the archives at Paris. Its author was at the time Governor of Namur, and for all his learning and predicted "unpracticality" made a most excellent administrator. A law-book, published by him, gives ample evidence that scientific research had not weakened his hold on the everyday realities of life. After the Revolution on 1830 he retired from public life. He returned at once to science. He now devoted himself less to independent research than to keeping up with the progress of the science. He published a manual of Geology, and gave much attention to problems at once scientific and philosophical e. g. the theory of evolution, and the conception of a "vital principle". His intellectual activity never weakened or wavered. At 91 years of age he was able to pronounce a discourse in the Belgian Academy, and a fortnight later he set out on a scientific excursion. It ended fatally. He was found lying unconscious in the open air, and never recovered from the stroke.

"In religion", says Dupont, "D'Omalius was a practical Catholic. The dogmas and duties, taught by the prescribed organs of the Church, always found in him a ready submission and obedience." [1]

On the relation of science to religion, D'Omalius has recorded his own convictions.

When the Belgian Academy celebrated on December 16th 1866 the fiftieth anniversary of its foundation, D'Omalius, as Director of the scientific department, was called upon to deliver the speech of the day [2]. He took as his subject the relations existing between science and religious belief. "I propose to lay before you some considerations", the speech begins, "which will show you how unjust is the charge so commonly made that the articles of our Christian faith are in contradiction with the established results of science." He then enumerates the stock objections to the Christian account of Creation, the Fall, the unity of the human race, immortality, and so on. His treatment of his subject is evidently inspired by the desire to go as far as he can to meet the scruples of science. "I admit", he proceeds, "that for our finite intellects there are grave difficulties in both these fundamental dogmas — the existence of an omnipotent, immaterial God, and the act of Creation — but it is still more difficult to conceive the existence of the universe and its marvellous order without postulating the prior existence of an omnipotent Being. And so science and reason can produce no valid objection in regard to either of the pro-

---

[1] En matière religieuse, d'Omalius était Catholique pratiquant. Les dogmes et les devoirs, enseignés par les organes légaux de la religion, étaient acceptés sans observations, et il montra pendant toute sa vie la plus grande soumission à l'Église. D'une grande tolérance, il s'abstenait de jamais prendre part aux discussions religieuses, laissant à chacun le soin de la responsabilité de rechercher la vérité où bon lui semble (Dupont in Annuaire of the Belgian Academy XLII 278).

[2] Bulletins de l'Académie Royale des sciences, des lettres et des beaux-arts de Belgique, 35e année, 2e série, XXII, Bruxelles 1866, 555—563. Reprinted without the introduction in the Revue générale V, Bruxelles 1867, 18—23.

blems in question." [1] He criticises sharply those champions of religion who, although without training or learning in science, presume to pronounce authoritatively on its conclusions. But on the other hand human pride and passion, burning to cast off the yoke of religion, are continually exaggerating the obscurities of religion and the mistakes of some of its defenders.

D'Omalius marshals in his discourse all the arguments familiar to the modern theologian. He concludes: "To sum up, I have no hesitation in saying that in my judgment there is no real opposition between our religious beliefs and the conclusions of science." [2]

André Dumont is another name of rare distinction in Belgian science. He was commissioned by the Government to make a geological map [3] of his native country, spent thirteen years (1836—1849) at the task, and produced a masterpiece. His "remarkable researches" exercised a "not inconsiderable influence on the whole development of tertiary stratigraphy". Born in 1809, Dumont was snatched away by an early and sudden death in 1857. "He honoured religion", it was said of him, "as much by his piety, as geology by his profound insight and industry." [4] As he lay on his death-bed

[1] Ante 556: Il est encore plus difficile de concevoir l'existence de l'univers et de son arrangement admirable, sans qu'il ait préexisté un Être tout-puissant. Cf. p. 561: Nous ne pouvons pas plus concevoir le mouvement des astres sans une cause première d' impulsion, que nous ne concevons la naissance d'un être vivant sans l'intervention d'un Être préexistant.

[2] En résumé, je n'hésite pas à dire qu'il n'existe, à mes yeux, aucune opposition réelle entre nos croyances religieuses et les démonstrations données par l'état actuel des sciences naturelles (ib. 563).

[3] v. Zittel, Gesch. der Geologie und Paläontologie 533 603 702.

[4] André Dumont, mort à la fleur de l'âge, laissant après lui de vastes travaux et des espérances plus vastes encore, a fait autant

his mind was busy with the relations of his science to Holy Writ. "On the day before his death, as he was about to receive the last Sacraments, he said to the Bishop of Liège: 'It is amazing how after all the labours of Geology we are forced to recognise that Moses, writing in an age so primitive and remote, was able to give a perfectly accurate account of the whole history of the earth, especially of the various orders of beings and of the line of succession in which they stand.'"[1]

D'Omalius and Dumont limited their researches to the geological conformation of Belgium, and bestowed but little attention on the fossils which are to be found in the various strata. The chief pioneer and authority in this latter department was the Louvain Professor Van Beneden about whom we shall have a word to say later.

If we turn to England we shall have no difficulty in finding great geologists who were at the same time loyal Christians. William Buckland[2] († 1856) devoted a special volume to the study of the relations between his science and natural theology[3]. Schönbein tells us that he heard him at the Scientific Congress at Birming-

---

d'honneur à la religion par sa fidélité qu'à la géologie par ses découvertes (Lefebvre in Revue des quest. scient. L, Louvain 1901, 67). A son of Dumont's consecrated himself to religious life in the Society of Jesus.

[1] Ami de la religion CLXXV, Paris 1857, 626.

[2] v. Zittel, Gesch. der Geologie und Paläontologie 162. — Cf. Mrs. Gordon, The Life and Correspondence of W. Buckland, London 1894.

[3] Geology and Mineralogy considered with reference to Natural Theology, London 1838. Cf. ante p. 224.

ham in 1839 declaim vehemently against the "groundless prejudice against science so prevalent in England at the time, which attributed to scientific men a hostility to religion".

The German geologist K. C. Von Leonhard[1] who spent a good deal of time in the company of Buckland at Heidelberg writes of him as follows:

"The great Oxford Professor insisted again and again — and for me his views were as congenial as they were instructive — on the reconcilability of geological research with Sacred Scripture. He had devoted long thought to religious as well as to scientific problems. It was a great joy to hear him speak out in his decided, attractive way. The account of creation given in Genesis he regarded as part of the infallible word of God, with which science must never allow itself to be betrayed into conflict. But none the less, certain modifications of the commonly accepted explanation of the Mosaic story were necessary, and science on its part could not yet claim to have established a complete history of the earth."

Writing of Buckland's Bridgewater Treatise "with which his name will long be associated and remembered" a famous brother-geologist, Roderick Impey Murchison († 1871), says: "Whatever new facts may be discovered, the book will always hold its ground as a proof of the rich and abundant insight which enabled him to reconstruct forms of a long vanished past, and bring them before our imagination, and so make visible to all the Providence of the Almighty as it manifested itself in the early history of creation."[2] Murchison repeats towards the end of his great work the belief here expressed in the existence of the Creator. The facts

[1] Aus unserer Zeit in meinem Leben II, Stuttgart 1856, 229.

[2] Journal of the R. Geographical Society XXVII, London 1857, CVI.

of Geology are to him "memoranda which the Creator has put before our eyes in the book of nature"[1]. In his contributions to the Geographical Society he takes frequent occasion to express his interest in the various Christian missions[2].

Edward Hitchcock († 1864), one of the leading geologists of America, wrote at large on the relations between the Scriptures and science. His excellent and popular book on the history of creation[3] "combines the ideas of Buckland with those of the theologians"[4]. Another writer on the same subject was the celebrated Scotch savant John Mac Culloch[5] († 1835). Hitchcock was a Congregationalist preacher; Buckland, like his colleagues W. D. Conybeare († 1857), and A. Sedgwick († 1872), was a minister of the Anglican Church[6]. Conybeare exchanged geology for theology so far back as 1832[7].

On April 14th 1895 America lost her greatest geologist, James Dwight Dana, then in his eighty-second

[1] Journal of the R. Geographical Society XXVII, London 1857, CV.

[2] Ib. e. g. XIV (1844) CIX; XXXV (1865) CLXXVII.

[3] The religion of Geology and its connected sciences (1851).

[4] Biographie gén. by Hoefer XXIV 807.

[5] System of Geology, with a Theory of the Earth and an Explanation of its Connection with the Sacred Records, London 1831. Proofs and illustrations of the attributes of God, from the facts and laws of the physical universe being the foundation of natural and revealed religion, London 1837.

[6] Hugh Miller, The Testimony of the Rocks; or Geology in its bearings on the two theologies, natural and revealed, Edinburgh 1857, 117. The author of this volume was likewise a diligent observer of nature.

[7] The Journal of the R. Geographical Soc. XXVIII, London 1858, CXXIX f.

year. "Dana", says Von Zittel[1], "was a most brilliant geologist, zoologist and mineralogist; his services in science won him in succession the Wollaston Medal, the Copley Medal, and the great Walker prize. He was accepted on all sides as the master of American Geology, and the development of that science owed much to his influence". He was a member of the famous Wilkes Expedition which spent fours years in investigating the coast of South America and the Pacific Ocean; the classification and systematisation of the materials obtained during the voyage occupied Dana for thirty years. "His studies of the geology of the Pacific, the volcanoes of the Sandwich Islands, the coral formations, and of various species of zoophytes and crustacea stand in the very forefront of the literature of travel."[2]

If we wish to know what the "first geologist of America" thought of religion, we have only to turn to the title-page of his "Manual of Geology"[3]. We find two quotations, the first from Juvenal: *Numquam aliud natura, aliud sapientia docet;* the second from Cicero: *Licet iam oculis quodammodo contemplari pulchritudinem rerum earum quas divina providentia dicimus constitutas.*

At the outset he offers praise to God as the great Guide and Law-giver who has shaped and directed to

---

[1] Ante 459. Cf. Dan. C. Gilman, The Life of James Dwight Dana, scientific explorer, mineralogist, geologist, zoologist. New York 1899.

[2] v. Zittel, Geschichte der Geologie 459.

[3] James D. Dana, Manual of Geology: treating of the principles of the science with special reference to American geological history, 4. edition 1896. Our references are to the 2nd ed., New York 1876.

its goal the history of the earth[1]. The book concludes with a discussion of the Biblical account of Creation. That account, writes Dana, is rich in so many truths which the human author could not possibly have derived from the science of his day that no explanation save that of divine inspiration is adequate.

"The record in the Bible", he writes, "is therefore profoundly philosophical in the scheme of creation which it presents. It is both true and divine. It is a declaration of authorship, both of Creation and the Bible, on the first page of the sacred volume. There can be no real conflict between the two books of the Great Author. Both are revelations made by Him to Man — the earlier telling of God-made harmonies, coming up from the deep past, and rising to their height when Man appeared; the latter teaching Man's relations to his Maker and speaking of loftier harmonies in the eternal future."[2]

Sir William Dawson († 1899), Chancellor of the University of Montreal, President of the Royal Canadian Scientific Society, was "one of the most eminent geologists of Canada, the scientific survey of which was in great measure his work"[3]. He was a Presbyterian[4] and published many apologetic studies on the relations of science to Revelation[5].

---

[1] . . . although Infinite Mind has guided all events towards the great end — a world for mind —, the earth has under His guidance and appointed law passed through a regular course of history or growth.

[2] Dana, Manual of Geology 770.

[3] Wildermann's Jahrbuch der Naturwissenschaften XV (1899 to 1900) 479. Cf. Henry M. Ami, Sir John William Dawson in The American Geologist XXVI, Minneapolis 1900, 1—48. Nature LXI, London and New York 1899—1900, 80.

[4] Ami ante 8—10.

[5] Archaia, or Studies of the Narrative of the Creation in Genesis. Montreal 1857. Archaia, or Studies of the Cosmogony and Natural

"There is surely", he writes, "a latent Gospel in nature which has always been proclaimed in it, though often to heedless ears, and which required the infinite knowledge and love of Jesus to interpret it clearly to us. No doubt this Gospel, like that of Christianity itself, is turned into gall and bitterness by modern pessimistic advocates of the mere struggle for existence; but to rightly constituted minds Christ's interpretation is better, as it is also more happy and hopeful" [1].

J. H. Fuchs, whose name we have already mentioned, deserves a special word as the great champion of what was called "Neo-Neptunism" [2]. In opposition to the theory of "Vulcanism" then dominant in Geology, he maintained in an academic thesis that the origin of the rocks is to be sought in an antecedent aqueous condition, and to be explained by chemical processes. "Although many of Fuchs' contentions have been dismissed as quite untenable, his work made and marks an epoch in the history of Genetic Geology. His 'Neo-Neptunism' was taken up and further developed by Bischof and others" [3].

Karl Gustav Bischof [4] (born 1792 at Woerth, died 1870) was at first a chemist; during his professorate at Bonn he turned his attention to Geology, and made

---

History of the Hebrew Scriptures. Ib. 1860. On the Antiquity of Man. Ib. 1863. Nature and the Bible. New York 1875. The Dawn of Life, Montreal 1875. The Origin of the World, according to Revelation and Science. Ib. 1877, 6th ed., London 1823, etc.

[1] Quoted by Ami ante 10.

[2] Uber die Theorien der Erde (1837). Gesammelte Schriften 199 to 218.

[3] v. Gumbel in the Allgemeine deutsche Biographie VIII 167

[4] Ib. II 665—669.

investigations into the geological formation of the Rhineland. At the outset he was a convinced "Vulcanist". His study of mineral springs (1824), and still more his "classical work" on the internal heat of the earth (1837) "won for the plutonistic theories, then struggling into prominence, an all but universal acceptance". And yet Bischof himself was to become later in life the most outspoken opponent of these theories. "An epoch-making and pioneer work" is the characterisation given of his "Text-book of Chemical and Physical Geology" (1848—54). In this Bischof developed the ideas put forward by Fuchs, and, as the work went on, changed over completely from the "Plutonist" to the "Neptunist" side. His notes on the part played in geological processes by water, and its manifold activity, hold a place among the master-pieces of Speculative Geology, and remain for all time an invaluable source of indispensable facts and stimulating ideas. "Bischof remains for all time one of the most powerful influences in the whole history of Geology."[1]

To complete the picture we should add that Bischof also did much for the application of science to practical life. It was at his suggestion that the now famous mineral well at Bad Neuenahr was bored. He also showed how copper could be extracted from ores regarded as worthless, and published a paper on the cause of hailstorms and certain preventive and protective measures that might be taken to diminish their harmfulness.

[1] v. Gumbel in the Allgemeine deutsche Biographie VIII 668 669. Also v. Zittel (Gesch. der Geologie und Paläontologie 306) praises Bischof's "bewunderungswurdige Sachkenntnis"; he has "die chemische Geologie zu einem neuen, selbständigen Wissenszweig erhoben".

In the years 1842 and 1843 popular lectures were delivered at Bonn by the teachers of the High School, the receipts of these lectures going to the building-fund of the Bonn Cathedral. We quote one or two passages from Bischof's course.

"We come then by a simple process of reasoning to this conclusion that the earth when it came forth from the hand of the Almighty must have been a fiery ball. . . . Is there anything strange in this? Have we not daily before our eyes an instance of such a fiery ball, though a far vaster one? I need not name it . . . it is that from which all life proceeds, and which, before the light of revelation broke upon them, was worshipped by many nations as their divinity." [1]

In another passage, having claimed, on the basis of experiments made by himself, a period of 353 million years to allow cooling-down of the earth, he goes on: "These vast figures in no way contradict what is written in Scripture. The 'days' spoken of in Genesis must obviously be taken to mean great periods of time. Do we not read in the Epistles of St. Peter (chap. 3, verse 8) that 'a day before the Lord is as a thousand years, and a thousand years as a day'?

"By a miracle God created the world; by a miracle the first plant appeared on the earth. For when we seek to analyse the causes of phenomena, and pursue the process stage by stage from the most immediate to the most remote, we always, in the end, come on an ultimate cause which lies outside the material world; we come on a miracle [2]. The question: How came the first plant on the earth? merges in the larger problem of the origin of all that is."

"Nothing on earth possesses its end in itself; everything has been created for an end higher than itself; man him-

---

[1] Populäre Vorlesungen über naturwissenschaftliche Gegenstände, im Jahre 1842 gehalten vor den gebildeten Bewohnern von Bonn, Bonn 1843, 5.

[2] The theologian will not call this work of God a miracle.

self exists only to glorify God, and to prepare himself for eternity."

"In this distinguished assembly I may feel sure that there are none of those short-sighted minds, that can see in nature only a planless welter. To those who think after that fashion, nothing can be more illuminative than a study of the extremely simple means by which great results are attained, and nothing can more fully convince them that planlessness is a quality absolutely alien to the Divine mind."

In the second part of the course, that of 1843, we find among other characteristic passages: "If we are unable to discern in all phenomena the directing hand of God, this is to be ascribed to our mental limitations. When we study things in their totality we discern everywhere the working of an Omnipotent Providence, Who governs the world with infinite goodness and wisdom."

In Bischof's purely scientific works we find the same ideas at least hinted at. He speaks of the "providential plan" after which "the Almighty" created the world and treats as self-evident the proposition that we find tokens, everywhere and throughout all creation, of purposiveness, and the wise ordering of things to the service of organic life. "That the Almighty, Who in the words of Genesis created the world out of nothing", he says on another page, "is able to transform one element into another is surely a proposition which nobody will dream of disputing." [1]

Gerhard Vom Rath († 1888) and Heinrich Von Dechen († 1889), who with Bischof, were the most distinguished geologists of Bonn University were both Protestants [2]. Von Dechen was a member of what

---

[1] G. Bischof, Lehrbuch der chemischen und physikalischen Geologie II 1, Bonn 1851, 9. Cf. I (1847) 981: "es ist eine weise Anordnung im Haushalt der Natur" etc.

[2] H Laspeyres in the Verhandlungen des naturhistorischen Vereins der preuß. Rheinlande etc. XLVI, Bonn 1889, 244—245; cf. 240 in which he, on the death of his son, writes of his "unbedingte Ergebung in den gottlichen Willen".

was called the Orthodox Church; Vom Rath belonged to a free Church, but was none the less ardent in conforming his life and opinions to the teaching of the Bible "which he made his daily reading, and knew as intimately as he knew his instruments"[1].

We come now to a name more distinguished even than that of Bischof. Friedrich August Quenstedt (born at Eisleben 1809, died at Tübingen 1889), a North German by birth, won his laurels at Tubingen. "For more than half a century", writes Q. Fraas[2], "Quenstedt taught in the Suabian Athens, honoured on all sides as one of the keenest and fruitfullest minds among German geologists. But although he enjoyed a University reputation he was still more widely known as a tireless traveller and investigator; indeed there was no part of Upper or Lower Suabia in which he was not a familiar and respected figure. He was a veritable *praeceptor Sueviae* in Geology." Von Zittel bears similar witness to Quenstedt's greatness; his study of the formation and fossils of the Suabian Jura was so thorough as to leave practically nothing of any importance to his successors[3].

Quenstedt has left his religious opinious on record in more than one of his works. Thus we read at the beginning of his "Epochs of Nature"[4]: "In proportion as research deepens, it seems to become more and more obscure. The fundamental design of the

---

[1] Leopoldina XXV, Halle 1889, 84.

[2] Nekrolog auf Quenstedt in the Neue Jahrbucher fur Mineralogie, Geologie, Paläontologie 1890, I.

[3] Gesch. der Geologie und Paläontologie 522.

[4] Tübingen 1861, 2.

Creator seems to retreat more and more from our gaze, in proportion as we push our investigations deeper and fancy ourselves to be on the point of grasping it." The processes of transformation and evolution which are to be observed in the organic world he refers back to the will and directing intelligence of God[1].

Of the Scriptural story of Creation he always speaks with profound respect; though we cannot accept all that he has to say on the theological questions raised by it. Having glanced rapidly at its outlines he remarks: "The picture given here is so rich in truth, that, considering the ancient and historic documents, we feel compelled to say that Moses, who lived 3400 years ago, was the greatest geologist of all times."[2] He dwells with obvious gratification on the many points in which the Mosaic account is corroborated by science[3].

Friedrich Pfaff (born 1825 at Erlangen; died in 1886 as a Professor in the University of his native town), was of a South German stock, and spent all his life in South Germany. He made contributions of great importance to Mineralogy, Crystallography, and Geo-Physics. He first attracted notice by his book "The Story of Creation with Special Reference to the Biblical Account" (1855). In this he sought to bring the results of Geology into harmony with the Bible. He writes from the same standpoint in the third edition of his "Story of Creation", published in 1882, and in his tractate

---

[1] Epochs of Nature 831.

[2] Die Schöpfung der Erde und ihre Bewohner, Stuttgart 1882, 8.

[3] E. g. ib.: "Jetzt erst, am vierten Tage, wird die Sonne fertig. Wie wahr! Denn die kleine Erde mußte sich lange vor der riesigen Sonne gestalten."

"The Evolution of the World according to Atomism"[1]. He wrote a long series of polemical works in criticism of the extravagances of the evolutionists, and of the materialistic ideas propagated by them in the popular mind. "Relying on the historical fact 'that a people, as soon as it has lost belief in a divine government of the world, falls into moral ruin', he went into battle; what he longed for above all, was to preserve in that German nation which he loved so ardently the sense of the ideal, and especially the belief in a moral order."[2]

A pupil of Quenstedt's, the Protestant pastor of Laufen, Oskar Fraas († 1897), writes on the question of the origin of the world[3]:

"Of speculations on the beginning of things there is naturally no lack; we find them recorded wherever men have been able to express their thoughts in language. What strikes one most in reading them is that humanity has not advanced by so much as a hair's breadth since the time of the Seven Sages of Greece. . . . Science can throw as little light on the problem as man can throw on the story of his own birth. Science finds nothing else, at all events nothing better, to say than what was said so long ago: In the beginning God created heaven and earth."

Hans Bruno Geinitz († 1900), whose appreciation of Barrande we have cited, was himself one of the first geologists of his day[4]. "He was one of the last, if not the very last, of that older school of geologists, who were at once thoroughly versed in the special literature of all branches of their science, and masters

---

[1] v. Gumbel in Allgemeine deutsche Biographie XXV 581.

[2] Leopoldina XXIV (Halle 1888) 216.

[3] Vor der Sundflut. Eine Geschichte der Urwelt, Stuttgart 1866, VIII.

[4] Biographical Sketch by his son in Leopoldina XXXVI, Halle 1900, 59—70 85—89 98—104.

of a general, synthetic view of it."[1] In his "Autobiography" Geinitz writes[2]: "It is not vanity that moves me to set down here a retrospect of a long life, so abundantly blessed by God." "Always blest with good health, I was able with God's help to overcome all the many obstacles which I encountered during my career as a scientist."[3] "With the most heartfelt thanks to God . . . and with inexpressible gratitude to the many thousands of friendly helpers" whom he had met during his life he concludes his personal reminiscences († 1898)[4].

Karl Von Raumer († 1865) is of an earlier period. An enthusiastic disciple of A. G. Werner, he was none the less among the first to oppose, on empirical grounds, the theories of his master. In his "Geognostic Sketches" we find the first attempt made by a German scientist to apply to Germany the ideas of French and English investigators. Raumer was "a gifted and many-sided man, of great religious fervour, and a rectitude of character which led him to take sides very often at the sacrifice of his own interests". He held that education should have "a strong religious tendency". During his Professorate in Erlangen he had to endure much unpleasantness and many attacks "because of his open and practical confession of Christian belief"[5].

The first Professor of Geology appointed (1843) to a German University (Munich) was K. F. E. Von Schafhäutl. He explored the Bavarian Alps, until then all

---

[1] Naturwissenschaftliche Rundschau XV, Braunschweig 1900, 131.

[2] Leopoldina XXXVI 59.

[3] Ib. 62. [4] Ib. 102.

[5] Allgemeine deutsche Biographie XXVII 420 f. Cf. Karl v. Raumers Leben von ihm selbst erzählt. Stuttgart 1866.

but unknown to Geology; discovered nitrogen in iron, and was the first to produce, by the aqueous method, artificial crystals of quartz.

Schafhäutl was an ardent Catholic; during the Döllinger trouble he, with Lamont and Kaiser, remained unwaveringly loyal to the Church[1].

"An amazingly active and fruitful mind in Palæontology" is the etimate given of Oswald Heer[2] . . . He was a Swiss, born at Niederutzweil in 1809, became a teacher of Entomology and Botany in Zurich High School in 1834, and died in 1883. His first great work on the fossil insects of Oeningen contains descriptions of about a thousand species. "It is" says Probst, "the pioneer book of this branch of Palæontology, and will long remain the chief source of our knowledge of these organisms". It was followed by work of even great importance. "Between 1855 and 1859 appeared his masterpiece, the great *Flora Tertiaria Helvetiae* . . . in which no less than 900 species, for the most part new, are described. Heer's specialized knowledge of his subject gave him a wonderful power of reconstructing tertiary flora, and of comparing them with the other tertiary remains, and also with those of our present age. By this means he was able to determine with amazing penetration the climatic and other conditions of the early world. The results of his labours were

[1] Allgemeine Zeitung, Augsburg 1871, Nr. 113, 1981.

[2] Nekrolog of J. Probst in Neues Jahrbuch fur Mineralogie, Geologie und Paläontologie 1884 I, Stuttgart 1884. v. Zittel, Gesch. der Geologie und Paläontologie 783 ff. de Saporta in the Revue des deux mondes, 1. juill. and 15 août 1884, 182 f 184 f. Notice of Heer's works in Schriften der physikalisch-ökonomischen Gesellschaft in Königsberg i. Pr. XXV 1, Konigsberg 1884, 16—26.

embodied in a popular manual 'Primitive Switzerland' (1864), and thus made accessible to a wider audience."[1] Heer was nearly seventy when he began the most elaborate of his works, the *Flora Fossilis Arctica*. This ran to seven quarto volumes, with more than four hundred illustrative tables. He described in it the fossil plant-remains which have been discovered in the highest latitudes, and showed that at the time of their growth the climate of those regions must have been considerably milder than it is now. Heer had at the outset intended to devote only a single volume to the undertaking. But fresh data continually accumulated on his hands, and demanded ampler treatment. During the greater part of the work Heer was constantly ailing, and had to keep his bed.

"I shall never forget", writes Probst[2], "the sight that met me when I called to see Heer at the beginning of his seventieth year, when he was busy on the third volume of his Polar Flora. He lay in bed with a kind of writing-table fixed up in front of him, crowded with the specimens which he had to examine, identify, and describe. He could not thank God enough, he said, for giving him strength to continue his work."

The cheerful piety, which these words reveal, finds frequent expression in his writings, especially in the conclusion of "Primitive Switzerland".

A retrospect of the plant and animal kingdoms of the various periods opens out to us, he says, "a succession of beautiful phenomena — phenomena which do not allow of a doubt that nature in the process of her evolution forms an infinitely beautiful and harmonious whole, inspired by a

[1] v. Zittel, Gesch. der Geologie und Paläontologie 783 ff.

[2] Ante 5.

systematic plan and purpose. Of this great fabric we know only the ground-piles, but the more we come to understand of the early world the richer and royaller the fabric seems; the gaps which the world, as we know it, presents, are filled up and vanish in the harmony of a minutely articulated whole. But the greatness and beauty of creation exist only for him whose spiritual eye is open to it. An image will make this clear. A page written over with the score of a symphony of Beethoven has meaning only for a musician. For him every note has its significance, and as he translates sign into sound there streams through his imagination a very world of harmony. So it is with nature. Individual phenomena, like the individual notes, reveal their significance only when taken in the unity of the context. Then they coalesce in a great articulate whole, and there arises in our soul a vast harmony, which like a musical symphony, lifts us above the world of sense and grants us a glimpse of a divine order. We should regard a man as very naive, indeed, who maintained that the notes of the symphony sprang from dots fallen by chance on the paper. But it seems to me that it is just as blind and unintelligent to maintain that the infinite and far more marvellous harmony of nature is the outcome of chance. The deeper we pierce into the secrets of nature, the more earnest and intimate becomes our conviction that nothing save a belief in an omnipotent and omniscient Creator, Who has created Heaven and earth after a definite and deliberate plan, will suffice to explain the twin riddles of the physical world and the human mind. Not only the heart of man, but nature itself, bears witness to God, and when we consider from this standpoint the wonderful story of the earth and of its plants and animals it seems to us for the first time to surrender its real meaning, and to stir us with all its ecstatic thrill." [1]

"In all his works", writes a biographer, "we find the same thought dominant, the same motive operative, and that is the desire to add something to our knowledge of the 'har-

---

[1] O. Heer, Die Urwelt der Schweiz. 2. Subskriptions-Ausgabe der 2. Aufl., Zurich 1883, 690—691.

mony of Creation', and of the glories of its Creator. For Heer was fundamentally religious; his piety had the character of a childlike surrender of himself to God. . . . He never began the work of the day without oblation to his Heavenly Father; he never brought an enterprise to a close without a fervent prayer of thanksgiving. And in his last days he held fast to his belief in the life eternal. And whatever we may think of this belief (!) we must recognise that to him it was the deepest of all realities; his personality was saturated in it. He would have no 'double-bookkeeping', but an absolute harmony between his scientific and his religious convictions. This was the source from which the old savant drew that peaceful, joyous courage of his, that childlike heart." [1]

Swiss scientists have always played an important part in the development of Geology, and its more recent progress is very closely associated with the name of Bernhard Studer. Studer (1794—1887) opened his career with a work published in 1825, "marked by his characteristic stamp of industry, accuracy, and insight". His main achievement was the "monumental work", "The Geology of Switzerland" (1851—1853), and a geological chart of the country, prepared in collaboration with A. Escher. "When we consider the enormous topographical, tectonic, and stratigraphic difficulties which had to be faced in the accomplishment of this enterprise, we readily concede to this chart a place among the master-pieces of Geology in the nineteenth century."

This judgment comes from the pen of Von Zittel [2]. He then goes on to the question which before all occupies our attention in this volume. Studer formally

---

[1] Vierteljahrschrift der Naturforschenden Gesellschaft in Zurich XXVIII, Zurich 1883, 306—307.

[2] Gesch. der Geologie und Paläontologie 536 Cf. L. Rütimeyer, Gesammelte kleine Schriften II, Basel 1898, 415—440.

defined his attitude towards religion in a lecture of which R. Wolf writes as follows:

"The lecture on 'Science and Religion' (Bern 1856), delivered by Studer before a popular audience, is designed to show that, to use the words of Secchi, there is no conflict between science and religion, and that if there seems for the moment to be such a conflict, it is because the representatives of these two human activities step outside their proper provinces. It is to my mind a very remarkable pronouncement, from which, even now, much may be learned. It is, moreover, thoroughly characteristic of its author, and exhibits his sound, clear intellect at its best." [1]

To Studer and Escher we must add a third Swiss geologist, Peter Merian, Councillor of Basle († 1883). Rütimeyer [2] writes of him in the following terms:

"Merian exercised great reticence with regard to his religious opinions. But two things are quite clear from his occasional utterances. Nothing was more alien to his mind than scepticism; he certainly did not feel himself called to be an indifferent or heedless witness to the course of the physical world. On the contrary, his whole being was fired with the conviction that the relationship between our human existence and the unknown totality of things is matter not for melancholy but for living faith; he believed that, as bearing on the meaning and destiny of man, the voice of conscience should assuredly have no less regard paid it than the testimony of the senses. So also we find expressions to the effect that to know the time and hour for the attainment of our goal is reserved to God alone.

"Such a life then, we may be certain, has not fallen back into the gulf of nature. . . ."

Merian was a believer in immortality. So much can be gathered from Rütimeyer's article. Rütimeyer himself (1895) "a scientist of the first rank, and a leading authority

---

[1] R. Wolf in Vierteljahrschrift der Naturforschenden Gesellschaft in Zurich XXXII, Zurich 1887, 102.

[2] Ante 411.

on mammals"[1], shared the belief of his friend. Emmanuel Ludwig Gruner († 1883 at Beaucaire) also holds a distinguished place in the line of Swiss geologists. He was an ardent Protestant, and laboured much for the re-establishment of the Sabbath, as a day of rest, in Paris, for the propagation of various Missions etc. In his Discourse "Dieu et la Création révélés par la Géologie" he arrayed the facts of science in criticism at once of pantheism after the manner of Renan, and of evolution after the manner of Darwin[2].

We have to add but two more names, both German, to our list of great geologists, Karl August Lossen († 1893) and Wilhelm Waagen († 1900).

"It is but rarely", runs an obituary of the former[3], "that the death of a colleague excites such deep and universal sorrow as that of Lossen. Every one who knew him had the sense of a great personal loss and even at this moment, six months after his death, we can hardly realise that he is gone from us for ever."

Lossen had left this impression on his friends as well by the extreme lovableness of his character as by his scientific attainments.

Born at Kreuznach on January 6th 1841, he had by 1866 entered on his career of geological research. "In the summer of that year he began his chart of that mountain-range with which his name will be for ever linked, the Harz." In 1867 and 1868 he published the

[1] v. Zittel, Gesch. der Geologie und Paläontologie 836.

[2] Vierteljahrschrift der Naturforschenden Gesellschaft in Zurich XXVIII, Zurich 1883, 297.

[3] E. Kayser in Neues Jahrbuch fur Mineralogie, Geologie und Paläontologie 1893 II, Stuttgart 1893. — Cf. also for Lossen Berendt in the Jahrbuch der k. preußischen geologischen Landesanstalt und Bergakademie zu Berlin fur das Jahr 1893 XIV, Berlin 1894, LXVII—LXXX; v. Hertling in the Jahresbericht der Görresgesellschaft fur das Jahr 1895, Köln 1896, 13—18.

first fruits of his labours. The paper on the formation of the older strata of the Eastern Harz "contains in germ the whole of his subsequent studies of that region", and "holds a place of prominence in his works". In 1877 he published the "magnificent" chart of the Harz, "a brilliant testimony to his genius and industry".

In 1870 Lossen became lecturer on Petrography in the Academy of Mines, and sometime later secured a similar position at the University of Berlin. In 1879 he completed one of his most laborious undertakings, an exhaustive study of the geological formation of the Berlin area. When the Prussian Geological Institute was formed in 1873 the eyes of the directors turned to Lossen as "one of the leaders" of this science. He did not obtain a Professorate until 1886, and never in fact became an Ordinary Professor, but this was certainly not for lack of scientific merit. "He enjoyed a European reputation, as is instanced by the fact that he was one of the authorities requested by the Committee of the International Geological Congress held at London, to put in writing their views as to the origin of crystalline slates."

As to his personality we may avail ourselves of the words of one his oldest and dearest friends, E. Kayser:

"Powerfully built and extremely attractive in appearance he had a mind to match. He combined in the rarest manner immense strength and seriousness with true Rhenish humour and enthusiasm for the goodness and beauty of life, intellectual greatness with the simplicity of a child. He was characterised above all by fidelity to duty, and inexhaustible goodness of heart. Religion lay at the very basis and intimate source of his life. He was all his life a strong and fervent Catholic, for whom obedience to the ordinances of his Church was no mere thing of custom but a service of the heart.

How often I have seen him during our wanderings together, when we slept in the same room, get out of bed again after the lights had been blown out and throw himself on his knees in prayer! How I used privately to growl at him in the Harz when instead of spending the Sundays with me resting after the week, he would set off to find a Catholic Church and attend Mass, journeying sometimes miles away from the mountains! His wonderful strength and cheery courage enabled him to bear without the least bitterness an affliction which sours so many lives: I mean his deafness. As a boy, he often told me, he had the keenest delight in the song of the lark; at thirty he could scarcely hear a thunder-clap. As years went by, his affliction increased; even with the help of an ear-trumpet he found it very difficult to hear what was said. In the social meetings of which he was so fond his deafness was the source of endless misunderstandings, and of infinite merriment. Notified by our laughter that he had made a blunder he would say smilingly that he had no right to be angry, for a man must suffer for his afflictions! Deafness did not, as is often the case, bring with it a monotonous, expressionless voice; his lectures, on the contrary, were as remarkable in delivery as in matter, and whoever had the chance of hearing him propose a toast in his rich, imaginative style will admit that a more effective speaker could not have been found.

"These few commemorative words will help to show what a dear and richly-endowed colleague we lost in Lossen. His death leaves a gap, never to be filled, in our circle, and in the institution with which he has been so long associated, in the history of which his name will hold a place of honour. . . ."

To complete the picture we add the verdict of another friend of his[1]:

"A thorough Conservative, he was also a faithful son of the Catholic Church, to which he clung with the piety of

[1] Berendt in the Jahrbuch der k. preuß. geolog. Landesanstalt XIV, LXXVIII.

a child till the end, till his eyes were fixed for the last time on the crucifix which hung above his death-bed. Curtius speaks of this trait of Lossen's character, so freely ridiculed by those who had never met him in argument, as 'the beautiful outcome of a belief unshaken by science'. But we should say not merely unshaken, but diffused through his whole life and being, and blended into one great harmony with his scientific conceptions. He was a man before whom one bowed the head in respect, a pure and stainless soul."

Wilhelm Waagen[1] was born in the same year as Lossen, June 23th 1841. He showed at a very early age great enthusiasm and aptitude for science. In the year 1866 five German geologists, of whom he was one, published a series of studies "which had a most important influence on the subsequent development of German science. There can be no doubt that of the five contributors Waagen was the most powerful and original mind". In the same year he obtained an appointment in the University of his native city, Munich, and taught there with brilliant success[2].

"While a *Privatdozent*", says Uhlig, "Waagen delivered no lectures but gave practical demonstrations, at which men like Neumayr, Von Willemons-Suhm, and Kowalevsky assisted. Thus he established in a very short time a distinguished reputation, but unfortunately no material recognition of it followed. At last he obtained in 1870 . . . a place on the 'Geological Survey of India'."

The explanation of Waagen's ill-success can be easily given:

---

[1] For Waagen cf. V. Uhlig in the Centralblatt für Mineralogie, Geologie und Paläontologie 1900, Stuttgart 1900, 380—392. Obituary notice in Beilage zur Augsburger Postzeitung Nr. 20, 7. April 1900, 133—134.

[2] Uhlig ante 383.

"He knew very well, and there was no lack of experienced and friendly colleagues to assure him, that, as things stood in Bavaria, a practising Catholic would have a hard time of it, and could not hope for position, reputation, or emolument. But the young scientist, full of courage and belief in himself, refused to abandon either his faith or his career, and determined to break down by zeal and industry the ban under which the Catholics of Bavaria had hitherto lain." [1]

In India Waagen collected an immense mass of material, but his health was unequal to the climate. He was prostrated by catarrh, and on his recovery attempted to resume his work. But he fell ill again, and was compelled to return to Europe in 1872. In 1875 he made a fresh attempt at a thorough exploration of India, but with the same result. He was once more driven out of the country, and on the voyage home a still greater calamity befell him; the vessel to which all his collections, books, and papers, had been committed was wrecked off Ceylon and sank with all her cargo. It was impossible to obtain a position of any kind in Bavaria, and Waagen emigrated to Vienna. "The most distinguished audience", writes Uhlig, "that ever a *Privatdozent* had, assembled to hear his first lecture (1878—1879) on the geology of India. There were to be found in it Hermann Abich, the Nestor of Viennese geologists, Suess, Hauer, Neumayr . . . and all the younger men." Soon after Waagen became Professor at the German High School in Prague, and in 1883 he published a supplement to Barrande's great work. He received a call to the Academy of Mines of Prussia in 1886, but refused it out of gratitude to his adopted country, and

[1] Beilage zur Augsburger Postzeitung Nr. 20, 7. April 1900, 133.

in 1890 he was raised to a Professorate in Vienna. "So rich was his Indian material that the classification of it absorbed almost his entire scientific activity at Prague and Vienna. The work in which he published his results is among the most noteworthy achievements of recent Palæontology." His laborious life came to a close on March 24th 1900. "His name", says Uhlig, "is inseparably bound up with Indian geological research."

"In Catholic circles in the Bavarian capital Waagen was, before his exile, a familiar figure. He took part in every phase of the Catholic revival which began there in the sixties [1]. "Among his writings we find a special paper in which he brings the Mosaic account of creation into comparison with the conclusions of Geology, and shows the complete agreement between them."

IX. PHYSIOLOGY.

"When Newton was setting about his study of the laws governing the movements of the heavenly bodies he is said to have exclaimed: 'O Physics, I appeal to you to preserve me from Metaphysics!' Whoever nowadays sets out to investigate the functions and properties of the human mind may well invoke the protection of philosophy against physiology. Nevertheless it is not science that leads to materialism, but the misdirection and misuse of science. True science is no more responsible for the misuse, than a knife is for the death of a man who is stabbed with it."

---

[1] Das Schöpfungsproblem, in Natur und Offenbarung XLIV, Munster 1898, 641—660 720—735.

This passage is taken from an address delivered by the great Austrian scientist, Andreas Von Baumgartner († 1865), in the Imperial Academy of Sciences[1]. The dangers, which he signalises as arising from the study of Physiology, are not however to be ascribed to the actual facts brought to light by that science, but to the minds of certain observers who fail to construe these facts in their right relations. If an Ehrenberg, when questioned as to the impression made on his mind by the temples of Egypt, could reply that he had not noticed the temples, that he had gone into them simply to study bats, and had not bothered about anything else; if a Roberval could ask disgustedly at a tragedy, "What does that prove?" — these are but naïve expressions of that concentration and narrowness which we so often find in specialists. A mathematician comes to despise and ignore everything that cannot be worked up into algebraic form, and a physiologist is in danger of becoming so absorbed in purely physiological processes as to overlook all facts of another order, including those which give token of the spirituality of the soul.

Humanity has a profound conviction that its life proceeds on a plan altogether higher than that of the other animals. But this conviction is not based on anatomical or physiological considerations. It rests on obvious and fundamental differences of activity, achievement, and progress between man and the lower animals. No one is in greater danger of overlooking these differences than the specialist whose mind is constantly occupied, not with points of difference, but with points of resemblance. He falls very easily into the mistaken con-

---

[1] Almanach der Akademie IX, Wien 1859, 39 f.

clusion that man represents simply a higher stage of evolution, and differs from the other animals not in kind but only in degree.

The characteristic development of science towards the middle of the nineteenth century added to this first error a second no less obvious. The older school of Physiology was always too ready to ascribe all processes of vegetative life to the immediate action of the soul or "vital force", as it was called. They represented this mysterious vital force as the direct and proximate efficient cause of all physico-chemical processes. Such a theory was bound to provoke a reaction. It was shown that the simpler changes that take place in organisms are due to the operation of the forces investigated by the chemist in his laboratory. It was further shown that many processes previously explained by the hypothesis of vital force could be explained without recourse to any such hypothesis. Wöhler, Liebig, and Berthelot produced in the laboratory chemical compound after chemical compound which had hitherto been regarded as producible only in a living organism. Bernard showed that even after death the liver, so long as the tissue withstands disintegration, continues to secrete sugar. Other scientists demonstrated that the heart can be made to beat after death by the introduction of fresh blood. The inference drawn from these facts went, however, quite beyond the warrant of sound reasoning. Certain processes, said materialistic scientists, hitherto ascribed to the immediate action of the soul, have been explained in another way, consequently we no longer need the hypothesis of a soul to explain anything, not even sensation or cognition.

We have not space to enter more deeply into these questions[1]. We can only hope in these cursory remarks to show that Physiology stands in no more intimate relation to the cardinal questions of Philosophy than any other branch of science, and that the leaders of that science in the nineteenth century were very far indeed from being hostile to the Christian teaching on these questions.

The greatest physiologist of the first half of the nineteenth century is admitted on all hands to have been Johannes Müller (born July 14th 1801 at Coblenz, died April 28th 1858 at Berlin, where he had occupied the Chair of Anatomy and Physiology). "The first physiologist not merely of our day but of our century, indeed one of the greatest of all time", R. Wagner[2], calls him; "the Haller of our generation, the Cuvier of Germany", says Du Bois-Reymond[3]. The extent and variety of his scientific works are simply astounding. It has been calculated that in 37 years he published

---

[1] Cf. L. Dressel, Der belebte und der unbelebte Stoff, Freiburg 1883 H. Malfatti, Über Lebenskraft, in Natur und Offenbarung XLVI, Münster 1900, 727—733. The purely mechanical theory of the origin of life has found in recent times many opponents among the scientists Cf O. Hertwig, Die Entwicklung der Biologie im 19. Jahrhundert, Jena 1900, 24: "Ebenso unberechtigt wie der Vitalismus ist das mechanistische Dogma, daß das Leben mit allen seinen komplizierten Erscheinungen nichts anderes sei als ein chemisch-physikalisches Problem. . . . Wenn es Aufgabe des Chemikers ist, die zahllosen Verbindungen der verschiedenartigen Atome zu Molekülen zu erforschen, so kann er, streng genommen, überhaupt nicht dem eigentlichen Lebensprobleme näher treten. Denn dieses beginnt ja überhaupt erst da, wo seine Untersuchung aufhört etc."

[2] Obituary Notice in the Allgemeine Zeitung, Augsburg 1858, 2029.

[3] Reden. Zweite Folge, Leipzig 1887, 143.

papers amounting in all to 950 sheets, i. e. about $3^1/_2$ sheets of hard and original scientific work every five weeks! And of these publications there is "not a single one that can be called weak". "The mass of facts which Müller's labours brought to light is simply incalculable, and in all his research work we hardly ever find an inaccurate or incomplete observation. On the contrary we find many instances in which his conclusions, although at first disputed, ultimately forced their way to acceptance."[1]

Müller was snatched suddenly away in the very fullness of his activity. In a brochure published in 1899, on the occasion of the erection of a memorial to him in his native city, we find the following extract from the Berlin "Nationalzeitung" of May 2nd 1858[2]:

"The funeral of Dr. Johannes Müller took place this morning with full religious service. A great procession of mourners followed the coffin from the Professor's residence to the cemetery. The Minister Von Raumer was present together with many of the leading members of his Council, as also others of prominence in the official world. The deceased had been a member of the Hedwig Guild of this city, and the Episcopal Legate Pelldram, Prior of the Guild, took part in the service and preached the funeral sermon. He dwelt on the brilliant and amiable qualities of Dr. Müller, and spoke of him as a man of stainless honour, a loyal friend, a loving and beloved husband and father, a master and pioneer of science. Unspoiled by the glory and renown which were his, he never wavered for a moment from the firm and humble faith of his boyhood; in public and in private he was the most religious of men, and the deeper he pierced into the secrets of science, the more ardently he cried out in praise of the wisdom and greatness of God....

[1] Ib. 278 280.

[2] Gamgee before the British Association 1882. Report 569.

The funeral proceeded by the Lust-Garten, up the Linden, and Friedrichstrasse, to the Catholic Churchyard in Liesenstrasse, where all that was mortal of the great scientist was interred with the full ceremony of the Catholic Church." [1]

Müller was not merely convinced of the presence of a spiritual soul in man; he went further, and like Berzelius and Liebig, postulated for the explanation of life a principle of an order other than the chemico-physical, namely, vital force. This hypothesis was however hotly contested even in his life-time by the younger school of physiologists. The slightest acquaintance with the fundamental conceptions of physics, argued his critics, was sufficient to show the complete inadmissibility of a force "which resides in no determinate substrate, acts at no determinate point, actuates billions of molecules of the most varying form and disposition without losing its absolute unity, attaches to matter and yet can exist apart from matter, and which can be destroyed without the intervention of resistance as it can be increased without the consumption of matter" [2]. All vital processes are, according to these critics, to be referred to known chemico-physical forces; life itself is to be explained by a purely mechanical theory. Such a dark and mystical agency as "vital force" is to be resolutely thrust out of the region of science. These maxims were eagerly put into practice; and scientific Europe placed before itself the task of elucidating the chemical and mechanical aspects of organic changes, and of explaining life without postulating a principle of life.

[1] Quoted in the pamphlet: Johannes Muller, Koblenz 1898, 19—20.

[2] Du Bois-Reymond, Reden II 218.

We cannot deal in any detail with the controversy. Most of our readers are aware that science is not so brusquely contemptuous to-day as it was ten years ago regarding the hypothesis in question. Reflection showed that the criticism cited above was effective only as against one conception of "vital force", the conception, namely, which regarded it as a force of the chemico-physical order, the immediate efficient cause of all organic processes of a chemico-physical nature. But if we conceive it as a principle of a higher order, standing to the agencies investigated by Chemistry and Physics in the relation of guide and controller, the criticism falls to the ground. But we are transgressing our limits. The question we set out to answer is this: Has scientific study of the processes of the organic life of man brought to light any facts which render it impossible or unnecessary to ascribe to him a spiritual soul, endowed with free-will and of its nature immortal? Let us see how this question has been answered by some of the pioneers of Modern Physiology.

According to Du Bois-Reymond[1], the founder of the modern school of Physiology was Theodor Schwann (born at Neuss 1810, Professor at Louvain 1839, at Liège 1848). It was his discovery of the animal cell which "banished from the sphere of vegetative life all conceptions, such as Muller had entertained, of an entelechy from which the total life of the organism was supposed to spring, and which raised the hope that ultimately all the processes of organic life could be explained by means of the general properties of matter".

[1] Reden II 219.

Schwann, "the world-renowned discoverer of the cell", who by this "triumph of Biology" has won a place among the deathless masters of thought [1], was in spite of his rejection of "vital force", anything but a materialist. In a letter of December 22nd 1858 he explains to Du Bois-Reymond the process of reasoning through which he reached the theory of organic life, "in which I rejected all teleological explanations which made appeal to a purposive vital force, and admitted only in the case of man (on account of his moral freedom), the presence of a principle substantially different from matter. This latter point to which I cling with absolute conviction, sets a gulf between my system and that of the materialists" [2].

In another passage he criticises with equal sharpness the vital force of the vitalists and the atheism of the materialists.

"I have never been able to understand the idea of a simple force which is assumed to be capable of altering its mode of action, although not endowed with the faculty of reason. I have always preferred to find the source of that purposiveness, of which the whole course of nature gives conclusive evidence, not in the thing created, but in the Creator. . . ." [3]

In the same year (1839) in which Schwann published his epoch-making study of cells "the great discoverer" in whom we find a rare union of consummate talent

---

[1] Gurlt in the Allgemeine deutsche Biographie XXXIII 188.

[2] Du Bois-Reymond ante 305.

[3] Toujours j'ai préféré de chercher la cause de la finalité dont témoigne à l'évidence la nature entière, non pas dans la créature, mais dans le Créateur . . . (quoted in the Annuaire de l'Académie royale des sciences de Belgique LI, Bruxelles 1885, 215).

for research and religious fervour, accepted a call to the Chair of Anatomy in the Catholic University of Louvain[1]. Schwann's acceptance of the position shows pretty clearly his inability to see the "necessarily anti-Christian" bearing of his discoveries in Physiology. He died at Cologne on January 11th 1882, unwaveringly loyal to the faith in which he had lived[2].

In his writings we find an occasional expression which may, perhaps, lend itself to misinterpretation. "But we must never forget", remarks Du Bois-Reymond[3], "that Schwann, although a strong opponent of vitalism was just as strong an opponent of materialism. In his conception of the soul of animals he adhered (as I gathered from a conversation with him at Neuss in Sept. 1849) to the standpoint of Descartes".

Ten years before his own death Schwann delivered the memorial address over a distinguished colleague and countryman, Friedrich Anton Spring († 1872), Professor of Physiology at the University of Liège. Spring was born in 1814 at Geroldsbach in Upper Bavaria.

---

[1] Gurlt in the Allgemeine deutsche Biographie XXXIII 189.

[2] Cf. the paper Germania of 17th and 20th January 1882, Nr. 25, 1 and 31, 1. Allgemeine Zeitung, Munchen 1882, Nr. 20, Beil., 294. Il a toujours été profondément religieux et prêt à se soumettre aux décisions de l'Église catholique, même en matière de science. Henle affirme que le manuscrit des recherches microscopiques fut volontairement présenté à la censure de l'archevêque de Malines, qui à ce moment ne trouva heureusement rien à redire à la théorie cellulaire. Dans la suite Schwann eut plus d'une fois recours aux lumières des théologiens lorsqu'il lui venait des scrupules sur l'orthodoxie de ses idées scientifiques, et il ne fut pas toujours aussi heureux qu'avec la théorie cellulaire (L. Fredericq in the Annuaire de l'Académie de Belgique LI 227).

[3] Reden II 321.

Like Schwann, he obtained a position abroad, and by his scientific achievements and his lovable character overcame the natural distrust with which strangers are greeted, and won universal respect and admiration. Spring was at one with Schwann in his attitude towards religion. "If he looked to the future with hope", says the latter, speaking of Spring's last illness, "it was because he did not leave God out of his reckonings. For, gentlemen, I must not and will not pass by the matter in silence, Spring was a man of a profoundly religious mind; he made no ostentatious parade of his faith, but he would have thought it disgraceful to deny it; and when occasion demanded he made open declaration of it. He lived a Christian, and a Christian he died. His supreme consolation was the certainty he had that he would meet again in a better world those whom he had loved in this." [1]

The celebrated Danish physiologist Daniel Friedrich Eschricht († 1863), was the first to grasp the full significance of Schwann's discovery. He regarded it as the death-blow of the hypothesis of "vital force". "Vital force has", he wrote, "lost its prestige, or — what is worse for it — has gone out of fashion." [2] The physical conception of life has quite supplanted the teleological. In this respect, indeed, Eschricht believes that science has gone a great deal too far.

---

[1] Il vivait d'ailleurs en Chrétien, et c'est en Chrétien qu'il est mort, — emportant avec lui, comme suprême consolation, la certitude de revoir un jour dans un monde meilleur ceux qu'il avait avait aimés (Theod. Schwann, Notice sur F.-A. Spring, in the Annuaire de l'Académie de Belgique XL, Bruxelles 1874, 261).

[2] D. F. Eschricht, Das physische Leben in populären Vorträgen dargestellt, Berlin 1852, 75.

"Vital force as understood by Van Helmold must undoubtedly be rejected; but if we use the words to denote a principle plainly operative in the life of every plant and every animal the case stands otherwise. Every phenomenon of life, taken by itself, may be explained by the general laws of nature. But these phenomena taken in their totality can be understood only as the outward manifestations of such a principle. The analogy which has been set up between the cell and the crystal I cannot accept; I believe, not that plants and animals originate through an arbitrary conjunction of matter of various kinds, but that on the contrary the material constituents of organisms, with their blind force, appear only in complete subordination to this vital principle. Such an hypothesis (which I call the teleological hypothesis) seems to me to be the only one in harmony with the actual facts of life."[1]

In a subsequent lecture Eschricht enters into a detailed defence of this teleological interpretation of life. He opens his case with an interesting and effective parable.

He imagines a remote island, the inhabitants of which have never seen a ship, and are totally ignorant of navigation. "Suddenly there appears off their coast a sailing vessel, battling against wind and tide. The natives are plunged in amazement at the strange sight. 'It is the work of a magician' they say. 'See how he lords it over wind and tide! See how the two join forces to cast and shatter him on the rocks; but his wisdom triumphs over their hostility. He has at command a power higher than theirs.' Then the savants arrive on the scene. They naturally begin to determine the precise circumstances and conditions under which the strange phenomenon presents itself. 'What! is this colossus to be exempt from the influence of the great natural forces, which are admitted to be the powers propelling every other body driven by wind and wave? You are astonished at

---

[1] Ib. 75.

seeing a change in the movement of a vessel without any corresponding change in wind or tide? But did you not see the board behind there shifting its position, and those huge sheets setting themselves into a new formation? These changes explain the change of direction.' The people, observing more closely, notice the rudder and sails, and recognise the truth of what the savants say. None the less they continue their study of the ship, of the harmony and singleness of purpose which its movements manifest, and cling to their intuition — some power, individual and compulsive, is at work there!

"Were they so completely mistaken, those primitive minds? They were certainly wrong in raising the hypothesis of a magical power . . . and the savants were clearly within their rights in rejecting such a conception. But the savants went wide of reality in limiting their vision to the individual phenomena exhibited by the ship, and declining to recognise the plain manifestation of mind given by the totality of these phenomena. For the fundamental question was always there. Had the forces of nature free play on the ship as on a piece of drift-wood, or were they guided by some power of another order to the accomplishment of a single definite purpose?" [1]

Eschricht adds a word on the immortality of the soul.

"It is a fact well known to you that many men of science declare the idea of a spiritual existence, continuing after bodily death, to be wholly untenable. How many things men will be led to pronounce impossible if they insist on subjecting the unknown to the limits of their imagination! Only a few years ago it was unimaginable that infusoria and parasites should originate in the usual way. Who would credit the possibility of sight and hearing, who would believe that an individual unit of life would maintain itself amid the endless changes and recombinations of its material elements unless these were facts of actual experience? Do you not agree with me that the body stands to the soul in

[1] Eschricht, Das physische Leben 78.

the relation of instrument to worker? That is how I reconcile my hope of immortality with the laws of physical nature."[1]

To Johannes Müller and Schwann we may add, among German savants, Rudolf Wagner, A. W. Volkmann, and Karl Von Vierordt.

Rudolf Wagner († 1864), held the Chair of Physiology at Göttingen. The violence with which his writings were assailed by Vogt is no doubt known to our readers. Wagner had, at the meeting of the Scientific Association at Göttingen, raised the question whether physiological research had made it impossible to conceive a spiritual principle in man different in kind from the body. In his own view, he said, Physiology had not made this conception one iota easier or more difficult of acceptance. For the grounds on which it rests are to be found in the province not of Physiology but of Ethics; free-will and immortality, without which there can be no question of morality, necessarily postulate a spiritual principle[2]. Wagner ended by declaring himself a loyal and fervent Christian[3].

Vogt attempted, as might have been expected, to belittle and deride the scientific performances of his opponent. But his abuse went wide of the mark; for Wagner, if not a man of great speculative depth, was in his own province thoroughly competent. His writings on Physiology and Anthropology are sufficient proof

[1] Ib. 511.

[2] Cf. Wagners Writings: Über Glauben und Wissen, Gottingen 1854; Menschenschöpfung und Seelensubstanz, ib. 1854; Der Kampf um die Seele vom Standpunkt der Wissenschaft, ib. 1857.

[3] E. g. in his philosophical letters in the Allgemeine Zeitung, Augsburg 1852, Nr. 20, Beilage 313.

of that. He had also some reputation as a pioneer. He shares with Meissner the credit of having been the first to investigate the tactile corpuscles of the skin, and to discover the germinal vesicle.

A. W. Volkmann († 1877, at Halle), "stands beyond question in the first rank of the physiologists of the 19th century"[1]. His works, "all of which bear the stamp of masterly completeness", relate especially to the movement of the blood, the physiology of the nervous system, and physiological optics. It is, however, to another source that we go for his direct utterances on the subjects with which we are concerned — to a speech delivered in 1874 on the then burning question of Darwinism[2].

Volkmann begins by stating his general attitude towards the theory of evolution. He declares that he has no *a priori* prejudice or objection against the theory as such, but he feels compelled to reject that form of it which is associated with the name of Darwin. Natural selection cannot of itself explain the origin of species. The whole of the first part of the speech is devoted to a vigorous criticism of Darwinism[3]. In the second

---

[1] Pagel in the Allgemeine deutsche Biographie XL 236.

[2] Zur Entwicklung der Organismen, in the Bericht über die Sitzungen der naturforschenden Gesellschaft zu Halle im Jahre 1874, 27—36 (Sitzung zur Feier des Stiftungsfestes am 5. Juli).

[3] Volkmann's conclusions are in short as follows: 1. The principle of heredity and that of constant change are contradictory. 2. An organ is only useful in the fight for existence, when it is completely formed; minimum additions to it are useless; consequently the organ cannot be formed by the addition of minimum changes. 3. Every definite form, which an organ of the body assumes, necessitates other definite forms for all the organs of the body. The

part he gives his own hypothesis of the uprise and development of species. The process becomes intelligible, he maintains, only when conceived as the working out of a purposive idea.

Purpose manifests itself everywhere in all products of human activity, and plays the part of a true final cause.

body is designed and framed after a certain type. This Darwin is not able to explain. 4. Still less can Natural Selection explain the difference between the species. If an individual is in the beginning capable of reproducing its own species, and, later on, is no longer so, the fact points to a deterioration and not to an amelioration in the struggle for existence. 5. For each particular animal that alone which is serviceable to, and suitable for the organs which have been given him, is fitting; therefore, the appearance of a new arrangement of organs, which would be suitable, depends on the pre-existence of the animal, according to which the new arrangement is to be regulated. No one will deny that a strong set of teeth is an advantage to a beast of prey; nor that in an animal whose whole bony skeleton, muscles, organs of digestion and sensation, nay, even the brain itself (the seat of instinct) are those of a beast of prey, a stronger set of teeth may be developed by natural selection. But whence comes it that all the organs formed themselves according to one single plan? The first beasts of prey must have been preceded by animals, which were not beasts of prey. It could not have been any advantage to the latter that their young should possess the beginnings of the organs of a beast of prey. 6. As we have no direct experience of the history of the evolution of animals, as set forth in the theory of descent, we are referred to the analogies between the evolution of a species and the birth and development of an individual. But in the latter case, numerous organs come into being simultaneously, preserving at the same time a tendency to an existence, that can only be realised provided that each separate organ does not depend more on the whole, than the whole on it; the animal is only developed with the development of its organs: it is not in existence before its organism nor can it be said that of the many different formations, which are possible, those only are actually realized, which are most suitable for the animal.

"Now the fact that there is a sphere in which purpose has a share in shaping events, deserves patient consideration when we come to study the history of the evolution of organic forms. For if there are special forces which bring a goal of action into conscious perception and direct the course of development towards that end, it is in the highest degree improbable that such forces are confined to our planet — or rather to a petty proportion of the dwellers on that planet. It is also repugnant to my mind to suppose that a Force, to whose potency we conceive no limit, has attained in the creation of man the highest point of its achievement.

"On the other hand we find many tokens that purposive activity works over wider areas than that of merely human consciousness. We are not indeed able to discern with eyes and hands the working of purposive force, but we are constantly meeting phenomena which can be explained only by such an hypothesis. It is by such a process of inference that Physics has penetrated to the atom, and the exact sciences lend the fullest support to such inference.

"If in the middle of a desert, apparently never inhabited, we were to come upon hewn stones, knitted together with mortar, would we not regard it as the merest nonsense to maintain that there was no reason to suppose that the building was the outcome of purposive thought? But, as far as co-ordination in view of a definite plan is concerned, living organisms stand far higher than any product of human art. Their structure bears so patently the stamp of purpose that the first sight of them sets us asking what is the function of this and that member. And such tokens of plan and purpose are not confined to the structure of a given individual organism, but extend also to the relations of one organism with another." A striking example of this necessity of postulating intellect behind the metamorphoses of the animal world "is to be found", says Volkmann, "in the evolution of sex". According to the theory of evolution every organism must at first have been able to propagate itself; only in a later period was the co-operation of two individuals required. Male and female organisms must therefore have come into existence at the same stage of evolution, and, under the same external conditions, pairs of beings of completely different structure and function must have been developed. But such a process is "completely unintelligible except on the assumption that there is a power which directs the process to an intended goal". Similar examples of inter-relation are to be found wherever we choose to look. "There are animals which serve as the indispensable food of others, and animals of prey that prevent the too great increase of specially prolific species. Insects are necessary for the fructification of certain plants, and, on the other hand, practically every insect species has had created for its use a plant which is its natural home and nutriment. Plants in general serve to support the life of animals, and animals to increase the diffusion of plants. In short, process after process, provided in the economy of the organic world, gives unmistakable evidence of an effort to attain ends deliberately pre-conceived. The fact that we are unable to penetrate in the same fashion to the purposive thought behind the larger cyclic processes of the universe is no ground for denying the existence of such thought: the infinitely great, like the infinitely small, transcends the limits of our understanding. "If anyone chooses to characterise as an 'hypothesis' this inferred idea of an intelligence which is at work in the universe, and which directs it in its totality to pre-conceived ends — in other words a Power which we call God —, I can find nothing against the term. But I do say that it is an hypothesis which nobody has yet succeeded in dismissing as superfluous." "I find the First Cause of all organic evolution in a directing Intelligence, which works towards deliberate ends, and creates the sum of conditions without which the process of Becoming could not go forward." [1]

---

[1] In the beginning of his essay Volkmann says "Eine Annahme wie die, daß der erste Mensch durch den Hauch Gottes aus einem Erdenkloß entstanden, ist für die Naturwissenschaft schlechthin unzulässig." But Holy Scripture does not say that Adam's body was first an "Erdenkloß", and was then changed into flesh. It makes two distinct

An exhaustive study of the brain by Volkmann concludes as follows[1]:

"My own views as to the relations existing between life and its physical envelope may be very briefly stated. Life and organism go together, and, therefore, either life is the causal agency behind the organism, or the organism is the causal agency behind life. But both must spring from a deeper causal source other than, and outside, themselves, for we know that there was a period when the earth was as yet barren of life. This ultimate source of causation I find in God. God conceived the idea of life, and made his idea actual in matter. But for matter, life must have remained a mere possibility, must have lain imprisoned in the Divine Mind, incapable of finding external manifestation. When the organism undergoes dissolution, life vanishes from the region of actuality, but the idea of it remains in the mind of God and may again be actualized in matter. Individuals die, but the idea of them persists in the race.

"Moreover the soul had need of matter in order to the development of its life. The substance in which it assumes concrete reality is the brain, and with the disintegration of the brain the manifestation of the soul in that particular form is at an end. But the ideal content of the physical envelope is imperishable, and no more disappears with the death of the brain than the idea of an animal species with the death of an individual member of it.

statements: 1. The material out of which Adam's body was formed in some way or other by the activity of God, was not created anew, but was taken from matter which already existed; in other words, by his body man belongs to the sphere of the lower order of creation. 2. The soul is derived directly from God. If Volkmann means to say that science can refute one of these two statements, this does not harmonize with his conception of a God, whose activity is free. If God is free, He can create men in whatever way pleases Him best.

[1] Handworterbuch der Physiologie mit Rücksicht auf physiologische Pathologie. Herausgeg. von Dr. Rudolph Wagner I, Braunschweig 1842, 596 f.

"In this view the survival of the soul after bodily death is merely a regression of it into the mind of God, and the possibility of rebirth always remains. How far immortality, as thus conceived, is personal it is not the function of philosophy to determine; but it may be remarked that philosophy can find no grounds on which to deny personal immortality. It is said that the total destruction of the organism by death is such a ground. But we must remember that from the physiological standpoint itself the personal soul is not controlled by the organism, but only conditioned by it. The idea finds outer expression in matter, and the organic processes themselves are no more than manifestations of the perpetually changing idea. Moreover, it must be borne in mind that we do not so thoroughly understand the process called 'death' as to be able to declare that it means the entire destruction of the organism. It is possible that the comparative grossness of our organs of observation may expose us to error. Fechner has very truly remarked that a foetus, if capable of studying its own physiology, would find good grounds for regarding birth as the death of its individuality. The organs which are of the greatest importance to it while in the foetal condition, the membranes and the organs of nutrition, are ruptured, but the real outcome of this apparent destruction, which is the death of the embryo as such, is an organic structure which serves as envelope for the true life of the individual."

Karl Von Vierordt († 1884), Professor of Physiology at Tubingen, did much to extend our knowledge of the circulation of the blood. He was the author of a widely popular treatise on Physiology, and of many studies on various problems of Physics. He has recorded his firm conviction of the existence of God, and of the spirituality of the soul in an address delivered to the students of the University [1].

---

[1] Uber die Einheit der Wissenschaften, eine Rede, gehalten in der Aula der Universität Tubingen am 6. März 1865, 9.

"With what justice Locke has said in his 'Essay on the Human Understanding': 'The propositions of morality are as demonstrable as the propositions of mathematics; for the ideas from which morality takes its origin are realities.' And if the English philosopher speaks of morality as the characteristically human science he means by this that the truth of its essential propositions is more fully recognised and more firmly held, alike by popular and by scientific thought, than are the central propositions of any other science. Spiritual reality has a basis as positive and 'factual' as material reality.

"The scientific blunder of materialism lies in a misunderstanding of the limitations of physical laws. However wide-reaching the laws may be, however successful the sciences which elucidate them, they furnish no shadow of explanation of spiritual processes."

Towards the close of his address he says to the students[1]:

"But before you proceed, with ripened insight, to fashion and formulate your views on religion, keep in your minds a word of friendly assurance. Faith in the divinity of the religion of Jesus is not imposed on your hearts in any deceitful disguise. True religion stands equally remote from a sick-souled, narrow pietism and from a too lucid and superficial rationalism; it allows the intellect its full rights, but it also teaches us to believe in a super-sensual and immortal life, and to place our reliance in Providence."

Gustav Adolf Spiess († 1875), a Frankfort physician, did work of great excellence in Physiological Pathology. His work on that subject attracted the hostile attention of Virchow, but even Spiess' severest critics recognised him as a savant of the first order.

"In his writings we find passage on passage in support of the theistic interpretation of the world, — a

[1] Über die Einheit der Wissenschaften 32.

philosophy in which he was able to unite and reconcile science and religion." [1]

Chr. George Theodore Ruete († 1867), won his reputation mainly in optical surgery. In the year 1863 he was chosen Rector of the University of Leipsic, and took as the subject of his inaugural address: "The Existence of the Soul, Regarded from the Standpoint of Science" [2].

"In direct opposition to the materialists who assert that the universe can be explained with logical completeness as the expression of a single principle, I find myself compelled to postulate two principles, a spiritual and a material, and to recognise that there are processes in nature which the human mind is incapable of understanding. I maintain that for the consistent materialist the facts of conscious perception are inexplicable, while the spiritualist is at least able to say that they point undeniably to the existence of a spiritual principle. In this conviction (that the phenomena of sensation can arise only as experiences of a spiritual, self-conscious principle) I am strengthened by a recognition of the fact that most of the great physiologists of our day... share it, although they do not always proclaim it."

According to materialism sense-perception, e. g. seeing or hearing, finds a complete explanation in the physico-chemical reactions evoked in eye and ear by light and sound-waves. There is no need of any active spiritual principle. Ruete opposes this interpretation of the phenomenon, and shows that the co-operation of the soul is needed in order to originate sensation. He does this by adducing instances in which all the external physical conditions of perception are present, without in fact producing conscious perception.

---

[1] Obituary notice in the Bericht uber die Senckenbergische Naturforschende Gesellschaft 1875—1876, Frankfurt 1877, 59.

[2] Uber die Existenz der Seele vom naturwissenschaftlichen Standpunkte, Leipzig 1863. — Cf. Rothmund in the Allgemeine deutsche Biographie XXX 39.

"Some one, for example, speaks to us, but we are inattentive and do not (consciously) hear what he says. A moment later, we gather ourselves together, and what he has said penetrates for the first time into our consciousness. But if too long an interval has elapsed we find it impossible to recover his words.

"I recollect that at the beginning of my professional career I had to perform a very painful operation on a young girl, the success of which was as important for my patient's welfare as for my own reputation. When the operation was over, the girl began to cry (we had no chloroform then), as I thought, for the first time. I did my best to soothe and quiet her, and expressed my surprise that she should not have begun to cry till everything was practically over, whereupon I was informed that she had been crying with far greater violence from the very beginning and that what I heard was only a feeble echo. My attention being wholly concentrated on the operation, I had remained quite unconscious of a physical stimulus far greater in volume than that which impressed itself on my mind as soon as my consciousness was released. The sound-waves had impinged on my ears, the inevitable vibrations and organic disturbances had been produced, but no auditory sensation had followed because the indispensable mental condition of attention had not been present." [1]

Of Theodore L. W. Bischoff († 1882), the Munich physiologist, Karl Kupffer says in a memorial address [2] of March 28th 1884: "Throughout his life he was full of pious affection towards the religion he had learned at his mother's knee, and he never wavered from an intense belief in the immortality of the soul which had there been implanted in his mind." In a posthumously discovered manuscript, "Thoughts of a Scientist on the Nature of Man and on Religion" (Bonn 1878), he explains his attitude towards religious problems. According to Kupffer's account [3], Bischoff's philosophical position is but inadequately developed. Many of his phrases

[1] Allgemeine deutsche Biographie XXX 17 f. [2] Munchen 1884, 6.
[3] Ib. 22 f 42.

have a materialistic ring "but Bischoff argues vehemently against the conclusions of materialism, while at the same time claiming the processes of organic life as falling within the domain of the general forces of nature"[1]. . . .

Du Bois-Reymond, as we have already learned, remarks that many passages of Schwann which show a tendency to monism are not to be pressed too far. The same remarks may be extended to the works of Claude Bernard († 1878), that great master of French science, and more than worthy successor of the vitalist Bichat, and the experimentalist Magendie. We must not look in his works for perfect accuracy of expression or steadiness of insight in the treatment of purely philosophical questions. Statements abound in his writings which on a hasty reading seem to imply a purely materialistic or positivist interpretation of life. But a deeper study nearly always reveals that the thought is better than the verbal form, and that not merely does Claude Bernard not deny the existence of a spiritual principle in man but that he expressly accepts it. This position is quite consistent with his general contention, namely, that it is not the duty of Physiology to decide the old battle of materialism and spiritualism, nor to put forward either system of thought as the ground and basis of its researches[2]. A glance into his "Physiologie Générale" will set us in the full stream of his thought.

The science of Physiology properly speaking came into existence, according to Bernard, with the discovery "that life is conserved by physico-chemical processes, which, so far as their immediate cause and character

---

[1] Ib. 23.

[2] De la physiologie générale par Claude Bernard, Paris 1872.

are concerned, do not differ from those which take place in non-living matter"[1]. It was Lavoisier who first made this proposition the starting point of scientific Physiology. He treated respiration as a process of oxidisation pure and simple. The heat of the body he showed, in conjunction with Laplace, to be due to a process of combustion, identical in essence with that which takes place in our ovens. Bernard signalises as the most fatal error of Physiology before Lavoisier "the assumption that vital manifestations proceed in complete independence of ordinary physico-chemical laws, and are produced and directed by vague, hidden forces (vital principle, spirit, physiological soul, vital force), which cannot be localised or scientifically understood".

The first impression which would be gathered by a hasty reader from this passage is that Claude Bernard was a materialist. But closer study will show that this is not the case. To dismiss the notion of a vital force or a physiological soul is, to his mind, to deny not the existence of a spiritual principle in man but merely that conception of it which makes it totally independent of physico-chemical laws. Physiology should not adopt as its basis either materialism or spiritualism, but should devote itself simply to the experimental investigation of organic life.

"Science (i. e. physical science) never reaches to ultimate causes, and the first cause of life, as of all else, will ever escape our researches. In order to understand and explain the mechanism of life it is no more necessary to know what is the nature of the creative power behind living matter, than it is necessary to know the nature of the creative prin-

[1] De la physiologie générale par Claude Bernard 4—5.

ciple behind a mineral before proceeding to investigate its properties." [1]

Physiology, according to this view of it, is incapable of raising obstacles against the existence of a spiritual soul, or against the existence of God. Such questions do not fall within the province of Experimental Physiology at all. But Claude Bernard, in casual expressions, rather transgresses the limits set by himself, and in so doing displays distinct hostility to materialism. The pen of a materialist would not "secrete" such phrases as "creative power". Still more definite in drift is a later passage in the book, the only one in which Bernard expressly discusses the conflict between spiritualism and materialism. Having declared that the question of the existence of the soul does not belong to Physiology, he continues:

"As science shows, neither organic nor inorganic matter produces phenomena: both serve simply to manifest phenomena through the properties which they exhibit under determinate conditions. It is a counter-sense to declare that a phenomenon of motion, whether it takes place in living or in lifeless matter, is not susceptible of a mechanical explanation. But on the other hand, matter, of whatever kind, possesses no spontaneity and no generative power; it is a mere expression of the thought of that mind which has created the machine. The organised matter of the brain, in which the phenomena of perception and intellection manifest themselves, is no more conscious of the processes of thought manifested in it than the dead matter of a mere machine, say for example, a watch, is conscious of the mo-

---

[1] Ib. 317. Similar opinions are of frequent occurrence in Bernard, e. g. p. 321: La cause première de la création, soit de la matière brute, soit de la matière vivante, nous échappe également; p. 306 to 307: Les causes premières des phénomènes nous échapperont partout etc.

vement of its parts. It is no more conscious of thought than the type of a compositor's case, or the paper are conscious of the ideas which they record. If it is said that thought is a secretion of the brain, it may with the same justification be added that time, or the idea of time, is a secretion of the watch. . . . To put the whole matter in two words: we must distinguish between causes and conditions. Matter is never the cause of anything, it is only a condition; and this holds as well of the changes which take place in lifeless as of those which take place in living matter. The savant must seek to explain the determinism of the processes by an analysis of their conditions; these, then, play the rôle of proximate causes. First causes, however, lie beyond his province, and he must not allow them to influence his researches. The determinism of phenomena is his domain. Therein lie the problems of experimental science."[1]

Passages such as this enable us to understand what Bernard means by the word "determinism", which occurs so often in his writings. He means nothing more than that every organic process is to be explained on its physico-chemical side by physico-chemical causes. This "determinism" does not clash with the conception of moral freedom. If, for example, I make up my mind to move my finger, this resolution sets going a whole series of processes. It produces a change in the brain, which projects an influence along the determinate nerve, the nerve moves a muscle, and the muscle the finger. In the whole chain there is only one link free, namely, the originating volition; all the others are the rigidly necessary outcome of their predecessors. But the scientist cannot subject to direct and immediate observation the volitional impulse, his view is limited to the series of changes by which that impulse is realised. He should

---

[1] De la physiologie générale 325.

confine himself to these changes without denying or asserting the freedom of the will. That Bernard desires to be understood in this sense, he expressly declares.

"If modern science accepts determinism, it so accepts it as to make it actually a condition of freedom. Indeed there can be no free act save at the moment when the process receives impulse and direction. Once set going, this impulse falls absolutely under the sway of determinism. During this latter period determinism is a compulsion to which the gods of old owned submission. Determinism, I re-iterate, does not exclude freedom." [1]

We have only to add that Bernard, while vigorously opposing the hypothesis of a falsely conceived vital force, is in no way hostile to the conception of certain directing forces which determine the formation and structure of the organism [2].

J. B. Dumas, speaking over the grave of Bernard, expounded the ideas to which the dead scientist had devoted himself in these words:

"Like Lavoisier, Laplace, Bichat, Magendie . . . Claude Bernard sought to unveil and understand the great secret of life, without professing to explain its ultimate nature and origin. The astronomer remains ignorant of the power behind the cosmic system, and yet is able to calculate with certainty the paths of the planets which that power main-

[1] Je le répète, le déterminisme n'exclut pas la liberté 334.

[2] Dans les corps vivants, les forces directrices ou évolutives des phénomènes sont morphologiquement vitales, tandis que leurs forces exécutives sont les mêmes que dans les corps bruts. The chemist may indeed reproduce the substances of which a bone consists, but can never make the bone with its specific form and characteristics (ib. 320). "La force vitale", dit Claude Bernard, "dirige les phénomènes qu'elle ne produit pas; les agents physiques produisent des phénomènes qu'ils ne dirigent pas" (Revue des deux mondes, 15 nov. 1878, 307).

tains in being and in motion. Claude Bernard held that in the same way the physiologist must be allowed to explain the phenomena of life in terms of physical and chemical forces, although life itself and thought, which direct and control these phenomena, lie outside his province."[1]

Another authority expresses himself in precisely the same sense:

"One last word: This pitiless physiologist, this champion of absolute determinism did not suffer himself to be misled into a denial of the truths of metaphysics. He believed himself to be conscious of, and dependent on, a Something, that did not fall under the scrutiny of science. He recognised a twofold order, a twofold kingdom of knowledge. In the one the experimental method held sway, and produced the richest results; in the other, pure reason and reflection were to be relied upon. In the one, determinism is absolute lord and master; in the other, reflection and introspection meditate on their characteristic problems, suggest solutions, and throw a little light on the sublime questions of our origin and destiny. . . . We have already quoted the last page of his book in which he characterises the truths of metaphysics by the bold term 'the sublimities of ignorance' (sublimités de l'ignorance). These sublimities cast their glow over the face of him who was the greatest experimentalist of his age, and it shone transfigured with the image of God, lacking which the countenance of man is a poor and lightless mask."[2]

To give these expressions their full weight we must add just one word. When Bernard saw that death was at hand, he sent for a priest and "had the happiness of ending a life, consecrated to the service of science, by a Christian death"[3].

---

[1] Comptes rendus LXXXVI, Paris 1878, 402.

[2] Revue des deux mondes, 15 nov. 1878, 310.

[3] Ce qui nous cause plus de joie que tous ces honneurs (at his state funeral), c'est l'assurance que cet homme de bien a eu le bonheur

Another master of Physiology, renowed for his researches into the functions of the brain, and for his contributions to the Anatomy and Physiology of the brain was Marie Jean Pierre Flourens († 1867). Despite the Catholic ring of his name he was a Protestant. He was a vigorous critic of materialism, and devoted special papers to a refutation of the materialistic theories of Gall, Spurzheim, and Broussais. We quote a passage from his work on the unity of the human species. The physical identity of the various races of man, as established by Blumenbach and Tiedemann, does not content him. We must, he maintains, re-inforce it by a consideration of another order.

"Even on the physical side of our organism, that which we can see and touch is not the most essential. 'The organs', says Bossuet, 'do not find their real essence in that which we see and touch. They really consist in the co-ordination of inconceivably delicate parts . . . the minuteness of which only the mind can conceive.' But what a huge step it is from even the most delicate of physical organs to mind! Physiology teaches us only one thing: the correspondence which exists between the development of function and the development of organ.

"The moment we touch on the veritable human function, intellect, we leave two sciences and step into a third, Psycho-

---

de terminer par une mort chrétienne une vie entièrement consacrée à la science. Quoique les médecins dont il était entouré, lui fissent illusion eux-mêmes sur la gravité de son mal, et qu'ainsi le prêtre a été appelé un peu tard, le malade jouissait de sa pleine connaissance à l'arrivée du ministre de Dieu, et il a témoigné, par ses réponses et surtout par la manière affectueuse dont il lui serrait la main, avec quelle reconnaissance il acceptait les secours de la religion (Études religieuses, philosophiques, historiques et littéraires XXII, Lyon-Paris 1878, 445). Cf. the reference in the Revue des deux mondes, 15 décembre 1878, 840; Allgemeine Zeitung, Augsburg 1881, 2301).

logy. Psychology has a characteristic province of its own. The activities of the mind can be understood only by the active mind. Spirit discloses its nature only to spirit.

"In the province of Psychology we can now draw the line of demarcation between instinct and intelligence; between intelligence as it exists in animals, and as it exists in man. This line is sharply and clearly defined. But between man and man, between race and race we can discover no more than grades, varieties, nuances. Man alone possesses a conception of a moral order and a conception of God, and these are the natural possession of all men. In relation to both, the intelligence of humanity is at one with itself. This unity of intelligence is the last and conclusive proof of the unity of the human race." [1]

Flourens had been for some time a free-thinker, but he returned to the Christian faith and fold [2].

"His mind became clouded (through weakening of the brain) in his last moments. He was unable to say, like Goodsir, on his death-bed: He is only a half-formed anatomist whose thought does not reach beyond the changes of the physical organism. But he had often given expression — this physiologist who so resolutely denied the possibility of localising the soul — to such a thought before his last illness came upon him." [3]

Flourens derived much assistance from the work of an English scientist, Sir Charles Bell († 1842). Bell

---

[1] P. Flourens, Recueil des éloges historiques lus dans les séances publiques de l'Académie des sciences, 3e série, Paris 1862, 279 f.

[2] Après s'être montré d'abord, comme c'était la mode du temps, penseur libre et indépendant, il fut un des premiers à revenir à l'orthodoxie; et sa science avait fini par être parfaitement d'accord avec la foi (Les Mondes XV, Paris 1867, 637).

[3] v. Martius in Sitzungsberichte der königl. bayr. Akademie I, München 1868, 464.

stands among the pioneers of Nerve-Physiology[1]. Haller had declared that he knew no afferent nerve that was not also an efferent nerve, but Bell showed that precisely the opposite is the case, and that the same nerve never fulfils both functions. The interest aroused throughout all Europe by this discovery was extraordinarily great. It is related of the French physiologist Roux, that when Bell entered his lecture-room, he dismissed his pupils, saying that they had done enough for the day, they had seen Charles Bell!

The great English savant was of a profoundly religious disposition. We have already made his acqaintance as author of one of the Bridgewater Treatises, and co-editor of Paley's Natural Theology[2]. In his lectures he was fond of drawing attention to the evidently purposive structure of organisms. On his private life his religious belief showed the most beneficent influence. "All his friends echoed from their hearts the judgment of Lord Cockburn: 'If ever I knew a good and happy man it was Sir Charles Bell.' 'He had too deeply-rooted a belief in that Providence, which rules the world, to fail ever in thankfulness for his lot in life.'"[3] One of his oldest friends, Lord Jeffrey, wrote on his tombstone the inscription: "Sacred to the memory of Sir Charles Bell, who after unfolding with unrivalled sagacity, patience, and success, the wonderful structure of our mortal bodies, esteemed lightly of his greatest discoveries, except only as they tended to impress himself and others with a deeper sense of the

---

[1] Flourens, Recueil des éloges III, Paris 1852, 47—159.

[2] V. p. 37 224.

[3] Dictionary of National Biography IV, London 1885, 156.

infinite wisdom and ineffable goodness of the Almighty Creator . . ." [1]

The name of Louis Pasteur († 1895) has almost as a great a claim to be included in the history of Physiology as in that of Chemistry. He is universally recognised as a discoverer of the very first order. Pasteur began his scientific career in 1848 with a series of discoveries with regard to crystals; he showed the interrelation between the crystalline form of certain bodies and their retention of light, and helped to found Stereoscopy. As early as 1860 he had formulated the fundamental ideas of this new science. He also analysed with great success the composition of wine and grape-acids. In 1875—1876 he was engaged in investigating the chemistry of fermentation. But it was his discovery in 1877 that certain diseases are due to the presence of minute organisms — bacteria or bacilli — that first won for him a world-wide renown. He followed up his discovery of bacteria by discovering further that in certain circumstances these agents of disease can be employed for therapeutic purposes. The experiments, by which in 1862 he demonstrated the untenability of the hypothesis of spontaneous generation [2], attracted universal notice, as also his studies of the diseases of wine and beer, and of the silk-worm. Alike theoretically and practically his discoveries were of inestimable value. The art of surgery was directed by them towards a new and brilliantly fruitful development; and Huxley did not

[1] Encyclopaedia Britannica III[9], Edinburgh 1875, 542.

[2] Pouchet, the obstinate opponent, who was fighting against him, was no materialist. On the contrary "il avait en horreur le matérialisme même alors que ses écrits semblaient l'affirmer" (Les Mondes XXX [1873] 2).

exaggerate the practical worth of Pasteur's researches when he declared that they would more than compensate France for the war indemnity of five milliards which she was compelled to pay to Germany[1]. In point of fact the great scientist saved the silk-industry of France from destruction. It was estimated that in the ten years before Pasteur came to the rescue this industry alone had suffered losses reaching in amount to 1500 millions (francs)[2].

Pasteur's place among the masters of science is certain beyond cavil, and equally certain is it that he was till the end a faithful and fervent Catholic. In his later years he was in the habit of approaching the sacraments very frequently[3]: "He gave up his soul to God at the last, clasping in his hands his little copper cross, and repeating fervently a confession of faith and hope." It is related that a student once asked him how it was that, after so much reflection and research, he could remain a believer. "It is just because I have thought and sought so much" replied Pasteur, "that I believe with the faith of a Breton peasant. If I had thought more and studied more I would have come to believe with the faith of the Breton peasant's wife."[4]

Pasteur made open profession of his belief on the occasion of his reception into the French Academy. He had been elected successor to Littré, the great Positivist, and had, according to custom, to pronounce a memorial

---

[1] René Vallery-Radot, La vie de Pasteur, Paris 1901; Duclaux, Pasteur, histoire d'un esprit, Paris 1898; J. F. Boutet, Pasteur et ses élèves, Paris 1898.

[2] Couette in La science catholique X, Arras 1896, 182.

[3] Van Tricht in Revue des quest. scient. XXXIX, Louvain 1896, 385 387.

[4] Revue des deux mondes, 15 octobre 1895, 917.

speech on his predecessor. He censured Positivism for the open contradiction of its principles involved in its manner of dealing with the idea of God. Positivism professes to found itself on the actual undeniable facts of experience, but brushes aside this most positive and undeniable of all facts, namely, that humanity as a whole has always believed in God and found its support in religion.

"The great and obvious gap in the system is its refusal to give any recognition to that greatest of all positive ideas, the idea of the Infinite.

"What exists on the other side of the starry heavens? New stars and new heavens. Be it so! And out beyond these, what is there? This is a question which the human mind finds itself drawn by an irresistible influence to formulate; it will never cease to ask it. Do we imagine it possible to come to a final term in space or in time? But the stage at which we would come to a stop is merely a vast something, greater than anything that has gone before, but yet finite; the mind perceives this, and the perception raises at once the old riddle, which is neither to be solved nor ignored. It is of no use to say: Out beyond there, there is time, there is space, magnitude without limit. It is impossible to rest content with such phrases. The mind that confesses consciousness of the idea of the Infinite — and no mind can fail to be conscious of it — accepts more of the supernatural than is contained in all the miracles of all the religions. For the idea of the Infinite has two characteristics; it imposes itself on the mind, and it baffles the mind's effort to comprehend it. When this idea takes possession of the intellect, nothing remains but to go down humbly on one's knees. In a mood of almost oppressive reverence and fear, one comes to beg forgiveness for reason: the whole mechanism of the mind threatens to leave its accustomed grooves; one comes near the sublime folly of Pascal. And this Positivist idea, this root-idea, Positivism brusquely dismisses without even assigning a reason. . . ."

Renan was chosen to reply to Pasteur's inaugural address. The scene had the air of a deliberately arranged trial of arms between the earnest savant and the brilliant dilettante. "In this clash of the crystal with the iron vessel it was assuredly not the latter that came to grief", wrote Melchior de Vogüé[1].

A biologist of considerable note died on Sept. 10th 1899 in the person of Jean Baptiste Carnoy, Teacher at the University of Louvain[2]. He was the founder of the new science of Cytology or Cellular Biology, which takes for subject-matter the cell as such; that mysterious structure which forms the ultimate basis alike of animal and of plant life. He was one of the first to discover the reticular structure of protoplasm. Carnoy established a review of his science, *La Cellule*, and an Institute at Louvain which bears his name.

Carnoy was not only a Catholic but a priest. Before his appointment to the position of teacher he had been for eight years curé in a small Belgian parish, and had shown the most ardent zeal for souls; during the whole course of his professorial career he never failed to begin his lectures with the sign of the cross.

To these names we might add a long list of others, distinguished in the history of medicine, but we limit ourselves to one or two. René Théodore Hyacinthe Laennec († 1826), was the first to employ auscultation and percussion in the diagnosis of pulmo-

[1] G. Gilson, Éloge funèbre de J.-B. Carnoy, in La Cellule XVII, Lierre-Louvain 1899, I—XXXIV. L. Gedoelst, Les progrès de la Biologie cellulaire, in Congrès scientifique international des Catholiques tenu à Paris II, Paris 1888, 543—555.

[2] J. J. Walsh in The Messenger XXXVIII, New York 1902, 50—68.

nary disease. His profoundly religious attitude of mind, maintained in an atmosphere of indifference and scepticism, was well known to his contemporaries. A story is told of him which illustrates this in a striking and slightly humorous fashion. He was travelling with his wife from Paris to Brest, when their carriage came into collision with another, and the occupants were thrown out on the road. There was naturally, a scene of great confusion, but in due time things were put in order again. Then Laënnec opened his lips for the first time. He said to his wife: "We left off our Rosary at such and such a place"; and they calmly resumed it as if nothing had happened[1].

"Like so many other masters of medicine, like Rivière, Baillou, Winslow, Bonnet, Baglivi, Morgagni, Boerhaave, Haller, he was led by his study of the human frame, the marvellous adaptation of its organs to one another and to the external world, to admire and love the Creator of such marvels. His mind was at one with that of his friend Bayle."[2]

Laënnec describes his discovery with characteristic simplicity. Hitherto, he says, two methods of investigation have been employed in the investigation of pulmonary disease, the application of the hand and of the ear. There are many cases in which neither is successful. For himself he has chanced upon a third and better one.

"In 1816 I was consulted by a young person who was labouring from the general symptoms of a diseased heart.

---

[1] Traité de l'auscultation médiate . . . par R.-Th.-H. Laënnec. Nouv. édition . . . augmentée d'une notice hist. sur Laennec. Bruxelles 1828, XXXI.

[2] Ante 4.

In her case, percussion and the application of the hand (what modern doctors call 'palpation'), were of little service because of a considerable degree of stoutness. The other method, that namely of listening to the sounds within the chest by the direct application of the ear to the chest wall, being rendered inadmissible by the age and sex of the patient, I happened to recollect a simple and well-known fact in acoustics and fancied it might be turned to some use on the present occasion. The fact I allude to is the great distinctness with which we hear the scratch of a pin at one end of a piece of wood on applying our ear to the other.

"Immediately on the occurrence of this idea I rolled a quire of paper into a kind of cylinder and applied one end of it to the region of the heart and the other to my ear. I was not a little surprised and pleased to find that I could thereby perceive the action of the heart in a manner much more clear and distinct than I had ever been able to do by immediate application of the ear.

"From this moment I imagined that the circumstance might furnish means for enabling us to ascertain the character not only of the beating of the heart, but of every species of sound produced by the motion of all the thoracic viscera, and consequently for the exploration of the respiration, the voice, the death rattle, and perhaps even the movements of fluid effused in the pleura or pericardium. With this conviction I forthwith commenced at the Necker Hospital a series of observations from which I have been able to deduce a set of new signs of diseases of the chest. These are for the most part certain, easily perceptible, and calculated, perhaps, to render the diagnosis of the diseases of the lungs, heart and pleura as decided and circumstantial as the indications furnished to the surgeon by the finger or the probe, in the complaints wherein these are of use." [1]

---

[1] Ami de la religion XXXI, Paris 1822, 118; cf. XLII, Paris 1824, 42: Comme Pascal il s'anéantissait devant la grandeur de Dieu etc. For Hallé's importance cf. G. Cuvier, Recueil des éloges III, Strasbourg-Paris 1827, 345—360.

Gaspard Laurent Bayle († 1816), of whom mention has been made, was one of the first physicians of his day. He made invaluable contributions to the study of cancer and phthisis. J. N. Hallé († 1822), one of the pioneers of hygienic science, was, as a notice from a Catholic pen puts it, "a man of note, not merely in respect of intellectual achievement, but also in respect of his religious principles" [1]. During the Revolution he displayed magnificent courage; he defended Lavoisier before his judges, and found a way to reach the sick in the prisons and convey medical aid to them. To these names we may add those of G. Dupuytren[2] († 1834), W. Hufeland († 1836) a Christian much honoured in Germany, and Dominique Jean Larrey († 1842), organiser of the modern system of army surgery. He made an end of the cruel practice of abandoning the wounded on the field of battle. He was a benefactor not merely of his own country but of the whole world, for the French system of ambulance corps was adopted by all civilized nations. Napoleon I. left Larrey in his will a legacy of 100000 francs characterising him as "the most virtuous man I ever knew. He left in my mind the image of the really good man". His edifying death showed to all the world that the great benefactor of so many wounded and dying soldiers shared the faith of the simplest and most humble-minded Christian [3].

---

[1] Journal historique et littéraire I, Liège 1834, 439.

[2] Ch. W. Hufeland, Esquisse de sa vie et de sa mort chrétiennes par A. de Stourdza, Berlin 1837; extract from Rev. germanique 3e série X, Paris 1837, 34—54.

[3] A peine instruit de la gravité du mal qui le saisissait, . . . M. le baron Larrey a voulu confier sa vie à Dieu et recourir aux sacre-

Other names that should at least be mentioned are those of Joseph Claude Récamier[1] († 1852); James Young Simpson[2] († 1870), the first to make use of chloroform in surgery; Wilhelm Baum[3] († 1883); Richard Von Volkmann[4] († 1889); Jules Émile Péan[5] († 1898); Joseph Hyrtl († 1894).

Hyrtl was born in 1810 at Eisenstadt in Hungary, in 1836 he became a University teacher at Prague, and in 1845 at Vienna. He published an immense number of papers on points and problems of Anatomy, and a text-book of his science which ran to twenty editions and was translated into many foreign languages. When, in 1865, the fifth centenary of the University of Vienna was to be celebrated, Hyrtl was elected Rector. It was in the fitness of things that the greatest name in science at Vienna should be prominently associated

---

ments de l'Église qu'il a reçus avec cette foi des camps qui ne connaît ni examen ni incertitude. Ami de la religion CXIV, Paris 1842, 230.

[1] P. Triaire, Récamier et ses contemporains, Paris 1899.

[2] Lexikon der hervorragenden Ärzte aller Zeiten X, Wien und Leipzig 1887, 416.

[3] Allgemeine deutsche Biographie XLVI 252 253.

[4] "Zur Idealität seines Wesens gehörte . . . vor allem seine wahre Frommigkeit, welche ohne Prunk und ohne Bekenntniseifer doch aus tiefer Uberzeugung von der Erlösungskraft des Christentums entsprungen war und die Welt seiner Gedanken auch in seinem Berufe und seiner Forschung durchdrang und belebte; ein neuer Beweis für den alten Satz, daß die halbe Wissenschaft von Gott hinweg, die ganze zu ihm fuhrt. Es war ihm aber mit stiller Aufnahme des Christentums nicht genug, sondern er empfand und verfolgte den Drang, das Verhältnis zwischen Wissen und Glauben wiederholt zu durchdenken und beide in sich selbst harmonisch zu verbinden." Fedor Krause in Leopoldina XXVI, Halle 1890, 44.

[5] Cosmos, 5 févr. 1898, 163.

with the celebration. Hyrtl took up the office of Rector on October 1st 1864 and chose for the subject of his Inaugural Address: "The Materialistic Theories of our Day" [1].

It was certainly not the first pronouncement made by men of science against materialism. But the condemnation by a man of Hyrtl's reputation of this favourite child of the modern mind, delivered amid all the pomp and solemnity of the public fête, attracted unusual attention, and aroused a storm of controversy in the Liberal Press of Vienna. We can understand the violent and angry abuse heaped on Hyrtl by his critics if we read his speech. He thrust materialism bodily aside as unscientific, and protested against the procedure of those who sought to make science responsible for this "extravagant expression of a system of thought that has allowed itself to be betrayed and benighted on a bye-way".

"To sum up..." said Hyrtl [2], "I cannot understand what scientific grounds have justified the resurrection of the old materialistic theories of Epicurus and Lucretius, or have assured to them a universal and permanent empire over the human mind. Observation and experience speak no more in their favour to-day than they ever did; the exact methods of modern science, so properly eulogised, have not led to any discovery that makes materialism easier of acceptance. It is now what it was then, a speculative hypothesis and no "cognitio certa ex principiis certis", to use the Roman orator's

---

[1] Reprinted in Allgemeine Bucherei, herausgeg. von der österreichischen Leo-Gesellschaft Nr. 4, Wien und Leipzig. Cf. Der Katholik XLV, Mainz 1865, 2, 641—651. Natur und Offenbarung X, Munster 1864, 569 f. For Hyrtl as scientist cf. Leopoldina XXXI, Halle 1895, 190 f 211 f.

[2] Allgemeine Bucherei Nr. 4, p. 36—37.

definition of science. It is an inference, resting, not on clear and irrefutable argument, but on boldness of assumption and assertion, and on the dominant temper of the day which finds such theories the more congenial, the more menacing they are to the established order of things. The earth-born Titan of materialism has not achieved a lasting victory over the kingdom of science. No such victory will ever be achieved so long as serious science refuses to abandon the fight, so long as science draws its strength and inspiration from the stable ground of fact, so long as it refuses to count its own cause as lost, or to sacrifice to false gods.

"But if science is able, as it is able, to shake itself clear of this proud rival, so many times defeated yet never slain, then do not avert your eyes from the work of the true and earnest investigator. He too is a priest of knowledge; for, to adopt the words of the poet prince:

> Willst du zuletzt zum Unendlichen schreiten,
> Dann geh vorerst im Endlichen nach allen Seiten."

X. ZOOLOGY AND BOTANY.

Like Pasteur, but in a very different direction, the German scientist Christian Gottfried Ehrenberg († 1876), won his reputation in the sphere of the infinitely little[1]. Having published many papers of original research, he undertook in the years 1820 to 1825 a scientific expedition to the Nile Valley. He was accompanied by Hemprich, and the two colleagues brought back with them to Berlin a large selection of Natural history specimens. In 1829 Ehrenberg made a second journey with A. Von Humboldt and G. Rose to the Ural and Altai region. But his most important work was his

[1] Max Laue, Christian Gottfried Ehrenberg. Ein Vertreter deutscher Naturforschung im 19. Jahrhundert, Berlin 1895. Joh. Hanstein in Allgemeine deutsche Biographie V 701—711.

determination of the properties of the infusoria. These had been brought within the range of science by the invention of the microscope, but before Ehrenberg's researches very little was known about them, and that little was interwoven with fables and delusions. It was still believed that they were spontaneously generated by decaying matter, and that the forms which they assumed were due to mere chance and passed easily into others. Ehrenberg put a very different complexion on the matter[1].

It was his discovery in the waters of one of Berlin's supply-stations of a swarming population of these minute organisms that first made Ehrenberg's name famous and familiar. Kings and princes summoned him and his microscope to their presence, and he was received with honour in Paris and England. His reputation was further increased by his demonstration of the important part played in nature by the most minute forms of life. To this section of his work belong his studies on marine phosphorescence, on the blood-like blotches to be observed on bread and other foods, on edible earths, on blood-rain and dust-rain. Still more important was his discovery that certain widely-diffused kinds of stone and earth are composed of lime and pebbles formed from the casings of primitive animals. "But Ehrenberg reached the height of his reputation among his fellow-citizens of Berlin when in 1841 he showed that the earth, on which their city stood, was made up, to the extent of one half or even two-thirds, of hard-shelled living animalcules, busily swarming hither and thither, and

[1] For further details v. R. Hertwig, Lehrbuch der Zoologie[5], Jena 1900, 157.

constantly bringing forth new broods out of their tiny green eggs."[1]

Many of Ehrenberg's contentions are, it is true, no longer admitted. Subsequent research has shown that he was wrong in ascribing to the infusoria an organism identical with that of the higher animals, in spite of its microscopical dimensions. Many organisms too, which he classified as infusoria have been removed from that class and transferred to Botany, and others are now ranked among various branches of the protozoa. But none the less he stands as the pioneer of the modern science of the protozoa, the first to fix the attention of science on the "infinitely little", and to show the relations of this latter to the "infinitely great".

Ehrenberg was a resolute opponent of materialism.

"From his youth", says Hanstein[2], "he held firmly to the idealistic interpretation of nature and conceived it as ordered by the reasonable, purposive laws of a conscious Creator. But as a scientist he was the purest and most dispassionate empiricist."

When "German science turned away from the sure method of unprejudiced empirical study, to which Ehrenberg was ever loyal, and gave itself up to airy and fantastic hypotheses, he resolutely opposed the new tendency. He was in no way hostile to sober consideration of the theory of descent as guided by intelligible laws, although for his own part he was content to put it aside for the time as an hypothesis incapable of demonstration. But the speculative extravagances which under the name of 'natural selection' were at that time setting all heads in a whirl, the wild imagining of transition-forms between plants and animals, the 'protist-kingdom' as they were called, these and the like airy spe-

---

[1] Laue ante 194.

[2] Allgemeine deutsche Biographie V 705.

culations he banished with just contempt from the region of inductive science to that of poetic fancy"[1].

Ehrenberg spoke frequently and forcibly in criticism of the materialism dominant in his day. Thus in a speech in the Berlin Academy on October 17th 1850.

"It is not out of place", he said, "to touch, though but superficially, on certain hypotheses, which, after the morbid manner of the day, have been widely represented as results of scientific research, and which have made a deep impression alike on learned societies and on the popular mind."

"Men of great name and authority have, speaking as scientists, put science in an attitude of hostility to religion — not merely to the dominant, but to every form of religion —, and maintained, that our conceptions of the present and the future of man must be based on the conclusions of a science which is supposed to lead inevitably to materialism and Epicureanism."

Ehrenberg then goes on to deal in particular with two "conclusions" of science (1) "that religion, in the only sense and significance which scientific research can allow it consists, solely of a feeling of dependence in relation to nature" and (2) that all vital processes are in essence nothing more than electricity.

With regard to the first of these "conclusions" he remarks among other things: "It is quite true that the scientist realises more keenly than anyone else the dependence, the paltriness of man, whose weakness it is to be too puny for the infinity of space and too gross for the imperceptibly small, which yet governs and moulds his life. But besides this 'dependence' he feels the sublime and beneficent order of the universe and bows, in humility, admiration, and hope, before it, and before its Creator. He feels himself in sympathetic relation with the Maker and Orderer of all. It is senseless to rail at the order of the world."[2]

---

[1] Allgemeine deutsche Biographie V 710.

[2] Monatsberichte der Berliner Akademie 1850, 397—398.

The sophism that, inasmuch as electricity is present in all vital processes, therefore, life is electricity, he criticises in the following terms: "Just as we know no life without the presence of moisture, and no essential organ of a living body which does not contain carbon, and yet do not say that either water or carbon is life, so electricity, with its varying currents, cannot be conceived as anything more than an instrument, an accompaniment, a medium of which life makes use in order to effect its ends." [1]

The rest of the speech is a criticism of the assertion that the progress of science has shown the continued existence of the soul after death to be impossible. We do not reproduce Ehrenberg's arguments. It is sufficient to draw attention to the spectacle of a great scientist repelling as utterly invalid the so-called "proofs" of materialism put forward in the name of science. As for Ehrenberg's positive development of his views, this does not possess the same interest, for there is no handbook of Christian philosophy but cuts deeper into the heart of the subject.

Similar protests against the misuse of the sciences might be multiplied out of every part of Ehrenberg's writings. We quote, by way of example, some passages from his micro-geological studies [2].

The results of deep-sea research have, as we know, been invoked in support of the theory of the spontaneous generation of life out of non-living matter. "Bathybius", "a remarkably tough, chalklike, white substance which has given rise to the conjecture that it is the

---

[1] Ib. 398.

[2] Ehrenberg, Mikrogeologische Studien uber das kleinste Leben der Meeres-Tiefgrunde aller Zonen und dessen geologischen Einfluß, in Abhandlungen der königl. Akademie der Wissenschaften zu Berlin aus dem Jahre 1872, physikalische Klasse, Berlin 1873, 1—398.

primitive form of life from which the various forms of life may probably have developed" is still fresh in our memories[1]. On this question of deep-sea research, and the conclusions to which its results lead, Ehrenberg writes:

"It is very natural that the restless fancy of scientists should have sought to employ the valuable empirical results, attained in this sphere, to explain the earliest geological formations, and to buttress up the theory of spontaneous generation. But these cloudy speculations, under the pressure of a more fundamental analysis, exhibit their limitations, and are seen rather to afford imaginative entertainment than sound scientific information."[2]

With regard to the school "which believes itself warranted to assume the mantle of plenary inspiration, and to imagine a beginning of things, quite beyond the reach of empirical investigation, in which the amoeba reveals itself as the source and origin of life", Ehrenberg remarks[3]:

"I can only say that I join with many others in deploring the fashion in which an age which summons us to active and earnest concrete studies is frittered away in fantastic theories. It is painful to see so many of our most brilliant young men much less interested in sound research than in scientific romances, which alike in their theories of the origin of life, and of 'natural selection' rely merely on chance and a sham teleology, and not on any serious purposiveness."

The whole of Section XI.[4] "Independent, Microscopic Life, and the New Theories of Nature" is directed against Darwinism.

---

[1] Ehrenberg, Mikrogeologische Studien 362; cf. 376.

[2] Ib. 347—348. [3] Ib. 338.

[4] Ib. 376—384.

In the year of Ehrenberg's death (1876) there died, also at Dorpat, the founder of Comparative Embryology, Karl Ernst Von Baer[1]. Born in Esthland in 1792 he made his studies for the greater part in Germany, especially at Würzburg, under Döllinger. He received his first chair at Königsberg, passing thence to St. Petersburg, and finally to Dorpat. His pioneer work in the embryology of the vertebrates was done mainly at Königsberg, the rest of his life being devoted to Geography, Ethnography, and Anthropology.

Von Baer never wavered in his adherence to a teleological interpretation of nature. The development of a chicken in the egg, e. g., proceeds, in his opinion, in no mere casual fashion, the unforseen result of which is an organism capable of independent existence. On the contrary it is a purposive process dominated throughout by the end which it is to accomplish. This appears plainly from certain characteristics of the life of the chicken while still in the shell.

"On the end of the bill of the still immature chicken we find a hard formation which divides into two sharp points, pressed against the shell, making an opening through which it is able to emerge. Such a formation is unknown in the case of mammals whose eggs are not guarded by a hard shell. Am I not justified in saying that the end and purpose of this hard protuberance is to facilitate the breaking of the shell? . . . Soon after the birth of the chicken the casing of the bill comes off, being no longer of any utility."[2]

Similarly in the egg, the yolk is so disposed that the embryo which lies on the top of it, turns constantly

---

[1] R. Stölzle, Karl Ernst v. Baer und seine Weltanschauung, Regensburg 1897.

[2] K. E. v. Baer, Studien aus dem Gebiete der Naturwissenschaften, St Petersburg 1876, 198—199.

upwards towards the body of the brooding hen; in a word, the whole process of development is governed and guided by the end to be obtained.

Naturally such a teleological conception implies a belief in the existence of God. Von Baer draws that conclusion and gives expression to it in many places.

"The harmonious working of the forces of nature", he writes, "leads us to the recognition of a common First Cause, and this can be no other than the sublime Being to whom the religious needs of man reach out." "None the less", he adds, "a true knowledge of God is beyond the grasp of science, and indeed of humanity." What he means, however, is a knowledge not of the existence of God but of His essence [1].

Many expressions of Von Baer have a pantheistic ring, although side by side with these we find a clear recognition of the existence of a personal God. It was not till a few weeks before his death that he expressly abandoned pantheism and returned to theism. In 1876 he read the younger Fichte's "Questions and Thoughts on the Next Development of German Speculation", and declared: "No book that I have read for years has made so deep an impression on me. I date from it a new movement in my thought." And he added later: "I had long believed in the possibility of reaching, through pantheism, a unifying conception of the universe. Fichte's book taught me better. Pantheism won't do." [2]

Three years before Von Baer, died (1873) Louis Agassiz, much of whose work was done in the same

---

[1] K. E. v. Baer, Studien 79. For Baer's position as regards religion v. Stölzle, Karl Ernst v. Baer und seine Weltanschauung 419 ff.

[2] Stölzle ante 438.

province as that of the Russian scientist. "Louis Agassiz" writes Rütimeyer[1], "holds a most distinguished place amongst Swiss scientists, not merely because of the range and penetration of his researches but of the recognition which he secured for his science in America. Not merely did he establish there a science of European, indeed of German origin — Comparative Anatomy and Embryology — but by his brilliant intellectual endowments, his genius for organization and his steady industry, he induced the government of one of the richest commercial nations of the modern world to endow the study of zoological science with a munificence for a parallel to which we must go back to Alexander or the Ptolemies."

Rütimeyer has in mind in this passage the great Museum of Natural History of Harvard College in Massachusetts. The idea behind this institution, "that certainly did inspire Agassiz to the creation of it, was to exhibit the animal kingdom as a manifestation of the Supreme Intelligence. As religious enthusiasm once built the Cathedral of Cologne and the Basilica of St. Peter, so, thought Agassiz, it might be hoped from the intellectual ardour of America, that that nation would build a temple for the Revelation deposited in the material universe. Such a temple could not be vast enough nor costly enough, since it was to contain the sacred documents of inexhaustible Wisdom and infinite Power."[2]

Agassiz gives frequent expression to such ideas in his writings. Thus he writes at the beginning of his great treatise on Zoology:

---

[1] Kleine Schriften II, Basel 1898, 349—350.

[2] Ib. 362—363.

"The animal kingdom merits our ardent study, not merely because of its manifold beautiful forms, nor because of its utility to man. It has a far higher significance than that. It is the visible manifestation of the thought of God, as expressed in one part of that marvellous whole which we call nature; and from this point of view it is full of the weightiest lessons.

"Man is incited by both parts of his twofold being, spirit and body, to the study of nature. Since his intellect has been created in the image of God he can lift himself up to the contemplation of the divine plan in creation. And since by the possession of a material body he is, so far, in the same plane of existence as the animals, he has a constant impulse to investigate the mechanism of their organs and the properties and functions of matter as well as the influence which matter exercises on intellect throughout the whole range of nature [1].

"The same Being that, contemplating the moral weakness of man, prophesied that the Son of the Virgin should crush the head of the serpent, has also stored up for him in the bowels of the earth huge masses of granite, marble, coal, salt and various metals, the products of her different revolutions." [2]

On January 8th 1894 there died at Louvain P. J. Van Beneden, Professor of the University of that town [3]. "His innumerable and important studies", said Carnoy, "won him a postion of the first eminence in the world of science. For us he represents in particular the union of religion and science in the most intimate and happy alliance. . . . Van Beneden found happiness in his belief.

---

[1] Naturgeschichte des Tierreichs mit besonderer Rucksicht auf Gewerbe, Kunste und praktisches Leben. Allgemeine Zoologie von Professor Dr Louis Agassiz und A. A. Gould, Stuttgart 1855, 9.

[2] Agassiz und Gould, Allgemeine Zoologie 202.

[3] J. Carnoy, Éloge funèbre, reprinted in the Revue des quest. scient. XXXVII, Bruxelles 1895, 336—348.

He practised his religion with the deepest sympathy and conviction; and in those hours of pleasure which the scientist experiences at times on his difficult journey, his heart breathed out many a sincere and ardent prayer. Every enumeration of the facts unveiled by his researches, of the manifold laws revealed in them, derived from his faith a light and a help which enabled him the better to fit them into the general scheme of creation, and to understand the divine harmonies of the animal kingdom.''[1]

Most of Van Beneden's work has reference to a species of being, which, while not so congenial to romantic poetry as the nightingale or the robin red-breast, is nearer to the rude realities of nature, and plays a role of the highest importance in sea and stream, in land and water, in dead and living bodies, in plants and animals — he devoted himself to an elaborate study of worms, especially parasitic worms. Before the time of Van Beneden this region of science was a complete chaos, full of riddles and contradictions; it was left to the Belgian scientist in collaboration with Von Siebold and Leuckart to bring light and order into it. In examining various small fishes he discovered that the worms to be found in their entrails all exhibited the same stage of development — one at which they could not be described as either male or female. It was obvious then that they must elsewhere pass through a higher stage of development, and as the smaller fishes examined by Van Beneden serve as food to the larger, the conjecture suggested itself to his mind that this process took place in the body of the larger fish. This proved to be the case, and led

[1] Ib. 337 348.

to a demonstration of the fact that intestinal worms attain their full growth only by passing through the bodies of different animals. The Paris Institute in 1858 awarded Van Beneden its chief prize for this striking discovery.

Van Beneden turned next to the study of polyps "the flowers of the sea which, for beauty and variety of form and brilliance of colour, rank among the loveliest of natural products", and in 1866 he published an essay on the subject which also obtained a prize. As early as 1842 he had conceived the idea of making a complete study of the littoral fauna of Belgium. In that year he founded a laboratory at Ostend at his own personal cost, and laboured for thirty years at his subject, diverging as he went on into Palæontology. Belgium was under water during the tertiary period, as is proved by the fossils found in its soil. The neighbourhood of Antwerp is particularly rich in these remains. During the reconstruction of the town's fortifications, such an immense quantity of fossil bones was unearthed that a special hall of 65 metres by 11 metres was found too small to contain them. Van Beneden was the first to publish a complete description of these fossils and his study of the 40 different species of cetacea discovered amongst them is of the first importance[1]. "If", says Carnoy[2], "we consider the vastness and variety of his scientific labours, and simply calculate the time which

[1] Van Beneden peut être considéré en paléontologie comme un successeur du grand Cuvier; ses travaux et ses observations sur les cétacés sont regardés par les naturalistes comme ayant la plus grande valeur (La Nature n. 1079, 3 févr. 1894, Paris, 150).

[2] Éloge funèbre, reprinted in the Rev. des quest. scient. XXXVII, Bruxelles 1895, 346.

at the very lowest estimate must have been required for his anatomical researches and his marvellous notes, we are plunged in amazement at the notion of a single scientist having accomplished such a Herculean task."

Van Beneden's colleague at the Antwerp excavations was Bernard Aimé Léonard, Vicomte Du Bus De Gisgnies, Director of the Natural History Museum at Brussels. His chief study was Ornithology, and the collection of birds which he made is admirably representative and systematic. He died in 1874 "in sentiments of faith and hope"[1].

Bernard Altum[2] († 1900), President of the German Ornithological Society established a wide and brilliant reputation by his work, "The Bird and its Life". Altum studied Theology from 1844 to 1848 in his native town of Münster, was ordained priest in 1849, subsequently studied science in Münster and Berlin, and in 1859 became a lecturer at the Academy of Munster. The publication of his book secured him, in 1869, a call to the Chair of Zoology in the Academy of Woods and Forests in Eberswalde, a position which he held till his death. During his tenure of it he published a manual of "Forest Zoology", which like his earlier volume ran to several editions.

Altum's predecessor in the Presidency of the German Ornithological society was Baron Ferdinand Von Droste-Hülshoff, a loyal and ardent son of the Catholic Church.

---

[1] Il est mort comme son père, dans les sentiments de foi et d'espérance (P.-J. van Beneden in the Annuaire of the Belgian Academy XLIX, Bruxelles 1883, 264).

[2] Obituary Notice of E. Wasmann S. J. in Natur und Offenbarung XLVI, Munster 1900, 193—204.

His chief work was an excellent study of bird life on the island of Borkum (Münster, 1869)[1].

The ornithology of China owns as its pioneers E. Oustalet, and a Lazarist missionary Armand David († 1900)[2]. The labours of the latter were not, however, confined to a single department of Zoology, nor to Zoology in general. David entered the Lazarist Order at the age of 22, and gave immediate token of his passion and talent for science. When in 1852 he was sent on the mission to Peking, he set about the establishment of a zoological museum in the mission-house. "He pushed on the project with great enthusiasm and ability, and showed himself a very genius in the work of arranging and collecting. He made journeys through the province of Tshili and the southern part of Mongolia, varied with stoppages at the various mission-stations, and in a short time had brought together at Peking a splendidly classified collection in which every branch of Zoology, Botany, Geology, and Palæontology was represented. The fauna of Northern China showed a variety of forms, rich beyond all expectation, many among which were species hitherto unknown and very remarkable. On the despatch of the greater part of

[1] Natur und Offenbarung XX, Munster 1874, 574. Verhandlungen der k. k. Zoolog.-botan. Gesellschaft in Wien XXIV, Wien 1874, 481.

[2] Annales de la Congrégation de la Mission XLVI, Paris 1901, 46—49. Karl Berthold, Die Forschungsreisen des französischen Missionärs und Naturforschers Armand David, in Katholische Studien, herausgeg. von J. B. Stamminger III, Würzburg 1878. For David's first two journeys v. Revue des deux mondes 1871, 15 févr. 718—737, 15 mars 368—394, 15 mai 317—335, 15 juin 611—632. David himself gives a comprehensive survey of his theory of evolution and his discoveries, in Les Missions catholiques XX, Lyon-Paris-Bruxelles 1888, 214 f.

the collection to Paris these species were soon exhaustively investigated. David was brought into intimate relations with the authorities of the *Jardin des Plantes* and at their instigation undertook still more adventurous journeys."[1] One of the most important of these was that made in 1869 to the capital of Se-tschuen. David's bishop allowed him to make a long stay in No-ping, where there was a large Christian population and an ecclesiastical seminary. "It was an Eldorado for the naturalist. . . . His scientific spoils exceeded all expectation. It seemed impossible in our day to discover anywhere on the earth's surface so large a number of new species of mammals as David was able, at the end of a year's labour, to send to the Museum of Zoology at Paris. The importance of his collection had been recognised by the most eminent authorities."[2]

David himself in a paper read in Paris in 1888[3]; wrote as follows[4]:

"Until quite recently scientists were acquainted with only a very limited number of the animal species of China, two or three of its birds and practically none of its reptiles, fishes, or molluscs. . . . As regards its flora, the precious but limited collections of Fathers D'Incarville and Cibot[5],

---

[1] Ferdinand Freiherr v. Richthofen, China I, Berlin 1877, 711.

[2] Ib.

[3] Congrès scientifique international des Catholiques tenu à Paris du 8 au 13 avril 1888 II, Paris 1888, 451—467.

[4] Ib. 452.

[5] Pierre d'Incarville († 1757) and Pierre Martial Cibot († 1780) were Jesuits. The former drew up a list of 260 Chinese plants, in 1742 sent drawings of 72 animals and plants to Paris to Anton and Bernard Jussieu, established the first herbarium of Chinese plants, which lay for many years disregarded in Paris, until 1882 when

together with Bunge's two or three hundred northern plants, gave only a very inadequate idea of the vegetable wealth of the kingdom.

"In short, now that this mighty and mysterious country has become more accessible, the labours of scientists, working in many ways, have so improved our knowledge of its natural products that I myself was able to indicate 200 species of wild mammals (63 of which were new) and 807 species of birds (65 of which were formerly unknown). A considerable number of reptiles, batrachia, and fishes, as well as of molluscs and insects of every kind have also become known to us. The herbaria sent from Yün-nan by M. l'Abbé Delavay, or collected by me in various parts of China, raise to the number of about 4000 the species of vascular plants of the Empire, classified by the distinguished labours of M. Franchet of the Museum. In passing I give you a hint of the unparalled wealth of certain well known genera. Thus the genus *Rhododendron* gives us 52 new species, *Primula* nearly 40, and *Gentiana,* in the mountains of Western China a still greater number [1].

"David ranks, as the most remarkable of the animals discovered by him, a species of bear *(ursus melanoleucus)* which exhibits a form intermediate between the bear and cat species. In Europe it is known only by the four specimens which David sent to Paris. Another remarkable 'find' is *Elaphurus davidianus,* the animal of which the Chinese say that it has the horns of a stag, the hoof of a cow, the neck of a camel, and the tail of an ass. He succeeded, after great trouble, in obtaining for his Paris friends a specimen of this famous long-tailed stag."

Franchet described it. Cibot composed works on certain remarkable plants of China, e. g. cotton, bamboo, Chinese Ash, apricot, etc C. Sommervogel, Bibliothèque de la Compagnie de Jésus II, Paris 1891, 1168 f; cf. 1141 f; IV (1893) 559 f. — For Abbé Delavay of the Society of foreign Missions v. A. David in the Missions cath. 1888, 226.

[1] Congrès scientifique international des Catholiques II 435.

Another untiring student of the animal world of China was the Jesuit missionary Petrus Heude[1] († 1902, January 3rd at Shanghaï). Despatched to China in 1868 he began in that year a series of scientific journeys, especially in Kiang-su and Ngan-hwei which occupied him almost without interruption for thirteen years. He established an admirable Museum of Natural History in Zi-ka-wei, returned to Europe in 1884—1885, and from 1892 till his death was once again engaged in scientific expeditions. He visited the Philippines, Singapore, Batavia, Celebes, and the Moluccas, reaching Japan and Wladiwostok in 1897, and Further India in 1899. At Tongking he was stricken with his fatal illness. Heude gained his reputation mainly by his work on shell-fish: "La Conchyliologie fluviatile de Chine" (Paris 1875—1885) in which he described many new species and variations. He also made valuable contributions to the study of the tooth-formation, and general anatomical structure of animals[2].

The department of Zoology which deals with insects counts among its pioneers a Catholic priest, Pierre André Latreille[3] (1762—1833). In his childhood he was abandoned by his parents and thus left dependent on the charity of strangers; in 1786 he chose the Church as his calling with the intention of devoting all his leisure to science. The outbreak of the Revo-

---

[1] Cf. for him Natur und Offenbarung XLVIII, Munster 1902, 625 to 627. F. v. Richthofen, China I, Berlin 1877, 712.

[2] Mémoires pour servir à l'histoire naturelle de l'Empire chinois, Shang-hai 1882—1901.

[3] Biographie générale XXIX 850—854. List of his writings by Carus-Engelmann, Bibliotheca zoologica II, Leipzig 1861, 1994.

lution compelled him to fly from Paris, and take refuge in his native town of Brive. Here he was arrested and sentenced at Bordeaux to deportation. A rare insect *(Necrobia ruficollis)* which crawled out the planks of his cell saved him: the prison doctor brought this "find" under the notice of Bory de Saint-Vincent, the naturalist, and the latter secured the liberation of Latreille a few hours before the convict ship was due to sail[1].

In 1797 Latreille was again in the clutches of the law, but once again his friends managed to save him. He was appointed later to a post in the Paris Museum of Natural History where he had charge of the entomological collection, and occupied important teaching chairs. "They give me bread", he said, "because I have no longer any teeth." Latreille's work relates to reptiles, crustacea, and insects, more especially ants. He was the author of the sections on crustacea, spiders and insects, in Cuvier's great work on Zoology, and also of the description of the collection of crustacea brought by Von Humboldt and Bonpland from South America. Latreille stands among "the leaders of natural science, and holds the first place in Systematic Entomology"[2].

Another most distinguished entomologist was Jean Théodore Lacordaire († 1871), brother of the famous pulpit-orator. He made four journeys to South America, and one to Senegambia, lived for a time in Paris by his pen, and in 1835 obtained a professorship in the University of Liège. His scientific reputation rests

[1] Details in Natur und Offenbarung XXX, Münster 1884, 701—703.
[2] Ib. XXX 701.

mainly on his work in ten volumes "Genera des Coléoptères", an epoch-making study which has not yet been surpassed. His "deeply religious attitude towards life" has been recorded by his biographers[1].

Arnold Förster († 1884) a native of Aix-la-Chapelle, and for many years Principal of the Real-Gymnasium in that town, won a name of great authority in every branch of Entomology, but especially in that relating to the microhymenoptera. "Reared in the most ardent piety he was all his life a loyal Catholic. He was one of the leaders of his party, but his Catholicity was not merely external . . . it was a matter of earnest, every-day practice. He showed the warmest interest in all works of charity; many were the needs which his benevolence unobtrusively relieved, and when his own recources fell short he was always ready to appeal to others.... "To the friends of his youth as well as to those whom he won in later years, he was always unwavering in his fidelity; and the two or three whom political or religious differences led to abandon him — he never abandoned anyone — received at his hands a respect and regard which made them in the end ashamed of their foolish rancour." [2]

---

[1] Il n'eut conscience de sa position que quelques heures avant de s'éteindre; mais à ce moment suprême la fermeté de son caractère, alliée à des sentiments profondément religieux, lui firent accepter sans défaillance l'arrêt qui allait recevoir son exécution (Annuaire of the Belgian Academy XXXVIII, Bruxelles 1872, 155). A daughter of his became a nun (ib. 156).

[2] Omar Wackerzapp in Verhandlungen des Naturhistorischen Vereins der preußischen Rheinlande, Westfalens und des Regierungsbezirks Osnabruck XLIII, Bonn 1886, Korrespondenzblatt p. 38. — On Joh. Egger († 1866), who "stets einen Ehrenplatz einnehmen

No purpose would be served by adducing any further names of distinction in Zoology. The objections to Christianity, drawn from that science, are bound up with the theory of evolution, and that we reserve for separate treatment. But a science closely akin to Zoology, Botany, will yield us some instructive examples.

The first to whom we appeal is Karl Friedrich Philipp Von Martius († 1868), a friend and colleague of Ehrenberg [1]. Von Martius was a student at Erlangen when in 1812 the Munich Academicians Von Schrank and Spix made his acquaintance during a passing visit, and induced him to change his residence to Munich. In the year 1816 he accompanied Spix on a scientific expedition to Brazil. In four years they covered 1400 German Miles, traversing seven Brazilian provinces, and ending with the Amazon. "From the point of view alike of the area explored, and of the brilliant discoveries made, it was the most important of all the expeditions to the South American continent." On his return Von Martius published an account of the journey "which possesses the same importance in regard to Brazil, as the works of Von Humboldt in regard to the other regions of tropical America" [2]. He followed this up with a work on Palm-trees of which Humboldt wrote: "So long as

---

wird" in the history of Entomology in Austria, we are told in the Verhandlungen der k. k. Zoolog.-botan. Gesellschaft in Wien (XVII, Wien 1867, 536): "Er starb ruhig und mit voller Ergebung in den Willen des Herrn."

[1] Wunschmann in Allgemeine deutsche Biographie XX 517 to 527. Ch. Rau, Memoir of C. F. P. von Martius, Washington 1871.

[2] Wunschmann ante 521.

we continue to speak of palms, and to study palms, the name of Martius is safe from forgetfulness." Von Martius undertook further the colossal task of writing a *Flora Brasileensis*, and at his death had completed the description of more than 8000 plant varieties.

On March 30th 1864 Von Martius celebrated his Golden Jubilee as a University Professor. In his reply to the address presented by the Academic Body we find the following [1]:

"Public opinion is in our day much too apt to assume that the study of natural science produces in those who pursue it a materialistic temper, which is hostile to every belief that lies beyond the range of the senses, and refuses to entertain the notion that the universe rests on a spiritual foundation. And yet who can grasp that truth more clearly than the scientist who stands, not on the mere crust of phenomena, but in the central stream of life? He recognises, 'that this great Whole can have been made only by a God', and that a something moves in it quite other than the laws of the phenomenal world. These he seeks, and in greater or less measure, discovers, and his intellect discerns their harmonious correlation as the expression of a supreme, a divine purposiveness. But to their source and first cause he can never penetrate, and his clear perception of the limitation of the human mind teaches him humility. . . . Mysteries encircle the path of the scientist. The disintegration of white light into the gay variety of the spectrum, the endless dissolution and re-combination of matter, the origin and growth of the simplest speck of life, its evolution and ascent through organisms rising higher and higher in the scale until we reach the human body: we see all these, we study them, we classify phenomena and determine the conditions of their uprise — but we do not penetrate into the essence of their being. . . . Deep down in abysses that we cannot fathom, lies

[1] Sitzungsberichte der k. bayr. Akademie der Wissenschaften 1864 I 190—192.

their source and ultimate ground, and the 'wonder' of Plato is not merely the first incitement to research, but also its final result. The scientist, finding that the beginning and the end of phenomena alike lie beyond his grasp, is driven in on the conception of a spiritual force, working behind and upbearing this sublime order of things in which life comes to mean death and death life, this surging ocean the waves of which rise and fall and take new shapes under the stress of a living infinite power, and not as mere dead spindles of an ingenious machine.

"Chance there may be in the material world, but not in that higher region of the intelligences which pursue their mysterious paths under the paternal eye of God. This was the faith of the great masters of science, of Linnaeus, of Kielmeyer, Cuvier, Humphry Davy, of my unforgettable teacher Schrank, and many another. It is also mine...." [1]

These words give us an unambiguous declaration of the philosophical position of Von Martius. From a private letter to C. G. Carus, of January 18th 1861, we learn how he stood with regard to Christianity. Carus had lost his eldest daughter; the letter, published by the recipient after the death of Von Martius, was one of comfort and condolence [2]:

---

[1] Von Martius wrote once to his pupil A. Spring, in Liège: C'est par la pensée et par l'aspiration vers l'Éternel que l'humanité a la chance de se soustraire à l'action aveugle des forces de la nature, à peu près comme certains êtres ont traversé vivants les cataclysmes géologiques, alors que leurs congénères n'ont transmis que leurs cadavres aux périodes suivantes. Deus autem, sempiternus rerum omnium auspex et iudex, sedet alta in arce et tremenda fata spargit per mundum. Combien, ajouta-t-il, je désirerais m'entretenir avec vous, à l'ombre d'un tilleul fleuri, sur les merveilles de l'être et de la pensée! (Annuaire of the Belgian Academy XXXVII, Bruxelles 1871, 293.)

[2] Leopoldina, Amtliches Organ der kaiserl. Leopoldino-Karolinischen deutschen Akademie der Naturforscher Heft 6, Nr. 12, Februar 1869, 109.

"Most wonderfully has God, Whose wisdom and justice I humbly reverence, fashioned us of sense and spirit, and where the body plays a part there follows on the light that passes the shadow of pain. When we enter within the circle of immortal life we find eternal joy, everlasting life. Yes! what eye hath not seen, nor ear heard, what it has not entered into the heart of man to conceive, that is the bliss which I hope to possess when I have put off the flesh. There is no more potent intimation given us of such an existence than the experience of pain....

"Since your last letter I have thought of you every night with unwearying sympathy while I lay awake in bed. The night before last there came a sudden brightness in my room, and the mightiest and noblest of humankind stood beside me, and lifted up his hands and blessed me. As I lay with my eyes fixed on the sacred scars I heard a gentle voice: 'Thus the destiny of every man lifts him up on his cross of pain, and lifts him nearer to heaven. The one feels it; the other, still in the darkness of primitive man, as so many are even now, does not see that it is towards heaven he is raised. But you who know this, bear in mind that the Calvary which every man must climb is written and appointed in the wisdom and justice of God, and long not after rest nor after love, for human life can give neither. What is your craving for bodily ease but mere weakness?'

"It was a lesson for my poor, weak, and anxious heart, and I said to myself while I thought of you: Be brave, hold your way unwaveringly, and do not long after the peace of heaven until the time is come...."

"The fervour of Martius' faith", writes a contemporary[1], "found expression even after his death: on the white hood of the habit which he had prepared for himself there was embroidered a green cross — 'a cross', as he said, 'because I am a Christian, green in honour of Botany'."

[1] E. Ringseis, Erinnerungen des Dr. J. N. v. Ringseis II, Regensburg und Amberg 1886, 274.

Karl Friedrich Kielmeyer († 1844) of whom Von Martius spoke in his address, was a professor at Tübingen, then director of the institutions in Stuttgart for both science and art; but as he wrote nothing he is to-day all but forgotten. But others as well as Martius, ranked him with the "masters" of science. Humboldt in dedicating to him the "Observations in Zoology and Comparative Anatomy" called him the first of German physiologists. Cuvier wrote that he "always regarded Kielmeyer as his master, and admired his genius no less than he loved his character", and it is certain that Kielmeyer exercised great influence on the ideas of Cuvier. Martius' account of his religious belief will be found confirmed in the biography of Kielmeyer by G. Jäger [1].

The botanist and zoologist Von Schrank († 1835) was a member of the Society of Jesus. On the suppression of his Order he turned to teaching, and in 1784 secured a professorate at the University which was at first in Ingolstadt and later in Landshut. In 1809 he went to Munich, where he was placed in charge of the Botanic Garden. Von Schrank rendered great services to Bavaria, and enjoyed a distinguished reputation. "There was a time in Germany", says a notice of his death [2], "when if it had been asked who was the greatest scientist in Germany, the reply would have been Von Schrank." He was called "the third Linnaeus". His pen was untiring, and he laboured in the most diverse departments of science. He was the author of more than 40 independent works, and 200 papers and minor studies. In Botany he will always bear a name of the most honourable repute [3]. His greatest work is his *Flora Monacensis* published in four folio volumes 1811—1818. Von Schrank was always a worthy and pious priest. "He never failed in the duties

---

[1] Verhandlungen der Leopoldinisch-Karolinischen Akademie der Naturforscher XXI, Breslau und Bonn 1845, 1 ff.

[2] Allgemeine Zeitung, Augsburg 1836, außerordentliche Beilage Nr. 22—24, p. 85 f 93 f.

[3] E. Wunschmann in Allgemeine deutsche Biographie XXXII 451. According to Von Martius he is the most fruitful of German writers (Akademische Denkreden, Munchen 1866, 53).

of his sacred office. One often found the old white-haired man on his knees reading his breviary; he said Mass every day, as long as he retained sufficient strength for anything." He was buried in the Jesuit habit which he had worn for half a century [1].

We could find among botanists a wealth of names friendly to religion as e. g. Jussieu [2] († 1836); Benjamin Delessert [3] († 1847); F. H. Link [4] († 1851); Karl Adolf Agardh († 1859), who was the first to undertake the study of seaweeds and who as Swedish Bishop of Karlstad [5] wrote against D. F. Strauss; Adalbert Schnizlein [6] († 1868); H. G. L. Reichenbach [7] († 1879); L. R. Tulasne († 1885); P. E. Boissier († 1885); M. Willkomm († 1895).

One of the most distinguished of the more recent Botanists was Alexander Braun († 1877).

"What distinguishes Braun's scientific works", writes a biographer [8], "is not merely their vast range — though there is no department of botanical science which he has not mastered and developed — and the depth and penetration of his mind, but also the steadiness with which he keeps his eye fixed on a higher goal. He is never content with the study of particular phenomena, master though he is of observational methods; his eye is ever fixed on the totality of nature, the living interrelation of all its parts, the great general laws through which we reach back to the ultimate

[1] Allgemeine Zeitung 1836, 94.

[2] A.-M Ampère, Essai sur la philosophie des sciences II, Paris 1843, XXXIV.

[3] Flourens, Recueil des éloges II, Paris 1857, 325—386.

[4] v. Martius in Bulletin der k. Akademie der Wissenschaften, Munchen 1851, 218—220.

[5] H. Steffens, Was ich erlebte IX, Breslau 1844, 144.

[6] Allgemeine deutsche Biographie XXXII, 178.

[7] Leopoldina XVII, Halle 1881, 35.

[8] Ib. XIII, Halle 1877, 68—69.

source of being. . . . In all his writings and addresses we find him insisting that all true science must lead from the created to the Creator. To him 'Nature is not dead matter, not a cunning mechanism kept in motion by unknown forces, but the ordered history of the evolution of life, life coming from that Creator, Whom through analysis of his own life he finds to be the source of all being and all force, and to Whom he reverently prays'" [1].

In his address on "The Significance of Morphology" (1862) and "The Significance of Evolution in the History of Nature" (1872) the freedom of mind with which he discusses Darwinism, not rejecting it, but pleading for a deepening of the theory so as to harmonise it with morphological laws, is very notable.

Of Braun's private life his biographer writes [2]:

"Under all these trials (family losses) he showed patience and humility; his profoundly religious mind accepted joy and sorrow as coming alike from the hand of God, Whose love is shown in taking away as in giving."

Johannes Hanstein († 1880), the Bonn botanist, maintained that "physico-chemical forces are quite insufficient to explain organic life". "Organic life becomes intelligible only when interpreted teleologically, and from the point of view of purpose." [3]

If Hanstein appealed to Botany against Darwinism it was from the same science that the most uncompromising and convinced opponent of that form of the theory of evolution drew his chief arguments. J. W. Albert Wigand († 1886), Professor in Marburg, may have

---

[1] A. Braun, Über den Zusammenhang der naturwissenschaftlichen Disziplinen unter sich und mit der Wissenschaft im allgemeinen, Leipzig 1855, 23.

[2] Leopoldina XIII, Halle 1877, 71

[3] Ib. XVII, Halle 1881, 77—78.

borne himself a little too savagely in polemics, but he certainly showed the inadequacy of the Darwinian theory to explain the actual facts of development. Wigand was a fervent Christian as well as a leader of science, and he died in the conviction that between science and religion there is no enmity or antithesis[1].

Ferdinand Von Müller († 1896), Professor of the Australian Geographical Society, and "admittedly the first authority on the flora of Australia"[2] — distinguished above all as a "systematiser" — "made it a practice to enrich his works with carefully chosen Latin mottoes, commonly drawn from the Bible, declaring the glory of the Almighty as manifested in the creation"[3].

Johannes Leunis († 1873), who won considerable distinction in Botany, was a Catholic priest[4]. His celebrated "Synopsis of the three Kingdoms of Nature" gives a survey of the subject, so exhaustive and systematic, that, brought down to date by various editors, it still holds its ground as a standard text-book. . . . Leunis' "Guide to Nature-study" gave a great impulse in that respect to his generation in Germany.

With Leunis we may associate an Austrian savant, Franz de Paula Hladnik († 1844 at Laibach). He was at once priest, professor, and botanist. As a teacher he raised scientific teaching in the Laibach

---

[1] Berichte der deutschen botanischen Gesellschaft V (1887), XLIX.

[2] Leopoldina XXXIII, Halle 1897, 15

[3] Ib. 149.

[4] L. Kellner, Lebensblätter², Freiburg 1892, 19—23. K. L. Grube, Joh. Leunis nach seinem Leben und Wirken, Hannover 1876. Natur u. Schule I, Leipzig u. Berlin 1902, 257—264. Frankfurter Zeitung vom 6. Juni 1902 (Wochenausgabe) Nr. 23, p. 362 (only School Anecdotes).

Gymnasium to a very high standard; he "held a foremost place in Botany", and enjoyed the friendship of all the masters of that science. His writings scientific, spiritual, and ascetic were never given to the public [1].

"One of the first, probably the very first", to combine photography with the microscope, was Francesco Castracane degli Antelminelli († 1899). He specialised on the diatoms, one of the minutest of the algae. The collection of diatoms obtained by the celebrated Challenger Expedition was sent to him for examination; he discovered three new genera, 225 new species, and some 30 varieties. His contributions to the biological study of his subject were perhaps of even greater importance than those made from the point of view of systematisation. Castracane was a Catholic priest, and a man of the most remarkable piety [2].

Equally fervent and simple in his Catholicity was Philipp Parlatore († 1877). His principal work in Botany was a *Flora Italiana*, six volumes of which had been completed at his death. He wrote the sections on Gnetaceae and Conifers for De Candolle's *Prodromus*. and those on umbellates and grasses for Webb's "Natural History of the Canary Islands" and published descriptions of the flora of the Mont-Blanc range and of Lapland founded on original observation. In his

---

[1] C. v. Wurzbach, Biographisches Lexikon des Kaisertums Österreich IX, Wien 1863, 60.

[2] Biologisches Zentralblatt XX, Leipzig 1900, 401—412 433—451. A short memoir by P. Damanti, I contributi del Clero italiano alla scienza botanica nel secolo XIX, Palermo 1902, enumerates some twenty members of the italian clergy, who have done good work in botany.

scientific works we find numerous passages in which he breaks out into reverent praise of the Author of creation [1].

Of the more recently deceased masters of Botany we may cite Max Westermaier († 1903), Professor at Freiburg (in Switzerland) from 1896, as an example of a scientist who combined the scientific with the religious temper [2]. On the religious significance of scientific research he writes as follows:

"Radical errors in science — in other words, a falsification of what stands written in the book of nature — is all the more capable of corrupting the human mind inasmuch as the reward set on a true knowledge of the physical universe is no other and no less than a true knowledge of God. This path to God is open to all men, even to those who have never heard of Christ or Christianity, and all reasonable men must perceive and pursue it. And it is because true science is so great and noble a thing, that false science must produce such bitter and fatal fruits." [3]

XI. THE THEORY OF EVOLUTION.

"It is evident", writes the celebrated zoologist Richard Owen at the end of his work "The Principles of Zoology", "that there is a manifest progress in the succession of beings on the surface of the earth. This progress consists in an increasing similarity to the living fauna, and among the verte-

[1] Gedenkrede von Kard. L. Haynald in Literarische Berichte aus Ungarn, herausgeg. von P. Hunfalvy III, Budapest 1879. Auszug in Natur und Offenbarung XXVI, Munster 1880, 177—183. Cf. Allgemeine Zeitung 1854, 1577; 1877, 3974.

[2] Kölnische Volkszeitung 1903, Nr. 502. Rev. de Fribourg XXXIV, Fribourg 1903, 296 f; XXXV (1904) 73 f.

[3] Jahresbericht der Görres-Gesellschaft fur das Jahr 1895, Köln 1896, 19.

brates, especially in their increasing resemblance to man. But this connection is not the consequence of a direct lineage between the fauna of different ages. There is nothing like parental descent connecting them. The fishes of the palæozoic age are in no respects the ancestors of the reptiles of the secondary age, nor does man descend from the mammals which preceded him in the tertiary age. The link by which they are connected is of a higher and immaterial nature; and their connection is to be sought in the plan of the Creator Himself. . . . Man is the end towards which all the animal creation has tended from the first appearance of the first palæozoic fishes." [1]

A problem and a double attempt to solve it are conveyed in these words.

One has only to glance at a comparative table in the first good scientific treatise that comes to hand to see, under the rich variety of forms presented by the fish, the mammal, or the bird family, a fundamental identity of structure. These resemblances obtain not only between the classes making up a given family but also between one family and another, whether fish, mammal, or bird. The skeleton exhibits certain invariable characteristics, and we find in the most widely different varieties the same sense organs, and nervous and nutritive systems. If we take as an example, any given organ, eye or ear or stomach, we can trace it from its simple beginning in the lower forms of life to the term of its development in the higher forms, and discover the same fundamental characteristics under endless variations. This unity under multiplicity obviously constitutes a problem of the first importance. How are we to explain it? The old answer was very simple? The whole animal kingdom is the

[1] Quoted by Hugh Miller, The Testimony of the Rocks, Edinburgh 1857, 210.

work of a Mind, a Supreme Intelligence which, delighting in order, fashioned the bewildering multiplicity of things after the same model, thus setting on them the seal of spirit. This explanation does not exclude the idea of "evolution" in animal life, but we must use the word in the sense which it bears when we speak of the Ionian and Corinthian styles as an "evolution" of the Doric. The evolution does not go forward in the things themselves, so that one actually develops out of another, but in the ideas of things as they lie, preordained and perfect, in the mind of the Creator.

But this theory does not meet all the facts of the case. On the contrary it immediately raises the fresh question: What means did God adopt in order to give actual existence to His plan of creation? Did He produce each species by a special and immediate act of creation, or did he produce one by genetic development from another? Such development, within certain limits, we have constantly before our eyes in the case e. g. of dogs, pigeons, and rabbits. Can we conceive the process as operating over a wider area, and regard the rabbit and the hare, the wolf and the fox as springing from the same original species? Can we go still farther and conceive the whole animal kingdom as evolving (as the oak evolves from the acorn) from a primitive germ of life, endowed by the Creator with an extreme plasticity and a power to acquire and perpetuate differentiations, the whole process being of course governed by an unchanging law of evolution?

These questions are very far from novel; they have been before Zoology ever since it entered on its modern phase. Buffon at the outset of his career set himself to answer them. He declared at first for the limitless mutability of species, then for their absolute immutability except as regards the origin of races. The theory of evolution is not in itself opposed to theism. It has unfortunately been misused in recent times to support atheism, and still lies under reproach and suspicion. But it is in no way irreconcilable with the most fervent belief in God [1]. This is evident as regards the more guarded and limited forms of the theory. As for the more sweeping form which conceives the whole organic world as sprung from one primitive protoplasmal germ, it is, so far, a pure hypothesis; and if it should come to be demonstrated, the total process will appear so immense and magnificent that it will be impossible for a stable intellect to contemplate it without invoking as its source an infinite Creator. . . But we are transgressing our limits in discussing the intrinsic validity and significance of the theory of evolution. Our busines in this book is simply to consult the pioneers of evolution, and learn their view as to the religious import of their work.

We begin with Lamarck [2] († 1829). The concluding words of his *Philosophie Zoologique* show how little ground there is for setting the authority of his name against belief in God, or against the idea of purposiveness in nature. In every department of nature, says the great

---

[1] Cf. J. Knabenbauer, Glaube und Deszendenztheorie, in Stimmen aus Maria-Laach XIII, Freiburg 1877, 69—86 121—138. E. Wasmann, Gedanken zur Entwicklungslehre, ib. LXIII (1902) 281—307. F. de Hummelauer, Commentarius in Genesin, Paris. 1895. 129. P. Schanz, Apologie des Christentums I[3], Freiburg 1903, 327 ff and the Literature cited.

[2] Cf. A. S. Packard, Lamarck, the Founder of Evolution, his Life and Work, London 1902.

founder of Evolution, we find an incessant cycle of change. But nature as a whole is "unchangeable" so long as it shall please the sublime Author to maintain it in existence. Nature should be regarded as a totality, constituted by all its parts, existing not exclusively for any of these parts but for an end known only to the Author of all. Each part being necessitated to change, and cease to be, in order to bring forth a fresh existence, has an interest contrary to that of the whole; and, if the part reasons, it pronounces the whole defective. "But in truth the whole is perfect, and completely accomplishes the end for which it is designed." In another passage Lamarck quotes with approval the saying of Lavoisier that, in creating light, God had diffused over the earth the principle of organisation, sensation, and thought [1].

Lamarck had traced back all animal forms to one primitive form, product of a primary act of generation, but the next great exponent of evolution took

[1] La Nature, cet ensemble immense d'êtres et de corps divers, dans toutes les parties duquel subsiste un cercle éternel de mouvements et de changements que des lois régissent, ensemble seul immutable, tant qu'il plaira à son Sublime Auteur de le faire exister, doit être considérée comme un tout constitué par ses parties, dans un but que son Auteur seul connaît, et non pour aucune d'elles exclusivement. Chaque partie devant nécessairement changer et cesser d'être pour en constituer une autre, a un intérêt contraire à celui du tout; et si elle raisonne, elle trouve ce tout mal fait. Dans la réalité, cependant, ce tout est parfait et remplit complètement le but pour lequel il est destiné (Lamarck, Philosophie zoologique II, nouv. éd. par Charles Martins, Paris 1873, 426). — Un savant célèbre (Lavoisier, Chimie I 202) a dit, avec raison, que Dieu, en apportant la lumière, avait répandu sur la terre le principe de l'organisation, du sentiment et de la pensée (Lamarck ante 76).

a less daring view. Étienne Geoffroy Saint-Hilaire († 1844) held that all living animals were sprung from antediluvian ancestors and that they were fundamentally identical in structure under infinite external differences. But he neither believed that the first living organism had come into being by spontaneous generation, nor did he regard it as the source and origin of the whole animal kingdom. He anticipated more recent ideas very markedly in tracing back modifications to the continuous self-adaptation of organisms to their external circumstances, and in drawing attention to the development of the embryo as a summary and model of the successive stages of evolution in general [1].

It is well-known that Geoffroy Saint-Hilaire had a fierce battle with Cuvier with regard to the unity of plan in animals. Contemporary opinion awarded the palm of victory to Cuvier. It is well to remember that to Geoffroy's mind this unity of plan was in no way an irreligious conception.

"But far from regarding the formula", writes J. B. Dumas [2], "as laying fetters on the freedom or power of the Creator,

---

[1] Cf. A. de Quatrefages in the Revue des deux mondes, 15 décembre 1868, 854—858.

[2] Mais loin de considérer cette formule comme mettant une entrave à la liberté du Créateur ou comme imposant une gêne à sa puissance, l'illustre anatomiste voyait dans la découverte de ce principe nouveau, au profit de la pensée humaine, un pas de plus vers la connaissance de Dieu. Son fils rappelle avec raison, à ce propos, que Newton, si profondément religieux, après avoir admiré l'unité de plan qui règne dans les cieux, après l'avoir signalée comme démontrant l'intervention de la sagesse et de l'intelligence de l'Être toujours vivant, en reconnaît une nouvelle preuve dans cette autre unité de plan et d'exécution, signe caractéristique de toute beauté, qui s'observe chez les animaux (Discours I, Paris 1885, 239).

the great anatomist regarded it as a principle the discovery of which brought the human mind one step nearer to the true knowledge of God. His son [1] recalled in this connection that a mind so deeply religious as Newton's, having celebrated and signalised the unity of plan discernible in the heavens as a proof of the presence of the Wisdom and Intellect of God, passed on to draw the same inference from the unity of plan, traceable in the animal kingdom, and to praise it as the characteristic stamp of all beauty."

In the story of Saint-Hilaire's life the most prejudiced will seek in vain for any token of hostility to religion. During the great Revolution he displayed wonderful courage and self-sacrifice in securing the liberation of imprisoned priests, and in aiding their flight from France. In the July Revolution of 1830 he gave shelter to the Archbishop of Paris, Mgr. de Quélen, in his house in the *Jardin des Plantes*. When he was in his last years stricken with blindness he saw in his affliction a friendly dispensation of Providence for which he should be grateful [2]. The same resignation marked his bearing at the approach of death [3]; and his first words to his daughter on hearing that his illness was fatal, were: "We must soon part, but we shall meet again." [4]

---

[1] Isidor Geoffroy St.-Hilaire († 1861), also wrote his father's life.

[2] He wrote to a young lady, a friend of his: Dieu a voulu cette douleur pour racheter l'excès de ma bien vive satisfaction. . . . Soyons reconnaissants des faveurs de la Providence (Isidore Geoffroy Saint-Hilaire, Vie, travaux et doctrine scientifique d'Étienne Geoffroy Saint-Hilaire, Paris 1841, 411).

[3] Ib. 414.

[4] Nous allons nous quitter; nous nous retrouverons (ib. 413). — Le 19 juin 1844 M. Geoffroy s'éteignit doucement . . .; recevant l'adieu de son enfant chéri, lui dit avec calme: Sois-en sûre, ô ma fille, nous nous reverrons (Flourens, Éloges hist. I 265).

Geoffroy's ablest supporter was a scientist whom we have already learned to know as an ardent Catholic — Ampère[1]. As early as 1803 he had hit upon the same guiding ideas as Geoffroy. He took his side in the controversy with Cuvier, and every declaration of the latter was submitted by Ampère in his lectures to searching and vigorous criticism. Ampère published an essay on the subject[2].

Cuvier's victory, or supposed victory in the polemical battle of 1830 put a check on the progress of the theory of evolution. One of the very few leaders of science to hold stubbornly to it was a Catholic, D'Omalius d'Halloy[3]. He maintained steadily that the animals now living have come in direct line of descent from ancestors, specimens of which are found in fossil deposits. He advocated these views in 1838 in his handbook of Geology, in 1846 in six public meetings in the Belgian Academy, and again in the Academy in 1873, in a lecture on transformism. To the assertion that this theory is necessarily irreligious in its drift D'Omalius gives a vigorous denial. Thus he writes in his Geology:

"It is not inappropriate to remark here, that from what has been said above as to the transformation and development of living forms, no argument whatever can be drawn against the immateriality of the human soul. We must not confound the physical with the moral order, and just as our religious beliefs must not prevent us from seeing the facts of nature as they actually are, so, but with still greater rea-

---

[1] See ante p. 120.

[2] C.-A. Valson, La vie et les travaux d'André-Marie Ampère, Lyon 1897, 333—336.

[3] V. ante p. 269.

son, we ought not to employ the observations of our gross senses to attack dogmas belonging to quite another order of being.

"Although I regard all organisms now living as sprung by way of reproduction from those of the earlier ages, I do not mean that man is to regard the polyps as the source of his nobler faculties. Though it be true that the human species has in the course of ages undergone modifications, this circumstance does not in any way affect the existence of that immaterial principle with which, as religion informs us, the Creator has endowed man, that principle being as compatible with other bodily forms as with that which distinguishes man to-day. But more than that, not a single one of the facts unveiled by geognostic observation can be regarded as refuting the account given in Genesis. . . ." [1]

---

[1] D'un autre côté, il n'est pas hors de propos de faire observer ici que l'on ne peut tirer de ce qui a été dit ci-dessus sur les changements de formes et sur le perfectionnement survenus dans la nature vivante aucun argument contre l'immatérialité de l'âme de l'homme, on doit éviter de confondre l'ordre moral et l'ordre physique; car de même que nos croyances religieuses ne doivent pas nous empêcher de voir les faits de la nature tels qu'ils sont, nous devons encore moins nous appuyer sur quelques observations faites avec nos sens grossiers, pour attaquer des dogmes qui tiennent à un ordre de choses tout différent.

Du reste, quoique je considère les êtres vivant aujourd'hui comme provenant par la voie de reproduction de ceux des temps anciens, je n'entends pas dire que l'homme doit reconnaître un polype comme la souche de sa noble race. Mais quand il serait vrai que l'espèce humaine aurait aussi subi des changements de formes dans la série des temps, cette circonstance ne ferait rien à l'existence du principe immatériel dont la religion nous apprend que Dieu a doué l'homme, ce principe étant tout aussi compatible avec d'autres formes qu'avec celle qui distingue l'homme d'aujourd'hui. Mais il y a plus, c'est qu'aucun des faits constatés par les observations géognostiques ne peut être considéré comme destructif de la relation contenue dans la Genèse . . . (Géologie par J. J. D'Omalius-d'Halloy, Bruxelles, Société pour l'émancipation intellectuelle, 259).

All those whose opinions we have so far cited came before Darwin, and, as everybody knows, Darwin gave the theory of evolution a new impulse and direction.

As for Darwin himself, obviously we cannot call him as a witness on behalf of religion. He was an unbeliever, or rather an agnostic. His education goes far to explain this. He lost his mother when he was only eight years of age: his father was a free-thinker, and the teacher of the school to which he was sent was a Unitarian, that is, substantially, a rationalist. In spite of this he was at first an orthodox Protestant, but in process of time he ceased to believe in the Bible, and in the existence of God.

The enemies of religion will, none the less, find Darwin an unsatisfactory standard-bearer. The grounds on which he based his disbelief in the existence of God are thoroughly unconvincing [1], and his attitude was never that of a man certain of his position. The Duke of Argyll records a conversation which he had with Darwin about a year before the death of the latter. "In the course of that conversation I said to Mr. Darwin with reference to some of his own remarkable works on the 'Fertilisation of Orchids' and upon 'The Earthworms' and various other observations he made of the wonderful contrivances for certain purposes in nature — I said it was impossible to look at these without seeing that they were the effect and the expression of mind. I shall never forget Mr. Darwin's answer. He looked at me very hard, and said: 'Well, that often comes over me with overwhelming force; but at other times', and he shook his head vaguely, adding, 'it seems to go away'." [2]

To W. Graham, Darwin wrote in 1881: "You have expressed my inward conviction, though far more vividly and clearly than I could have done, that the Universe is not the result of chance." To this declaration he adds an ex-

---

[1] V. its refutation e. g. in Bern. Boedder, Natural Theology, London 1891, 182—200).

[2] Good Words, Ap. 1885, 244; cited by Francis Darwin, The life and letters of Charles Darwin I, London 1888, 316).

pression of the "terrible doubt" that always beset his incipient conviction on this point[1] — a doubt namely as to whether the human mind was capable of attaining certainty on such questions. But if we begin by distrusting our reason we shall find ourselves brought to an absolute stop, and unable even to determine whether two and two make four or five.

Darwin's position on all the higher issues of life remained one of suspended judgment and irresolution. He was never, he tells us himself, "an atheist in the sense of denying the existence of God". He goes on to say that on the whole (and as he grew older the description became more and more accurate) "agnosticism" was a much truer characterisation of his philosophical outlook[2]. He wavered between theism and atheism. If we bear in mind that he never spent much systematic thought on religion and its relations with science, and that speculation proper was very far from being his forte, we shall see with what little effect his authority can be invoked on the side of unbelief.

We have shown that, before the appearance of Darwin there were many Christian savants who found no difficulty in reconciling evolution with religion. Is this still possible, or has everything been radically changed by the fact that evolution has been used as a battering-ram to beat down Revelation? We do not incline to this latter view: despite the tumult of Darwinism we have always had both theologians and scientists who were able to show that there are evolution-theories and evolution-theories.

Let us take as an example Wilhelm Waagen († 1900), a great scientist, and a Catholic whose faith bore the test of pain and suffering. He was the first to extend to Palæontology the theory of evolution, in a book dealing with a species of ammonites.

[1] Ib. 316.

[2] F. Darwin, Life of Ch. Darwin I 304.

"Up to the present, Palæontology has been regarded as a science all but identical with Zoology, the only difference being that the one dealt with dead, the other with living, animals. But one point has been overlooked, namely, that in Palæontology the chronological element is an essential feature.... The method of exposition of the one must therefore differ widely from that of the other; for while in Zoology we have simply to determine and describe the form of a living species, in Palæontology we have, before all, to elucidate the historical relations of various types, and the organic evolution of one form out of another in process of time.

"It is natural that such a conception should lead us to set up some form of the theory of transformism. If I cannot profess any great affection for that extreme form of it which is popularised to-day in so many books and lectures, I am yet convinced that, within the area on which I have specialized, such transmutations of species are to be met with.... But whether the whole organic world forms an unbroken chain, every link of which is connected with and dependent on its neighbour is a question which a scientist can hardly hope to investigate to its depths: we are practically without data for the determination of it." [1]

Waagen, having, as he believes, established the fact of evolution as far as the *ammonites subradiatus* is concerned, continues:

"The ground of this remarkable phenomenon is to be sought, not in the external surroundings of the *ammonites*, but in a law of its inner being, which guides and governs its long evolution. This is an essential point on which I am compelled to disagree with Darwin, for he ascribed all variations to the sole influence of environment." [2]

"It is", concludes Waagen [3], "still undemonstrated whether the leading types ot be found in the organic world are genetically connected, or, on the contrary, whether after the creation

---

[1] W. Waagen, Die Formenreihe des Ammonites subradiatus, Munchen 1869, 4—5. (E. W. Benecke, Geognostisch-paläontologische Beiträge, Munchen 1876, Heft 2.)

[2] W. Waagen ante 61. [3] Ib. 77 f.

of the first organism, new organisms were not called into existence by new acts of creation. Here is a vast field for research. When once an hypothesis has been formulated and given a sufficiently clear expression, it is the business of science not to spin the hypothesis out in the air, but to endeavour to bring to light irrefutable facts which shall definitely establish or overthrow it. This is the proper and sole use of research. . . ."

A not less loyal Catholic than Waagen was K. A. Lossen. In 1874 he expressed himself as follows on the question of evolution:

"As for the theory of descent I distinguish sharply between its application to the lower animals and its application to man. As far as bodily structure goes, man stands in such intimate relations with the lower animals, especially with the monkey (he is much more akin to the latter e. g. than the monkey is to the whale) that the more minute differences which Zoology is able to discover between the human frame and that of the ape, and of which so much used to be made, do not seem to me to count. I find . . . the real gulf between them in their psychical qualities, which differ, not in degree, but in kind." "Language is and remains the impassable chasm between man and the lower animals. Assertions such as 'As language grows, mind comes into existence', or 'language creates reason' are so obviously nonsensical that we must treat them as deductions from a materialistic theory, not as ideas of independent origin."

As for the theory of descent in general, Lossen declines to make any final pronouncement. "To do that one needs long experience, rich material, and zoological genius, three things which I have not at command, though indeed a number of people manage without their aid to become enthusiastic Darwinians. But whether Theology and Philosophy have any real interest in setting themselves absolutely against every form of Darwinism, even the narrowest and most guarded, I very much doubt. It is quite easy to conceive the whole non-human, organic world as originating from a primitive germ endowed by God with the capacity of development; in that case the whole rich variety of existence would have been contained potentially in the first act of creation." He believes most firmly "that this conception is in no way hostile to the idea of a positive, revealed religion." [1]

Armand David also speaks in support of a modified form of the theory of evolution [2].

"It is a remarkable fact that certain classes of birds are confined to certain districts; they are represented there by numerous species, which are nearly related to one another, which play the same part in the same place. In other regions they are completely lacking, although it would be equally possible for them to live there, and their place has not been filled by equivalent races. Thus the remarkable and numerous family of the phasianidae includes more than forty species, all of which are to be found in the neighbourhood of the Tibet Tableland, whilst on the rest of the globe, no similar species are found. Similarly there are from 20 to 40 species of the family of the crateropods, which live in the East and are very rich in individual specimens there, but have no relations in Europe. Can we believe, in the face of these and similar facts, that such a great number of related species have been created from the beginning exactly as they are now, and have all been located in one single spot on the earth? Is it not more natural to look at the matter in this way: When the chief types of animals had made their appearance on this earth, when and how it pleased God — for this will always be a secret for man — they underwent transformations which separated them by degrees into different varieties, races and species; they emigrated and spread themselves about in the neighbourhood of their place of origin? Thus we could understand how America, for instance, possesses more than 400 species of colibri, whilst in the rest of the tropics where these tiny creatures would

[1] Jahresbericht der Görres-Gesellschaft für das Jahr 1895, Köln 1896, 16.

[2] Les Missions catholiques 20, Lyon-Paris-Bruxelles 1888, 247 f.

find it just as easy to live, not a single one is in existence. Any one who has studied Nature attentively, knows that among all classes of animals, similar facts can be observed and similar observations made."

Oswald Heer and Fr. A. Quenstedt in their scientific writings give constant expression to the firmness of their religious belief. Bóth were opponents of Darwinism, but not of every form of the theory of evolution. Heer's position may be stated in the words of a memorial article published shortly after his death [1].

"In the last chapter of his 'Primitive World' Heer propounds his ideas on the development of the organic world.... They are broadly these: All the members of the organic world are genetically connected one with another; the development of species from one another takes place however, not by a gradual, continuous process, but in a sporadic fashion, the periods during which species remain fixed being much longer than those in which new species are suddenly brought into existence. Heer thus maintains that in the history of the earth, relatively short 'periods of creation' alternate with longer periods during which species remain fixed and unchanging. Heer thus accepts in its completeness the kernel of Darwinism, but he rejects the notion of continuous variation, and consequently that also of natural selection. In lieu of the origin of species through evolution he posits origin through 're-coining'. How this 're-coining' is effected he leaves in doubt; the development of one species (from another) remains for us a riddle." [2]

---

[1] Reprinted in the Vierteljahrschrift der Naturforschenden Gesellschaft in Zurich XXVIII, Zurich 1883, 313.

[2] Regarding Darwinism Heer says: "Es ist die Furcht vor der Zweckmäßigkeit in der Natur und noch mehr vor dem dadurch notwendig gewordenen Zwecksetzer, welche manchen Naturforscher veranlaßt hat, sich an die Lehre von der naturlichen Zuchtwahl als rettende Planke anzuklammern. . . . Es ist dies aber ein sehr zerbrechliches Rettungsmittel, wie K. E. v. Baer, der größte Forscher

Quenstedt also accepts a theory of evolution, though not the Darwinian theory. After treating of the species of animals which succeed one another in the history of the earth he says[1]:

"Were we to suppose that these countless species were called into life by repeated acts of creation only to be in time utterly destroyed, what explanation would be possible of the fact that types once established continue to repeat themselves after the same model? For example, the thin-shelled lingula runs back in an unbroken line to the oldest mussels: more than one hundred species of it have been unearthed in transition rocks, and they are not confined to these, but are to be found in every marine formation. In our clay-coals every blow of the hammer in certain layers brings a large number to view, and this toughest of all organisms is to be found to-day, alive and flourishing, in the tropics. In spite of superficial differences they are as like one another as eggs. Surely we are warranted in concluding that the life-thread of this family was never broken, but that all its members have sprung from the same source..."

As a further example Quenstedt[2] instances the *Nautilus* which is found in the oldest formations, and which is as like the living *Nautilus umbilicatus* of the Indian Ocean "as mother to daughter". "Since the very beginning of my scientific career I have been an enthusiastic supporter of the theory of evolution. As I have often said jestingly, though the saying greatly shocked some of my older colleagues, were I the Lord God, I should have managed things in just the same way. To create a conscious life, and then let it die out in its agony, were the work of a cold though perhaps an infinite Power; there is warmth and wisdom in the plan of creating a primitive germ in which all creation lies

---

auf dem Gebiet der Entwicklungsgeschichte . . ., nachgewiesen hat" (Die Urwelt der Schweiz, Zurich 1883, Vorwort x).

[1] Die Schöpfung der Erde und ihre Bewohner, Stuttgart 1882, 39 f.

[2] Ib. 41.

implicit, and in evolving from it all that is to be called into existence by the kindlier way of generation. . . ."

On the theory of a struggle for life, "which can be accepted only in a limited number of cases", and on that of natural selection, Quenstedt comments as follows[1]:

"Yonder giraffe (as Darwin would say) got its long neck, not by continual stretching, but by natural selection. Africa was once visited by a great drought, everything on the surface of the soil was withered; only those animals survived whose long necks enabled them to feed on the leaves of the trees, and all the short-necks perished utterly. The long-necks transmitted their peculiarity to their descendants; and such famines, frequently repeated, inevitably produced the giraffe. These are the sort of notions that delight our present-day men of science, and in spite of that they still have the impudence to turn up their noses at Noah's Ark."

Twenty years earlier the great geologist had written:

"It is a much more probable conjecture that at no time did nature completely break the thread of life, but that she developed one living species from another. . . . Over the 'How?' of this process, nature has dropped a veil which perhaps we shall never lift. In such questions where the mind finds nothing to lay firm hold of, feeling comes in to supply the lack. And for myself, a Power which destroys to-day what to-morrow it will be compelled to rebuild, appeals less to me than one which deposits all creation germinally in a primitive being and unfolds it by a gradual and ordered evolution."[2]

We have already quoted the criticism of the physiologist Volkmann on evolution.

Alexander Braun, the botanist, accepts the theory in its essentials. But he follows Heer in positing

[1] Ib. 46 f.

[2] Epochen der Natur, Tubingen 1861, 60; cf. 831.

periods of fixation of species as well as periods of transformation. "A process of evolution without such resting points can hardly be conceived." [1]

Amongst English-speaking evolutionists we may appeal first of all to Dana. Of the evolutionary hypothesis in general he writes:

"There is no discordance with the Biblical account of Creation, since, in it, there is one 'fiat' for the first introduction of life and only three others for that of the animal kingdom; and moreover, the language implies growth for the rest, through laws established by the fiats." [2]

And to explain the creation of man he invokes [3]:

"the special act of a Being above Nature, whose supreme will is not only the source of natural law, but the working force of Nature herself".

The American botanist Asa Gray published a book in which he set himself to prove that the theory of natural selection is in no way at variance with theology [4]. Lord Kelvin, the first of English physicists, has written strongly, not against evolution as such, but against that form of it which dismisses as superfluous

[1] A. Braun, Über die Bedeutung der Entwicklung in der Naturgeschichte, Berlin 1872, 25.

[2] Manual of Geology 603—604. [3] Ib.

[4] Natural Selection not inconsistent with Natural Theology, London 1861. — Asa Gray (1810—1888) enjoyed a very high reputation in America. "Everyone wanted to see him. Strangers waited in the garden to catch a glimpse of his venerable head at the window of his favourite room" (Memoirs and Proceedings of the Manchester literary and philosophical Society, 4. Ser., I, Manchester 1888, 95). Cf. Berichte der deutschen botanischen Gesellschaft VI, Berlin 1888, XXXI f. Ib. XXXVII: "Obgleich Gray ein frommes Mitglied der orthodoxen Kirche war, konnte er doch keinen Widerspruch zwischen Darwinismus und Religion sehen."

all idea of purposiveness or finality [1]. An upholder of the theory of evolution was the celebrated geologist, Charles Lyell. Concerning its philosophico-religious bearing he says, for example, at the end of his book on the Age of Man [2]:

"None of the authors above cited, while they admit fully the analogy which exists between the faculties of man and the inferior animals, are disposed to underrate the enormous gap, which separates man from the brutes, and if they scarcely allow him to be referable to a distinct order, and much less to be a separate sub-class, on purely physical grounds, it does not follow, that they would object to the reasoning of M. Quatrefages, who says, in his work on the Unity of the Human Species, that Man must form a kingdom by him self, if once we permit his moral and intellectual endowments to have their due weight in classification." Lyell then quotes the passage in which Quatrefages sums up what he takes to be the characteristic marks distinguishing man from the animals. These the French scientist finds, not in anatomical differences, nor even in the functions of perception and evolution, but in the exclusively human faculty of apprehending abstract ideas of good and bad, right and wrong, virtue and vice, in the exclusively human belief in a supernatural world and supernatural beings — or a single such Being — whom man fears and reverences. Quatrefages, in two words, finds the *differentia* of man in his capacity for religion and morality [3].

"But", adds Lyell, "he omits to notice one essential character which Dr. Sumner, the late Archbishop of Canterbury, brought out in strong relief fifty years ago in his 'Records of Creation'. 'There are writers', he observes, 'who have taken an extraordinary pleasure in levelling the broad di-

---

[1] Ante p. 36.

[2] The Geological Evidences of the Antiquity of Man, with remarks on theories of the origin of species by variation, London 1863, 495 f.

[3] Cf. A. de Quatrefages, Hist. générale des Races humaines, Paris 1887, 4—6.

stinction which separates Man from the brute creation. Misled to a false conclusion by the infinite variety of Nature's productions they have described a chain of existence connecting the vegetable with the animal world, and the different orders of animals one with another so as to rise by an almost imperceptible gradation from the tribe of Simiae to the lowest of the human race, and from these upwards to the most refined. But if a comparison were to be drawn, it should be taken not from the upright form, which is by no means confined to mankind, nor even from the vague term reason, which cannot always be accurately separated from instinct, but from that power of progressive and improvable reason, which is Man's exclusive and peculiar endowment.

"It has been sometimes alleged, and may be founded in fact, that there is less difference between the highest brute animal and the lowest savage than between the savage and the most improved man. But in order to warrant the pretended analogy, it ought to be also true that this lowest savage is no more capable of improvement than the Chimpanzee or Orang-Outang.

"'Animals', he adds, 'are born what they are intended to remain. Nature has bestowed upon them a certain rank, and limited the extent of their capacity by an impassable decree. Man she has empowered and obliged to become the artificer of his own rank in the scale of beings by the peculiar gift of improvable reason.'"

Having quoted a passage from Agassiz in which the latter writes in a somewhat exaggerated strain of the points of resemblance between man and the animals, Lyell goes on:

"We cannot imagine this world to be a place of trial and moral discipline for any of the inferior animals, nor can any of them derive comfort or happiness from faith in a hereafter. To man alone is given this belief, so consonant to his reason, so congenial to the religious sentiments implanted by nature in his soul, a doctrine which tends to raise him morally and intellectually in the scale of being, and the fruits of which are therefore most opposite in character to those which grow out of error and delusion."

Lyell concludes by saying: "We may imagine that events and operations in general go on in virtue simply of forces communicated at the first and without any subsequent interference, or we may hold that now and then, and only now and then, there is a direct interposition of the Deity, or lastly, we may suppose that all the changes are carried on by the immediate, orderly and constant, however infinitely diversified action of the intelligent, efficient Cause. They who maintain that the origin of an individual, as well as the origin of a species or a genus, can be explained only by the direct action of the creative Cause, may retain their favourite theory compatibly with the doctrine of transmutation." [1]

Albert Gaudry, Professor of Palæontology at the Natural History Museum of Paris, formulates as follows the central idea of his book "On the Interrelations of the Members of the Animal Kingdom during Geological Times": "So long as we confine our attention to actually living animals it is impossible to establish genetic relations between them. But Palæontology comes to our aid, and shows that, in addition to those actually living, a multitude of others have appeared on the earth at various times. To these earlier earth-dwellers, science now has to put the question: 'Are you isolated existences that have sprung up here and there in the immense tract of time, without any clearer or more comprehensible order than that of the flowers in our meadows? Or are you in bonds of relationship one with another, and under the apparent diversity of nature shall we discover in time the plan through which the Infinite Author has stamped on all things the stamp of His unity?' This effort to unveil the plan of creation is the task to which all science is to-day applying itself."

[1] The Geological Evidences of the Antiquity of Man, London 1863, 505.

"Palæontologists are not agreed as to the manner in which the plan has been realised. One school, impressed by the many lacunae in the history of the earth as known to us, believes in the independence of species, and maintains that the Creator brought the plants and animals of geological times into existence one by one, but in such a way, as to suggest in their structure that filiation which really exists only in thought. Others, impressed on the contrary by the rapidity with which these lacunae are filled up, maintain that this filiation is material and genetic, and that the divine method was to evolve each successive species from a living predecessor. Personally I prefer this latter hypothesis, but whether it be adopted or not, it would be impossible to doubt the actual presence of a plan. The day will come, I doubt not, when Palæontology will unveil this plan, and that day will be a glorious one, for if the details of nature are so magnificent, how sublime must its inspiring idea be!"[1]

"If I have attempted", concludes Gaudry, "in this book to bring forward certain arguments in favour of evolution, I have deliberately avoided discussion of the methods by which the Creator has produced those changes of which Palæontology shows us the picture. One theory of the means adopted is what is called Darwinism.

. . . Assuredly the subject is one which demands the attentive study of scientists. But I have to confess my incompetence to deal with it. My task has been simply to draw attention to those tokens of interrelation which I think I perceive between the earth-dwellers of geo-

[1] Les enchaînements du monde animal dans les temps géologiques. Fossiles primaires, Paris 1883, 3.

logical times. It is for the physiologists . . . to tell how the variations are produced to-day, and consequently how they were probably produced in remote ages."[1]

We find nothing here of the "atheistical implications" of evolution. Gaudry himself says, with regard to the remarkable discoveries made by him at Pikermi in Greece, that they filled him with reverence and gratitude to God[2].

G. J. Romanes († 1894), a friend of Darwin, began his career as a resolute opponent of the teleological interpretation of nature, but the course of time and of reflection led him back to a conviction of the existence of God and to Christian faith and practice[3]. The circumstances of his life are still fresh in the general memory and it is unnecessary to detail them.

"Through the misuse", writes E. Wasmann[4], "which Monism, especially the Monism of Haeckel, has made of evolution, through the employment of it as a weapon against theism, many conservative theologians have been persuaded that the idea of evolution is intrinsically and irreconcilably at variance with Christian belief." We

---

[1] Les enchaînements. Mammifères tertiaires. (Nouveau tirage conforme à l'édition de 1873.) Paris s. a. (1895), 257.

[2] Quelle ampleur de formes et quelle variété sur le théâtre de la vie! Bêtes géantes et innombrables de Pikermi, la pensée de vos imposantes cohortes a souvent transporté mon esprit; je ne peux songer à vous sans m'élever jusqu'à l'Artiste infini dont vous êtes l'ouvrage, et sans lui dire merci de nous faire assister aux grandes scènes qui semblaient reservées pour lui seul, jusqu'au jour où a été soulevé le voile sous lequel la paléontologie était cachée L. c. 259.

[3] G. J. Romanes, Gedanken uber Religion. Die religiose Entwicklung eines Naturforschers vom Atheismus zum Christentum. Herausgegeben von Ch. Gore. Übersetzt von E. Dennert, Göttingen 1899.

[4] Stimmen aus Maria-Laach LXIII, Freiburg 1902, 296.

have shown by our appeal to men of science how groundless is this view. We have quoted the words of scientists of the first rank who were evolutionists without ceasing to be Christians, and who vehemently denied that the two were opposed to each other. The theory of evolution is not, therefore, atheistical. Whether it is in accord with the actual facts of nature, as observed and analysed by science, it is not the purpose of this book to enquire.

RETROSPECT.

We have now completed our survey of the various departments of science. The question which we set before ourselves was this: Must the science of the nineteenth century as a whole be regarded as hostile to religion? Or in other words: Do the leaders of science in that century exhibit such unanimity on ultimate problems, and such vehemence of unbelief as justifies popularizers of anti-Christian thought in resting their case on the authority of "Science" and "the scientist"?

To that question a resolute "No!" must be returned by any honest enquirer. It is perfectly true that in many of our Universities, professors can be found to support the interpretation of science which we have combated; and that this temper of mind forces itself from time to time on public notice. But how many of these University Professors are likely to live in the history of research for as long even as a hundred years, or to be called up as witnesses to the religious or the irreligious import of science? Not very many, we should imagine; but we are content to leave them, in common with other living scientists, to the appraisement of posterity. One thing is certain. If in our survey of the nineteenth century we have regard only to the pioneers and torch-bearers of physical research, the result of our enquiry will be far from inimical to religion.

We have not in these pages adopted a merely statistical point of view. In other words, we have not made out a list of great scientists who died between 1800 and 1900, ascertained whether each was a believer or an unbeliever, and then counted up the numbers on both sides. Such a proceeding was both impossible, for lack of adequate data, and unnecessary.

The scientists to whom we have made appeal may be divided into two classes. In the first are to be ranked those who accepted at least the existence of God, and of a spiritual principle in man, whatever further development they gave to their religious views. We are warranted in calling these as witnesses favourable to Christianity. For if the assault of science is to be successful, the points of attack must be those natural truths which form the basis of Christian belief. How else could the two be brought into conflict? The possibility of miracles, the question as to whether God, for the purpose of a special revelation, is able to suspend the uniform course of natural laws, must be decided by a study of the nature of God and not by physical science. For physical science has as its sole purpose and province the study of the uniform course of natural laws. The historical fact that, in Christ, God gave a Revelation to the human race, can by no possibility conflict with the laws of Chemistry and Zoology. The content of that Revelation can in no way clash with Astronomy and Geology. The theologian concerns himself only with the primal source and cause of things, and leaves an absolutely free hand to the scientist in determining their established qualities and uniformities. The points of contact of science and theology, therefore, are confined to the two problems specified. As to the bearing of the one department of knowledge on the other we have appealed to a great number of authoritative names, and we might without much trouble, have largely increased the list [1].

The second group comprises those who were in the fullest sense Christians, very many of them being Catholics. Our list is very far from complete, but we have been able to adduce a goodly number, and every name is a name of the first importance. To put in concrete form the result of our investigation, let us

[1] Among geologists may be mentioned, as representing S. America, Ignatius Domeyko, Professor of Mineralogy and Geology at Santiago; he was a Pole by birth and died in 1889; as representing S. Australia J. E. Tennison Woods, died at Sydney 1889, Vicar General of the Bishop of Adelaide, an authority on the geology of the southern Continent. Most of these sections, which we have purposely not treated in detail, can naturally be further developed, e. g. the section on Zoology. Henri-Marie Ducrotay de Blainville († 1850), a zoologist of high merit, made no secret of his belief in Christianity, laid great stress on the activity of final causes, and wrote a work on the relations between religion and science. J. F. Blumenbach († 1840) speaks in his works of God as the Creator of nature. Henry Milne-Edwards († 1885), one of the most celebrated of modern zoologists, declared openly that he could not understand the wonders of nature as being the result of mere chance. The botanist Tulasne, whose name has been mentioned above bequeathed his botanic library to the Catholic Institute in Paris, and wished to further the honour and glory of God by his works. Of the celebrated surgeon Joh. Nep. Nußbaum († 1890) even the Munchener Allgemeine Zeitung writes (1890, Beil. 260): "Nußbaum war ein glaubensstarkes Glied seiner Kirche; ohne diese Kraft des Glaubens, ohne das Positive desselben wäre seine ganze Persönlichkeit gar nicht zu denken und zu verstehen." His last words were: "Gelobt sei Jesus Christus" (Germania, 4. November 1890, Nr. 254, 2. Blatt; cf. Nr. 253, 1. Blatt). Among those who have recently died may be mentioned Adolfo Cancani Montani († 29. May 1904), an excellent seismologist and a Catholic of child-like piety.

imagine a Samaritan of unbelief, a man so passionately hostile to Christianity as to reject in science and in practical life all aid or help that comes from a Christian hand. In what a sorry plight would he not find himself! If he turns to Chemistry he will have to go his way without Berzelius, Dumas, Liebig, Sainte-Claire Deville, Chevreul; in other words, he will have to rediscover practically the whole of modern Chemistry. If he fixes on Electricity he will have to put aside the work of Galvani, Volta, Ampère, and Faraday; if on Optics, he must step back over the despised discoveries of Fresnel, Fraunhofer, and Fizeau to the old theories of emission; if on the Theory of Heat he must reject Mayer and Joule. As for Astronomy, when he has shorn away the discoveries made possible by Fraunhofer's telescope, and the work of Leverrier and Laplace, there will be very little left. So much for speculative science. And what of practical life, of trade and commerce, art and industry?

Our consistent unbeliever will have to light his house with tallow candles, for stearine comes to him from the Catholic hands of Chevreul; and he cannot use electricity without tribute, in the very quantitative terminology in which his bill is calculated, to the Catholic names Ampère and Volta. Aluminium he must refuse and abandon, for he owes it to the Catholic Sainte-Claire Deville. He cannot continue to pasteurize his wine; he cannot use Schönbein's collodium in photography, nor can he use water-glass or cement. His medicine will have to manage without Pelletier's quinine, Laënnec's auscultation, and Pasteur's whole fabric of bacteriology. The list of necessary abnegations might be continued almost at pleasure. It has been pushed far enough to show the retrogression and utter bankruptcy in which science would be plunged by the rejection of the work of Christian, or even merely of Catholic, pioneers.

It is to be hoped that nobody will raise the objection that many scientists of the first eminence, such as Virchow, Du Bois-Reymond, Tyndall or Berthelot, can be called up on the side of unbelief. That we have made no attempt to deny. We set out simply to show that there is no justification for writing of "Science" as intrinsically and necessarily hostile to religion, and that the alleged unanimity of scientists on the matter simply does not exist. It does not in the least weaken our contention to show that many of the admitted leaders of science were unbelievers, and enemies of religious belief. We have been concerned simply to exhibit the spectacle of men of genius in the full glory of their renown as scientists, accepting the teachings of Christianity with fervour and simplicity of mind. When a disciple of the school of Elea, had proved conclusively to another Greek philosopher that the idea of motion is self-contradictory, and that, consequently, motion is impossible, his hearer replied, not by argument, but by simply walking up and down. He adduced the fact of motion as a proof of the possibility of it. We have ventured to follow the same tactics in reply to the assertion that religion and science are irreconcilable. There are in this case other methods of reply, but the one which we have chosen is perhaps the simplest.

Nobody has, so far as we know, attempted to show that the majority of scientists of the first order have thrown the weight of their authority against religion, nor would such a project have much hope of success. On the contrary the greater minds of science have ever shown warmer friendship and reverence for religion than the lesser, and the more they meditated on the fundamental problems of life the more friendly they became. Men like Ampère, Volta, Cauchy, and Maxwell found in science not a confutation but a confirmation of Christianity. There never was a more earnest and passionate opponent of materialism than G. A. Hirn. At the meeting of the British Association at Belfast in 1874, Tyndall used the presidential chair as a pulpit of materialism, but one had to go no further than his audience to find a man like Maxwell, at least his equal in science, who absolutely rejected his manifesto and dismissed it in a set of doggerel verses. In the writings of the French Positivists we find all speculation as to the ultimate nature of things brusquely dismissed as "metaphysical" and unscientific. But against this sentence of death on metaphysics we can appeal to the declaration of Heinrich Hertz[1] († 1894). "No idea that forces itself on the intellect is in any way weakened by being called metaphysical. The intellect, as such, has its needs which certain scientists are pleased to call metaphysical."

We find also a great many scientists who began with Monism, but diverged further and further from it with the progress of their researches. We may appeal for instances to Haeckel who is certainly not a prejudiced witness in this regard. He cites as examples of this "psychological metamorphosis" the two most famous scientists of our time, Virchow and Du Bois-Reymond, and later Wundt, and Von Baer[2]. Virchow was at first a convinced materialist, and in 1856 he declared his

---

[1] Die Prinzipien der Mechanik, Leipzig 1894, 28.

[2] Die Welträtsel, Bonn 1899, 108 f 116 f 118 207 f.

firm conviction that he would never waver from that position. "Unfortunately this 'conviction' proved a grave delusion; for 28 years later, he put forward principles completely at variance with those which he had formerly advocated."[1] Wundt came to regard the first edition of his "Lectures on Comparative Psychology" as a "sin of his youth", and in the second edition he expressed radically different opinions. The first edition was "purely monistic and materialistic", the second "purely dualistic and spiritualistic"[2]. Haeckel's statement of the change in Wundt's position is somewhat exaggerated, but he is quite right in signalising the fact that the scientists, whom he quotes, came in process of time and thought to a more and more complete recantation of their original declarations[3].

---

[1] Ib. 109. [2] Ib. 117.

[3] In one of his last essays (on Neo-Vitalism) printed in the Deutsche Rundschau 81, Berlin 1894, 384—401) Du Bois-Reymond († 1896) recognises the statement, that the world derives its existence from an act of divine omnipotence, as a conclusion confirmed by science. One can only think with Leibniz that divine omnipotence "vor unvordenklicher Zeit durch Einen Schöpfungsakt die ganze Materie so geschaffen habe, daß nach den ihr mitgegebenen unverbruchlichen Gesetzen da, wo die Bedingungen fur Entstehen und Fortbestehen von Lebewesen vorhanden waren . . . einfachste Lebewesen entstanden, aus denen ohne weitere Nachhilfe die heutige organische Natur, von einer Urbazille bis zum Palmenwalde . . . ward" (p. 400). This is almost identical with St. Augustine's view of creation by a single act of God, and his theory of *rationes seminales*. Du Bois-Reymond is in complete accord with these sentiments, because Darwinism has not justified the hopes which were placed in it. "Nachdem die Darwinsche Lehre den oben geschilderten Triumphzug gehalten hatte, verflog nach einiger Zeit der Rausch. Von verschiedenen Seiten her erhoben sich lauter und immer lauter Zweifel an der Strenge von Darwins Beweisfuhrungen" etc. (p. 397).

Lichtenberg says somewhere that in society he often professed to be an atheist, *exercitii gratia*. Sebastian Brunner, a man of great insight and experience, relates that while in his youth, he was wont to scoff at those of his comrades who were openly pious, he none the less never failed to say the prayers "in his little prayer-book", morning and evening, and he adds that on enquiry he found this to be a very common "psychological phenomenon" [1]. If this was the case in Brunner's day, still more is it so in ours; unbelief is the ruling fashion, and to confess one's faith in Jesus Christ and his Church is to ensure bitter criticism and contempt. It needs courage to stand out against so strong a current of opinion. But in spite of this "psychological phenomenon", it is a fact as firmly established as any observation of science, that mankind in general has ever been on the side of belief, and that religion has its root deep in the core of the human heart. The mass of humanity gives way very readily to superstition, but not to scepticism. The Cagliostros, Saint-Germains, and Mesmers of the eighteenth century, the table-turners and spiritists of the nineteenth are a conclusive proof of this. Man is naturally religious in mind and heart; and the blatant unbelief of the newspapers and the popularizers springs from no profound and ingrained conviction. A great part of it, at least, must be regarded as a mere current fashion, a phenomenon not of philosophy but of "good tone".

It will perhaps be said in reply to our contention that if science is not hostile, yet it certainly is not

---

[1] G. Chr. Lichtenbergs Vermischte Schriften I, Göttingen 1867, 15. S. Brunner, Woher und Wohin III 94.

actively favourable to Christian belief. That, at all events, is its general reputation; and how could this reputation be acquired without some adequate cause? To this latter question we cannot undertake to reply in detail. We have shown that it rests on no defensible basis. Its origin is probably to be sought in the fact that the scientific apostles of unbelief possess, in a much fuller measure than their Christian colleagues, the faculty of getting themselves talked about. Everybody in Germany knows the names of Haeckel and Karl Vogt, and everybody in England knows the names of Tyndall and Huxley. Men who count for very much more in the progress of general research are not known beyond an extremely limited circle. One meets many and many an educated man, who has only the vaguest acquaintance with such names as Fresnel and Fizeau, Dumas and Chevreul, or perhaps no acquaintance at all. It is not hard to understand how this state of affairs has arisen. Scientists are no more than human; and in the nineteenth century many of them, growing weary of the stern and solitary business of research, strayed into easier paths, and put their imaginations at the service of unestablished but fascinating hypotheses. Some of them set up as wandering missionaries of the new "scientific" gospel, and went from town to town drawing all the world to their lectures; others, in brilliantly inaccurate manuals and treatises, "brought the new philosophy within the range of everybody of average education". The newspapers were filled with their names; they became the storm-centres of controversy, the staple of conversation. They were the only scientists known to the great public, and every word that fell from their lips was accepted as the authoritative pronouncement of "science". The appeal made in their writings to the conquests of science never failed of sympathetic listeners; and they, the spokesmen of science, must they not have her authentic word? But all the while the true masters of science were busy at something other than lecture tours; they spoke, indeed, but not in halls given over as a rule to concerts and dances. They were labouring with a fierce zeal in their laboratories, lecturing and writing to audiences of trained scientists, and in a learned idiom. They shrank from publicity, partly perhaps because they lacked the facile fluency of the popularizers, partly because they had no desire to be drawn into newspaper controversies. They remained silent, and the impression produced by their silence recalls a homely image. In a pond while the fishes hold their peace the frogs do not fail to croak with raucous vehemence; and common speech, ignoring the fishes, describes the whole as a frog-pond!

We find something of the same state of affairs in popular biographies of the great scientists. Full details are given of the personal life and political convictions of the subject of the biography, but we often seek in vain for so much as a hint of his attitude towards the fundamental questions of philosophy and religion. It will have been observed throughout our quotations that, as a rule, the commemorative notices of great scientists — though one or two exceptions are to be noted — contain appreciations of the religious convictions of the deceased only when the author of the notice chances to be himself on the side of religion. One may read, for instance, the memorial speech of Arago on Volta, from the first syllable to the last without finding a single hint that Volta was a fervent believer. Gumbel's notices of famous geologists in the "Compendium of German National Biography" exhibit the same extraordinary omission. When a statue of Ampère was, in 1888, erected in his native town of Lyons none of the orators adverted to the fact that he was a loyal and ardent Catholic. Moreover the statue exhibits him standing with a pile of books behind him, and on one of them is carved in large capitals, *Encyclopédie!* [1] The natural inference of the uninformed must be that Ampère was an adherent of the Encyclopaedists, whereas his sole relation to them was that he read them in his youth, and rejected them in his maturity. In an issue of "Die Natur" (1883, Nr. 2, p. 18) we came upon a memoir of Joule, in which the passages which we have quoted on an earlier page were embodied. Joule's references to the Creator were, however, excised without a word of explanation or comment [2]. We also call to mind reading, in another popular review, an article on Schwann in which the great discoverer of the animal cell was represented as a thorough materialist. We, on the Catholic side, display a culpable indifference with regard to such matters as these. It is true that we rest on the authority of Christ, and not on that of this or the other scientist. But our indifference, combined with active concealment or misrepresentation on the part of our opponents, casts a veil of obscurity over the true state of things in science.

Still another cause may have contributed to bring science into ill repute. It was not assuredly in our day

---

[1] V. sketch in La Nature II, Paris 1888. 337.

[2] Joule, according to the translator, was born in 1818 at Salford in Christmas-Eve. Christmas-Eve is, in German, Weihnachtsabend, and Salford is not situated in "Weihnachtsabend", but is a large town adjoining Manchester.

that controversialists, friendly and hostile, began to represent science as essentially irreligious. In the seventeenth century the English Royal Society incurred the denunciation of religious opinion in London as tending to belittle the Holy Scriptures, and to draw people away from the Christian belief. Critics of to-day form a very different estimate of the seventeenth century; they hold up the firmness and fervour of its belief as a reproach to our "godless" age. In a newspaper of the year 1841, which came casually into our hands, we read an article defending the scientists of that day against the imputation cast on them of atheism and revolutionary ideas. To-day some of us are willing to cast the same imputation on our contemporaries, but we speak of 1841 as the "good, old time" of unshaken belief. How is this puzzling phenomenon to be explained?

If we are not mistaken, it results from the fact that we judge past epochs by the names which have survived the sifting process of time. English science of the seventheenth century means for us Newton and Boyle. Newton and Boyle were both deeply religious men, and we transfer the attribute to their age in general, being content to pass over those of their less distinguished contemporaries, who were also, perhaps, less pious. At the end of the eighteenth century the Professors of the University of Pavia were very far from being all Christians, and some of them made the life of their colleague Volta sufficiently miserable. But the twentieth has found no reason for remembering any of them except Volta, and Volta alone.

St. Thomas Aquinas says somewhere that a true knowledge of nature fashions the mind of man more fully to the image of God, for such knowledge is not too low for the Divine Reason. St. Thomas goes on to praise the useful function of science which delivers men from fantastic superstitions such, for example, as astrology[1]. The attitude of the Church towards science is, then, very far from hostile; and if we have seemed in these pages to take up a position of distrust and defence, it is not of true science that we are distrustful, but of the misuse of it, attempted by many popular writers. Our first object has been the vindication of religion, but our second has been the vindication of science itself as against extravagant fantasies.

Mathias Claudius writes at the end of a passage in which he makes appeal to Bacon, Boyle, and Newton[2]:

"I do not deny, Andres, that I find great joy in the words of Francis Bacon, of Robert Boyle, of Isaac Newton. Not indeed, for the sake of religion; religion can neither gain nor lose at the hands of scientists, be they great or small. But I feel cheered by this spectacle of men of much industry and resolution, men who have grown grey in the service of science, and who know more of nature and the ways of nature than all the world beside. . . . I feel cheered to see men of such character and genius, not priding themselves on their wisdom, but, hat in hand, humble and eager to learn, drawing close to the altar of the sublime mysteries of God. I feel cheered, Andres, and I recover all my old enthusiasm for learning, which crowns her servants with the richest gifts without allowing their reason to be clouded by pride, and themselves to be degraded to foolish scoffers and mockers. And it has an amazingly different effect, Andres, to see, on the other side, the crowds of light sciolists defiling by, their hats on their heads, their noses contemptuously in the air. . . ."

More than one savant has bitterly lamented the ill repute into which science has been brought by "scientists"

---

[1] Contra Gentiles lib. 2, cap. 2 3. [2] Werke VI, Wien 1844, 161.

of this stamp. We have quoted Joseph Hyrtl to this effect. We may well conclude with the words of another Austrian master who regards science, not as something to be excused and defended, but as the most effective of all weapons for the overthrow of materialism. Andreas Von Baumgartner says[1]:

"Natural science is able, above all, to expose the contradictions of materialism, and to show its untenableness, whether it has sprung from the soil of history, or from that of philosophy, or some other science. This consideration should suffice to dissipate the anxiety of those who regard the study of nature as fraught with peril to the young. In point of fact, science, rightly directed, is the best and most stable barrier against error; and, more than any other branch of learning, it leads us to recognise the universe as the temple of the Almighty."

We agree; but the "right direction" is to be found only in a solid discipline in philosophy.

[1] V. p. 295.

LIST OF NAMES.

1503769R0

Printed in Great Britain by
Amazon.co.uk, Ltd.,
Marston Gate.

Les Belles
HISTOIRES

ISBN : 978-2-7470-6048-6

18, rue Barbès – 92120 Montrouge – France
Dépôt légal : septembre 2016
Imprimé en Italie
Loi n° 49-956 du 16 juillet 1949
sur les publications destinées à la jeunesse

10 histoires à lire et à relire

Les Belles HISTOIRES

bayard jeunesse

Sommaire

J'ai un lion à la maison !

Une histoire de Claude Prothée,
illustrée par Anne Wilsdorf

C'est arrivé comme ça :
j'étais sorti un instant
pour récupérer mon courrier
dans la boîte aux lettres
et, quand je suis revenu,
il était là, dans le salon.

– Alors, m'a-t-il dit, les nouvelles sont bonnes?
Il était installé dans mon fauteuil préféré.
J'étais si étonné que je n'ai pu m'empêcher de lui demander:
– Mais…? Que faites-vous là?
– Tu le vois, Julien (Julien, c'est mon prénom), je suis assis près de la table…
Puis il a repris: –… table, hélas, bien dégarnie, car je ne te cache pas que j'ai une faim de…

– … de loup ? ai-je ajouté.
– Non, une faim de lion !
En disant cela, il a agité sa crinière
et il m'a regardé d'une drôle de façon.
Je me suis empressé de lui dire :
– Attendez ! Je reviens tout de suite !

J'ai couru chez monsieur Tripoux, le boucher.
Il m'a demandé :
– Que désirez-vous, monsieur Julien ?
Un petit steak haché comme d'habitude ?
J'ai approuvé d'un signe de tête :
– Oui… et vous ajouterez aussi un gros gigot,
quelques kilos de jambon,
et puis aussi ces chapelets de saucisses, là…
Cela a drôlement étonné monsieur Tripoux,
qui s'est exclamé avec admiration :
– Eh bien, quel appétit, monsieur Julien !
Moi, je me suis dépêché de filer
à la maison.

J’étais à peine rentré que, déjà,
toutes mes courses étaient avalées.
– Ouf, ça va mieux !
m’a dit le lion en se curant les dents.
Puis, il m’a serré chaleureusement
la main en ajoutant :
– Julien, tu es un vrai copain.
Au fait, appelle-moi Sultan,
c’est mon prénom.

Le lion et moi, on s'est vite bien entendus.
Il y avait une chambre d'ami dans la maison,
et Sultan s'y est installé.
Je lui ai prêté une paire de pantoufles
et une vieille robe de chambre.
Naturellement, dans la journée,
j'allais au bureau comme d'habitude
et, pendant ce temps,
Sultan restait à la maison.

Celle qui a été un peu
étonnée au début,
c'est madame Plumeau,
la femme de ménage.
Elle trouvait que j'avais
de drôles d'amis !
Mais, comme Sultan
se comportait en parfait lion
au foyer, madame Plumeau
y trouva vite son compte :
Sultan faisait la vaisselle
et il passait l'aspirateur
sur les tapis.

Bref, quand elle arrivait,
madame Plumeau n'avait presque plus
rien à faire.
Du coup, elle passait son temps à lire
l'avenir dans les lignes de la patte
du lion, et il adorait ça.

Cependant, quand le soleil rougeoyait à l'horizon,
Sultan se souvenait de sa lointaine savane.
Le soir venu, il ne pouvait s'empêcher
de pousser quelques rugissements.
Ces bruits bizarres inquiétaient fort
madame Le Greffier, ma voisine.
J'ai dû lui expliquer, en faisant semblant
de tousser, que c'était moi
qui avais un chat dans la gorge.
– Un gros chat alors,
m'a répondu madame Le Greffier.
Vous devriez consulter un médecin.

Un jour, les frères Filoux,
qui sont de célèbres brigands,
ont tenté de cambrioler ma maison.
Moi, j'étais au bureau,
mais Sultan les a entendus.
Il est sorti brusquement de sa chambre,
et un seul rugissement a suffi
pour que les trois brigands, terrorisés,
courent se réfugier au commissariat
du quartier.

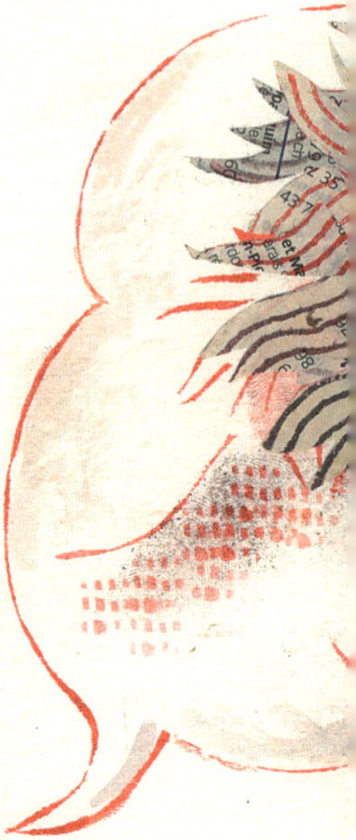

Quand je suis rentré chez moi,
le commissaire en personne m'a félicité :
– Vous vous êtes défendu comme un lion.
J'ai dû faire enfermer les frères Filoux
dans une maison de fous : ils prétendaient
que vous vous étiez transformé en fauve !

La nouvelle de mon exploit s'est répandue
dans la ville. On me regardait maintenant
avec admiration, mais aussi avec un peu
de crainte. On me trouvait changé.
Monsieur Tripoux, le boucher,
prétendait que c'était à cause
des bons steaks qu'il me vendait
en abondance.

Notre vie aurait pu se poursuivre longtemps ainsi.
Mais, un soir, en rentrant du bureau,
j'ai trouvé madame Plumeau en pleurs.
– Je l'avais prédit !
a-t-elle dit en me tendant la lettre
que Sultan avait laissée avant de partir.

Désolé, Julien,
mais je rentre chez moi.
Ma savane me manque trop.
Merci pour tout, mon copain !
Je t'enverrai des cartes postales.
Sultan

Sultan a tenu parole.
Depuis, nous nous écrivons régulièrement.

C’est encore un secret, mais,
aux prochaines vacances,
je compte aller visiter sa savane.
Il se peut donc qu’un beau matin,
Sultan me trouve sur sa terrasse,
installé dans son grand fauteuil
à bascule.

– Alors Sultan, lui dirai-je
malicieusement,
les nouvelles sont bonnes ?

Le loup vert

Une histoire de René Gouichoux,
illustrée par Éric Gasté

Il était une fois un loup vert, aussi vert qu'une belle pomme verte. Il s'appelait Raoul.
Un jour, Raoul arrive dans la forêt des loups gris.
Or, ce jour-là, les loups gris jouent au foot.
Comme Raoul adore le foot, il s'approche, et il dit :
– Salut, les potes, ça boume ?
Les loups gris s'arrêtent de jouer
et se tournent vers Raoul.

6
2
5

L’un d’entre eux commence à rire :
– Vert ! Mais ce n’est pas une couleur pour un loup !
Il bombe le torse, et il dit encore :
– Gris ! Voilà la seule couleur digne d’un loup !
Raoul dit timidement :
– Mais vert, c’est ma couleur…
Le loup gris répond en se tapant les cuisses :
– Eh bien, change de couleur !
Les autres loups gris rient
en se tapant les cuisses, eux aussi :
– Ben oui, change de couleur !
Raoul s’en va, et en chemin il se dit :
– Gris ! Il faut que je devienne gris.

Raoul court jusqu'à la ville,
et il entre dans une boutique de vêtements.
La marchande lui demande : – Vous désirez ?
Raoul répond : – Des habits, s'il vous plaît.
La marchande propose : – Du vert peut-être…
pour aller avec la couleur du visage ?
Raoul s'écrie : – Ah, ça non ! Pas de vert. Plus de vert.
Du beau gris, s'il vous plaît.

Et c'est ainsi que Raoul s'en retourne dans la forêt,
gris de la tête aux pieds : bonnet, jogging,
chaussettes, baskets…
Il porte même un masque gris.
Quand il arrive, les loups gris jouent à la course.
Justement, Raoul adore la course.
Il dit : – Bonjour, les amis, ça va ?

5
6

Les loups gris cessent de courir.
L'un d'eux remarque la queue,
la longue queue de Raoul.
Il murmure :
– C'est bizarre, un loup gris à la queue verte…
Au même instant, Raoul pense :
« Zut, j'ai oublié d'habiller ma queue ! »
En s'enfuyant, Raoul entend les ricanements
des loups gris qui se tapent les cuisses.

Mais Raoul n'est pas un loup à se laisser décourager.
Il prépare un grand feu. Quand le feu est refroidi
et que les cendres sont bien grises,
Raoul s'en couvre le corps tout entier,
sans oublier sa longue queue verte.

Raoul est si content de lui qu'il sifflote
tout le long du chemin menant chez les loups gris.
Il réfléchit : « Que vais-je leur dire ?
Bonjour, les potes ! ou : Salut, les amis ? »
Soudain, un orage éclate, un de ces orages
à ne pas mettre un loup dehors.
Raoul, lui, est si pressé qu'il poursuit sa route.
Il court pour arriver plus vite.
Mais la pluie tombe si fort
qu'elle emporte les cendres grises.

Bientôt, Raoul se retrouve plus vert que jamais,
aussi vert qu'une belle pomme verte sous la pluie.
Il rage, il trépigne :
« Puisque c'est ainsi, employons les grands moyens. »
Et il retourne à la ville acheter de la peinture,
grise évidemment.

Raoul se couvre de peinture, il s'en badigeonne, il s'en étale partout : sur la tête, sur les oreilles, sur les pieds et sur le derrière. Sans oublier sa queue, naturellement.

Pendant ce temps, le soleil revient. Il brille tant que le pauvre Raoul a bientôt trop chaud sous sa couche de peinture. Il transpire, il commence à étouffer, ouvrant tout grand sa gueule pour tenter de mieux respirer.

Heureusement, à ce moment-là, une fée passe.
Rien qu'à voir Raoul se tortiller,
elle comprend immédiatement.
Elle lève sa baguette magique
et, hip ! hap ! hop !
elle délivre Raoul de sa carapace grise.
Puis la fée demande :
– As-tu encore besoin de mes services ?
Raoul gémit :
– Gris ! Je voudrais être gris !

La fée lève de nouveau sa baguette.
Hip ! Hap ! Hop !
Et Raoul devient… poisson. Un poisson rouge.
– Ah ! Raté, dit la fée. Mais, dis-moi,
ça ne te plaît pas d'être un poisson ?
C'est beau, un poisson, ça nage,
ça se promène au fond de l'eau…
Raoul pleurniche :
– Gris ! Je voudrais être gris !

– Bien, dit la fée. Elle agite sa baguette.
Hip ! Hap ! Hop !
Et Raoul devient… oiseau.
Un merveilleux oiseau aux mille couleurs.
– Oh, zut ! dit la fée.
Remarque, un oiseau, c'est agréable :
ça vole, ça traverse le ciel, c'est libre.
Raoul sanglote :
– Gris, je voudrais être gris.

La fée agite encore sa baguette.
Hip ! Hap ! Hop !
Et Raoul redevient… loup. Un loup vert.
La fée soupire : – Excuse-moi,
je ne suis pas très douée comme fée.
Moi, j'aurais préféré être danseuse à l'opéra.
Raoul dit en reniflant :
– Je te trouve très bien en fée.
– Vraiment ? demande la fée.
– Vraiment, répond Raoul.
La fée dit : – Eh bien, moi, je te trouve très mignon
en loup vert. Mais qu'est-ce que tu voulais devenir, déjà ?
Raoul répond : – Finalement… je vais rester comme ça.

La fée dit : – Comme tu voudras.
Bon courage et bonne chance !
Puis elle disparaît.
Raoul court à toute vitesse chez les loups gris.
Ils jouent à cache-cache.
Cache-cache, c'est le jeu préféré de Raoul.

Alors Raoul s'avance au milieu des loups gris, et il dit :
– Salut, c'est moi !
Et, avant que les loups gris ne disent un seul mot,
il ajoute :
– Oui, je suis vert.
Et après, qu'est-ce que ça peut faire ?

Le prince Olivier ne veut pas se laver

Une histoire de Odile Hellmann-Hurpoil,
illustrée par Régis Faller

Il était une fois un roi, une reine
et leurs deux enfants.
Les habitants du pays étaient très fiers
du roi Hubert, de la reine Isabelle
et de la princesse Marinette, mais
ils avaient un peu honte du prince Olivier.

Il était pourtant toujours gai,
toujours prêt à rendre service.
Il n'avait qu'un seul défaut,
il ne voulait pas se laver !
Aussi l'avait-on surnommé
le prince mal débarbouillé.

Le matin, la reine Isabelle lui disait en l'embrassant :
– Prince Olivier, mon fils, il faut vous laver !
Vos joues sont toutes noires
et vos mains toutes collantes !
Mais le prince Olivier répondait :
– Reine Isabelle, ma mère, pourquoi me laver,
puisque je vais me salir
en jouant dans le parc ?

À midi, le roi Hubert lui demandait :
– Prince Olivier, mon fils,
vous êtes-vous lavé aujourd'hui ?
Et le prince Olivier lui répondait :
– Non, Roi Hubert, mon père,
je ne me suis pas lavé aujourd'hui.
Mais je me suis lavé les pieds le mois dernier,
c'est bien assez !

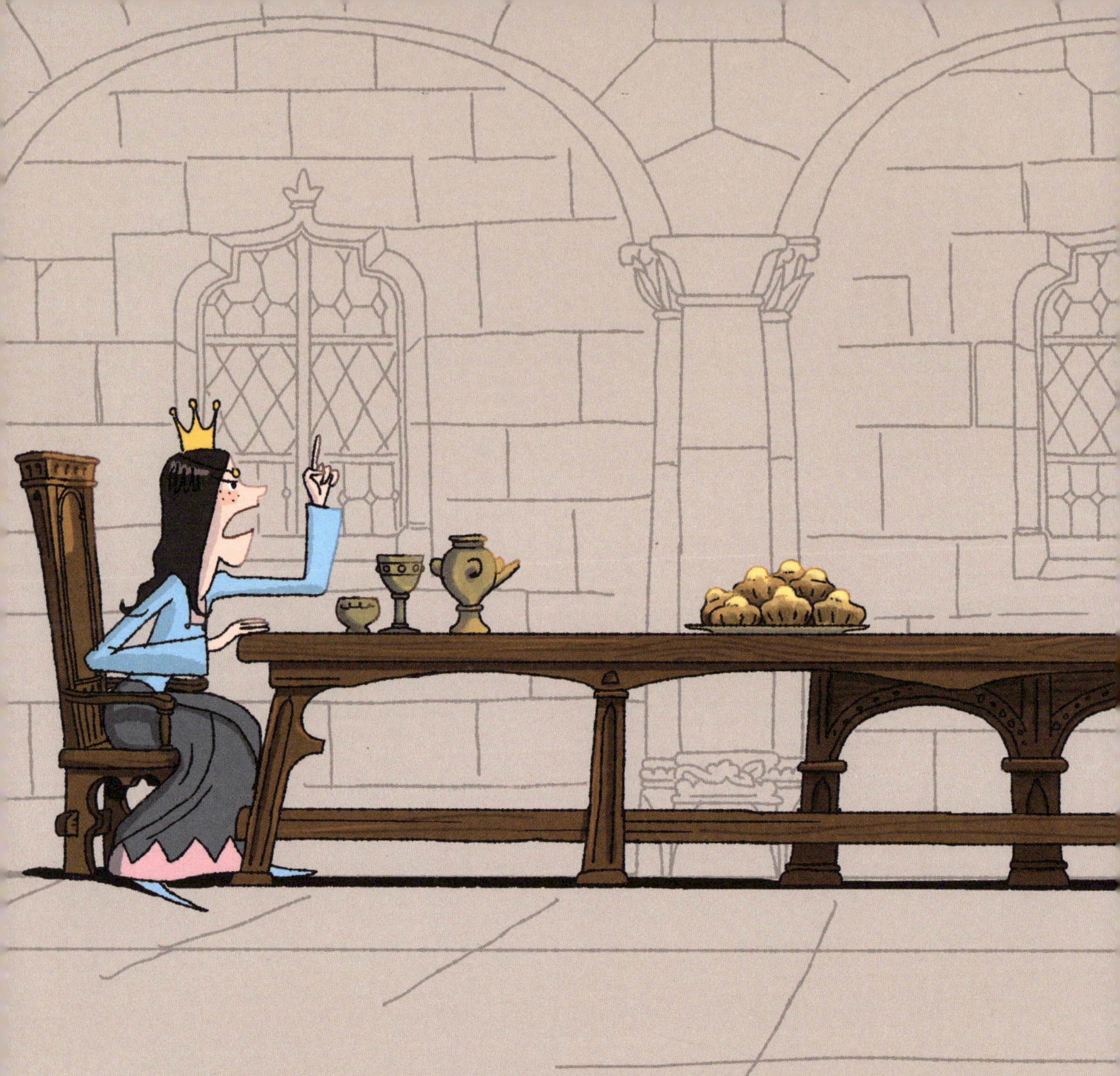

À l'heure du goûter, la princesse Marinette s'écriait :
– Quelle horreur ! Prince Olivier, mon frère, vous avez des poux et vos oreilles sont crasseuses !

Le prince Olivier essuyait sur sa chemise
ses doigts pleins de chocolat et il répondait :
– Princesse Marinette, ma sœur,
j'entends très bien avec mes oreilles.
Alors, pourquoi les user en les lavant ?

À la cour, tout le monde est triste
d'avoir un petit prince aussi sale.
Le roi Hubert prend sa grosse voix :
– Prince Olivier, mon fils,
si vous ne vous lavez pas,
vous irez dormir avec les cochons !
Mais le prince Olivier ne se lave pas.
Il sait bien que son père l'aime trop
pour l'envoyer dormir avec les cochons.

La reine Isabelle le menace :
– Prince Olivier, mon fils,
si vous ne vous lavez pas,
vous n'aurez plus de gâteau
au chocolat !
Mais le prince Olivier ne
se lave pas. Il sait bien que
sa mère l'aime trop pour
le priver de gâteau au chocolat !

La princesse Marinette ne veut plus
s'asseoir à côté de lui.
– Prince Olivier, mon frère,
vous sentez mauvais !
Alors là, le prince Olivier se met
à pleurer très fort en criant que
ce n'est pas vrai, qu'il ne sent pas mauvais,
que sa sœur est une menteuse
et une méchante !
La princesse Marinette aime trop
son petit frère pour le laisser pleurer.
Elle retourne s'asseoir à côté de lui.

Et le prince Olivier
ne se lave toujours pas !

Un soir, la grand-mère
du prince Olivier,
la reine Marguerite, arrive au palais.
On lui raconte que le prince
ne veut toujours pas se laver.

Alors, en grand secret,
pour ne pas réveiller le prince,
la reine Marguerite réunit tout le monde,
le roi, la reine, la princesse Marinette,
les gardes, les valets, les servantes, les cuisiniers.
Tous ensemble, ils établissent un plan de bataille.

Le lendemain matin, le prince Olivier est très étonné
de trouver des bols et des cuillères sales
sur la table de la salle à manger.
Il demande un bol et une cuillère propres.
La servante lui dit qu'il n'y en a plus, qu'elle ne fait plus
la vaisselle pour ne pas user les bols ni les assiettes.

Et que, d'abord, ça ne sert à rien de les laver
puisqu'on les resalit en mangeant dedans.
Le prince Olivier trouve que c'est vraiment dégoûtant
de déjeuner dans un bol qui n'a pas été lavé !

Le prince Olivier traverse le palais. Que se passe-t-il? Des papiers de bonbons, des mégots de cigarettes, des épluchures de cacahuètes traînent par terre. De la poussière, des toiles d'araignées recouvrent les meubles.

Un valet passe par là. Le prince Olivier lui dit :
– Il faut faire le ménage !
Mais le valet répond :
– Prince Olivier, j'ai balayé hier, c'est bien assez !
Et les araignées ne vont pas vous manger !

En l’honneur de la reine Marguerite, la famille royale est réunie dans la grande salle de gala.
La reine Isabelle, vêtue d’une vieille robe de chambre, a de gros bigoudis sur la tête.
Son rouge à lèvres a coulé et lui barbouille le menton.
Le roi Hubert n’est pas rasé. Il est coiffé d’un vieux bonnet de laine et il est encore en pyjama.

La reine Marguerite ressemble à une vieille sorcière. Ses cheveux blancs, tout emmêlés, pendent sur un vilain châle plein de taches. Ses orteils prennent l'air dans ses savates percées. La princesse Marinette a la figure barbouillée de chocolat et elle essuie ses mains pleines de boue sur son chemisier rose.

Le prince Olivier croit rêver.
Il pense que, vraiment,
tout va de travers au palais !
Que sa mère, son père,
sa grand-mère et sa sœur sont sales !
Ils sont trop moches !
Et ça n'a même pas l'air
de les gêner !

Toute souriante,
la reine Marguerite lui dit :
– Prince Olivier, mon petit,
nous avons décidé de nous laver
seulement une fois par an.
C'est bien suffisant !
Après tout, vous avez raison,
pourquoi se laver tous les jours
puisqu'on se salit tous les jours ?
Et nos vieux habits tachés,
nos cheveux mal coiffés
ne nous empêchent ni de dormir
ni de manger !

Le prince Olivier ne répond pas.
Il n'est pas content, pas content du tout.
Tant que lui seul ne se lavait pas,
ne se coiffait pas, portait
des vêtements crasseux,
il trouvait ça très bien.

Mais si tout le monde fait comme lui,
ça ne va plus !

Le lendemain matin,
il s'enferme dans la salle de bains.
Alors, un bruit court dans tout le palais :
– Le prince Olivier se lave ! Le prince Olivier se lave !

Tout est redevenu comme avant au palais.
Enfin, pas tout à fait comme avant.
Car on n'entend plus jamais la reine Isabelle dire :
– Prince Olivier, mon fils, il faut vous laver !

Le petit empereur de Chine

Une histoire de Michel Amelin,
illustrée par Ulises Wensell

Il était une fois, dans un immense palais appelé la Cité Interdite, un petit empereur de Chine et son petit chien qui s'appelait Ouâ-Ouâ.

Ce palais était si grand qu'il fallait un jour entier pour le traverser. Il n'était habité que par des ministres, des suivantes et des soldats.
Personne d'autre n'avait le droit d'y entrer.
Le petit empereur de Chine le savait,
c'est le ministre des Habitants qui le lui avait dit.

Et personne n'avait le droit de regarder
le petit empereur de Chine.
Il fallait toujours lui parler
en baissant la tête, car, si on le regardait
dans les yeux, on était transformé
en statue, c'est le ministre
du Bonjour-Bonsoir qui le lui avait dit.

Alors le petit empereur de Chine
restait tout seul dans son palais.
Il agitait sa tresse pour faire sauter
son pékinois Ouâ-Ouâ,
et il changeait chaque jour
ses habits tissés d'or,
car un petit empereur de Chine
ne doit pas porter les mêmes beaux
vêtements plus d'une fois dans sa vie,
c'est le ministre des Habits
qui le lui avait dit.

Le trône était surmonté d'un dragon,
tout en or et en jade.
Le dragon portait des mots sur son front.
Le petit empereur de Chine demandait toujours
une explication à son ministre de l'École :
– Racontez-moi l'histoire du dragon
qui a des mots écrits sur le front.
Je n'ai pas de ministre des Contes,
et je m'ennuie.
Alors, le ministre de l'École
baissait la tête et il disait :
– C'est le Dragon Aux Yeux Verts,
le plus méchant, le plus terrible.
Personne ne peut le combattre,
sauf l'empereur de Chine.
Mais vous êtes trop petit !
Restez avec nous dans la Cité Interdite.

Le petit empereur de Chine
n'était pas content,
et son pékinois Ouâ-Ouâ non plus.

Un jour, il demande :
– Racontez-moi comment il faut combattre le Dragon Aux Yeux Verts.
Et le ministre de l'École répond :
– Si l'empereur de Chine réussit à parler au dragon sans mentir et s'il parvient à écrire les mots EMPEREUR DE CHINE sur son front, alors, le dragon sera vaincu, et il lui obéira toujours.

Le soir, dans son grand lit, le petit empereur de Chine ne joue plus avec sa tresse ni avec son pékinois Ouâ-Ouâ. Il rêve au dragon et à l'aventure.

Soudain, quelqu'un le secoue. C'est une petite fille.
Le petit empereur de Chine a du mal à se réveiller :
– Qui… qui es-tu ?
Comment es-tu entrée dans la Cité Interdite ?
La petite fille caresse le chien, et elle chuchote :
– Je m'appelle Tsi-Tsi, je cours vite, je suis petite, et je sais escalader les murs et passer par les fenêtres. Je viens du quatrième village après la Cité Interdite pour vous demander de nous sauver.
Nous sommes en danger !
– Mais de quoi parles-tu, Tsi-Tsi ?
– Il faut nous sauver du Dragon Aux Yeux Verts ! Il a enfermé tous les habitants de mon village dans sa grotte. Venez vite ! Tout le monde dit que seul l'empereur de Chine peut combattre le dragon. Et vous êtes l'empereur de Chine !
Le petit empereur de Chine est très étonné.
Tsi-Tsi l'a regardé dans les yeux sans être transformée en statue.
Le ministre du Bonjour-Bonsoir lui aurait donc menti ?

Il se lève, prend Tsi-Tsi par la main, et lui dit :
– Je vais venir, Tsi-Tsi. Je m'ennuie dans mon palais, et je connais l'histoire du Dragon Aux Yeux Verts.
Et ils sortent tous les deux de la Cité Interdite, suivis du pékinois Ouâ-Ouâ.
Ils ne réveillent ni les ministres, ni les suivantes, ni les soldats.

Au premier village, les gens meurent de faim.
Ils ne reconnaissent pas le petit empereur de Chine.
Ils disent : – Le Grand Dragon nous a pris toute notre nourriture et nous n'avons plus rien !
Donne-nous l'un de tes beaux vêtements d'or.
Nous le vendrons, et nous pourrons acheter quelque chose à manger.
Le petit empereur de Chine se déshabille et leur donne tous ses beaux vêtements. Tsi-Tsi sourit, elle lui prend la main pour le conduire, et le pékinois Ouâ-Ouâ marche devant.

Au deuxième village,
les gens meurent de soif. Ils disent :
– Le Grand Dragon nous a volé toute notre eau.
Nous n'avons plus qu'un puits, trop profond
pour notre seule petite corde.
Donne-nous ta longue tresse
pour l'attacher au bout de la corde.
Le petit empereur de Chine
coupe sa tresse et l'attache à la corde.
Le seau peut descendre jusqu'au fond du puits
et remonter de l'eau.
Tsi-Tsi sourit au petit empereur de Chine,
elle lui prend le bras pour le conduire,
et le pékinois Ouâ-Ouâ marche devant.

Au troisième village, les gens pleurent
à qui mieux mieux :
– Le Grand Dragon nous a pris notre joie de vivre.
Depuis, nous sommes toujours malheureux.
Donne-nous ton petit chien,
il nous amusera et nous rendra la joie.
Le petit empereur de Chine est bien triste,
mais il donne son cher petit pékinois Ouâ-Ouâ.
Tsi-Tsi sourit, et elle prend le petit empereur de Chine
par la main pour le conduire jusqu'à son village,
le quatrième village, encore plus loin.

Dans le quatrième village, il n'y a plus personne.
Le Dragon Aux Yeux Verts a emprisonné
tous les habitants dans sa grotte.

Quand le dragon voit
arriver Tsi-Tsi et son ami,
il gronde en crachant des flammes :
– Tu t'es enfuie, Tsi-Tsi ! Je devrais te manger !
Tsi-Tsi réplique :
– Pour me faire pardonner,
je te ramène un nouveau prisonnier !
Le dragon gronde :
– Qui es-tu, misérable ami de Tsi-Tsi ?
Si le petit empereur de Chine dit qu'il est l'empereur de Chine, le dragon va le dévorer, c'est sûr !
Mais il ne doit pas mentir, c'est le ministre de l'École qui le lui a dit. Et le petit empereur de Chine répond :
– Je suis l'empereur de Chine !
Le Dragon Aux Yeux Verts éclate de rire :
– Toi ? Ce n'est pas possible ! Où sont tes habits tissés d'or, ta longue tresse et ton petit chien ? Je connais l'empereur de Chine. Il a peur de moi, là-bas, dans sa Cité Interdite ! Ha ! ha ! ha ! ha ! Entre dans ma grotte, petit mendiant menteur, je te mangerai plus tard. Ha ! ha ! ha ! ha !

Quand la nuit arrive,
le dragon ferme ses grands yeux verts.
Tsi-Tsi fait signe à tout le monde de se taire,
et le petit empereur de Chine se lève.
Doucement, tout doucement,
il grimpe sur la patte aux griffes pointues.
Il a si peur qu'il tremble.
Il lui semble que les griffes remuent.
Et s'il allait se faire dévorer ?
Mais il sait ce qu'il doit faire, et sur le front du dragon,
vite, vite, il écrit les mots EMPEREUR DE CHINE.
Le dragon ouvre alors ses yeux devenus bleus et dit :
– Tu ne m'avais pas menti,
tu es bien l'empereur de Chine !
Demande-moi ce que tu veux, je t'obéirai,
car je suis pour toujours ton serviteur !

中国小皇帝

Le petit empereur de Chine a demandé la liberté
pour Tsi-Tsi, sa famille et tous les habitants du village.
Il a demandé de l'eau, de la nourriture,
des fêtes et des feux d'artifice.
Il a demandé son pékinois Ouâ-Ouâ.
Et il a fait ouvrir les grandes portes de la Cité Interdite.

Et maintenant c'est le petit empereur de Chine
qui a beaucoup de choses à apprendre à ses ministres.

Le secret de la petite souris

Une histoire de Alain Chiche,
illustrée par Anne Wilsdorf

Aujourd'hui, en rentrant de l'école, Raphaël a très faim.
Il mord à pleines dents dans son goûter quand, soudain, il fait :
– Ooohh ! Ça y est, dit Raphaël, ma dent est tombée ! Regardez !
– Bravo, dit son papa. Tu ressembles à un vrai pirate, maintenant !
N'oublie pas de mettre ta dent sous l'oreiller ce soir…
Parce que, lorsqu'on perd une dent, la petite souris vient la chercher pendant la nuit et elle donne un cadeau en échange.
– Mais, demande Raphaël, qu'est-ce qu'elle va faire avec ma dent ?
– Hum... C'est son secret ! dit Papa.
– Ouaf ! fait le chien Bouli qui a l'air d'avoir tout compris.

Le soir, Raphaël veut découvrir
le secret de la petite souris.
Il guette son arrivée en se demandant :
« À quelle heure va-t-elle venir ?
Comment connaît-elle mon adresse ?
Et puis, qui l'a prévenue que j'avais perdu ma dent ? »
Mais les paupières de Raphaël sont lourdes, très lourdes…

Au moment précis où il s'endort,
le chien Bouli se lève
et il sort tout doucement de la chambre.
Il grimpe sur la chaise du couloir, saisit le téléphone
et, avec sa patte, compose un numéro.

CPS

Loin de là, au pays des souris
chercheuses de dents,
une petite souris blanche
s’active dans son bureau.
Elle consulte ses messages sur Internet
quand, soudain,
le téléphone sonne :
– Allô, oui ? Compagnie
des Petites Souris, bonjour !
Tina à votre service !
– Ouaf, c’est moi ! dit Bouli.
Je vous appelle pour vous prévenir
que mon jeune maître, ouaf, a perdu
sa première dent, ouaf ouaf !
Surtout, n’oubliez pas son cadeau.
Il s’appelle Raphaël.
Je vous donne notre adresse…
Tina répond : – C’est noté !
Merci de votre appel, monsieur Bouli.
J’arrive !

Aussitôt, Tina, la petite souris,
s'élance à toute vitesse.
Quand elle arrive à l'aéroport
international des Rongeurs,
un pigeon voyageur l'attend
dans la zone d'embarquement.
– Bonjourrr, miss Tina ! dit le pigeon.
Vous êtes à l'heurrre...
Je suis Jules, bienvenue à borrrd !
– Salut Jules, répond Tina
en montant sur le dos de l'oiseau.
Cap sur la maison de Raphaël !

Après un long voyage,
Jules se pose doucement
sur le toit de la maison de Raphaël.
Tina se glisse dans la cheminée.
La voilà dans le salon :
– Ouaf, je vous attendais, dit Bouli
en remuant la queue. Suivez-moi !

Dans la chambre de Raphaël,
la petite souris se faufile
et grimpe sur le lit.
– Objectif dent atteint !
dit-elle en découvrant
la dent de lait.
Tina met la dent dans son sac à dos.
Puis elle prend un petit cadeau
qu'elle glisse sous l'oreiller de Raphaël.
– Objectif cadeau atteint ! dit-elle. C'est du bon boulot.
Oups, j'allais oublier quelque chose !
Tina se penche alors vers l'oreille
de Raphaël et elle chuchote tout bas :
– Bonne nuit, Raphaël. Et merci pour la dent !

SERVICE
DES DENTS DE LAIT

De retour à la Compagnie des Petites Souris,
Tina se dirige au pas de course
vers le guichet « Service des dents de lait ».
– Salut collègues ! dit-elle en croisant d'autres petites souris.
– Salut Tina ! répondent les souris. On repart en mission !
Et elle s'approche d'un mulot.
– Bonjour, professeur Mulot ! dit Tina.
Voilà une belle quenotte d'enfant de six ans !
– Merci, dit le professeur Mulot. Quel beau spécimen !

C'est exactement ce qu'il nous fallait.
Suivez-moi, miss Tina,
je vais vous présenter
nos dernières innovations.

– Regardez, dit le professeur Mulot à Tina, c'est ici que nous trions les dents de lait. Voilà nos nouveaux paniers de tri pour les dents des enfants de cinq, six, sept et huit ans.

– Très ingénieux ! s'exclame Tina.
– Et ici, nous les transformons
pour leur donner une forme utile !
Voilà le résultat...
Et en effet, au bout du tapis roulant,
apparaît une grande défense d'éléphant.
– Ma-gni-fique ! s'écrie Tina.

A
Weight (2)
lb.
oz.
12
FRAG
CP

Le professeur Mulot continue sa présentation :
– Et regardez notre organisation :
avec cette défense qui vient juste d'être terminée,
on va pouvoir soigner le grand éléphant d'Afrique
qui nous a appelés il y a trois jours.
Regardez, notre équipe est déjà prête à partir
en Afrique pour lui apporter
sa nouvelle dent !

Le lendemain matin, Tina retourne dans son bureau.
Elle trouve un énorme paquet de lettres
en provenance du monde entier.
– Voyons qui a encore besoin de dents
chez nos amis les animaux.
En Chine : Domi le panda.
En Inde : Lotta le tigre.
En Allemagne : Shakia le poney.
Kala le morse au pôle Nord…
Eh bien, nous en avons du travail !
Tiens, j'ai déjà un message d'Afrique
sur mon ordinateur !
« Merci pour la dent !
Signé : le grand éléphant. »
Ça, c'est une bonne nouvelle !
Mais le téléphone sonne.
Bip ! Bip ! Bip !
– Allô ! Compagnie des Petites Souris, j'écoute !
répond Tina. Comment ? Oui, j'arrive !
Et Tina, la petite souris, repart en mission.

CPS

Au même moment, Raphaël se réveille
et il se dépêche de regarder
sous son oreiller :
– Ma dent a disparu !
Mais… ouah, j'ai un cadeau !
C'est un petit éléphant en peluche.
– Super ! s'exclame Raphaël.
– Bonjour, mon grand ! disent Papa
et Maman.
Raphaël leur dit :
– Et mes autres dents,
elles vont tomber quand ?
Parce que moi, je vais commencer
une grande collection… de cadeaux !

La sorcière qui rapetissait les enfants

Une histoire de Véronique Caylou,
illustrée par David Parkins

Il était une fois une sorcière
qui s'appelait Pichnouille.
Elle était bête et méchante.
Elle portait au bout de son nez crochu
une énorme verrue.
Et son seul grand plaisir,
c'était d'embêter ses voisins.

La nuit, Pichnouille faisait grincer leurs volets,
elle transformait les fleurs en cactus,
les bébés en microbes,
elle faisait voler les chiens et courir les escargots.
Les enfants avaient si peur d'elle
qu'ils n'osaient plus jouer dehors.
Dans le village, tout le monde rêvait
d'en être débarrassé.

Celui qui en rêvait le plus, c'était Séraphin,
son plus proche voisin.
Il passait son temps à se cacher
pour échapper aux mauvais tours de Pichnouille.
Mais un beau matin, il en eut assez.
En prenant son petit déjeuner, il dit :
– Je vais me débarrasser
de Pichnouille.
Et il sortit de la maison.

Séraphin se dirigea vers la maison de Pichnouille.
Il marmonnait entre ses dents :
– Par le nez ou le bout du chapeau,
maudite sorcière, j'aurai ta peau !
Au moment où Séraphin allait frapper à sa porte,
Pichnouille sortit. Furieuse, elle saisit Séraphin
par le fond du pantalon en hurlant :
– Ah, tu veux entrer chez moi ?
Eh bien, tu entreras...
par le trou de la serrure !

Paf ! Dans un grand éclair,
Pichnouille rendit Séraphin minuscule,
aussi petit qu'une fourmi,
pas plus gros qu'un moucheron.
Puis elle lui claqua la porte au nez.
Vlan !

Séraphin ne se découragea pas.
Il escalada la porte, et il entra…
par le trou de la serrure !
Hélas ! le chat de Pichnouille l'aperçut.
Il hérissa ses poils en crachant furieusement.
Pichnouille l'entendit…
– Qui ose me déranger ? cria-t-elle.
Ses petits yeux cruels se posèrent sur Séraphin.
Elle hurla : – Encore toi ! Mais il faut donc
que je te mange pour avoir la paix !
Et, slurp ! elle l'avala tout rond.

C'est ainsi que commença
l'étrange voyage de Séraphin
au cœur du corps de la grande,
de la redoutable Pichnouille.
Séraphin découvrit
un escalier en colimaçon.
Courageusement, il descendit.
Il faisait sombre,
les marches étaient glissantes.
Séraphin s'accrochait aux parois
pour ne pas tomber.

Séraphin se trouva bientôt devant une porte
blanche et lisse comme la porte d'un réfrigérateur.
Il sauta sur la poignée : la porte grinça et s'ouvrit
en laissant s'échapper une bouffée d'air glacé.
Là, un énorme caillou se balançait :
c'était le cœur de pierre de Pichnouille.
Pour ne pas geler sur place,
Séraphin s'éloigna rapidement,
mais il laissa la porte ouverte.
Aussitôt… Ratatchoum !
Ratatchoum ! Ratatchoum !
Par trois fois, la sorcière éternua.
« Hé hé, bien fait ! » se dit Séraphin.

Tout grelottant, Séraphin monta
le long de la colonne vertébrale.
Il grimpa, grimpa…

Et il arriva dans une grotte obscure :
c'était le crâne de Pichnouille.
Les murs étaient entièrement recouverts de tiroirs,
portant chacun une étiquette : danser, pincer, bâiller…
Séraphin s'amusa à décoller les étiquettes
des tiroirs pour les recoller sur d'autres.
Comme ça, au lieu de bâiller,
Pichnouille se mettrait à aboyer,
au lieu de manger,
elle se mettrait à sauter !
« Hé hé, bien fait ! »
se dit Séraphin.

griffer
manger
aboyer
terroriser
siffler
tourneboulér
ensorceler
sauter
zigouiller
emberlificoter

Un peu plus loin, Séraphin découvrit
deux drôles de fenêtres :
c'étaient les yeux de Pichnouille.
Au milieu, pendaient deux longues cordes, assez fines.
Séraphin attrapa le bout de chaque corde.
Il tira, tira si fort qu'il réussit à tordre les fenêtres.
Aussitôt, Pichnouille se mit à loucher abominablement !
« Hé hé, bien fait ! » se dit Séraphin.

Satisfait, Séraphin chercha la sortie.
Il courut, courut dans un long tunnel.
Il sentit un petit vent frais comme un courant d'air :
la sortie n'était pas loin… Enfin il fut dehors !
Il se pencha… Malheur !
Il était au bord de l'oreille de Pichnouille !
Il fut pris de vertige.
Il ne pouvait pas sauter de si haut :
il allait se fracasser par terre…

À ce moment, Pichnouille,
qui n'y voyait plus rien, tellement elle louchait,
se cogna contre un mur. Boum !
Le pauvre Séraphin perdit l'équilibre et tomba.
Heureusement, il se rattrapa de justesse
au nez crochu de la sorcière.
Il s'accrocha de toutes ses forces à l'affreuse verrue.
Soudain, il entendit un « CLIC ! ».
La verrue s'enfonça,
comme un bouton sur lequel on appuie.
Sans le savoir, Séraphin venait de découvrir
le point faible de Pichnouille :
le bouton rétrécisseur.

Dans un grand éclair, la sorcière se mit à rapetisser.
Elle devint minuscule, aussi petite qu'une fourmi,
pas plus grosse qu'un moucheron.
En même temps, Séraphin grandit, grandit, grandit…
Lorsqu'il eut retrouvé sa taille normale,
il regarda la minuscule Pichnouille à ses pieds.
Séraphin se pencha, il la prit dans ses mains
et décida de l'emmener dans son jardin
pour l'installer sur une feuille,
tout près d'une petite chenille affamée…

Lorsque sa maman le vit au bout du jardin,
elle se précipita pour le serrer dans ses bras.
Ils s'assirent sur un banc,
et Séraphin lui raconta son étrange voyage
au cœur du corps de la grande,
de la redoutable Pichnouille.
À leurs pieds, une petite chenille
bien rondelette les écoutait.

Un bébé...
et MOI, alors ?

Une histoire de Kidi Bebey,
illustrée par Anne Wilsdorf

Je m'appelle Weï :
ça veut dire « soleil »,
dans la langue de mon papa.

Pendant longtemps, mon papa, ma maman
et moi, on était bien contents de vivre
tous les trois ensemble.
Maman disait toujours :
– Tu es le plus beau gars du quartier !
On ne peut pas avoir de plus bel enfant !
Tu es mon amour, tu es le meilleur
petit Weï que je connaisse !
Je vais te manger, manger, manger !
Elle essayait de m'attraper
et on éclatait de rire.

Mais un jour, j'étais en train de jouer dans ma chambre. Papa et Maman m'ont appelé. Quand je suis arrivé dans la grande pièce, ils étaient assis l'un près de l'autre sur le canapé. Ils ont dit :
– Nous avons une grande nouvelle à t'annoncer : tu vas avoir un petit frère ou une petite sœur.

Un petit frère ou une petite sœur ?
Je n'aurais jamais cru que mes parents pouvaient me faire ça ! Et moi, alors ? On n'était donc pas bien, tous les trois, ensemble ? On s'est mis à attendre.
On parlait tout le temps du bébé.
Un jour, dans la rue, quelqu'un a dit :
– Si le bébé est aussi beau que votre petit garçon, vous aurez une bien jolie famille !
Mais ça, c'était impossible, puisque Maman m'avait dit, à moi : Tu es le plus beau gars du quartier ! Tu es mon amour, le meilleur petit Weï que je connaisse !

Alors, un soir, j'ai demandé à ma bonne fée :
– Chère fée, toi qui me veux du bien, s'il te plaît, est-ce que tu peux faire un bébé moins beau que moi ? Je ne sais pas, moi... Est-ce qu'il ne pourrait pas, par exemple... être rayé... comme un zèbre ?

Alors, l'air de rien, je demanderais à mes parents :
– Vous ne trouvez pas qu'il a l'air d'un zèbre ?
– Un zèbre ? crieraient en chœur mes parents.
Mais bien sûr, tu as raison, c'est un bébé zèbre !
Mais, qu'est-ce qu'on va en faire ?
Alors…

Alors, je leur dirais d'aller vite au zoo
pour présenter le bébé à une famille de zèbres.
Les zèbres s'approcheraient, ils renifleraient
le bébé rayé. Ils croiraient peut-être, au début,
que c'est un zèbre. Mais soudain, le bébé
se mettrait à pousser des cris de bébé,
des cris vraiment forts.
Alors…

Alors, les zèbres sauteraient dans tous les sens, tellement ils seraient surpris. Les zèbres, ça connaît les cris des zèbres, mais pas ceux des bébés, même rayés comme eux. Finalement, ils partiraient en faisant de drôles de têtes. Ils ne voudraient plus garder le bébé rayé. Ah ça non!
Alors…

Alors, je dirais à Papa et Maman d'emmener le bébé rayé dans un cirque. Les gens du cirque essaieraient de lui apprendre à faire le clown. Mais quand il entrerait en scène, personne ne rirait. Parce qu'un bébé, même rayé, ça ne sait pas faire le clown ! Alors…

Alors, les gens du cirque repartiraient sans lui.
Il serait obligé de se débrouiller tout seul.
Les gens trouveraient ça bizarre,
un bébé qui a l'air d'un zèbre, tout seul dans la rue.
Ils lui demanderaient :
– Où est ton papa ? Où est ta maman ?
Mais le bébé rayé ne pourrait même pas
répondre, parce qu'il ne saurait pas parler.
Il y a même des gens qui auraient peur
de lui, à cause de ses yeux tristes.
Tout le monde partirait en courant.
Alors…

Alors, il irait s'installer au pied d'un arbre, dans un parc. Des enfants s'approcheraient de lui pour lui donner à manger.
Ils lui offriraient des bonbons, de la barbe à papa.
Mais un bébé, même rayé, ne boit que du lait.
Je ne sais pas comment il pourrait manger.
Oh le pauvre !
Alors…

Alors, Maman est arrivée,
j'ai essayé de lui raconter tout ça.
Elle a écouté toute l'histoire.
Elle m'a dit : – Ne t'en fais pas.
Dès qu'on le verra, ce bébé,
je suis sûre qu'on saura
comment s'en occuper, toi et moi.
Et puis, tu seras toujours mon petit soleil !

Et le ventre de Maman a continué à pousser.
Parfois, je me mettais tout contre elle
pour parler au bébé.
Je lui disais :
– Toi, tu peux venir,
rayé, ou à carreaux, ou à pois !
Moi, je serai quand même gentil
avec toi, tu sais ?

Quand, un jour, le bébé est né,
il n'était pas du tout rayé.
C'était une petite fille. Elle s'appelle Rose.
Normalement, je n'embrasse pas les filles,
mais pour une fois, je l'ai fait.
De toute façon, je suis toujours Weï,
le plus beau gars du quartier !

La bataille de l'alphabet

Une histoire de Eglal Errera,
illustrée par Giulia Orecchia

d'après une légende du Talmud, avec l'aide de Louma Errera

Dans la grande prairie des hommes,
il y a longtemps de cela,
il y avait des paroles et des mots,
mais il n'y avait pas d'écriture.

Pas une recette écrite de gâteau au chocolat,
pas une liste de cadeaux pour le Père Noël.
Ce n'était vraiment pas drôle !

Les hommes décidèrent
donc d'inventer l'écriture :
ils dessinèrent les lettres
et ils donnèrent un nom à chacune.
Puis ils dirent :
– Maintenant,
nous allons vous trouver un ordre
que les enfants du monde apprendront
quand ils auront l'âge de savoir écrire.

Ils décidèrent donc de donner rendez-vous aux enfants et aux lettres pour choisir ensemble cet ordre.

 s'écria : – Si on faisait un pique-nique ?

 dit :

– Avec des biscuits et des bonbons !
Ils s'assirent en rond sur l'herbe fraîche.
Mais voilà que, poussant les autres,

 s'écria en zozotant :

– Avec mon corps en zigzag, c'est moi le plus zoli. Ze serai donc la première lettre de vous tous.

Les autres lettres lui crièrent :
– Espèce de zigoto qui se vante !
Il n'est pas question qu'on te laisse la première place.
Puis, elles se mirent à se battre entre elles.

Alors  bégaya :
– Aaaaaattention,
vous allez vous faire mal !
Les enfants ouvraient de grands yeux étonnés.
ça commençait mal !

Les hommes crièrent à  :

– Z, ça suffit ! Tu sèmes la zizanie !

 demanda :

– Ça veut dire quoi, zizanie ?

On appela , le savant qui sait tout.

 dit à :

– Tu n'es qu'un ignorant!

Les enfants se mirent en colère. Ils dirent:

– Nous non plus, on ne sait pas ce que c'est, la zizanie. Ce n'est pas un crime, quand même, de ne pas savoir !

Calmement, les hommes expliquèrent:

– Semer la zizanie, cela veut dire fâcher tout le monde contre tout le monde.

Et pour te punir, Z, tu seras la dernière lettre de la liste.

 dit: – Zut!

 cria: – Youpi! C'est bien fait !

Et pourquoi ce ne serait pas moi le premier de la liste ?

Y a pas plus joyeux que moi !

Les enfants applaudirent.

C'est vrai, la joie, y a rien de mieux.

dit :
– C'est juste. Et comme le début du mot joie, c'est moi, le premier ce sera moi.

– Oh, dit  en se dandinant,
mais tu es aussi la première lettre
du mot jalousie et ça, ce n'est pas joli joli, hein !
La bagarre allait recommencer.

supplia :
– Aaaarrêtez, je vous en prie !
Les hommes grondèrent :
– Silence, ou on n'y arrivera pas…
Les lettres ne bougèrent plus.
Mais les enfants dirent aux adultes :
– Les disputes, ça fait partie de la vie.
Vous ne supportez ni le bruit ni le désordre.
Vous n'êtes vraiment pas rigolos !
Et ils leur tournèrent le dos.

Dans le silence revenu, on entendit

qui sanglotait avec de grands hoquets de tristesse.
Il dit :
– Ça m'est égal de ne pas être le premier de la liste.
Mais je vous en prie, ne me séparez pas
de mon cher vieux V !
Parce… que… je suis… je suis… le double de V.
C'était d'un triste ! Tout le monde pleurait.

Dans la grande prairie du monde,

s'avança et dit :
– Ne t'inquiète pas, mon cher W,
moi aussi j'ai besoin de toi.
On ne se quittera pas.
Les lettres hurlèrent en chœur :
– Vive V !
Et les enfants répétèrent :
– Vive V !

Alors, dans les herbes hautes,  se leva.

Il poussa doucement  qui somnolait,

 qui dormait

et  qui rêvassait.

Qu'il était mignon, ce  !
Il sourit et murmura :
– Et la première lettre de « maman »,
ça ne vous plairait pas pour démarrer votre liste ?
Tout le monde – ou presque – était d'accord.
Miracle ! Les enfants suçaient leur pouce en souriant.
Mais voilà que dans les hautes herbes,
la tête de  apparut.

Il roulait des yeux terribles en disant :
– Et les papas, ce n'est pas aussi important
que les mamans, peut-être ? Plus important, même !

Quelle peste, ce  !
Les enfants s'écrièrent :
– Non, pas plus ! Pareil !
Dans la grande prairie du monde,
il y eut un grand découragement.

Quand, tout à coup, 
trottina entre les lettres en disant :
– Tout doux… écoutez-moi !
Je suis timide, c'est vrai, et taquin aussi,
je trébuche et je tombe tout le temps.
Mais si vous saviez comme j'ai envie
– tellement, terriblement, trop envie –
d'être à la tête de notre liste !
Les hommes dirent :
– Tope là ! T, tu seras le premier.
En plus, tu es la première lettre du mot temps,
qui est si important.

Tout le monde était content.
Sauf les enfants, qui s'écrièrent :
– Non, non et non ! Nous ne voulons pas
de la lettre du temps à la tête de la liste !
Quand nous allons vite,
on nous dit de prendre notre temps.
Quand nous allons lentement,
on nous dit que nous perdons notre temps.
On vous prévient : si vous choisissez T,
on refuse d'apprendre à lire !
Les hommes se turent
parce que les enfants avaient raison.

Alors, dans le silence,
la voix de  s'éleva :

– Et A ? Notre A d'amour et d'amitié,
n'est-ce pas lui dont nous avons le plus besoin ?
Les enfants hurlèrent :
– Hourra pour A !
 cria : – Bravo ! Quel bonheur !
Les hommes dirent : – Mon cher B, tu es la bonté même.
Tu seras la deuxième lettre de la liste.
Elle portera vos deux noms : l'alphabet.
Les autres lettres se fâchèrent :
– Et nous ?
Dans quel ordre allons-nous nous mettre ?
Les enfants dirent :
– On a une idée, regardez.

Et ils commencèrent à se mettre les uns derrière les autres.

D'abord Alma, Annabelle et Adrien.

Ils portaient  en criant : – A !

Bianca saisit . Les enfants hurlèrent : – B !

Céleste et Cécile les rejoignirent avec 

David avec son ,

Emma et Éliott avec .

et François avec .

Georges et Gérard portaient ,

Henri brandissait  et Ibrahim son .

Jeanne, Joséphine et Jonathan se mirent derrière eux avec ,

Kévin avec , Louma, Luna,

et Lillah avec leur cher ,

Margherita et Mélanie avec leur doux ,

et Nicole avec son petit .

Oscar apporta ,

Prunelle et Pietro, , Quentin, .

Raphaël et Romane tenaient leur grand ,

Suzanne, Stella et Salomé leur joli ,

Théo son , Ursule son , Véra son .

Wagner les suivait avec , Xavier avec ,

Yves avec .

Enfin, Zoé et Zéphir se mirent en bout de rang,

puisque leur pauvre  était puni.

Pour le consoler et parce qu'on l'aimait beaucoup,

les lettres crièrent en chœur : Z !

Et depuis lors, rien ni personne n'est venu déranger
l'ordre de l'alphabet qui avait été choisi
en ce grand jour de l'invention de l'écriture.

Le gros chagrin d'Edgar

Une histoire de Xavier Gorce,
illustrée par Yves Calarnou

De mémoire de cochon, de mémoire de canard,
jamais dans une ferme,
on n'a vu d'âne plus heureux qu'Edgar !
Car jamais dans une ferme
on n'a vu d'âne plus gâté.
Parce que le seul travail d'Edgar,
c'est manger le plus possible de chardons
dans le Grand-pré-d'en-bas.
Les chardons, Edgar, il adore ça !
Il les mange si consciencieusement
qu'il en a gagné un bon petit bidon bien rond
d'âne-mangeur-de-chardons.

Mais la principale raison du bonheur d'Edgar, c'est l'amour que lui porte son maître, Gaston.
Car, si l'on n'a jamais vu d'âne plus heureux qu'Edgar, jamais on n'a vu de maître plus aimant que Gaston.
Tous les matins, Gaston apporte à Edgar trois ou quatre bonnes grosses carottes fraîchement cueillies.
Gaston dit : – Bonne journée, Edgar !
– HI-HAN ! répond Edgar.
Puis Gaston emmène Edgar manger ses chardons au Grand-pré-d'en-bas.

Dans la ferme, il y a bien quelques jaloux qui disent :
– Edgar, c'est le chouchou !
Il y a bien quelques poules qui papotent,
quelques canards qui cancanent,
et quelques jars qui jasent…
Bof ! Edgar s'en moque.
Edgar est heureux, et voilà tout.

Jusqu'au jour où Gaston revient du marché
avec une dinde sous le bras.
C'est une simple petite dinde
dans son joli costume de plumes noires.
Dès qu'elle arrive à la ferme,
les poules se précipitent vers elle :
– D'ou viens-tu ?
– Sais-tu jouer à gobe-caillou ?

Mais la dinde, qui s'appelle Marie-Delphine,
fait la fière.
Très vite, les poules la prennent en grippe.
– Non mais, pour qui se prend-elle, celle-là ?
disent-elles.
– Marie-Delphine, quelle pimbêche !
Les jours passent,
et Marie-Delphine n'a encore adressé la parole
à personne. Mais il y a pire : on s'aperçoit très vite
qu'elle est la mieux nourrie de tous…

Gaston la nourrit deux fois par jour !
Parfois, il la prend sur ses genoux
pour lui tâter les cuisses.
Il veut être sûr
qu'elle ne manque de rien.
Les poules sont furieuses !
Edgar aussi trouve
que Gaston exagère.

Pourtant Gaston n'oublie pas Edgar.
Tous les matins, il lui apporte de bonnes carottes.
Oui… mais voilà : de jour en jour, Edgar les trouve…
un peu moins juteuses,
un peu moins croquantes,
un peu moins sucrées…
Si bien qu'à la fin il les touche à peine.
Il n'arrête pas de penser
à cette idiote de Marie-Delphine,
toute fière d'être cajolée par Gaston.
Et tandis que, chaque jour, elle devient plus grasse
dans son beau costume de plumes noires,
petit à petit, Edgar perd son bon petit bidon
d'âne-mangeur-de-chardons.

Une nuit qu'il neige à gros flocons,
Edgar est réveillé en sursaut.
Il voit Gaston dans la cour de la ferme
qui court de tous côtés en criant :
– La dinde, où est donc passée
cette idiote de dinde ?

Gaston entre dans l'étable, il plonge dans la paille,
il fouille, il fouille, mais il ne trouve rien.
Alors, déçu, il se confie à Edgar :
– Depuis des semaines, je bichonne cette dinde,
je l'engraisse pour la manger le soir du réveillon,
et voilà que, juste la veille, paf ! elle disparaît.
J'ai beau la chercher partout, elle s'est envolée !
À ces mots, Edgar comprend tout ! Il se dit :
« Comment ai-je pu me rendre malade
à cause de cette malheureuse dinde ? »
D'un coup, il se sent soulagé.

Le soir du réveillon passe… sans dinde pour Gaston.
Le lendemain, pour fêter la nouvelle année,
Gaston emmène Edgar au Grand-pré-d'en-bas.
– Ce n'est pas parce que je n'ai pas eu de dinde
que tu n'auras pas de bons chardons, lui dit-il.
Régale-toi, mon brave Edgar !
Et Edgar travaille donc à se refaire
un bon petit bidon d'âne-mangeur-de-chardons.

Mais, soudain, un drôle de sac de plumes
lui tombe dans les pattes. Marie-Delphine !
C'est bien elle, mais dans quel état !
Ses plumes sont grises et trempées,
elle grelotte de froid et de peur, et elle supplie :
– Edgar, s'il te plaît, cache-moi !
Je ne veux pas être mangée…
Et elle s'effondre, épuisée.
Edgar est stupéfait.
Est-ce cette Marie-Delphine, si fière,
qui lui parle ainsi ?

Alors, Edgar la conduit vers son étable,
et lui fait dans la paille
une cachette bien chaude.
Il a envie de s'occuper de Marie-Delphine,
de l'aider à se refaire une santé.
Mais… que va dire Gaston ?
Voudra-t-il toujours la manger ?
En voudra-t-il à Edgar de l'avoir protégée ?

Or, ce soir-là, quand Gaston va voir son âne,
il aperçoit bien la dinde
couchée entre les pattes d'Edgar,
mais il ne cherche pas à l'attraper.
D'abord, parce que le réveillon est passé ; mais surtout,
parce qu'elle n'est plus très appétissante, cette dinde !
Gaston fronce les sourcils,
puis il sourit et dit d'un air moqueur :
– Tiens, tiens, Edgar,
tu as une nouvelle amie, à présent ?

Depuis ce jour-là,
Edgar et Marie-Delphine ne se quittent plus.
Oh, il y a bien quelques poules qui papotent,
quelques canards qui cancanent,
quelques jars qui jasent, mais Edgar s'en moque !
Car, de mémoire de cochon,
de mémoire de canard,
dans une ferme,
on n'a toujours pas vu d'âne
plus heureux qu'Edgar !

Le grand voyage de Nils Holgersson

Adapté par Catherine de Lasa,
illustré par Carme Solé Vendrell

d'après *Le merveilleux voyage de Nils Holgersson à travers la Suède* de Selma Lagerlöf.

Il était une fois un petit garçon qui s'appelait Nils.
Ses parents se désolaient,
car il ne pensait qu'à faire des bêtises.
Nils courait après les poussins.
Ceux-ci avaient si peur qu'ils s'éparpillaient
de tous côtés, et la poule s'essoufflait à les rassembler.

Puis Nils renversait la gamelle du canard,
il jetait son sabot dans les pattes de la vache
et, surtout, il lançait des fléchettes
sur le beau jars blanc que sa mère aimait tant.

Le jars essayait de se sauver mais, après quelques pas…
plouf ! il s'étalait dans la boue ! Et Nils riait comme un fou.

Un matin, Nils est tout seul à la maison.
Il se chauffe devant le feu en bâillant quand, tout à coup, il sursaute : un petit bonhomme au chapeau pointu est assis sur le vieux coffre de sa mère !
Nils n'en croit pas ses yeux.
Il se met à ricaner :
– Quel drôle de lutin ! Je vais lui faire une farce !
Nils attrape le filet à papillons...
Zip ! il le rabat sur la tête du lutin !
Et il se dit : « Je vais appeler le chat : ça va lui faire une de ces peurs ! »

Nils se dirige vers la porte pour inviter le chat à entrer. Il ne voit pas le lutin qui soulève doucement le filet pour se libérer, et qui chante en sautant à cloche-pied :

– Méchant tu es, petit tu seras.
Petit tu es, gentil tu deviendras.

Au même moment, Nils rapetisse, rapetisse…

Dehors, une vache géante gronde à ses oreilles :
– Tiens, te voilà, toi qui m'as lancé ton sabot, hier !
Attends que je te fasse danser sur mes cornes !

Un canard énorme manque de le faire tomber :
– C'est toi qui as jeté ma gamelle dans le fumier !
Attends un peu que je te pousse dans la mare !

Une poule gigantesque le menace :
– C'est toi, hier, qui as fait peur à mes poussins !
Approche, tu vas tâter de mon bec pointu !

Nils croit rêver :
ces animaux sont immenses !
Et il comprend qu'il est devenu
tout petit, aussi petit que le lutin.

Nils court se cacher. En trois minutes,
il escalade le mur derrière le poulailler,
et il se retrouve près du ruisseau.
Ouf ! Il est sauvé.
Derrière une feuille de pissenlit,
plus personne ne peut le voir.
Alors Nils se met à pleurer :
« Que puis-je faire, maintenant
que je suis tout petit ?
Les animaux vont sans cesse
s'amuser à me faire peur…
Il vaut mieux que je m'en aille. »

À ce moment, une bande d'oies
sauvages traverse le ciel.
Aussitôt, le jars de la ferme bat des ailes :
– Emmenez-moi ! Emmenez-moi !
Les oies répondent :
– Viens avec nous ! Viens avec nous !
Nils s'accroche au jars :
– Non, ne pars pas,
Maman serait trop triste sans toi !

Mais d'un bond le jars s'élance.
Il monte si vite dans le ciel
que Nils n'ose pas le lâcher, de peur de tomber.
Pour ne pas glisser, il s'agrippe à son cou.

Bien installé sur le jars, Nils regarde tout en bas.
Il découvre une grande nappe au-dessous de lui,
pleine de petits carreaux de différentes couleurs :
ce sont des champs, des forêts, des prairies ou des fermes.
Les oies survolent une ferme, et elles demandent :
– Comment s'appelle votre ferme ?
Comment s'appelle votre ferme ?
Le coq tend le cou pour répondre :
– Notre ferme s'appelle Petit-Champ,
cette année comme l'an passé,
cette année comme l'an passé !

Nils éclate de rire,
oubliant un moment ses malheurs.

Le soir venu, les oies sauvages se posent sur un lac gelé.
La plus vieille d'entre elles dit :
– Je pense que, là, nous serons à l'abri du renard.
Et les oies s'installent pour dormir.
Le jars prend Nils par le col de sa chemise :
– Toi, dit-il, ne t'endors pas.
Va voir si le renard ne se cache pas là-bas,
dans les buissons !
Aide-nous, et nous t'aiderons !
Nils s'éloigne vers la forêt.

Dans la forêt, il entend soudain des caquètements.
Un renard file devant lui à toute allure.
Dans sa gueule, il tient une oie.
Sans réfléchir, Nils court à sa poursuite.
Il attrape la queue du renard,
mais le renard, la bouche pleine, s'écrie :
– Lâche-moi, riquiqui,
chinon che te manze zaussi !
Furieux d'être traité de riquiqui,
Nils prend appui sur une racine
et il tire un grand coup
sur la queue du renard.

Surpris, le renard ouvre la gueule :
l'oie en profite pour se sauver.
Le renard se retourne et, faisant face à Nils, il crie :
– L'oie m'a échappé, mais toi, tu ne m'échapperas pas !
Nils s'enfuit, et il grimpe
au premier arbre qu'il aperçoit.
Le renard se couche au pied de l'arbre,
et il attend, il attend toute la nuit.
Et toute la nuit, dans l'arbre,
Nils grelotte de froid,
sans fermer l'œil une seule fois,
tant il a peur de tomber.

Au petit matin, Nils voit le soleil se lever.
Il entend les cris des oies qui se préparent à partir.
Son cœur bondit. Il se dit : « Vont-elles partir sans moi ? »
Il est sur le point de pleurer
quand, tout à coup, il voit une oie qui vole
tout près du renard et s'amuse à le frôler.
Le renard saute pour l'attraper, mais l'oie lui échappe,
il la poursuit de plus en plus loin…
Alors le jars arrive, il tend son cou vers Nils,
et Nils s'accroche à lui.

Depuis ce jour, Nils est devenu l'ami de toutes les oies.
Mais c'est le jars qu'il préfère.
La nuit, Nils dort au creux de ses plumes.
Le jars l'appelle Poucet et, quand il a des ennuis, il n'hésite pas à crier : « À l'aide, Poucet ! »
Nils en est très fier.
Un jour, les oies survolent la campagne, et Nils reconnaît la ferme de ses parents.
– J'aimerais tant les revoir ! dit-il au jars.

Nils et le jars atterrissent
dans la cour de la ferme.
Pendant que le jars se promène
fièrement, Nils se cache dans un trou du mur.
Mais un cri lui fait tourner la tête :
– À l'aide, Poucet ! À l'aide !
C'est le père de Nils qui a attrapé le jars par le cou
et qui appelle sa femme :
– Viens voir la belle bête pour notre dîner !
La mère de Nils répond :
– Ne le serre pas si fort !
Il me fait penser à notre beau jars blanc
qui a disparu l'an dernier
avec notre petit Nils.
Le jars hurle de plus belle :
– À l'aide, Poucet ! À l'aide !

Nils bondit et, à son tour, il crie :
– Père ! Mère ! Ne tuez pas ce jars, c'est votre beau jars blanc ! Sans lui, je serais mort depuis longtemps !
Le père et la mère se retournent, bouche bée :
– Nils ! C'est toi ? Notre petit Nils ?
Comme tu es devenu grand !
Nils regarde autour de lui : la vache, le canard et la poule ont retrouvé une taille normale.
Et lui aussi ! Il est même plus grand qu'avant !
Très ému, il se serre contre ses parents :
– Me voilà enfin revenu, dit-il.
Libérez mon ami le jars !
Je vais tout vous raconter !

Collection Les Belles Histoires

Jacqueline Cohen
Bernadette Després

Xavier Gorce
Yves Calarnou

Claude Prothée
Anne Wilsdorf

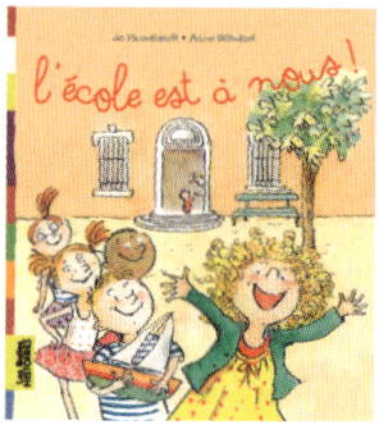

Jo Hoestlandt
Anne Wilsdorf

Mimi Zagarriga
Didier Balicevic

Céline Claire
Aurélie Guillerey

René Gouichoux
Éric Gasté

Anne-Laure Bondoux
Roser Capdevila

Agnès Bertron
Axel Scheffler

Anne-Marie Chapouton
Amélie Dufour

Marie-Hélène Delval
Pierre Denieuil

Mildred Pitts Walter
Claude et Denise Millet

Véronique Caylou
David Parkins

Michel Amelin
Ulises Wensell

Marie-Agnès Gaudrat
Colette Camil

Marie-Agnès Gaudrat
David Parkins

Thomas Scotto
Jean-François Martin

Hélène Leroy
Éric Gasté

Jo Hoestlandt
Claude et Denise Millet

Alain Chiche
Anne Wilsdorf

Eglal Errera
Giulia Orecchia

Claire Clément
Jean-François Martin

Anne Leviel
Martin Matje

Kidi Bebey
Anne Wilsdorf

Anne-Marie Abitan
Ulises Wensell

Anne Mirman
Éric Gasté

Catharina Valckx

Claude Prothée
Didier Balicevic

Françoise Moreau-Dubois
David Parkins

Catherine de Lasa
Carme Solé Vendrell

Gwendoline Raisson
Anne Wilsdorf

Chantal de Marolles
Boiry

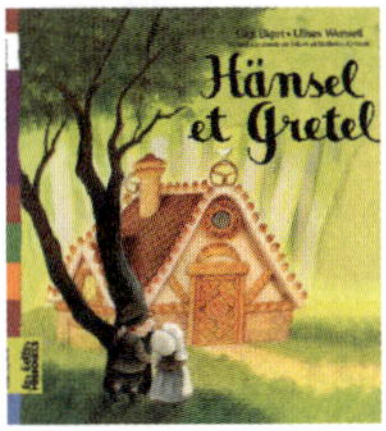

Gigi Bigot
Ulises Wensell

Marie-Hélène Delval
Ulises Wensell

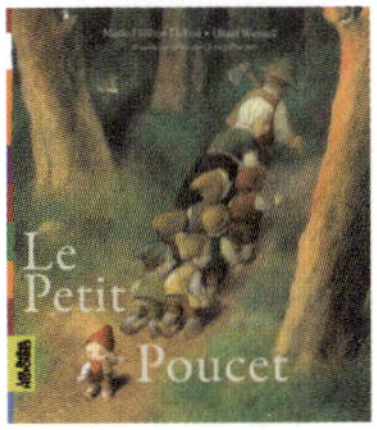

Marie-Hélène Delval
Ulises Wensell

Pascale Chénel
Britta Teckentrup

René Escudié
Ulises Wensell

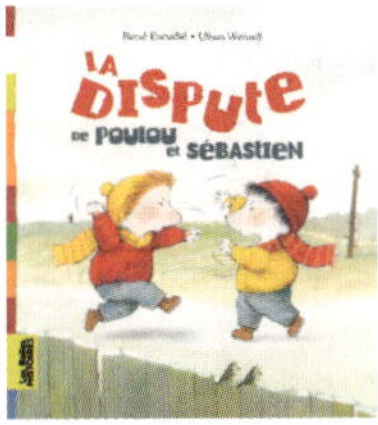

René Escudié
Ulises Wensell

Marie Bataille
Ulises Wensell

Catherine de Lasa
Yves Calarnou

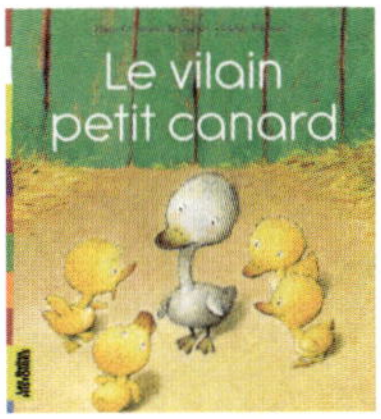

H C Andersen
Ulises Wensell

Rémi Courgeon

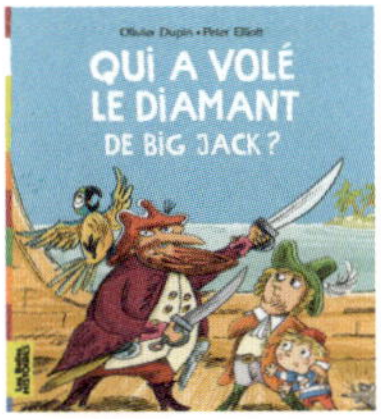

Olivier Dupin
Peter Elliot

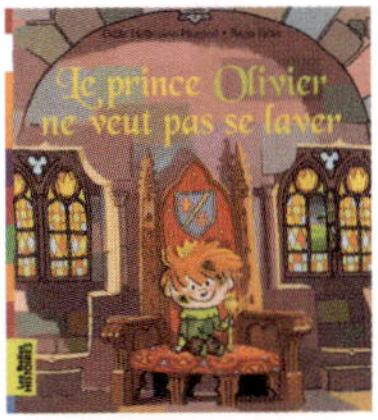

Odile Hellman-Hurpoil
Régis Faller

Marie-Hélène Delval
Maude Legrand

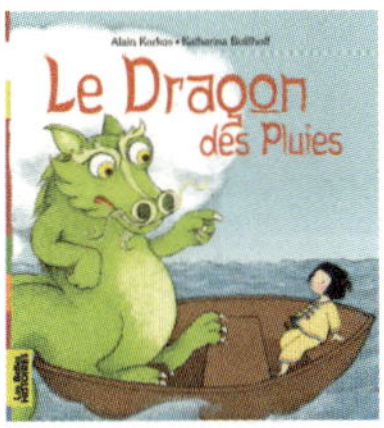

Alain Korkos
Katharina Bußhoff

Antoine Lanciaux
Samuel Ribeyron

Pierre Bertrand
Michel Van Zeveren

Laurence Pain
Claude et Denise Millet

Marie-Agnès Gaudrat
David Parkins